CANADIAN
BUSINESS HISTORY

CANADIAN
BUSINESS HISTORY

Selected Studies, 1497-1971 / David S. Macmillan

McClelland and Stewart Limited

The Canadian Publishers
McClelland and Stewart Limited
25 Hollinger Road, Toronto 374

Printed and bound in Canada

Contents

Extra-National Control: An Early Case Study

Introduction

It is surprising that in Canada, a country which owes more than most to private enterprise and initiative, there should have been a comparative neglect of business and entrepreneurial history. This is all the more remarkable since, as F.H. Armstrong points out in his survey chapter in this volume on the writing of Canadian Business History to date, economic historians in this country, such as that pioneer, Adam Shortt, and notably Harold Innis, were among the first to appreciate the driving motivation and the personal dynamic in such important business contributions to economic development and political achievement as the Montreal-based fur trade and the early Canadian railways.

The increasing interest shown in business history in the United States, Germany, France, Britain and Australia over the last twenty-five years, based on the preliminary work done at Harvard and in London in the period between the Wars, reflects an awareness of a new, long-neglected aspect of modern history. It is hoped that this, the first collection of studies in Canadian Business History, will stimulate further interest in the field in Canada, and that it will show the range and quality of the work that is already being done, by established historians and by their younger colleagues, in this area of study.

"Business History" is a broad term, which covers not only "case studies" of individual firms, and quantitative, statistical surveys of the growth of particular trades and industries, but also the investigation of the social backgrounds, the political and religious connections of the business classes, the impingement and implications of government policies on business, and, in short, every aspect of the development of business in its setting within the community. It is hoped that this collection of chapters will be representative of the study in its many facets, for it includes "case studies," quantitative surveys, and papers on bibliography, archives, political and "connectional" aspects of the subject. The "connectional" themes (which consider the importance of French, Scottish, English and American influences on Canadian business and economic development) give some indication of how far Canadian enterprise and the country's business class was shaped by outside forces, and of how the Canadian business community in turn, even in the early, colonial phase, came to exert its influence on the commercial and industrial scene in the outside world. R.C. Overton's chapter on the Burlington Railway, though not treating a specifically Canadian theme, has particular interest as an example of the way in which the close study of the internal "politics" of a corporation in the American manner can yield valuable results. Its author is a distinguished product of the Harvard school of business history. The contrast between early railway development in Canada and the United States is brought out clearly by a comparison between Douglas McCalla's chapter on the Great Western Railway and Professor Overton's study of a railroad system which extended its influence right up to the Canadian border and beyond in the great days of the "railroad promotion mania."

These studies are diverse in subject, approach, and technique, and this is deliberate, for recent collections of business history studies in other countries – "Studies in Scottish Business History" (London, 1967), and "Wealth and Progress: Studies in Australian Business History" (Sydney, 1968) are examples – have shown that entrepreneurial history cannot be considered "in a vacuum" if it is to yield its full measure of profit and clarification, especially for members of the intelligent reading public. To achieve a balanced, informative picture of business development, the men of enterprise, their firms and partnerships, their methods and procedures must all be viewed in the setting of the contemporary community at large, in its social, political, economic, and constitutional aspects. Just as Canadian political historians in recent years have improved the quality and perception of their work by bringing economic, social and urban aspects into consideration, so must the business historian pay due regard to the forces other than enterprise, the profit-motive, and the internal structure and achievements of the business organisations which are his primary concern.

It will be interesting to see the pattern, or patterns, that Canadian business history will follow in the future. Will it be influenced by the English approach which tends to view the business firm or the group of firms as part of an industry or trade within an overall national or international economy, or will it follow the American or German lines, of concentration on the analysis of a firm or industry's performance, its internal organisation, with painstaking charting of its personnel, capitalization, and growth? It is possible that both the "broader" and "specialized" approaches will be followed in a country which is influenced so strongly, in both business techniques and research methods, by both Britain and the United States. Indeed, the achievement of an amalgam of British breadth in business studies and American quantitative and analytical expertise may well be the distinctive contribution which Canada can make in this field.

The study, if not in its infancy here, is still at the stage where it is not yet accepted as part of the formal range of fields for investigation in the Universities and schools, though its importance has long been realised in progressive circles. It seems ironic that while so many exotic new areas of study in the social sciences are being opened up for research and teaching, the development of the study of one of the principal strands in the texture of Canadian life should receive so little attention. Almost certainly, the historians of two hundred years from now will regard our Canadian society as largely conditioned by the needs, the drives, and the successes and failures of what we call "business," in its wider implications of investment in the "private sector," the enterprise of individuals, the initiatives shown by management, and the reactions of businessmen to external and internal pressures.

An attempt has been made in this collection to trace the main stream of commercial development in Canada, omitting such already well-charted waters as the fur trade and the lumber industry. It is obvious that many important aspects cannot receive the attention they deserve in this preliminary outline. The early development of the wheat-growing industry of the Prairies, the growth of the automobile industry, and the beginnings of the iron and steel, shipping, brewing, distilling and textile industries, and of insurance and investment companies are examples that come readily to mind. These and hundreds of others are subjects which deserve to be explored, and there is a desperate need for basic studies in these fields.

Michael Bliss's chapter on the stresses and divisions within the Canadian business community, and on the obstacles which were encountered in what has generally been regarded as the "halcyon days" of 1880-1914; points the need for more detailed biographical studies of business leaders – their background, motivation, operating methods, and their relations with each other. It is only when we have studies of this kind – Alan Wilson's *John Northway, Blue Serge Canadian* (Toronto, 1965) is an example – in sufficient number that the synthesis necessary for the drawing of "general conclusions" can be made. The tragedy is that so much of the "raw material" for business history research, in the form of early company records, has already been destroyed. Even more tragic, the destruction of business records goes on apace, almost daily, especially in our cities, where storage space and record-keeping staff are at an increasing premium.

Many of the industrial and commercial "giants" we know today in Canada represent amalgamations, federations and combinations of much larger numbers of smaller firms, often "private" companies or family concerns. Surprisingly few records of such small-scale "seminal" enterprises have survived. When they have been preserved, they are of vital importance for the social, economic and business historian; yet almost certainly, in lawyers' offices (a common dumping-ground for the archives of firms which have passed out of separate existence) and in attics, storage repositories, and in private hands all over the country, such books and papers must exist, and all too often, their owners must have slight realisation of their significance. It is to be hoped that some form of systematic survey will be undertaken in the near future to ascertain the existence and location of such holdings. In national terms they are irreplaceable and priceless.

The variegated nature of the chapters which follow, in subject, style, approach, and content, may be advantageous in two regards. Firstly, it will show how much work there is to be done in a field that these studies open up for further research; secondly, the chapters show the range of aspects from which the subject can be treated – political, social, economic, and urban. Perhaps the development of business history in Canada will be all the richer for being pushed forward by researchers with such varied interests and viewpoints. This, too, may counteract the narrowness which has tended to circumscribe the study in some other countries. Canada may have been slow to consider its commercial past from other than strictly political or constitutional angles, but that, in the long run, may be beneficial if a "balanced" approach to the subject can be developed, an approach which views the activities of businessmen as playing an integral part in our modern society, a part just as significant as those played by political and social reformers, statesmen and educationists. Much has been accomplished in the making of Canada through the co-operation of business and governments, and possibly even more has been accomplished through the exercise of business initiatives despite governments. The question of whether the untrammelled activities of free enterprise have achieved more since the days of New France than the collusion of businessmen with the state is only one of the many significant issues which an intelligent and considered approach to business history can resolve. Others include the elucidation of the roles of outside capital and enterprise, the relations between capital-management and labour, and the contributions made by the small business to national development in the various stages of growth, from the formative colonial stage of 1763-1793 to the present. The study of business history, in its wider sense, can add a new dimension to our approach to these vital problems. Most important of all, it can provide new insights into the attitudes of sections of the community which played key parts in the shaping of our society. As G.M. Young, the distinguished historian of Victorian England, put it: "History is not so much the assembling of facts about happenings in the past as an attempt to find out what people felt about these events when they were occurring."

It is not always easy to ascertain the attitudes of traders, merchants, manufacturers and other entrepreneurs to the economic, social and political context in which they lived. Such people seldom expressed their views in print and John Galt, that entrepreneur in Upper Canada on the grand scale, was almost unique in his time in being a businessman with a literary flair, with access to the columns of the periodicals of his time. The thoughts, plans and aspirations of most of the others who shaped the commerce, the industries and the communications systems of the country must be sought out in letterbooks, diaries, journals and in their scattered correspondence. Their activities and their projects can often only be analysed through quantitative studies, based on their daybooks and ledgers. They were not "vocal" men in the sense that their views were seldom published.

J.H. Archer's chapter in this volume lists the principal groups of such business records preserved in accredited repositories, and it is to be hoped that more attention will be paid in future by researchers to these riches. The superb Baring Brothers banking collection in the Public Archives in Ottawa is an example. It is also to be hoped that much more material of this type will be lodged in places of safety, and that more of the larger firms in Canada will follow the lead of the corporations which have already established their own archives systems for their old records.

There are hopeful signs of spreading interest in the subject. The Canada

Council has sponsored research into commercial development and business history, and several of the universities are building up collections of business archives. Significantly, historians of the first rank are giving due weight to commercial considerations and the role of businessmen in "general" histories – the work of Fernand Ouellet on Lower Canada is an example.

In the studies contained in this volume an attempt is made to trace some of the main features of business development in Canada, to show what has already been effected in the field of business history, and to indicate possible lines which future research and investigation might take.

The primary aim of the book, though, is to break through the crust of indifference towards aspects of the nation's past which have been unduly neglected. If this appraisal of "Enterprise and Initiative" stimulates a greater interest in the commercial side of Canadian history, in the social implications of the entrepreneurial system, and in the changing attitudes and aims of the men who shaped the country's economic destinies, it will have served its purpose.

David S. Macmillan
Trent University

1/Outside Influences and Internal Developments

Exploration and Enterprise – The Newfoundland Fishery c.1497-1677

John Gilchrist, Professor of History, Trent University

The early history of trade and commerce in the Maritimes presents special problems to the historian. The records are poor and scattered and they encourage value-judgements rather than factual analysis. But this is not necessarily a bad thing. Such judgements can often provide us with insights into events of a later period. For example, the present-day difficulties of the resettlement program in Newfoundland appear to be deep-rooted in the early socio-economic development of the island.

In primitive economies dominated by such industries as fishing and fur trading, the human element becomes heavily conditioned by environmental factors, which dictate the working methods, the means of financing the enterprise, the distribution of profits, and the control of labour. Environmental adaptation, which seems to be a predominant factor in the early period of exploration and enterprise, suggests that, in dealing with the fisheries of Newfoundland, we should not retain the artificial distinctions implicit in the treatment of the fishery under such headings as French, English, Spanish or Portuguese.[1] The various governments' intervention in the fishery was spas-

---

[1] On the fishery see the following: M. Carroll, *The Seal and Herring Fisheries of Newfoundland* (Montreal 1873); H. A. Innis, "The Rise and Fall of the Spanish Fishery in Newfoundland," *Transactions of the Royal Society of Canada*, Third Series, Vol. 25, Sect. II, (1931) 51-70; R. F. Grant, *The Canadian Atlantic Fishery* (Toronto, 1934); R. G. Lounsbury, *The British Fishery at Newfoundland, 1634-1763* (Yale University Press, 1934); A. P. Usher, "The Influence of the Cod Fishery upon the History of the North American Seaboard," *Canadian Journal of Economics and Political Science* 6 (1940) 591-599; H. A. Innis, *The Cod Fisheries: The History of an International Economy* (Yale University Press 1940; revd. edit., University of Toronto Press, 1954); W. C. MacKenzie, "Fisheries," *Encyclopedia Canadiana*, 4 (1958) 146-159; C. de la Morandière, *Histoire de la pêche française de la morue dans l'Amérique septentrionale des origines à 1789*, 2 vols (Paris 1962); G. T. Cell, *English Enterprise in Newfoundland, 1577-1660* (University of Toronto Press, 1969).

modic and, until the middle of the seventeenth century, mostly unsuccessful. Despite a growing awareness of the national importance of the fishery, it ran a poor second to the attraction held out by the search for a North-West passage, and, in some instances, the Newfoundland fishery was subordinated to or even sacrificed to other national concerns, as in the case of the Spanish fleet.

Treating the fishery as a whole does not mean that there was no rivalry among the fishermen. But it does mean that, in the early period at least, the rivalry among the fleets was more economic than national, and a strong argument can be made for the thesis that these fishermen as a group had more to lose than to gain by pursuing the separateness dictated by national interests. For example, the fishermen evolved their own system of allocating harbour sites which worked reasonably well, until it came into conflict with the seventeenth century attempts at settlement.

In concentrating upon Newfoundland, I do not intend to overlook the importance of other fisheries which eventually emerged to play an important role in the settlement of New England and New France. In some cases, I use evidence from the one area to supplement the paucity of records in the other. But because my intention is to illustrate the degree to which the commercial development was subject to several "determined" situations, I feel it is justified to concentrate on the one region. For another reason, I do not commence with exploration and then follow up with enterprise. In the natural order of things it was fishing first, exploration and settlement second, and it is this order which I follow. Nor shall I adhere strictly to the chronological limits of 1497-1677. Where evidence is lacking in the one period, it may be available in another, and it seems proper in this type of study to apply such evidence to fill gaps in our knowledge. Hence the speculative character.

This speculation can be justified if we consider the extent to which, of all industries, fishing is subject to the ties of tradition and exhibits strong tendencies to resist change. Despite the impact of the discovery of the New World, and the Reformation of the old, there was as far as the fisheries went an unbroken development from the fifteenth century onwards. From the Icelandic fishing voyages c.1420 to fishing off the Grand Banks in the seventeenth century, there is a continuous and unified history.

The Reformation, at least in the early stages, seems to have left untouched West Country and Basque fishermen alike, and it makes nonsense of all that we know of the fishing industry to ask whether the Weber-Tawney theses are relevant here or not. The fishermen went to Iceland or to Newfoundland for profit or they did not go at all. Seamen were generally held in contempt by Catholic and Protestant alike:

> since sailors, who form the greater part of our parishioners are ordinarily quite deficient in any spiritual feelings, having no sign of religion except in their oaths and blasphemies, nor any knowledge of God

beyond the simplest conceptions which they bring with them from France, clouded with licentiousness and the cavilings and revilings of heretics. . . .[2]

These introductory remarks may suggest that, in treating of the fishing industry, we are dealing with a primitive and therefore uncomplex industry. But the contrary is true. The industry was a highly structured, labour-intensive one, with heavy overhead costs, low profits, and the employment of a larger proportion of basic skills than any other industry. The financing of voyages, the preparing and provisioning of boats, the fishing operation itself, the marketing of the product, and the additional hazards of piracy, bad weather, and falling markets created an industry in which there was little room for mistake.[3]

The Atlantic coast line from Grand Manan to Hudson Strait (including Newfoundland and other islands) is some 12,000 miles in length. The coastal waters, including the Bay of Fundy and the Gulf of St. Lawrence, are some 200,000 square miles in extent. From New England to Labrador stretches the continental shelf, whose shallow waters, if we include the Grand Bank, constitute the largest demersal fishing grounds in the world. In Newfoundland some 20,000 fishermen in 1,000 villages depend on the sea for a livelihood. The dominant species of fish are the salmon, lobster, cod, herring, halibut, whitefish, perch and its relations, but in the early stages the fishing industry was founded on the cod, walrus, and whale, and of these three the cod became the staple product.

The cod is a cold-water fish that thrives best in water about 40°F and with a high degree of salinity. The warm Gulf Stream and the cold Labrador current carry ample marine life so that when they meet near the Grand Bank, they produce the right conditions in which the cod grows fat. Throughout the middle ages and well on into the modern period, the Western World depended on fish for a high percentage of its protein intake. Fish was a substitute for meat, just as it is today in those countries where climate and natural resources make meat a luxury. During the middle ages proper, the salted herring was the main fish, then, with the discovery of the Icelandic grounds in the fourteenth century, the stockfish took over. Unlike most other fish, the cod seems to have been destined for a special function in man's history. Innis points out that it "is different from other fishes like the salmon and herring; its flesh is rich and gelatinous without being fatty, and readily lends itself to a simple and efficient cure by salting and being dried in the

---

[2] Letter from Father Pierre Biard to the Reverend Father Provincial, in Paris. Port Royal, January 31, 1612: cited in *The Jesuit Relations and Allied Documents* edited by R. G. Thwaites, Vol. II, pp. 8-9.

[3] These aspects are well brought out by H. A. Innis in his *Select Documents in Canadian Economic History, 1497-1783* (University of Toronto Press, 1929).

sun." Fish so cured is easily restored to its natural state by replacing the water.[4]

In the fifteenth century the various fishing fleets left each spring for Iceland and both fished and traded for fish so it seemed that there was no need to venture elsewhere. Why then did the West Country and Basque fishermen turn to seeking out other sources? The answer lies partly in the action by the Bergen monopolists who sought to exclude foreigners from direct trade with Iceland. The records are few, but if we attempt to reconstruct the events of the last quarter of the fifteenth century, it appears that the Bristol merchants heard rumours, possibly from Portuguese venturers, of rich fishing grounds to the North West and they began to send out fishing expeditions into the Western Atlantic destined for the famed "Island of Brazil." Here they intended to establish a fishing station and, keeping the knowledge to themselves, accumulate all the profits. The expeditions located Newfoundland and the Bank fishery, and the West Country fishermen as long as they kept silent enjoyed a monopoly. There is nothing strange in their silence. Among fishermen the knowledge of good fishing grounds is not to be shared, not even with friends. Thus when Cabot rediscovered Newfoundland in 1497 and bruited abroad the fact of the rich fishing there, he was breaking a secret well-kept rather than presenting the world with a new discovery.[5] English ships from the east coast had continued to go to Iceland and, during the first half of the sixteenth century, at least, they provided the home country with most of her needs. There is no official mention of the English fishery at Newfoundland until an Act of 1541-2 for prohibition of buying fish at sea, instead of catching it, which was alleged to be injurious to the common weal. However, the Act was not to extend to the buying of fish in Iceland and Newfoundland.

If we supplement the official records with other sources, such as the evidence of the *portolanos*, we can conclude that by 1534 "the fisheries extended along the entire Atlantic coastline from southeastern Labrador to southern Nova Scotia. With the advent of Cartier's discovery the industry rapidly expanded into the Gulf of St. Lawrence and up the river."[6] Although we are concerned with Newfoundland, at this point I should emphasise the extent to which all enterprises were conditioned by climatic fac-

[4] Innis, *The Cod Fisheries* p. 6. See R. H. Tawney, *Business and Politics under James I* (Cambridge University Press, 1958) p. 25.

[5] For the modern treatment of this problem consult E. M. Carus-Wilson, *The Overseas Trade of Bristol in the Later Middle Ages* (Bristol Record Society Publications, Vol. 7, Bristol, 1937); T. J. Oleson, *Early Voyages and Northern Approaches 1000-1632* (Toronto, 1963); E. Brazão, *La découverte de Terre-Neuve* (Montreal, 1964); B. G. Hoffman, *Cabot to Cartier: Sources for a Historical Ethnography of Northeastern North America 1497-1550* (University of Toronto Press, 1961); and D. B. Quinn, "The Argument for the English Discovery of America between 1480 and 1494," *Geographical Journal*, 127 (1961), pp. 277-285.

[6] Hoffman, *op. cit.*, p. 198.

tors. In the case of the English fishing fleet, in order to reach the Bank or to arrive offshore in time for the summer fishing, the vessels had to leave England between January and April and, using the prevailing easterlies, go north after clearing Ireland. Near the American coast the Arctic current would take them south to Newfoundland. On the return voyage the fleet had to leave in August and, providing the westerlies were good, it could arrive home within seventeen days. But the average was four weeks. Thus the fishing fleet crowded western ports such as Plymouth and Dartmouth in the months of September and October. The alternative route described by Hayes in his "A direction of our course unto the New found land," although it is a good example of sailing directions, represents the early summer route – too late for the fishing fleet.[7] In the absence of accurate charts, the pilot took a dominant role and this was fully reflected in the shares allocated to him from the profits of the voyage.

Given the conditions imposed by the European market for the fish, the fishermen had little incentive to undertake controlled exploration. Nor did the land offer itself as an attractive proposition. There are several descriptions of Newfoundland in this period. The following account by Hayes given in Hakluyt is probably the best known:

> Touching the commodities of this country, serving either for sustentation of inhabitants, or for maintenance of traffique, there are and may be made divers: so that it seemeth Nature hath recompensed that only defect and incommoditie of some sharpe cold, by many benefits: viz. With incredible quantitie, and no lesse varietie of kindes of fish in the sea and fresh waters, as trouts, salmons, and other fish to us unknownen: Also Cod, which alone draweth many nations thither; and is become the most famous fishing of the world. Abundance of whales, for which also is a very great trade in the bayes of Placentia and the Grand bay, where is made Traine oiles of the Whale: Herring the largest that have been heard of, and exceeding the Malstrand herring of Norway: but hitherto was never benefit taken of the herring fishery. There are sundry other fish very delicate, namely the Bonito, Lobsters, Turbut, with others infinite not sought after: Oysters having pearle but not orient in colour. I tooke it by reason they were not gathered in season.[8]

Elsewhere Hayes adds that the inland commodities are better than any

---

[7] "A report of the voyage and successe thereof, attempted in the yeere of our Lord, 1583, by Sir Humfrey Gilbert Knight . . . written by M. Edward Haies. Gentleman . . . " in R. Hakluyt, *The Principall Navigations, Voiages and Discoveries of the English Nation* (London, 1589, Hakluyt Society, Extra Series No. XXXIX, Cambridge University Press, 1965), Vol. II, p. 684.

[8] Cited by H. S. Burrage, ed., *Early English and French Voyages 1534-1608* (New York 1906; reprinted 1959), p. 203.

"which our East and Northerly countries of Europe doe yeelde. . . Namely rosen, pitch, tarre, sopeashes, dealboard, mastes for ships, hides, furres, flaxe, hempe, corne, cordage, linnen-cloth, mettals and many more." He defines the Banks with some accuracy, and his description of the French and Portuguese fishery upon them is a brief and excellent summary of the "wet fishery."[9] Lescarbot writing his history of New France in 1608 claimed most of the honour for developing the fishery for France and for the seamen of Dieppe, St. Malo, and La Rochelle. These and other mariners "from Havre de Grace, Honfleur, and elsewhere are wont to make voyages into these countries in search of codfish, wherewith they feed nearly all Europe, and supply all sea-going ships." Lescarbot turning his back on the false lures that motivated those who searched for the Western passage, found the cod fisheries to be the true "mines," the profits of which compensate for the cold climate.[10] Eventually other fishermen found better fishing grounds than the Newfoundland ones, but none succeeded in surpassing the availability and quantity of fish in that region.

Newfoundland and the Banks provided an abundance for both the wet and dry fishery. Apart from the English who concentrated on the dry fishery, other nations employed both methods. It is sometimes suggested that the availability of salt or, as in the case of the English, its scarcity, determined the type of fishery a fleet pursued. The salt supply was certainly crucial to the industry, but other factors need to be taken into account. Those who fished the Banks had no choice about which method to follow. The cod fish caught on the Banks was generally large and unsuited for drying: it had to be put down green. Again the fishing months on the Bank (April-July) were usually the fog months, and the Banks were far from land so it was uneconomic to try to dry the catch. The offshore fishery started later in the year and coincided with better drying conditions. The fish was also smaller and suitable for drying. In terms of documentary evidence the French were the first to establish the seasonal offshore fishery. In the decade from 1520 to 1530 some sixty to ninety ships are estimated to have gone to Newfoundland, from Dieppe and Rouen, whereas reports of English vessels are very few. But fifty years later the English controlled the east coast of Newfoundland fishery and the French had moved round to the west coast. The explanation of this reversal of role will be discussed later.[11]

An adequate and guaranteed source of supply of salt was basic to the industry. In the case of France, Portugal and Spain there was no problem. With the English it was different. They had to secure supplies from their rivals. The history of the supply of salt emphasises the extent to which the

[9] *Ibid.*, p. 194, 203-4.

[10] M. Lescarbot, *The History of New France*, trans. and introduced by W. L. Grant and H. P. Biggar in 3 vols. (Toronto, The Champlain Society, 1907), Vol. II (1911) pp. 22, 41.

[11] Innis, *Cod Fisheries*, pp. 14-16; and *idem, Select Documents*, pp. 4-5.

fishing industry in the sixteenth century was heir to the medieval tradition and that its fortunes depended not on royal or official authority but on market conditions of supply and demand.[12]

Salt in this period had a variety of uses, among which were leather curing and the manufacture of distillates from wine, but its main use was for the preservation and flavouring of food – meat, bacon, butter, cheese, and fish. For trading ventures, it represented an ideal return cargo for vessels that otherwise would have to return in ballast. Without it there could have been no fishing fleet. The chief source of supply was France, Spain and Portugal, but it is important to realise that this had not always been the case and that the sixteenth century arrangement had taken two hundred years to evolve.

Rock salt, apart from the cost factor, was the most desirable salt to use. But the main producing centres in the middle ages had begun to decline by the fourteenth century. Thus rock salt was in relative short supply and considerably dearer. In 1494, according to the Great Chronicle of London, "Bay" salt could be landed at London for less than 4d a bushel, whereas salt from Nantwich, in Cheshire, fetched 6d.[13] "Bay" salt was from Bourgneuf Bay in France, where it was produced by the solar evaporative process. This method was simple and low cost; on the other hand seawater retains salts that can harm the curing process of fish, with the result that the inner core of the fish remains uncured and may prove, by the end of the voyage, to have gone bad. Bourgneuf Bay became the major salt producing region, and at the centre of the salt trade lay the town of Brouage, otherwise insignificant, close to La Rochelle and within easy reach of the islands of Ré and Oléron, all of which were important fishery areas. The proximity of the French fishing vessels to the main production centre for salt gave them an advantage over their rivals, but it also forced them into large scale green curing processes, whereas the English, who had some natural supplies of higher grade salt, became skilled in the dry fishery in which smaller quantities were used and a longer lasting curing process achieved. But the English still had to purchase large supplies of foreign salt. Resentment at this dependence is reflected in the numerous suggestions throughout the period that overseas discoveries might enable England to do without French and Spanish sources.[14] Dutch vessels predominated in the salt-carrying trade. The Netherlands imported salt on so vast a scale that after meeting the requirements of their own fish curing industry and supplying the region served by the Rhine, they managed to re-export something like 90,000 tons a year.

[12] A. R. Bridbury, *England and the Salt Trade in the Later Middle Ages* (Oxford University Press, 1955) is valuable for the salt trade in general.

[13] Cited by Bridbury, *op. cit.*, p. 95.

[14] See "Notes framed by M. Richard Hakluit . . . given to certaine Gentlemen that went with M. Frobisher in his Northwest discoverie" in R. Hakluyt, *The Principall Navigations* (Hakluyt Society, Extra Series No. XXXIX), Vol. II, p. 637. See also "A briefe and summarie discourse upon the intended voyage to the hithermost parts of America: written by Captaine Carlill in Aprill 1583" in *Ibid.*, Vol. II, p. 721.

The presence of salt in large quantities among the cargo of some of the exploring vessels suggests that the object of the voyage was to discover fishing grounds. In the early part of the sixteenth century much of the English imported supplies came from Bourgneuf Bay, but in 1566 when supplies of French salt threatened to fail, Burleigh noted that ". . . we of England and other countrys shalbe enforced to make our provysione from Spayne and Portingale and other places more farther off. . ."[15] A strong relationship with Portugal was established, which explains why the English regularly guaranteed the safety of the Portugese vessels in Newfoundland. But the supplies were not always consistent. From evidence furnished by John Guy in 1612, it seems that salt was shipped in bulk for use by the English fleet:

> . . . [we] came to Harbor de Grace as farre in as the Pirates forte, wheare the Banke shippe roade, wheare we remayned untill the 17th day of the sayde month and in the meane time did bring the Banke shippe a shoare, land the Salte upon the higheste parte of the ground thereaboutes, putting yt to preserve yt . . . the quantitie of salte was about fifteene tonnes.[16]

The failure of the salt supply meant the ruin of the whole voyage. It is clear that even the explorers expected to recoup some of their costs by returning with a cargo of fish. Thus, Anthony Parkhurst complained bitterly that he had been "deceived by the vile Portingales descending of the Jewes and Judas kind" who broke their promise and "disappointed me of the salt they should have brought me in part of recompense of my good service in defending them two yeeres against French Rovers that had spoyled them, if I had not defended them." As a result he suffered a loss of £600. Failing compensation from the King of Portugal, he sought leave of the Queen's Council to allow him to distrain Portuguese goods "as they have damnified mee, or els that I may take of them in New found land, as much fishe as will be worth 600 li. or as much as the salte might have made." He sought counsel for himself as well as for "the poore fishermen, who with me have sustained 300 pound losse in that voyage."[17]

The interdependence of the fisheries is most marked in the financial organisation that equipped and supported the fishing vessels. Of all industries, the fisheries possessed one of the most complex financial structures, for the

---

[15] Bridbury, *op. cit.*, pp. 56-7.

[16] "A Journall of the voiadge of discoverie made in a barke builte in Newfoundland called the Indeavour begunne the 7 of October 1612 and ended the 25th of November following. By John Guy of Bristow," reproduced, in part, in J.W.D. Powell, "The Explorations of John Guy in Newfoundland," *Geographical Journal*, 86 (1935), pp. 512-18, here, pp. 513-4.

[17] "A letter written to M. Richard Hakluyt of the middle Temple, conteining a report of the true state and commodities of New found land, by M. Anthonie Parkhurst Gentleman, 1578," in R. Hakluyt, *The Principall Navigations*, (Hakluyt Society, Extra Series No. XXXIX), Vol. II, p. 676.

degree of risk imposed solutions that would not have been tolerated in other industries. The financial structure, in origin, dates back to the thirteenth century, and one of the most obvious ways in which this appeared was the continued use of subterfuge to avoid the accusation of usury. As in the middle ages there was plenty of open usury (at rates varying from twenty to thirty-five per cent), but also hidden usury.[18] The common form was the loan on bottomry, that is, the owner mortgaged the ship to the backer for a guaranteed figure on return, but gave no compensation if the ship were lost. The following extract has a special significance, which I summarize in calendar form:

Sept.-Dec., 1533. Minutes of M. Gaschet, notary. Yvon Raymond, merchant and master of the ship *Xpristotle* of Plusmanac. Raymond has received money to the sum of 30 livres tournois from Julien Giraud, merchant and bourgeois of the town of La Rochelle. He has received the money "renoscent, sur ce ledit Raymond, à l'exception de ladite pecunie non avoir heue, non receue, non comptée, et à toutes autres manière et exception et dexxetions quelxconques. . . ."

Giraud in return for his 30 livres tournois is to have "deux milliers de moullues parées, ainsi qu'il les amenera moyennent qu'elles soyent bonnes et marchandes."[19] The form of this notarial agreement is very ancient, going back to the twelfth century, and it contains the common *exceptio de non numerata pecunia*, which is designed to prevent the borrower from appealing to the courts against hidden usury charges.

It has been suggested that the "essential characteristics of the industry had evolved during the middle ages when few merchants enjoyed extensive reserves of capital."[20] But this does an injustice to the middle ages and fails to understand the fishing industry. In a high risk industry a merchant, however wealthy, preferred to spread his risk rather than to put all his money in the one enterprise. For the merchant investor, fishing was just another outlet for his capital. The operation and continuity of this system is obvious from the time that our records commence (in the case of England with the Iceland fishery) and there seems no difference between the possible arrangements here and those on the continent. A typical agreement is the following relating to the *Catherine*, about 160-180 tons, "to provide all necessary victuals, for the boat to leave from Honfleur and to proceed direct to Brouage, there to take on salt and from there to go make its fishing on the Banks, off the Isle de Sable, the vessel to have 33 seamen, as well as soldiers."[21]

[18] On usury in the middle ages see J. Gilchrist, *The Church and Economic Activity in the Middle Ages* (London, 1969), pp. 62-70.

[19] Cited by H. P. Biggar, *The Precursors of Jacques Cartier 1497-1534, a Collection of Documents* (Ottawa, 1911), Doc. LX, pp. 181-2.

[20] Cell, *op. cit.*, pp. 6-7.

[21] Cited by Innis, *Select Documents*, pp. 75-8. (Translated from the French by the present author).

Fishing ventures were all insured. According to Cell, "the insurance policy had become an established instrument in the financial organisation of Newfoundland industry by 1580." The earliest extant copy of such a policy covered a voyage made by the *Hopewell* of London in 1604. The owner insured the cargo of fish from time of loading at Newfoundland to time of discharge at London or Marseilles. The risks concerned were ". . . of the seas men of warre, Fier, enemies, Pirates, Robers, Theeves, Jettesons, Letters of Mark and counter Mark, Arrestes, Restraintes, and detaynements . . . barratrye of the Master and Marriners of all other perilles, losses and misfortunes whatsoever they be. . . ." The owner paid £7 for every £100 worth of goods insured.[22]

Equally complicated were the arrangements for paying the fishermen. The various systems of paying seamen go back to the medieval Laws of Oléron, which give three possible systems (1) a proportionate share of the ultimate profits, (2) a share of the cargo space, and (3) wages. Nicholas Denys, in his account of Acadia (1672), provides much evidence of the seventeenth century practice.[23] It seems that the varying skills of the fishermen produced variants of the three systems. The élite of fishermen were the Basques. The owner of the vessel made an estimation of the capacity of the ship, divided this into two or three hundred shares and gave so many shares to the captain, beach master, pilot, dressers, masters of boats, stowers, boatswain, and boys. If the final catch of the venture was less than calculated, then the shares were proportionately reduced. The men of Bordeaux worked for a third of the cargo. The other two thirds went to the owner of the vessel and victualler respectively. The captain arranged his crew and allocated one-third proportionately, that is, before the voyage commenced. The men of La Rochelle, Isle of Ré, and Isle d'Oléron took a quarter of the catch. This has been explained on the grounds that they were less skilled than the men of Bordeaux, but a more likely explanation is that each man also received a small "premium" in advance of the voyage, provided by the ship owners as a sort of gratuity. Each person on the boat had his premium, a good indication of the hierarchical structure of the industry by the sixteenth century.

More interesting, however, were the arrangements by which, in chartered vessels, the charterer allowed the crewmen an amount of cargo space that the crewmen could fill or was filled by the merchant who paid freight charges to the crewman. This system of "portage" had been common in medieval Europe but it practically died out except for the fishing industry. The pursuit of profit became so strong that owners of vessels complained that their interests were neglected or inferior fish brought back while the seamen kept the best part of the catch for themselves. Everyone had his price. Even the

---

[22] Cell, *op. cit*, p. 12.

[23] Nicolas Denys, *The Description and Natural History of the Coasts of North America (Acadia)* ed. W. F. Ganong (Toronto, 1908), pp. 271-2. See also Innis, *Cod Fisheries* 18.

ship's doctor received a premium for his medicine chest of some 200-300 livres out of which he had to provide medicines and instruments. He kept the chest on return, and he could, I suppose, make an additional profit if the voyage had been uneventful. He also received twenty sols for each man for barbering him, and a share of the fish.

London and La Rochelle were the main financial centres. In the case of London, this created conflict with the fishermen of the West Country. These two centres produced for the fishing industry a system of finance based on the charter-party, which gave the investor the maximum of control and the minimum of financial risk. The Dutch too got involved and it seems that by the seventeenth century the fish re-export trade was financed and handled by Dutch, Irish and French as well as English interests. A typical instance of a charter-party is the agreement between Phillpott and Barrett (1563) to send the ship *Jesus* on a fishing voyage to Newfoundland. The agreement contains a general average clause, the sharing of good "aventures," and spoil. The charter stipulates that if the vessel is robbed it

shalbe leyde and putt in a generall average solvendum per libras videlicet pounde for pounde lyke. And of good aventures that shall happen or chaunce unto the said shippe . . . then the said owners vitlers the master and his companye to have the said good aventures betwen them equallye devyded in three severall partes one parte to the owners thother part to the vitlers and the thirde parte to the master and his companye towage sownage and petye lodesmanshippe with all other accustomed averages to be at the costes of the said merchants and laders.[24]

These terms should be compared with the following agreement between merchants and masters of fishing vessels to supply the vessels in return for

leur droict et cotité des pesches, huilles, gaings et prouffictz qu'ilz ont faicts en leur voiages de la Terre Neufve, selon qu'ilz estoient associez par les ditz maistres de navire, selon les chartes parties sur ce faictes et passées auparavant.[25]

Such charters could be for a full season or for some specific part. In 1636 the *Mary and John* of London was hired by a group of merchants at £ 220 a month to collect fish worth £ 2500 at Newfoundland and proceed directly to the Straits. In 1650 the *Adventure* went to the Canaries, Newfoundland and back to St. Lucar for £ 110 a month. Such vessels were known as Sack ships, that is, vessels that went to Newfoundland to buy fish, and they could have several partners, for example, the *Alethia* and *Diamond* of London had

---

[24] *Select Pleas in the Court of Admiralty* (Selden Society Publications), Vol. II, *The High Court of Admiralty* (A.D. 1547-1602) (London, 1897), pp. lxviii, 64.

[25] Doc. LII, in Biggar, *The Precursors of Jacques Cartier*, p. 160. See Doc. LIII for a similar agreement, *ibid.*, p. 161.

eleven and twelve owners respectively. But a small West Country fishing vessel might have only one owner, and the charge for a nine months' voyage to Newfoundland and thence to Marseilles cost £40 or less a month.

In equipping a fishing fleet, there is a great deal of miscellaneous evidence which can be pieced together to give us some idea of the type of vessel, outfitting costs and complement of men needed for the voyage. The ideal ship was from seventy to one hundred tons. A seventy ton vessel would cost £200 to build and equip and would require a crew of twenty-four. Whitbourne recommended a ship of one hundred tons and a crew of forty. And here it should be obvious to the reader that in such ventures each man had a dual role to fill, that is, he had to be a seaman as well as a fisherman. For the English offshore fishery, the fishing was done from small boats of three to five tons, which could hold about one thousand fish and carried a crew of five men. The parent ship would have perhaps five such boats, from which all the fishing was done during the season.[26] Meanwhile the parent ship was unrigged.

As an example of a detailed outfitting we have the account of Martin Frobisher's expedition in 1577 in which three ships totalling 240 tons and 115 men cost £4500. Among the provisions were biscuit, meal, beer, wine, beef, pork, peas, stock fish, butter, cheese, oatmeal, rice, honey, salad oil, aquavita, mustard seed, candles, sea coal, charcoal, prunes, raisins, almonds.[27] A typical fishing vessel of one hundred tons with a complement of forty men cost £420-1-4d a year to provision and outfit. Whitbourne estimated that such a ship would carry eight, three-men fishing boats catching an average of 25,000 fish per boat, therefore a total catch of 200,000 cod. If the catch were taken to Marseilles or Toulon, it could be sold at 12s a quintal which would gross £1320 (at 16s a quintal = £1760). The crew of forty would count twenty-four fishermen, seven skilled headers and splitters, two boys, three salters, three men to wash and dry fish. In addition the venture would yield twelve tons of cod oil at £10 a ton in Newfoundland (£18 or £20 in England), plus 10,000 green fish. All for a grand total of £2250.

I cite these figures because it is not readily seen that the jump from being a fishing vessel to undertaking a voyage of exploration was a big one, and, considering the financial commitment, an impossible one. We may wonder why the fishing vessels that called at Newfoundland and established seasonal bases on shore did not undertake more exploration and settlement? The answer lies in the simple fact that their outfitting did not allow such luxuries. As we shall see, once the vessel reached Newfoundland every man was committed to a tight schedule that excluded the luxury of exploration. Ships

[26] Cited by Innis, *Cod Fisheries*, pp. 59-60.
[27] Cited by Innis, *Select Documents*, pp. 11-13. See also Cell, *op. cit.*, p. 7; and Biggar, *The Precursors of Jacques Cartier* Doc. LVI, p. 163.

that delayed their return might find themselves confronted with the situation at Plymouth in 1595 when fifty Newfoundlanders reached the port within the fortnight and caused a glut in which some 2,000,000 fish were available to the foreign buyers. In 1615 Whitbourne preferred to risk danger at sea rather than wait for a convoy, which would have meant the ships arriving in port together, flooding the market with fish, and so lowering prices. As fishing was a profit sharing venture, it was in every man's interest to beat the competitors.[28]

An example of the tight schedule followed by the fishing fleets, which precluded any strong interest in anything but fishing, is found in the account given by Denys of the Dry fisheries in Acadia. On the voyage out the men were occupied in preparing for the fishing such as sail making, fitting out the boats, preparing the lead sinkers and so on. Once on shore each step followed by the crew was like the fitting together of some gigantic puzzle. There was a rigid order of priorities that determined who should have the shore sites where the stages could be built for salting and drying, and how fishing boats that had been left behind the previous season but were unmarked should be divided up. The hierarchy was elaborate, the division of duties highly specialised – on shore every man changed his job, except the captain, and took up the new duty to which he had been assigned. Before fishing could begin, lodging for the captain, crew, and for the provisions had to be prepared. Stagings had to be built. Denys remarks that "when once the work has commenced, it is almost useless to speak of sleeping, eating, or drinking unless by stealth, except for the supper. Whilst some are transporting all the logs, others are at work preparing the stagings." Even the ship's doctor and the apprentices took on new roles, preparing the flakes on which to dry the cod and becoming responsible for supplementing rations with hunting game and tending a vegetable garden.[29]

When the fishing commenced, the margin for error had gone. The process of catching, splitting, salting, and drying cod was an elaborate one from start to finish, which, among other things, involved great care in the use of the salt and in ensuring that once the process of drying had begun, the flesh of the fish was never allowed to get wet again. This last condition applied until the fish arrived at the market. Each day's catch had to be kept separate from the others, during the long drying process. The fishing day was an arduous one. The men rose at dawn and fished until 4 p.m. It was usually about 6 p.m. before the first boat reached the staging to unload the catch.

As for the working conditions, we know that there was an elaborate equality of work and provisions among the fishermen; the ship's provisions belonged "as much to all the crew as to the captain, and he cannot dispose of them in favour of any one whatsoever except by consent of all the crew,

[28] Cell, *op. cit.*, pp. 25, 108.
[29] *Edit.* W.F. Ganong, p. 274 ff.

although he has the right to drink the wine pure at his table during the voyage and during the stay."[30] The crew drank their wine pure at sea three days a week and the other days half and half, and on shore they drank it more diluted. The diet was monotonous, except on Sundays. The men sat in messes of seven by seven, while the captain, beach master, pilot and doctor "who is the one who has charge of the cooking" ate in the captain's lodging.[31] Seamen could rebel against their diet. Davis on his first voyage (1585) experienced such an incident, which led to an improvement in which "every messe being five to a messe should have 4 pound of bread a day; 12 quarts of bere; 6 newland fishes: and the flesh days a gill of pease more: so we restrayned them from their butter and cheese." On his third voyage (1587) the mariners in one of the vessels were again dissatisfied with the food and decided to discontinue the exploration and instead to "goe on their voyage a fishing."[32]

At the end of the season, there was still some time before the drying process was completed, and during this period the crew was occupied in preparing the vessel for the return voyage. Again the profit motive loomed large, and the following text from Denys illustrated this. After making up the cod into lots of 33, which make 132 cod to the 100, to allow for spoiling and breaking:

> The finest and largest of the dry fish are separated out every time the piles are spread in the sun; and they are placed in the store-room. That is where the bread or biscuit is kept as being the dryest place. That which is left of the biscuit for the return voyage is placed between decks as is also all the rest of the drink, provisions, and the baggage of the sailors. . .[33]

The fishing boats were left behind, hidden in the woods, and any surplus provisions sold to those that sought them. If it had been a good season, the ship might have as many as 200,000 dry cod, as against a vessel from the Banks which would carry 45,000-50,000 fish.

The industry just described was clearly a labour intensive industry, with the additional difficulty of being one in which the actual fishing itself was but a part of the total time taken for the voyage. Thus overheads were high, and the question may be asked at this point whether the industry could not have been streamlined by introducing such, apparently, labour saving devices as

[30] Denys, op. cit., p. 263, 316.

[31] Denys, op. cit., p. 316.

[32] "The first voyage of Master John Davis, undertaken in June 1585, for the Discoverie of the Northwest Passage written by John Janes Marchant, servant to the worshipfull M. William Sanderson," in R. Hakluyt, Hakluyt Society, The Principall Navigations (Extra Series No. XXXIX) Vol. II, p. 779. Sanderson was the leading investor in the venture; see Quinn, ibid., Vol. I, p. xliv. For the third voyage, see ibid., Vol. II, p. 790.

[33] Denys, op. cit., p. 339.

maintaining the shore establishments all year round? For it is obvious that all this fishing activity had not, by the end of the sixteenth century, done much to improve the settlement of Newfoundland.

For several reasons the question of settlement is tied up with export markets for dry fish and therefore in particular with the English fishery. The French had a large domestic market for green fish and so, when her fishermen sought sites for the dry fish, they did in the knowledge that, should conditions be poor for drying, they could always find a market for fish put down green. But the English West Country fisherman did not have the same security. Despite the existence of the statutory fish days, it proved difficult to persuade the English to consume more fish. Therefore the industry, which was largely financed by London interests, found itself obliged to produce for the export markets, which meant dry fish. Moreover, the fishermen, under pressure from the financial backers, felt compelled to be more vigorous in the struggle to secure the best sites on the east coast of Newfoundland. Having once secured the sites, the same financial interests considered whether it would not be better to replace the seasonal fishing with a permanent sedentary type, in other words, settlement. At this point, the clash of interests between West Country fishermen and London capital becomes obvious. The financiers wanted fish, and as cheaply as possible. They became accustomed to hiring Sack ships to carry Newfoundland fish to the Mediterranean markets. If the fishing season could be extended by forming permanent bases in Newfoundland, with the marketing operation separated from the fishery, then increased profits could result. It is not therefore surprising that the period of prosperity in the English Newfoundland fishery (1600-1625) coincided with the first attempts at settlement, from 1610 onwards. After 1625, the prosperity was gone and it did not return before 1660.

Although the carrying trade showed profits, it did not encourage the West Country fishermen to heed the advice of the London merchants who wanted a sedentary fishery, based on settlement and monopoly. And here we confront the paradox which explains why the fishery brought the European nations close to Newfoundland but then drove them into active opposition to permanent settlement. The London interests which drew profits from the three cornered trade of purchasing the West Country catches, carrying them to the Mediterranean and returning with the price of the catch in specie, and luxury goods, could make a profit even when fish prices were depressed, which tended to deepen the antagonism between the fishermen and the financiers. Contemporary economists praised this type of trade, for it was done without draining bullion away from England. Monopolistic control was, of course, a necessary condition in order to ensure maximum profits.[34]

This type of classical thinking, which nevertheless encouraged settlement,

[34] See Thomas Mun, *England's Treasure by Forraing Trade* (London 1664 reprod. Oxford, 1959) art. 6, pp. 9-10

ran counter to the spirit that motivated the fishing interests. Both in France and England the fishery demanded what Innis called "an aggressive commercialism" which was in contrast to large-scale company organisations and which "opened a breach in mercantilistic control which was progressively widened." The industry involved a number of supplementary trades, listed by Whitbourne in his *Discourse and discovery of Newfoundland* (London 1622), as "bakers, brewers, coopers, ship-carpenters, smiths, netmakers, rope makers, Hooke-makers, pully makers, and many other trades."[35] During a century of fishing the fishing fleets increased from the "eleven sails of Normans, and one Brittaine, and two Portugall Barkes, and all a fishing" reported by John Rut as found by him in St. Johns in 1527, to the following figures by Parkhurst in 1578:

> Now to answer some part of your letter touching the sundry navies that come to New found land, of Terra nova, for fish, you shall understand that some fish not neere the other by 200 leagues, and therefore the certaintie is not knowen, and some yeeres come many more than other some, as I see the like among us: who, since my first travell being but 4 yeeres, are increased from 30 sayle to 50, which cometh to passe chiefly by the imagination of the Westerne men, who thinke their neighbours have had greater gains than in very deed they have, for that they see me to take such paines yerely to go in proper person, they also suppose that I find some secret commodotie by reason that I do search the harbors, creekes and havens, and also the land much more than ever any Englishman hath done ... I am informed that there are about 100 saile of Spaniards that come to take cod (who make all wet, and do drie it when they come home) besides 20 or 30 more that come from Biskaie, to kil Whale for traine.[36]

In 1586 Thevet put the number of vessels engaged in the fishery as about 300 sail. Finally, Whitbourne in 1615 estimated the English vessels alone as some 250 in number, with a total tonnage of 15,000, employing some 5000 seamen, and yielding a total catch valued at £120,000. In 1634 there were some 27,000 tons of shipping, employing some 18,600 men, yielding a gross value of £178,880.[37]

Despite the decline of the Spanish and Portuguese fleets, leaving France and England as the chief contenders, it is obvious that the fishing never became the monopoly of any one nation. By the time permanent settlement came to be considered, the English fishery was consolidated on the east coast

[35] Innis, *Cod Fisheries*, p. 42; idem, *Select Documents*, pp. 16-17.

[36] For John Rut, see Hoffman, *Cabot to Cartier*, p. 119, where he cites the account of the 1527 expedition as found in *Purchas his Pilgrimage* (1625): Vol. III; p. 809. For Parkhurst's figures see the text in Haklyt, *The Principall Navigations*, Vol. II, p. 674.

[37] Cited by Innis, *Select Documents*, p. 16. For the later figures see Innis, *Cod Fisheries*, pp. 69-70.

south of Cape Bonavista, and this tended to force the French to more distant parts of the island. How then did the fishing interests react to suggestions of monopoly settlement and control?

The basic organisation of the fisheries was opposed to permanent settlement but paradoxically, the fishermen were drawn towards some form of settlement by the same interests that opposed it. The growth of the fishing fleets gradually involved the national governments' supervision and then control of the activities of the fishing vessels. The ships were exposed to various natural and man-made hazards. Nothing could be done about the first kind – Hayes recounts how, with the loss of the *Delight*, a group saved themselves and spent six days at sea without food or water and with "no better sustenance than their own urine"[38] – but for the second kind, which consisted largely of reprisals, privateering and pirate attacks on the fishing ships, the royal authorities attempted to provide a remedy by convoying the fishing fleets. An interesting example of both privateering and piratical attack is found in the English Admiralty Pleas of 1582. A Roger Poyton had shipped a cargo of Newfoundland fish by a French vessel, *Pelican*, which was captured by one John Grainger and his accomplices. This in turn was recaptured by one Francis Langherne who took, as recompense, 15,000 fish "besides and beyond the number of 10,000 fish by our order." The court ordered Langherne to restore the 15,000 fish, valued at 26s 8d per 100 fish.[39] The Admiralty Court did not automatically favour the English party. In a case in 1598 the Court passed sentence for restitution of a French "banker," the *Marquis d'Olonne*, and fish in her, captured by Thomas Broughton on her way home from Newfoundland.[40] Pirates were numerous especially in the seventeenth century, and there was the additional hazard of automatic seizure by the enemy whenever war broke out. It has been estimated that in the period 1612-20 the damage done to English Newfoundland fishermen amounted to £40,800; plus loss of 180 cannon, and 1080 fishermen and merchants carried off by force. Convoys by the English navy became frequent but sometimes the fishing fleet suffered as much from them as from the supposed enemy.

Royal intervention placed the fishing interests in a quandary. They needed the protection but not for the same reasons as motivated the crown. Royal intervention came about because it saw the fishery as a nursery for seamen – both French and English fleets were often forbidden to sail for Newfoundland, until the respective navies had reached their full complement of men – and also as a source of income. Sometimes royal officials were over zealous in taxing the fishery, so special legislation was needed such as the Act of

---

[38] Cited in Burrage, *Early English and French Voyages*, p. 213.

[39] *Select Pleas in the Court of Admiralty*, Vol. II, pp. 160-1.

[40] *Documents relating to Law and Custom of the Sea*, ed., R.G. Marsden, Vol. I, *A.D. 1205-1648* (Navy Records Society, Vol. 49, 1915), pp. 293-8.

Edward VI "an Act against the exaction of money or any other thing by any officer for licence to trafique into Iseland, and Newfoundland. . . "[41]

Royal intervention in the fishery came also from another direction, namely under pressure from the organisers and promoters of the voyages of exploration and settlement. These voyages, like the Newfoundland fishery itself, were really a continuation of the medieval outreachings towards the West, the one by the northerly route – Iceland, Greenland, Labrador, the Belle-Isle Strait and Cape Breton, the other – dating from the Portuguese voyages of the fourteenth century – by the south-west routes. Who discovered Newfoundland first is immaterial to our purpose, what is important is that all the early explorers shared common aspiration and common techniques, which may be summarized as first the westwards "voyage" towards Asia, which gradually turned itself into a search for the North-West passage, and then by the end of the sixteenth century into the knowledge that Newfoundland was an island, that the Gulf of St. Lawrence did not yield the desired route, and into a desire for wealth that the "mines" of the fishing banks – to use Lescarbot's phrase – did not satisfy.[42]

Any estimation of the impact of the fishing fleets upon the formation of settlements must take into account not only the fact that the dry fishery brought men to Newfoundland, in search of shelter, supplies of wood, fresh water, bait, and drying stages, as well as safe harbours, and which then ground to a halt any attempt at exploration by reason of the demands of the fishing season that occupied every man's labour, but also the fact that "the European image of North America actually seems to have developed through a process of slow and painful accretion . . . This seems to have been particularly true in the Newfoundland area where a combination of rugged and complex coastlines, persistent fogbanks, and dangerous ice conditions caused the loss of many expeditions and kept the cartographers baffled for over a century."[43]

In retrospect we know that the returns from this part of the world were small during the sixteenth and seventeenth century, apart from the profits of fish and fur, but the explorers were not to know that and what inspired them was their ignorance of the true position. All the royal charters possess common

---

[41] In Hakluyt, *Principall Navigations*, Vol. II, p. 521.

[42] *The History of New France* ed. Grant and Biggar, Vol. II, p. 317. On the voyages of exploration, see J.E. Oleson and E.G. Bourne, eds., *The Northmen, Columbus and Cabot 985-1503* (1906, reprint 1959); H. P. Biggar, *The Voyages of Jacques Cartier* (Ottawa, 1924); J.D. Rogers, *Newfoundland* (New edit. rev. by C.A. Harris, Oxford, 1931); L.J. Burpee, *The Discovery of Canada* (Toronto, 1944); F.F. Thompson, *The French Shore Problem in Newfoundland: An Imperial Study* (University of Toronto Press, 1961); M. Trudel, *Histoire de la Nouvelle France*, I, *Les vaines tentatives 1524-1603* (Montreal-Paris, 1963); R. Maran, ed., *Jacques Cartier (1491-1557), Voyages de découverte au Canada entre les années 1534 et 1542* . . . (Paris, 1968).

[43] Hoffman, *op. cit.*, p. 101. See Trudel, *op. cit.*, p. 77, 251.

characteristics, the grant for a number of years, the relief from taxes and customs, the return to the crown of a fifth or sixth part of the profits. For the first forty years, after Cabot, there was a great deal of activity, but then the English and French became frustrated at finding no return for their outlay. After Cartier's voyages, Canada was largely forgotten, except for the fisheries. When the next spate of exploration began the aims were more realistic and they included some very practical possibilities that saw Newfoundland as a source of naval supplies, as well as fish. The aims had also come to include the desire to convert the native peoples. But in the meantime the fisheries had established their claim to the shore line of Newfoundland on a seasonal basis, and had established customs and a way of life that was seriously threatened by the possibility of a permanent colony.

After the failure of Sir Humphrey Gilbert's patent in 1584, Hayes worked on a plan for a commercial company to finance a colony in Newfoundland, which would have a monopoly of the fishery and control of distribution at home. When the first colony was so established – John Guy's in 1610 – it was along such lines, even though it was thirty years in inception. About the same time (1588) as Gilbert's grant, Jacques Noël and Étienne Chaton de la Jannaye got from Henry III, for twelve years, the monopoly of Canada and adjacent lands, whose conditions were the same as the 1540 commission to Jacques Noël's uncle but, this time, material exploitation was dominant.[44] Such grants not merely threatened to exclude the fishermen from the enterprise directly, but any settlement would by its nature give an advantage to residents who wintered in Newfoundland, in the form of first choice of the best sites, fishing stages, boats and so forth, over the seasonal fishermen who would arrive in April to find themselves ousted by the settlers. Thus we see the West Country merchants of England and those of St. Malo and La Rochelle up in arms against the monopolists. It was in fact a struggle of free trade versus regulated trade. The St. Malo merchants petitioned for a revocation of the grant which they secured on 5 May, 1588. In England the conflict resolved itself into one between London financiers and the Western merchants and their allies, the gentry. The fishermen could not settle the island, they were determined that no one else should.

Actually the fishing interests underestimated the difficulties facing any attempt to settle Newfoundland. The climate made agricultural settlement highly unprofitable, for the growing season coincided with the fishing season which was a successful competitor for labour. Moreover, contrary to their fears, the basic skills of the seasonal fishermen were not easily transplanted from the native homeland and adapted to different living conditions. These factors are all in evidence in the history, from 1610 onwards, of the London and Bristol Company for the Colonization of Newfoundland. John Guy, after choosing Cupet's Cove (Port de Grave) on the west coast of Concep-

[44] See Trudel, *op. cit.*, I, pp. 222-4.

tion Bay for his capital, issued ordinances fining subject and foreign fishermen for various offences, and the fishermen counter-charged that the settlers took the best fishing places, stole what the fishers left behind, and tried to deprive the fishermen of bait-birds from Baccalieu Island. This first colony went through various transfers and subdivisions. Its capital was never enough. Despite Star Chamber regulations to enforce the ordinances of John Guy, these were easily disregarded. The documentary evidence for the seventeenth century shows that the settlers suffered from a number of economic and physical ills that made them less efficient than the seasonal fishermen. Settlers lost initiative for work, they showed lack of enterprise, they could not retain the hired fishermen who came out for the season except by offering high wages. There was lack of winter provisions, and the consequent spread of disease and scurvy. In order to protect the fishery as a source of seamen, the mother country imposed difficult conditions on the settlers, such as the six mile prohibition of settlement near the coast, which was subsequently changed into a quarter mile limitation without improving the lot of the settlers. In 1677 details were published for the first time of the English settlements. In all there were some 523 settlers scattered in 28 settlements, all of which except Trepassey were on the east coast, between Cape Race and Cape Bonavista. The largest settlement was St. Johns (87), Bonavista (63), and Carbonear on Conception Bay (55), but the average settlement was Ferryland (21), Renewse (19), and Trepassey (10). Of these, 361 were women and children. In addition, there was a fluctuating body of 1342 boatmen, servants, and the like, only 23 of whom were women. They came out each year with the fishermen, who left them behind to save freight and food. To survive, the groups fished in summer and boat-built in winter.[45]

But the settlements were at least established, government intervention had become normal, and the stage was set for the Anglo-French conflict for control. But the extent to which the traditions of the fishery had determined the fate of the island and would continue to so determine it, is seen in the fact that the French retained offshore fishing rights till 1904. Newfoundland and, if one may generalise, the whole of the Maritimes provides a perfect example of the impact of environmentally determined factors on the emergent colonial society of the pre-conquest period.

[45] See Innis, *Select Documents*, pp. 84-97.

Commerce in New France

James Pritchard, Lecturer in History, Queen's University

Commerce in New France stood in stark contrast with that of the mother country. Whereas the French pre-industrial economy was dominated by agriculture, and commerce by the exchange of agricultural products, in New France commerce was governed by the exchange of North American furs for products of French manufacture.[1] Prior to the last decade of the French regime, Canada held few values in the eyes of French authorities that were not associated with the fur trade. Fur was not only the major export of New France, but the characteristics of the trade shaped the colony's domestic economy and society. The high land-to-man ratio required by the trade made metropolitan merchants unwilling to encourage or to support immigration. Hopes for profits to be derived from fur drew scarce manpower and local capital away from investment in colonial enterprises in the St. Lawrence valley into the West and Hudson Bay. The fur trade also gave rise to and cultivated the boom-bust psychology of many of the colony's leaders. Combined with *poor geographic location* for supplying the large West Indian market, it limited diversity of exports and retarded development of commercial agriculture, fishing, lumbering and local shipping.[2]

The establishment of a commercial military settlement on Cape Breton Island in the years following the signing of the Treaty of Utrecht presented New France with market opportunities that were exploited for about twenty years, but the period of time was too short and the proportion of total exports too small to provide a basis on which to establish an indigenous entrepreneurial group in French colonial society. In 1739, when New France had reached the apogee of its economic diversification, fur still constituted seventy per cent of the total value of the colony's exports.[3] New France never experienced the period of consolidation that witnessed the emergence of a self-conscious commercial class in several of the colonies to the south. Instead, by the middle of the eighteenth century, when the settled English colonies were preparing to cross the Appalachian Mountains into the Ohio

[1] E. Labrousse, *et al.*, *Histoire économique et sociale de la France*, Tome II, *Des derniers temps de l'âge seigneurial aux préludes de l'âge industriel (1660-1789)*, (Paris, P.U.F., 1970), p. 180.

[2] H.A. Innis, *The Fur Trade in Canada: An Introduction to Canadian Economic History*, Rev. ed., (Toronto, 1956) continues to provide insights into the nature of Canadian economic development, but the chapters on the French trade require considerable revision in the light of more recent scholarship. See, for example, A.J.E. Lunn, "The Illegal Fur Trade out of New France, 1713-1760," *Canadian Historical Association Report*, 1939, pp. 61-76; E.R. Adair, "Anglo-French Rivalry in the Fur Trade during the Eighteenth Century." *Culture*, VIII, (1947), pp. 434-55; and G. Frégault, "La Compagnie de la colonie," in *Le XVIIIe siècle canadien: études*, (Montreal, 1968), pp. 242-88.

[3] J. Hamelin, *Economie et société en Nouvelle-France*, (Quebec, 1960), p. 47.

valley, agents of the French fur-trading colony already had erected posts on the Saskatchewan River and viewed the "Shining Mountains" still farther west. Little energy remained for other economic activity. Commerce in New France was always weak and relatively shapeless, for over it ruled the fur trade controlled largely by metropolitan merchants.

If the central feature of trade in New France was the exchange of North American furs for French products and manufactures, the central problem was finding means to pay for imports required by the colonists. As population grew, largely through natural increase, so too did the difficulties for the ever increasing demand for imports was tied to demographic growth in New France rather than to the fur trade. Colonists were hard put to find currency, media of credit, and capital resources that would enable them to create an economy in New France at a level beyond mere subsistence. It was owing chiefly to the fur trade that they did not resolve all of their difficulties, but also to the enterprize of some colonists that they did not entirely fail.

During the early years, when New France was exploited by private monopolists, population remained very low. Until 1643 the Company of One Hundred Associates had the sole right to move goods in and out of New France. Trade was an extension of metropolitan commerce carried on by subsidiary companies of the chartered body at the level of barter. Each year trade goods and supplies for the colonists were shipped to New France while furs and hides were sent to France. Local commerce was carried on through direct exchange, or with the use of beaver skins as a circulation medium.

Most of the cargo space in ships from France was required to transport food, clothing and building supplies for the colonists rather than trade goods. Furs occupied little bulk in relation to their value; and, except for the tremendous risk involved, could be carried in a single merchant ship. This feature of the trade never changed. During the eighteenth century the main cargo of beaver pelts normally was sent to France in the armed naval transport that called annually at Quebec. Consequently many ships departed Quebec in ballast. Throughout the regime, but especially during the era of private monopoly, there was present every incentive to prevent colonization in order to reduce the demand for extra ships whose outfitting costs ate into the potential earnings of furs shipped to France.

In later years, failure to obtain return cargoes from New France became a constant feature of trans-ocean trade; and was the major factor leading ships' captains departing Quebec to sail to the West Indies where they hoped to find a cargo to lade for the return voyage to France. This activity by metropolitan shippers obstructed development of a colonial carrying trade during the seventeenth century. In the years when an agricultural surplus was produced, metropolitan vessels were available to carry it to the Islands. When colonists finally appeared as competitors such was the mercantilist orthodoxy of the minister of marine, that in 1702, he forbade any exchange between

New France and the French West Indian Islands in colonial bottoms.[4] The fur trade and official policy frequently combined to discourage colonial efforts to diversify the economy.

Early commercial activity in New France was carried on with little need for coin, as the colonists dealt only with the monopoly holders. Specie entered the colony in the form of considerable donations sent by the devout in France to religious orders. The Jesuits alone are thought to have received 160,400 *livres* during the thirty years before 1655.[5] Additional small private holdings of capital belonging to a few of the French gentry who immigrated to New France may also have contributed to the supply of coin in New France, but the total amount was small. Most colonists were indentured servants, with nothing but their salaries on which to depend.

The founding of Montreal in 1642, the loss of the general trade privileges by the One Hundred Associates a year later, and the transfer of the beaver monopoly to a colonial company based at Quebec all led to a need for a regular currency in New France. The center of the fur trade soon shifted to Montreal. Currency would facilitate exchanges between the center of the trade and the colony's sea port. A need for currency arose also, soon after it became legally permissible for any French merchant to outfit a ship and send it to Canada with supplies and merchandise required by the colonists.

During the 1640's control of New France's external trade passed first, from the Company into the hands of a local group known as the *Communanté des habitants*; although everyone in the colony was entitled to membership, in reality the new company was controlled by a small group of fur traders at Quebec. Towards the end of the decade, New France's trade passed once more into the hands of metropolitan traders, located chiefly in La Rochelle. The directors of the *Communanté des habitants* attempted to carry on trade from New France, but lacking sufficient capital of their own, were forced to borrow in France. The initial arrangement appeared successful and for a few years colonists were able to avoid reliance upon French merchants. Whether due to incompetence, internal rivalry, consumption of profits, or to the disastrous consequences arising from the destruction of the Huron trading system, the *Communanté* was unable to meet its obligations and forced to borrow additional capital. By 1651 the colonial company was in the hands of its creditors who numbered nearly fifty merchants in La Rochelle.[6]

[4] Archives Nationales, *Colonies*, B. XXVI, f. 78v. Instructions to Governor Beauharnois, 6 May, 1702.

[5] G. Lanctôt, *A History of Canada*, Volume I, *From Its Origins to the Royal Regime, 1663*, trans. J. Hamilton, (Toronto, 1963), I, p. 218.

[6] M. Delafosse, "La Rochelle et le Canada au XVIIe siècle," *Revue d' Histoire de l'Amérique francaise*, IV, (1950-51), pp. 476-8.

At the same time, individual traders from La Rochelle were beginning to carry goods into the St. Lawrence valley, often in their own ships. This new practice reflected the colonists' inability to raise their own capital or credit, and their growing demands for supplies. The decade of the fifties was marked by the almost constant blockade of the western frontier of New France by the Iroquois and the consequent absence of means to pay for goods being imported into New France.

Specie very quickly drained from the colony as witnessed, in 1654, by the first of several attempts to fix the value of coins remaining in New France above their French rate.[7] During the remainder of the century French authorities struggled with this form of solution to the problem of the constant drain of coin, but without visible success. Although Canadian specie was valued at twenty-five per cent above the French values, money continued to leave New France. For several years after 1663, temporary relief was obtained because New France became a royal crown colony. Specie to pay troops sent for the colony's defence and increased government expenditure placed substantial amounts of coin in circulation, but only postponed a return to earlier conditions.

The troops, who numbered nearly two thousand also provided colonists with a large market of local consumers, which stimulated agriculture. The presence of an intendant, Jean Talon, in New France, led to several efforts to diversify the economy. Talon encouraged agriculture, lumbering, local industry including shipbuilding, and the carrying trade. But the small success enjoyed by these undertakings, despite all of Talon's efforts, was due also to the unsettled conditions in the West that prevented full exploitation of the fur trade. Following the departure of the majority of the troops and the intendant, and the re-opening of the West, conditions for economic diversification quickly faded from New France.

The outbreak of war with Holland in 1672 led the French home authorities to halt their subsidies to immigration and to economic diversification, and to cease the export of specie. Little coin was sent to New France for several years. Also, after 1672 a new aggressive governor, the comte de Frontenac, began to develop the policy of western expansion first initiated by Talon. Three years later, the beaver monopoly became attached to the royal tax farm of the Western Domaine and the price of beaver skins was fixed. The conditions were established for rapid western expansion. Thereafter, until the end of the century the small resources of manpower and capital in New France were poured into the fur trade. Only a few individuals attempted to exploit other resources in New France.

By the mid-eighties the exchange problem was as desperate as twenty-five or thirty years earlier. Expenses for military supplies and soldiers' pay mounted owing to growing preparation for war against the Iroquois, while in

---

[7] A. Shortt, ed. *Documents Relating to Canadian Currency, Exchange and Finance During the French Period*, 2 vols., Ottawa, (1925-26), I, p. 3.

France, agents of the ministry of marine grew increasingly reluctant to send specie.[8] A similar situation had been reached long before in private commerce where, in order to avoid additional risks to trans-ocean trade, which itself was filled with dangers, a system of private bills of exchange had been developed. This procedure only operated successfully in cases where institutions and individuals had funds on which to draw in France. Small merchants located in New France quickly came under the sway of metropolitan traders, either through credit arrangements or when dealing with the latter on the beach at Quebec.

As early as 1676, the Sovereign Council acted in the interest of a colonist who was unable to pay cash for cargo delivered from France. The metropolitan trader was ordered to furnish proof that any offer to pay in coin was contained in the prior agreement to deliver the goods or else to accept payment from the colonist in the form of a note drawn on the local partner of the lessee of the Western Domaine.[9] At least twice before the Council had ordered that wheat be accepted at fixed rates in exchange for goods, owing to some merchants' refusal to accept it at all, or because they did so only at ludicrously low values.[10] In 1684, merchants were again ordered to accept wheat in payment for muskets delivered from France after the colonial authorities had enjoined all residents in New France to provide themselves with firearms for their own defence.[11]

The repeated appearance of these orders indicate that no long term solution to the currency problem could be found by fixing either currency or commodity exchange rates. Jean Talon had advised the government to send the colony's annual budget in merchantable goods rather than in specie. He imported merchandise in lieu of his emoluments in order to force greater competition among private traders, or to profit from the existing practices.[12] Talon also favoured striking a special colonial coinage.[13] Private traders legitimately protested against Talon's first solution, which would have allowed colonial authorities to import merchandise without paying duties or freight, while the latter recommendation ran counter to the bullionist ideas of the central government and was dropped on the outbreak of the Dutch War.[14] No solution appeared to prevent the drain of coin from New France or to facilitate commercial transactions.

Despite the Sovereign Council's actions on behalf of colonists, the latter

---

[8] Shortt, ed., *Documents*, I, p. 65, Demeulles to Arnoul, Quebec, November 12, 1684.

[9] *Judgements et delibérations du conseil souverain de la Nouvelle-France*, 6 vols., (Quebec, 1885-91), II. p. 78.

[10] Shortt, ed., *Documents*, I, pp. 15 and 23.

[11] Shortt, ed., *Documents*, I, p. 53.

[12] *Rapport de l'archiviste de la province de Quebec*, 1930-31, p. 126 (hereafter *R A P Q*). Talon to Colbert, Quebec, November 10, 1670; *ibid.*, p. 147, King to Talon, February 11, 1671.

[13] *R A P Q*, 1930-31, p. 161 "Mémoire sur le Canada," November 2, 1671.

[14] *R A P Q*, 1930-31, p. 169. Colbert to Talon, St. Germain, June 4, 1672.

were unable to negotiate from a position of strength. Although metropolitan traders were ordered to accept notes drawn on others, the drawee was able to choose his own time and method of reimbursement, always to his own benefit. Rarely did a merchant offer to meet notes drawn on himself except in merchandise of his own choosing and at a value set by himself. It was not long before merchants with a source of supply of goods anticipated the colony's wants and lack of currency to their advantage by issuing promises to pay to their local creditors rather than await a draft issued on them. Inevitably these individuals were from France or had metropolitan connections. The notes used in private transactions, known as *bons* (from *bon pour* etc.), began to circulate in New France as an exchange medium. Their usefulness was such that they were employed extensively throughout the colony's history and continued to be used by British merchants after the conquest. It was from this commercial paper that the intendant, Jacques Demeulles, may have obtained the idea for his first issue of card money.[15]

After complaining to the minister of marine concerning the stupidity of the naval agents at Rochefort who had not sent sufficient coin to pay the troops in New France, or to meet immediate expenses, and after forbidding fur traders to take any coin or bills of exchange in place of trade goods into the interior, Demeulles was forced back on his own resources. Finally, after ten companies of regular colonial troops had hired themselves out to colonists because he was unable to meet their pay, in June 1685, Demeulles issued his own currency to pay the troops and to meet his most pressing expenses until additional funds arrived from France. The currency, issued in three denominations to enable one month's pay to be made up for both officers and men, was made from individual playing cards bearing the intendant's own arms and signature.[16] Backed by Demeulles' personal, private promise to redeem the cards, they met with ready acceptance in New France. The temporary increase in the money supply was beneficial. Commerce received a boost from the new ease with which it was carried on.

This first issue was not designed to relieve the problem of the constant drain of specie from New France (i.e. as a circulation medium), but to pay the troops. The danger of forgery was real and viewed by the home authorities as the chief weakness of all colonial paper. Counterfeit cards appeared during the summer so that three months after the first issue the cards were withdrawn following the arrival at Quebec of the king's ship carrying coin.

Neither the governor nor the home authorities approved Demeulles' action and although he resorted to the practice the following February, his new instructions ordered him to cease. Henceforth, the intendant followed a more orthodox and expensive practice of issuing bills of exchange each fall, drawn on the General Treasurers of the Marine, to the departing French merchants in return for their coin. In 1690, however, Demeulles' successor again resort-

[15] Shortt, ed., *Documents*, I, p. 61, n.2.
[16] Shortt, ed., *Documents*, I, pp. 69-71, Ordonnance, June 8, 1685.

ed to cards; and the following year, when much of this issue remained in circulation the first reference to cards functioning as a circulation medium was made. As merchants presented cards for redemption before the arrival of new supplies of coin the intendant issued treasury notes, temporary credits drawn on the Marine Treasury against future colonial funds.[17] No provisions for redemption of the cards issued in 1692 were made, and in several instances during the next decade unauthorized cards were introduced and permitted to circulate unknown to the home authorities. The effect rapidly increased the cost of imports and gave rise to a dual price list for coin and paper in New France. In order to forestall the obvious disadvantage to holders of colonial paper (i.e. soldiers and government officers) the intendant began to issue bills of exchange on the marine treasury each fall, and sell them to French merchants in return for their coin. The advantage to both merchants and government quickly became apparent and the practice continued. It was by far the best solution to date, but by the end of the century the old complaints of lack of coin, metropolitan merchant control of trade, and inadequate funds for future expenditure had reappeared, reinforced, now, by conditions arising from the collapsing fur market in France.

Owing to the steady excess of colonial government expenditures over funds allotted, losses of supplies and specie at sea, and growing financial difficulties in France, little could be done to prevent intendants in New France from solving their problems by releasing commercial paper into general circulation. The practice was not harmful. The ready redemption of cards established confidence and controlled inflation as too did the apparent expansion of commercial activity in the years between the Treaty of Ryswick and the outbreak of the War of the Spanish Succession.

This was not to be the case after 1704 when owing to the home government's refusal to send specie to New France the intendant no longer redeemed the paper cards. Instead, he released additional cards into circulation. At the same time the treasurers of the marine refused to meet all of the bills of exchange drawn on the colonial budget. Confidence was shaken and metropolitan traders either withdrew from New France or demanded specie. Inflation spread rapidly in the colony. By the end of the war nearly 2,000,000 *livres* worth of cards were in circulation.[18] In order to reduce inflation at the war's end the government redeemed the cards at half their nominal value, but the task was finally completed only in 1719. New France appeared to have returned to the conditions of fifty years before.

After 1717 all money in the colonies was to circulate at the same value as in France; three years later, card money was abolished. Included in the

---

[17] Shortt, "Introduction"; *Documents*, I, pp. li-lii.
[18] G. Frégault, "Essai sur les finances canadiennes," in *Le XVIIIe siècle canadien: études*, (Montreal, 1968), pp. 289-363, for the best account of financial developments in New France during the eighteenth century, and which lays particular stress on the influence of government spending on economic development.

return to financial orthodoxy was the abandonment of intendants' former practice of issuing bills of exchange drawn against future Canadian allotments in the treasury to French merchants in return for their coin. These multiple reforms almost paralysed colonial commerce owing to the immediate drain of the little coin remaining in New France. The situation was not aided by the common practice among habitants of hoarding small supplies of cash. Some relief was provided through the illegal fur trade that operated between Montreal and Albany, New York, but the existence of the traffic hardly met with approval in France. Finally after being inundated with complaints that his policy had paralysed internal commerce, in 1729, the minister of marine once more permitted local paper currency to circulate on a regular basis in New France.

French authorities recognized the need for a colonial circulating medium, but remained highly suspicious of paper. In a compromise directed towards maintaining control over the amount in circulation, cards with a nominal value of 400,000 *livres* were authorized. Each year 250,000 *livres* were to be redeemed leaving the remainder in circulation to facilitate trade. Cards redeemed in one year were to be re-introduced into circulation the next. In addition to cards, however, other forms of financial paper had been developed during the shortage of the twenties and also were presented for redemption with the result that more cards remained in circulation, fewer were available for re-circulation as colonists began to save them, and new demands were made for additional amounts to be put into circulation.

Owing to the steady expansion of the fur trade and the need to supply the western posts a means had been devised to pay for local labour and supplies beyond what was carried out through regular contracts. During the twenties the practice had developed among officials in the West, acting on the authority of the intendant, of issuing drafts on the marine treasury. When presented at Quebec and receipted by the intendant, they were known as vouchers and allowed to circulate. As the practice grew, and the distance between the drawee and payee was great, the drafts frequently were not presented for redemption, but also circulated endorsed by each successive recipient. Consequently, the colonial authorities had no means of maintaining an annual audit on the supply of paper in New France. Yet growing demand forced new issues of cards into circulation. By 1749, a total of 1,000,000 *livres* worth of cards was authorized to circulate, but the nominal value of paper in New France was far higher.[19]

The steady increase in the money supply during the thirties probably was not detrimental to colonial commerce. Unlike the situation during the War of the Spanish Succession, peace prevailed and local commercial activity was expanding. Redemption on demand restored confidence and the money supply grew with the economy. Diversification undoubtedly was aided by the

[19] Shortt, ed., *Documents*, II, pp. 641-5, 707-11 and 775-83.

new ease in making commercial transactions. Colonial merchants were able to exploit market opportunities without always relying on metropolitan exchange facilities. But each year the system became riper for exploitation, especially after 1744 when enlarged demands for military expenditures led to an unprecedented increase in drafts being issued. As warfare increased, local commercial activity declined giving rise to greater inflation. Paper savings were threatened and in many cases wiped out. Several merchants abandoned New France. Commerce in New France was in the throes of inflation and the colony's commerce in trouble well before the outbreak of the Seven Years' War.

Following the expansion of trade beyond barter, private traders were faced, in addition to the problem of currency, with finding sources of capital and instruments of credit. Although influenced by developments in the fur trade, the difficulty asssociated with obtaining capital and credit was governed by the fact that all commerce in New France was based on seaborne trade; furthermore it was trans-oceanic. Such trade involved the use of risk capital, which was not easily obtainable in France owing to general and particular conditions in the seventeenth century. After the 1630's European credit resources shrank considerably owing to the decline of precious metal imported from the Spanish colonies. Until new gold imports reached Europe from Portuguese Mozambique and Brazil in the opening years of the eighteenth century credit was difficult to obtain.[20] In France, the practice of buying judicial and administrative offices that carried with them increased social position absorbed capital; so too did the practice of purchasing *rentes*, or low interest bearing annuities. While in reality, the purchaser loaned his capital, the long terms involved owing to the Church's insistence upon the perpetual alienation of the principal in order to avoid the sin of usury, meant that the capital involved was very secure but yielded a low interest. Like investment in venal offices, *rentes* diminished the amount of French capital available for speculative commercial ventures.[21]

Individuals searching for risk capital had difficulty finding any beyond what was produced by the merchant community. But as many successful merchants sought to remove themselves from trade through the purchase of offices or *rentes*, risk capital itself was steadily drained away.[22] Although Paris was an important money market its attention was focused chiefly on the demands of the crown. Little capital was available for commercial investment. Merchants seeking capital and credit to venture to New France were restricted largely to the French seaports where risk capital of the special nature required by seaborne commerce was available.

---

[20] Labrousee, *Histoire économique et sociale de la France*, II, pp. 363-4.

[21] G.V. Taylor, "Non-capitalist wealth and the origins of the French Revolution," *American Historical Review*, LXXII, (1967), pp. 479-80.

[22] R.B. Grassby, "Social Status and Commercial Enterprise under Louis XIV," *Economic History Review*, XII, (1960), pp. 20, 28.

Unfortunately additional difficulties faced the French merchant. Not only was risk capital difficult to obtain but owing to its dispersal around the periphery of France in the ports, it was often available only in small amounts. The French never developed a central bank during the old regime or any similar institution designed to accumulate large amounts of private capital. Also, no comprehensive system of marine insurance was available to the private trader. Throughout the French regime, merchants insured their ventures where possible at London or Amsterdam. Owing to this lack of a large marine underwriting capability, French merchants often were unable to obtain any insurance during the seventeenth century, and then, only at excessively high rates. During wartime the situation could be especially difficult. In 1747, for example, cargoes bound for Quebec from La Rochelle could be insured for lower premiums in London than in France even though the two nations were at war.[23] During the previous century merchants relied instead upon bottomry loans, or loans *à la grosse avanture*, for both capital and insurance. Bottomry loans were obtained at rates of between twenty-five and thirty percent. They were the backbone of seventeenth century seaborne commerce.

Like *rentes*, bottomry loans avoided the sin of usury owing to the unusual conditions under which they were made. Loss of a ship or cargo financed by such a loan led to cancellation of the borrower's obligation to repay. But in making such a loan, the lender rather than the borrower accepted the risk; thus, unlike contemporary bond and debenture credit, control remained with the lender, and resembled direct equity investment. Owing to the lack of marine insurance available in French ports, this type of loan was generally impossible to avoid; merchants borrowed *à la grosse avanture* in order to cover their own capital investment in ships and goods bound overseas. Commerce carried out under such conditions provided little opportunity for an entrepreneur anxious to exploit new markets, for this was not a matter of excess capital seeking outlets for investment, but the reverse.

Only as English and Dutch marine insurance grew to include French shippers, and local groups in the seaports formed small mutual protection associations, did the practice of bottomry loans decline among those sending vessels to New France. This does not seem to have occurred before the restoration of financial stability in France during the 1720's. At least one example survives of a bottomry loan taken out during the War of the Spanish Succession on part of ship sailing between La Rochelle and Quebec bearing interest of sixty percent.[24]

Few colonists were able or willing to initiate commercial activities from New France, beyond what was associated with the fur trade. Some mer-

---

[23] Archives Nationales, 62 A2, "Papiers Dugard," Carton 40, *Insurance Policy*, August 8, 1747.

[24] Archives departementales de la Charente-Maritime, Minute Rivière et Soullard, Registre 1705, May 14, 1705.

chants at Quebec in the 1690's were described as indifferent rich and fitting out ships on their own bottom. But while these individuals were acknowledged to have correspondents at La Rochelle to send out and take in cargoes from their ships, the business relation between colonist and French agent was less likely that of merchant and broker than of partner or younger son.[25] Under the conditions in trade, the difficulties facing colonial merchants at Quebec or Montreal in their search for backing frequently were insurmountable.

The private traders to New France were few, but most were bound to the colony by marriage ties. The permanent family rather than the transitory firm was the major institution for carrying on commerce during the seventeenth and eighteenth centuries. Hardly any important merchant resided in New France who was not tied by marriage or direct family links to metropolitan France. For nearly a century after 1650, Catholic merchants at La Rochelle dominated the Canadian trade. Close to sources of capital and credit, they controlled the movement of goods and ships to New France until after 1737 when poor agricultural harvests and war imposed new conditions on trans-ocean trade, and led to their being supplanted by merchants from Bordeaux. During the intervening period La Rochelle merchants sailed to New France, established themselves or their sons in the colony and married among the important fur trading families. These merchants were not colonists in the accepted sense of the word, for they always maintained their metropolitan connections, frequently crossed the Atlantic, and sometimes after decades of residence in New France, returned home permanently. If the La Rochelle merchant Antoine Grignon sent his sons and son-in-law to New France, where his grandchildren married into the LeBer, Jolliet and Fleury families, sons of the Fleury, LeBer, and Lemoyne connections established themselves at La Rochelle; and these are but examples. Other French merchants served an apprenticeship in New France then returned home where they established themselves or took charge of a family business and continued to trade to the colony for many more years. Perhaps the best example of such activity is found in the career of Antoine Pascaud who lived in New France for a score of years after 1688 and returned to La Rochelle where first he, then his wife and two sons continued to outfit and send ships to New France until the Seven Years' War. During the interval one of Pascaud's sons became mayor of the port. It was in relations such as these that control of commerce in New France lay.

Metropolitan control of trans-ocean trade was especially strong during the seventeenth century when New France's sole export commodity was fur. During the early decades, trade was in the hands of private and state monopolists. At mid-century, the debts of the colonial company led to the opening of trade to its creditors. Free trade reigned until 1664 when the West India

---

[25] Louis-Armand de Lom d'Arce Lahontan, *New Voyages to North America*, R.G. Thwaites ed., 2 vols., (Chicago, 1905) I, p. 374.

Company was established, but its monopolistic trading privileges were exercised only for five years. The West India Company did not send its own ships to New France owing to lack of numbers, but instead allowed the old private traders to fit out ships on its behalf. When trade was later re-opened to all on account of the company's own difficulties and the monopoly's injurious effect on the colonists, the small group of La Rochelle outfitters had obtained a secure hold on trade to New France.

Shortly afterwards, Governor Frontenac accused two of these merchants of carrying on a knavish if not illegal practice of charging full payment in advance from colonists for freight shipped to New France.[26] The practice was new and probably originated with the freeing of trade. Owing to the new procedure ships' captains or dishonest merchants could then insure their ventures at no risk to themselves by using the freight payments exacted from colonists to pay the premiums on bottomry loans. Some of Frontenac's other accusations were probably the product of an active imagination. The minister of marine paid them little attention although the charges were renewed a year later. But the recently introduced practice of charging for freight carried to New France in advance of sailing did discriminate against colonists who wanted to ship their own goods or to carry on commerce.

Metropolitan shippers obtained a tremendous advantage by using the advance freight payments from colonists to cover the cost of insuring their own trade goods and even the ship's hull. Little wonder that metropolitan traders were being referred to as foreigners (*forains*). The use of the term suggests more than a mere description of activity, but also a pejorative distinction. Frontenac later described La Rochelle merchants as "tyrans et . . . corsaires."[27] Baron Lahontan agreed; he thought the Canadian merchants (i.e. those trading to Canada) no different from the "pyrates that scour the seas."[28] Nevertheless, with little coin, capital or credit to pay for imports in New France, metropolitan merchants continued to demand payment in advance for shipments. Unable to obtain return cargoes, French traders sought to earn profits from their outbound voyages to New France. This practice, however, gave rise to carelessness in handling cargo, damaged goods on arrival and occasions for fraud. Colonial merchants were forced to pay for freight in bills of exchange drawn the previous fall for goods to be shipped in the spring. Canadians with complaints were forced to seek redress through the courts which often proved a lengthy procedure that tied up scarce capital and hindered local commercial activity. The judicial records of New France's appeal court abound with cases between colonists and metropolitan merchants or their local agents concerning damaged or incomplete cargo and failure to make delivery.

The minister of marine once hoped that merchants from other French

---

[26] *R A P Q, 1926-27*, p. 10. Frontenac to Colbert, Quebec, November 2, 1672.

[27] *R A P Q, 1927-28*, p. 24. Frontenac to Seignelay, Quebec, November 17, 1689.

[28] Lahontan, *New Voyages*, I. p. 374.

ports could be persuaded to send ships to New France in order to provide competition against La Rochelle, and some relief for colonists. But the outbreak of the War of the League of Augsburg, King William's War, prevented the plan from developing. Instead, Canadians were caught in another squeeze between metropolitan shippers and the government owing to the crown's inability to pay for its own freight. In their efforts to compensate for poor harvests in New France and to send extra stores and munitions required by war, the home authorities requisitioned one quarter to one third of the cargo space on merchant ships bound for Quebec. The growing strain on the treasury forced the government to defer paying for freight. Under the circumstances shippers in other French ports refused to venture to New France, and those in La Rochelle raised their own freight rates fifty percent passing the increase on to the colonists.[29] Thus, fewer goods at higher prices reached Quebec. The minister of marine failed in his bid to encourage merchants from St. Malo and Nantes to New France and the increases remained.[30]

During the War of the Spanish Succession the financial difficulties of the government increased and combined with the weakness of the navy to push trans-ocean freight rates to more than one hundred percent above the previous wartime rates. In addition, the collapse of the fur trade led several French traders to withdraw their commerce from New France and turn elsewhere to more profitable ventures. Colonists in New France were left largely on their own. Trade all but disappeared as many ships ceased to sail for Quebec. Canadian merchants had little choice but to marshal their small capital resources and attempt to diversify their commercial export activities. Originally, they were unwilling to accept the situation in the European fur market and spent several fruitless years attempting to prosecute the fur trade from New France.

Independent efforts to ship furs to Northern Europe in a German ship met with failure. Lack of credit forced Canadians to accept Danish trade goods which were unacceptable to the Indians, while the absence of international exchange facilities controlled by the Dutch made it impossible to trade directly with north German ports. The colonists turned to other activity. They built ships, initiated several privateering expeditions in search of booty, and began to carry cargoes of food stuffs and construction materials to the French garrisons at Placentia, Newfoundland and Port Royal, Acadia. Under cover of negotiating an exchange of prisoners, trade was even carried on with New England. Beginning in 1706 and continuing for several years, local merchants also sent cargoes of flour, fish and lumber to Martinique in the

---

[29] Archives Nationales, Colonies, CIIA, XI, f.288, Champigny to Pontchartrain, Quebec, October 12, 1691.

[30] Archives de la Marine, B2, 78, ff.637v-8, Pontchartrain to Bégon, Versailles, April 25, 1691; also B3, 64, ff. 114v-5, Degustines, Ordonnateur, to Pontchartrain, Nantes, April 21, 1691.

Windward Islands. All of these activities had been brought about by conditions created by the war and in the fur trade. Local resources in New France quickly proved inadequate.

By 1707, the intendant was complaining that resources for ship construction were exhausted. He was unable to send supplies to Acadia owing to a lack of seaworthy vessels in New France.[31] Privateering did not prove very profitable. Prizes were disposed of with difficulty owing to a lack of potential purchasers. Market conditions in the West Indies only temporarily favoured colonists owing to the war and bad harvests in France. Port Royal was lost in 1710 and Placentia by the terms of the Treaty of Utrecht. Conditions at the new establishment on Cape Breton Island turned favourable only later during the 1720's. The initial efforts of the colonists to diversify their economic activity died with the coming of peace. Agricultural production appeared unable to meet export demands for several years. Also, the fortunes of the fur trade improved following the destruction of the excess supply from the 1690's; and rising prices led the colony's major attention to become focused once more on the West. Inflation and the abolition of paper currency did the rest. Commercial activity stagnated during the decade after the war.

Several factors that appeared during the war, however, led to improved conditions during the twenties and thirties. Especially before 1735, land in New France was cleared and placed under cultivation at nearly double the rate of demographic increase. An agricultural surplus, chiefly wheat, appeared. At the same time, the structure of the French cod fishery changed from green to dry production which meant a greater increase in inshore fishing, the growth of a resident population on Cape Breton Island, and a new demand for foodstuffs where none had existed before. Local merchants in New France were quick to exploit the new opportunity. Between 1725 and the outbreak of war twenty years later, merchants outfitted small ships in increasing numbers to carry food-stuffs, chiefly flour, peas and biscuit to Louisbourg. The size of this trade is difficult to determine, but until the mid-thirties, New France was the major source of food supplies for the fishing industry.

Changes in the West Indies also led to more regular contact with New France. Growing demands for food and construction lumber increased prices, leading some Canadian merchants to ship cargoes south. Local products were exchanged for rum, molasses and sugar required in New France, but the quantities involved were too small to encourage island planters to favour Canadians at the expense of much better New England customers. Furthermore, the shorter distance between the French islands and New England favoured the latter over New France. As the demand for cod fish increased in the Islands some Canadians laded cargoes at Louisbourg and

---

[31] Archives Nationales, Colonies, CIIA, XXVI, f.230v, Raudot to Pontchartrain, Quebec, November 12, 1707.

sailed to the Islands, but New France's poor geographic location generally worked to the colony's detriment in the Caribbean trade.

The demand for fish in the French islands also operated against the commercial interests of New France. French fishermen were unable to supply the low quality demanded (the fish was mostly for slave consumption), and Louisbourg merchants, acting as fish buyers, dealt increasingly with New England fishermen rather than as before when their major activity involved food purchases for distribution to fishermen. By the mid-thirties a common interest between New England and Louisbourg had grown up, to the exclusion of Canadian traders dealing chiefly in food-stuffs. Under these altered circumstances, the impact of crop failure in New France in 1737 was doubly disastrous. In addition to reducing the colony's total trade by a third and preventing exports, great impetus was given to Louisbourg-New England relations.

Poor harvests in 1741 and the two succeeding years re-enforced the exclusion of New France from intercolonial trade. Unable to guarantee regular supply, Canadian merchants began to lose confidence in themselves. The outbreak of war in 1744 completed the process. Despite a good harvest in the next year, the loss of Louisbourg and conditions at sea made it impossible to derive any commercial benefit. Success afterward was short-lived. Crop failures in 1748 and again three years later combined with increased local demand owing to westward imperial expansion and the presence of increased numbers of troops to lead to the destruction of New France's intercolonial trade. From 1752 onwards "ordonnances" were issued annually to forbid the export of flour from New France. Beginning the same year increasing quantities of flour were imported from France.

The intercolonial carrying trade, based on commercial agriculture, had led to the development of a small shipbuilding industry which in turn encouraged some lumbering. The decline in wheat production was followed by the replacement of the local shipbuilding industry by a royal shipyard where several vessels were produced for the French navy. Although this new endeavour introduced capital into New France, little aid was given to colonial commerce. The warships produced were of poor quality owing to lack of timber of sufficient strength for large scale construction. The enterprize also absorbed all of the manpower available. Local shipbuilding ceased. From 1744 onwards commercial interests in New France were sacrificed to the demands of empire and war.

Commerce in New France declined steadily from levels established during the thirties when a good deal of economic self-sufficiency from France was enjoyed. During the thirties, the volume of trade from France actually declined while colonial exports grew. A small but increasing portion of New France's exports came under local mercantile direction. The fur trade also became more independent as the number of beaver pelts declined in proportion to other furs *(menues pelleteries)*. But with the return to war, the volume of shipping increased dramatically between France and New France. During the last decade of the old regime, New France became tied to France in a way never before experienced as men, munitions and stores poured into the colony. Local merchants did not participate in this activity nor did those from La Rochelle dominate the trade. Instead, a new type of merchant with large capital resources, more financier than trader, able to grant credit in large amounts to the government, and chiefly interested in supply and freight contracts, rather than trade with the colonists emerged to dominate the transocean traffic to New France.

Canadian merchants had always to contend with metropolitan control of the beaver monopoly, scarce manpower and capital, a permanent imbalance in trade that gave rise to exchange and currency difficulties, and poor geographic location, but an additional factor, the outlook and attitudes of their fellow colonists, also operated to the detriment of commercial activity. Much of the wealth, such that it was in New France, belonged to fur traders, men whose knowledge and experience were essential to collecting furs in the west and bringing them down to Montreal and to Quebec. Often from seigneurial families, and receiving an emolument that went with a position in the colonial military establishment, these individuals looked upon wealth in a different manner from profit oriented entrepreneurs whose aims were focused on accumulation. With an aristocratic and military outlook that was fostered by the fur trade and the opportunities for service that were present in New France, money appears to have been viewed chiefly as a means to increase personal consumption in order to live "nobly." Many contemporary observers, among them the historian Charlevoix and the biologist Kalm, drew attention to this aspect of Canadian life.[32] At the same time, the leaders of Canadian society were necessary to merchants wishing to exploit commercial opportunities, seeking special grants of land, trade privileges and silent capital in return for a share in the profits. Evidence exists, and more remains to be examined, that local colonial enterprises often failed because the merchant himself was not sufficiently profit-oriented, or because one of his associates destroyed the business through excessive consumption of working capital and profits, mis-management of affairs, inattention to opportunity, or to a combination of all three.[33] Rivalry and fraud also contributed to failure. Although isolated instances only can be cited, there seems to have been a shortage of like-minded, profit-oriented individuals in New France. Canadian society and economy were directed towards the west and the fur trade

---

[32] F. X. de Charlevoix, *Journal of a Voyage to North America*, trans., 2 vols., (London, 1761), I,; and P. Kalm, *Travels in North America*, ed., A. B. Benson, 2 vols., (New York, 1964), II, p. 431.

[33] See the suggestive comments concerning the behaviour of Augustin Legardeur de Courtemanche in F. Ouellet, "M. Michel Brunet et le problème de la Conquête," *Bulletin des recherches historiques*, LXII, (1956), pp. 97-8; further discussion is contained in the author's *Histoire économique et sociale du Québec*, 1760-1850, (Montreal, 1966), p.6

where the largest profits, which went chiefly to metropolitan merchants, were earned. The trade itself encouraged intensification rather than diversification of resources. Individual activity, hard physical work, personal courage and pride of life were recognized among the highest social virtues in New France. Canadian society contained little wealth but a great deal of pretension and ostentation. Currency difficulties were not unique to New France but a part of colonial commerce. Scarce manpower, capital and credit were problems but the greatest commercial difficulty arose in New France from metropolitan control of the chief export commodity, and the attitudes nurtured by the major economic activity carried on by the society taking root in the valley of the St. Lawrence River.

The "New Men" in Action: Scottish Mercantile and Shipping Operations in the North American Colonies, 1760-1825

David S. Macmillan, Associate Professor of History,
Trent University

Considerable attention has been given in the writing of Canadian history to the contributions made by Scottish agricultural settlers, both Lowland farmers and Highland crofters, to the pioneering of this land. Similarly the prowess of the military settlers, the disbanded Highland regiments, and the role of the professional men, in Kirk, law, education and medicine, have not been neglected.[1] The class among the Scottish immigrants which has, remarkably, received surprisingly little attention is the race of entrepreneurs, – merchants, shipowners, traders, shipbuilders and master craftsmen working on their own account who, in their contribution to the development of the North American Colonies after 1776, embodied the most distinctive of their home country's contemporary characteristics – the phenomenal surge of its commerce and industry, and its refusal to be trammelled by the limitations of an outmoded mercantilist system. The fifty years between 1776 and 1826 saw Scotland in the most revolutionary phase of its economic and social evolution. It was only natural in the circumstances of the time that the energies of the commercial Scots should seek a new outlet, and there were good reasons why it should be found across the Atlantic.

There is one important exception to the general neglect the Scottish entrepreneurs have suffered at the hands of historians – and that is the group of fur traders who operated from Montreal in various company groupings. These colourful and forceful men, and their great opponent, Lord Selkirk, have received the treatment merited by their achievements and exploits from a number of Canadian historians over the last few decades, but the work and role of the Scottish general merchant, the shipowner, the timber merchant and the shipbuilder have not had the same appeal for the writer or research worker. Inevitably, too, the colour and high adventure of the great staple fur trade has exercised its lure on many a writer.[2]

---

[1] To mention only three examples, from the extensive literature which treats these groups so fully, there is the important two volume work, *The Scot in British North America*, by W. J.Rattray, (Toronto, 1880), William Gregg's comprehensive *History of the Presbyterian Church in the Dominion of Canada*, (Toronto, 1885), and John Murray Gibbon's survey, *Scots in Canada*, (Toronto, 1911).

[2] On the fur trade, apart from Harold Innis's classic study, there are such definitive works as G. C. Davidson's *The North West Company*, 1918, republished by the University of California Press in 1967; and W. Stewart Wallace's scholarly *Documents Relating to the North West Company*, Champlain Society Publications Vol. 22, (Toronto, 1934). On Selkirk, his schemes, and his contest with the North West Company, there is John Gray's fine interpretative study *Lord Selkirk of Red River* (London, 1963).

The "staple" theory itself, in its intensive application, has also tended, perhaps, to diminish unduly the role of men who saw the small, but growing colonial communities as markets as well as simply sources of commodities and raw materials. In his penetrating study *The North American Assault on the Canadian Forest*, A.R.M. Lower suggested that Canada always had been, and always would be dependent on outside markets.[3] The thesis is valid from a producer's point of view but it ignores to some extent the sheer desperation for markets and outlets that can exist in other producing societies, especially those undergoing rapid industrialization. It was precisely because of the pressing need for customers for their new manufactures that the Scottish merchants, manufacturers and shipowners made their ventures in British North America in the period under review. If they felt increasingly the "pull" of cheap lumber, they felt too the "push" of exportable commodity surpluses at home. The search for markets was an even more pressing consideration in Scottish merchant circles at any given time in the period 1776-1825 than the quest for furs, timber, corn or fish.

Essentially, the society of central Scotland was one which had "taken off" by 1770 into a phase of rapid industrial growth and its capacity thereafter, in the manufacture of linens, cottons, iron and a range of other commodities, including ships, was increasing at a rate that startled English and French observers, as well as the men who were engaged in forwarding the process.[4] Industrial growth was matched by an even more remarkable increase in foreign trade. Between 1750 and 1800 its overseas commerce grew by nearly three hundred per cent, as compared with England's remarkable growth rate of two hundred per cent in the same period. Such rapid change from a largely agricultural country in the first half of the century was bound to shatter the old structure of Scottish society, and the "new men" who came to the fore in commerce and industry bore the marks of the changed economic and social environment. From their ranks were drawn the great majority of the entrepreneurs who came near, in the half-century between 1775 and 1825, to making British North America into a sort of Scottish commercial preserve, almost an "informal empire." To their new colonial environment they brought the characteristics that had been moulded by the changes they had known at home, and these were to condition their conduct, their outlook and their aspirations in the very different setting of Newfoundland, Nova Scotia, New Brunswick, Canada, and the other colonies.

These features may be summed up as 1) an attachment to the idea of Free Trade and an impatience with the mercantile pretensions of England, especially the dominating role of London, the Port and City; 2) a tendency towards secession as "anti-Burghers" or under various dissenting labels from their own established "moderate" Kirk, dominated by the gentry and the

---

[3] *Op cit.*, (Toronto, 1938), Preface, p. xxi.

[4] For the fullest account of this phenomenal development, see Henry Hamilton, *An Economic History of Scotland in the Eighteeenth Century*, (Oxford, 1963), Chapters V-VII.

nobility with their powers of patronage; 3) a belief in Parliamentary and Burgh Reform, in both of which Scotland stood in much greater need of an alteration than any part of the United Kingdom; and 4) a belief in the efficacy of education as an improver of mankind (which seems rather touching now in retrospect, but which was perhaps a natural enough belief to hold at the time when Scotland's educational system was distinctly superior to that of England, and Henry Brougham and many another beat their way North across the Border to grace the benches at Edinburgh and other Scottish Universities). They also held strongly to the conviction that "Scotland's time had come at last," as Kirkman Finlay of Glasgow put it, and that no opportunity must be lost to bring their country's commerce and prosperity up to a par with that of England. Apart from these five characteristics, which might be considered "progressive," if not entirely admirable, there were other possibly less attractive features of the "new mercantile men" of Scotland, which they were to display to the full in the colonial settings of British North America. One was their intense localism. Scotland, for all the rapid rate of industrial change, was still a country of "regions" within which population movement was as yet slight. This bred a "clannishness" and, sometimes, a narrowness of viewpoint. Scottish merchants and shipowners in the colonies tended to trade with their home ports, to recruit their partners, clerks, shipmasters and other associates from their own home districts, especially from among their own kinfolk, if suitable candidates were available. In colonial centres like Halifax and Saint John and Montreal, it led them to form "cliques" and "coteries" and "rings" among themselves, sometimes to promote such worthy ventures as the building of churches, but occasionally for such questionable purposes as the virtual defrauding of the authorities through "rigged" sales of prize ships and cargoes.[5] This latter activity, which reached its peak in Halifax during the War of 1812, was probably the most lucrative type of venture in which Scottish merchants during the period are found to be acting in collusion. Like the "trading on the Line" with the United States which was being carried out at the same time in the War of 1812, and the illicit sale of Nova Scotia and New Brunswick gypsum, used as a fertiliser in the Southern States, to American vessels, and the shipment of this commodity to Boston and ports north of Boston after 1816, it was "technically" illegal, but it must be remembered that Scottish overseas trade in its earliest phase could only have existed, far less grown, through the exercise of a calculated indifference to the law as laid down in London.[6]

[5] For examples of Scots activity in the various fields, and of the ways in which localism prevailed among them, see the Reverend Robert Campbell, D.D., *History of the Saint Gabriel Street Church, Montreal* (Montreal, 1887), pp. 84-149; James S. MacDonald, *Annals of the North British Society*, 1768-1903 (Halifax, 1905), pp. 39, 63, 107, 122; Navy Board Records – Disposal of Prizes 3/143-8, 1813, Public Record Office, London.

[6] For "trading on the Line," see the account of Christopher Scott's activities at Saint Andrews below; see also D. C. Harvey, "Pre-Agricola John Young," in *Collections of*

Prior to the Union of 1707, when all Scottish trade with the English colonies was prohibited, the merchants of Glasgow circumvented the regulations by having their vessels registered and "owned" in the northern English port of Whitehaven, in Cumberland; even after the Union, Scottish merchants blatantly carried on a thriving trade with Russia in defiance of the monopolistic charter of the Russia Company of London, despite a ruling by Attorney General Edward Northey in 1711 that "The North Britains (sic) are by the 18th article of the Treaty of Union subject to the Regulation of their trade by that Company, and cannot trade to the North without taking their freedom" (i.e. without joining the Company).[7] In 1735, the Edinburgh merchant, William Hogg, junior, openly contested the right of the Russia Company to charge dues on imports from the Russian Empire into Scotland, in the face of the Company's threats to seize all Scottish vessels engaged in the trade, and even had the temerity to declare that he "doubted the usefulness of such Companies in General," a statement that provoked a near-apoplectic response from the London Governors.[8] The incident is interesting because it reveals something of the contemporary Scottish mercantile attitude towards monopoly and to Chartered companies, and to the privileged position of London. This critical attitude was shaped and developed further in the later part of the century by Scottish writers and commercial theorists, and it pervaded the thought and influenced the activities of the Scottish mercantile class who traded and shipped to British North America, and of those who went out to settle there.

The Scots shared with the merchants of such English "outports" as Liverpool, Bristol, and Hull an especial detestation for the virtual monopoly of privileged London in the East India trade and for the favoured status of the metropolis in West India trade as well. As Ralph Davis has pointed out in his survey of eighteenth century foreign trade, large quantities of Scottish goods were channelled because of these circumstances through London for export (a practice which has led, incidentally, to the serious distortion of available trade figures for the period prior to 1755).[9] In view of all these encumbrances and restrictions on their export and trading activities, it was only natural that the Scottish merchants should be receptive to Free Trade doctrines when they appeared later in the century. It was also natural that they should increasingly focus their attention, after 1707, on the rapidly developing market in the British colonies in North America, where the popu-

---

the *Nova Scotia Historical Society*, vol. 32, 1959; Esther Clark Wright, *The Saint John River and Its Tributaries* (Toronto, 1949); and Guy Murchie, *Saint Croix: The Sentinel River*, (New York, 1957). For the traffic in gypsum, see W. S. McNutt, *New Brunswick: A History, 1784-1867*, (Toronto, 1963).

[7] Records of the Russia Company, MSS. Box 11749/1, The Guildhall Archives, London.

[8] Minutes of the Court of the Russia Company, Vol. 4, 1734-56, entries of May 1, 1735; May 22, 1735; July 2, 1735; August 20, 1735, Guildhall Archives, London.

[9] Ralph Davis, "English Foreign Trade, 1700-1774" in *The Growth of English Overseas Trade*, edited by W. E. Minchinton (London, 1969), p. 100.

lation increased from 300,000 in 1700 to three millions in 1774. Colonial wealth and purchasing power, and living standards as well, were rising steeply during that period and Scottish linens and other manufactures found a ready sale.[10] The era between 1750 and 1774 saw the high water-mark of the Glasgow tobacco trade with Virginia, and the loss of the Colonies forced many who had participated in it to turn their attention to the North American settlements which remained under the British flag.[11]

Meanwhile, in Scottish business circles, increasing antagonism was building up against what Eli Heckscher called "the outmoded power theory of British mercantilism." David Hume in his study "On the Jealousy of Trade" (1758) and Duncan Forbes in his "Essay on the History of Civil Society" attacked the pressure groups, "the great overpow'ring, odious interests and monopolies," which Michael Kammen has recently shown to have been so influential in provoking the crisis of 1774.[12] In the light of Hume's strictures and Forbes' tirades, which reflected the views of mercantile men in Scotland, it is easy to understand how large-scale smuggling should have gone on steadily along large stretches of the Scottish coastline, especially in the South-West, throughout the eighteenth century. It was condoned in commercial circles to a degree unknown in England, and the illegal trading activities of Scottish merchants in the Maritimes in 1794-1815 must be considered against this home background. Just as the works of Hume and Forbes led on naturally to Adam Smith's classic statement of the case for Free Trade in 1776, to John Galt's essay on "a Free Commercial Policy" in 1805 and to Lauderdale's diatribes against restrictions and monopolies in the 1820's, so did the permissive attitude among all classes in Scotland towards smuggling of French produce from the great base in the Isle of Man, and the evasion of monopolistic trade restrictions lead to such open defiance of regulation as Kirkman Finlay's dispatch of ships to Bombay and Canton in 1813 and 1818 in contravention of the East India Company's charter, and Christopher Scott's and "Agricola" John Young's "Trading on the Line" of the Maine-New Brunswick border from 1812 to 1815. Finlay, in his attempts to build up Scottish trade, felt as little compunction about injuring the susceptibilities of the "nabobs" of East India House as he had felt at infringing Napoleon's Continental System with large-scale smuggling activities carried on through Anholt, Heligoland, and Malta during the Wars.

Even ultra-conservative Scots, like the veteran merchant David Loch of Over Carnbie, who tended to regard the British government as godlike in its

---

[10] *Ibid.*, p. 112.

[11] For an account of the tobacco trade, see Jacob M. Price, "The Rise of Glasgow in the Chesapeake Tobacco Trade, 1707-1775," in *The William and Mary Quarterly*, April 1954; and M. L. Robertson, "Scottish Commerce and the American War of Independence" in *Economic History Review*, 2nd Series, Vol. ix, No. 1, 1956.

[12] See Michael Kammen, *Empire and Interest: The American Colonies and the Politics of Mercantilism* (Philadelphia, 1970).

omniscience, fawned on the Scots nobility, and outlined a scheme for the forcible convoy of colonial ships to British ports "under sailing orders" in 1775, railed against the regulations and bounties which promoted the Scottish linen industry as "unnatural and vicious." Loch favoured a woollen manufacture as against a subsidized linen industry, and regarded all colonists as "less than equal" to Britons, but Scots, he considered, should have equal rights with the English and be free of "fanciful regulations and unwise fettering of trade."[13]

After 1783, many Scots, especially those who had been engaged in the profitable tobacco trade, were even more resentful against the vested monopoly interests of London, for they felt that the final breach with the thirteen insurgent colonies had been largely occasioned through the pressures brought to bear by shipowning and mercantile groups in London and Bristol. In their determination to "make the best" of a changed situation, by expanding their commerce with the remaining North American colonies, the Scots merchants were resolved that their trade should not be trammelled by restrictions, that it should be immediately profitable, and that the contacts already established in Newfoundland, the Maritimes and Canada should be utilized to the full. In this they were helped by the commercial activities of their countrymen in these areas, which had begun in 1759-60, and by the flow of Scottish emigration at an increasing rate after 1770.

The subject of Scottish emigration to Canada, as indicated earlier, has received adequate attention at the hands of Canadian historians, and the exhaustive quantitative surveys recently made by Dr. James M. Cameron, to be published soon, will undoubtedly round out the picture already sketched by Helen I. Cowan and W.A. Carrothers.[14] What concerns us here is the part played by that emigration in promoting the shipping and mercantile contacts between the two countries, for it was highly significant as a source of freights for Scottish shipowners and as a means of stimulating the market in these colonies for Scottish products and manufactures of all kinds. To the Scots merchant, the industrialist and the shipowner, the need for markets was of paramount importance in this period, more pressing than the need for raw materials. And in no part of Scotland was this need felt more acutely than in Greenock, the country's rising port, centre of the initiatives and the enterprise that were to bring Canada within the orbit of Scottish commercial

---

[13] For the Scottish attitudes to smuggling in the eighteenth century see P.W.J. Riley, *The English Ministers and Scotland* (London, 1964). For Kirkman Finlay's activities see *James Finlay and Co.: A Company History* (Glasgow, 1962). Galt's "Essay on Commercial Policy" was published in *The Philosophical Magazine* of London, vol. 23, 1805, pp. 104-112. Loch's views are presented in his *Letters concerning the Trade and Manufactures of Scotland* (Edinburgh, 1774), and his *Essay on the Trade, Commerce and Manufacture of Scotland* (Edinburgh), 1775.

[14] Helen I. Cowan, *British Emigration to North America* (Toronto, 1961); W. A. Carrothers, *Emigration from the British Isles* (London, 1929).

expansion. It is not surprising that the first petition against the renewal of the Honourable East India Company's monopoly should have come in 1806 from its merchants and shipowners.

THE CLYDE – FOCUS OF THE TRADE

By 1783 Greenock, with a population of 15,000, had become the recognised port and outlet for the booming city of Glasgow, centre of Scotland's rising industry. Just as Glasgow was bidding fair to outstrip the ancient capital, Edinburgh, in population and economic importance, so was Greenock well on the way to surpass Edinburgh's ancient port of Leith as the chief centre of shipping operations in the Scottish kingdom. Its shipyards, especially that conducted by the family of Scott, were already achieving a reputation throughout Britain. Between 1784 and 1791, according to a "View of the Situation and Trade of Greenock" in *The Scots Magazine* of January, 1805, "Inward" shipping rose from 2,600 tons to 43,400 tons. "By 1800," claimed David Macpherson, "Greenock owned 377 ships employing some 4000 men." Its merchants, and those of Glasgow, had established trading connections with the West Indies and the Americas as early as the 1670's.[15] The result of the American War of 1776-1783 was to make the merchants of Greenock and Glasgow look very closely at the more northern parts of the Americas, and in this field they were no novices. As early as 1620 a small group of Glasgow merchants, straining their meagre resources, had given financial assistance to the Newfoundland Company, founded and chartered in 1610 in Bristol and London.[16] This was the time when many Scots fondly believed that they would be allowed to share the fruits of empire and trade with the English, who shared their king; when Sir William Alexander was forming his feudal domain of "New Scotland" and Lord Ochiltree was forming his "Scots Barony or Stewardry" in Cape Breton Island. The schemes for Scottish settlements in Acadia to rival the English colonies of Virginia and New England broke down in the confusion and financial turmoil that beset the first two Stuart Kings of Great Britain, but the Glasgow merchants maintained their interest in the area, because it provided some useful subterfuges in the increasingly popular national sport of evading the English Navigation Acts.

Edward Randolph, Surveyor-General of Customs for the American Plantations in the last twenty years of the seventeenth century, plaintively reported to the Commissioners of the Customs in June, 1680, that "many ships full laden with tobacco" gave bonds at the Naval Office in Boston that they were bound to Newfoundland, but proceeded in fact to "Scotland, Canada and other foreign countries."[17] This useful pretext, in addition to the trick of registering their vessels at Whitehaven, helped the Glasgow merchants to get

[15] See Daniel Weir, *History of the Town of Greenock* (Glasgow, 1829).
[16] R. G. Lounsbury, *The British Fishery at Newfoundland*, Archon Reprints, 1969, p. 44.
[17] Lounsbury, *op. cit.*, pp. 198-9.

established in the tobacco and plantation trades long before the Act of Union of 1707 gave them legal entitlement to participate. By 1699 the traffic in tobacco, carted north through Pennsylvania, and shipped in the ports of that colony, or of Massachusetts, to Newfoundland and thence to the Clyde, was considerable enough to cause grave concern to the Board of Trade. In this dubious trade the Scots made full use of the legal questions and uncertainty that surrounded the status of Newfoundland, for some English legal authorities contended that it was "no true plantation" but rather "a part, nay an extension of His Majesty's realm of England" with which the Scots were in fact allowed to trade openly, since the Acts of Trade did not apply in such areas. In March, 1701, Randolph reported to the Board of Trade the further enormity that a combine of Scottish merchants had shown the audacity to establish a "factory" on the coast of Newfoundland, and, that through this warehouse, set up purportedly as a fishing station, they were sending large quantities of enumerated commodities, especially tobacco, and sugar, back to Scotland, Holland and other places.[18] After 1707 the Scots were not slow to engage fully in such trades and they developed further their skills in breaching the Navigation Laws and the trade regulations. By 1725 Greenock had three sizeable vessels at the Newfoundland fisheries, and the number increased steadily as the years passed.

This may seem surprising, in view of Scotland's own natural wealth in fish-resources, which were exploited increasingly in the eighteenth century. But it is less surprising when one considers that Newfoundland and its fisheries were being used increasingly as a "cover" not only for the shipping out of colonial produce from the Southern plantation colonies and the West Indies to foreign European ports, but also as a "blind" for importing large quantities of European goods, such as French brandy, laces, silks, Dutch spirits and German Osnaburgh linens into all the British colonies of the North American seaboard and the West Indies.[19] The "nature" of the "Newfoundland Fishery" conducted from Greenock in the eighteenth century, and even into the early 1800's, is perhaps revealed by the fact that the Greenock vessels participating by 1807 (there were thirty-nine ships from the port engaged, as against sixty from Liverpool and fifty-eight from Poole, putting Greenock third on the list of British ports involved) were, with those from Liverpool, the largest of the entire fleet. They were also the most heavily gunned.[20]

The records of Johnstone and Co., of Lang and Co., of the Greenock-connected firm of Hamilton, Graham and Co., all operating in Newfoundland in the 1770-1810 period, leave no doubt that there was much more

---

[18] Lounsbury, *op. cit.*, p. 201.

[19] Lounsbury, *op. cit.*, pp. 203-6.

[20] A. C. Wardle, Chapter on "The Newfoundland Trade" in *The Trade Winds: A Study of British Overseas Trade During the French Wars 1793-1815* (London, 1958), pp. 243-244.

concern in the Newfoundland trade than codfish, sealskins, and the provisioning of the scattered settlements.[21] The absence of any effective government authority for most of the year, or of any naval patrol, rendered the area a natural *point d'appui* for smuggling and illegal trade activities, and the naval officers who performed their annual tours of duty as "justices" had little interest in checking the traffic. After 1776, there was a noticeable increase in Scottish trade with the island, though it is difficult to know how to interpret the figures, in view of the wholesale illicit trade which was obviously being transacted on its shores and in the waters about it. The useful Glasgow Chamber of Commerce Abstracts (to which fuller reference will be made later) show the following figures (in pounds sterling).[22]

Table 1. Scottish Trade with Newfoundland (official figures) 1764-1801

Year	Scottish Imports from Newfoundland	Scottish Exports to Newfoundland
1764	—	340
1765	—	2453
1769	4984	962
1775	2783	4053
1778	5668	14077
1781	3720	17836
1786	1292	13784
1790	5499	11991
1793	3098	18498
1797	18846	13745
1798	6125	27683
1799	13953	23291
1801	18830	46888

A list of exports from Scotland to the island in the years 1770-1785, sent from the headquarters of the Scottish Customs at the order of the "Lords of the Committee of Council for Trade and Foreign Plantations" in January, 1786, showed the principal items sent out as meal flour, fresh pork, linens, leather goods, barrelled beef, and sailcloth, totalling in value for the fifteen year period no less than £133,000. It is difficult in the light of these figures to avoid the conclusion that the Wars of 1776-1783 and 1793-1801 gave a considerable stimulus to the trade, and that the export figures are much

---

[21] The Lang Papers are housed in the Business Archives Collection in the Department of Economic History, the University of Glasgow.

[22] Abstract of the General Customs of Scotland 1755-1801, Archives of the Glasgow Chamber of Commerce, probably compiled by George Chalmers; Customs account book, Newfoundland, 1771-85 R. H. 20/22 in the Scottish Record Office, Edinburgh.

higher than can be accounted for by the returns from the fisheries, even allowing for direct shipments of fish to foreign ports. Obviously the illicit trade was plied with particular vigour in wartime, and it is worth noting that when Chief Justice Reeves made his third report on the state of the island in 1793, several Greenock and Port Glasgow firms had recently established Newfoundland agencies. These were the four important houses of Messrs. Andrew Thomson and Co., Crawford and Co., Stevensons and Co., and Stuart and Rennie.[23] The predominance of Scots in the trades masked by the fisheries and in the fish-trade itself was noticeable to several observers, and the Scots operated not only in St. John's and other island settlements and from Greenock but from other colonial centres as well. When War came in 1776 the thriving firm of Messrs. Cochrans, at Halifax, took over the New-foundland trade in fish to Bermuda from the Boston concern of Russell and Co. It is significant that it was a Scot, Nathaniel Atcheson of London, holding such large Nova Scotian and Newfoundland interests that he was regarded as mercantile agent for these colonies, who secured the exclusion of foreign fish from the West Indies in 1813, earning for himself the title of "saviour of our livelihood" from the islanders.[24]

THE EARLY PHASE OF OPERATIONS, 1759-1776

As interest in the Newfoundland trade extended to the other North American colonies north of Massachusetts after 1760, Greenock steadily maintained its lead in this new field for enterprise. Already the principal port for Scotland's Virginia and West India trades, a key centre of the Scottish coastal and fishing trades, and helped by a growing commerce with the Mediterranean, Norway and the Baltic, especially after the completion of the Forth and Clyde Canal in 1790, Greenock was well situated at the throat of industrial Scotland, and on the best sea route to the Saint Lawrence River, to avail itself of the opportunities.

The port, and its neighbouring city of Glasgow, which it served as an outlet to the overseas world, shared in the general growth precipitated by the continual wars of the eighteenth century, which stimulated the Scottish economy as a whole, bringing rapid developments in the iron industry and in shipbuilding and shipowning.[25] The war of 1739-1748 saw considerable advances in those fields of activity, and there was even greater progress in the Seven Years' War, when the new conquests appeared to many in Scotland to be opening up vast areas for the exercise of the country's commercial skills, for its rising shipping trade, and for exploitation as markets for its new manufactures. Apart from the Scottish troops who served in the campaigns

---

[23] H. A. Innis, *The Cod Fisheries: The History of an International Economy*, Revised Edition, (Toronto, 1954), p. 289.

[24] *Ibid*, pp. 297, 212, 245.

[25] See Henry Hamilton, *An Economic History of Scotland in the Eighteenth Century*, (Oxford, 1963).

in North America, there were Scottish merchants active on the fringes of mainland Canada – a few at Halifax, and some in the Albany and Schenectady areas where profits to be made in the fur trade were already proving attractive. Some of these Scots received concessions to operate in certain French areas in North America between 1748 and 1756, but little is known of their background or activities. Unlike the Hudson Bay and North West Company venturers, whose histories have been meticulously recorded in detail, the men of the "dark age" of free enterprise and endeavour in the North American fur trade have been sadly neglected. Here the finding of an account book or a letter book may one day add another important chapter to the story of the trade. There were also Scots among the "four hundred and fifty contemptible sutlers and traders" to whom General Murray made scathing reference as being an embarrassment to him in the new conquest of Canada.[26]

The course of the War for Canada was followed with keen interest in Glasgow and Greenock, for it was realized among commercial circles that here was indeed a promising new field for enterprise that might well supplement the Virginia and West India trades in furthering the advance of Scottish trade. John Rutherford, Scottish commentator on mercantile matters, expressed the view of many of his countrymen when he wrote in 1761: "colonies will render us independent of the world, in point of trade." In this new area, there would be no chartered monopolies. The London shipping interests would have no preference, it was felt. Hence the progress of the War in North America was watched more closely than operations in any other theatre. In June, 1759, the weekly *Glasgow Journal*, the most widely circulated and influential of the area's newspapers, ascribed the "imminent threat of a French invasion of Britain" solely to the concern of the enemy to save their "precious" possessions – Louisbourg, Cape Breton and Canada, and the fisheries.[27] Greenock and Glasgow merchants engaged in the Newfoundland "fisheries" trade had realised by this time that there was another lucrative angle to the business, and were directing their vessels to load extra supplies of provisions at Cork in Ireland for sale to the British forces engaged in the Canada campaign. In this trade Scottish shipmasters made their first acquaintance with the waters of the Saint Lawrence River. Naval pressgangs were active in the Clyde throughout the war, but despite losses of seamen to them, and very often ignoring the strict injunction to sail in convoy, the Greenock ships continued to ply their Newfoundland-Canada trade, and no fewer than twenty-three departures are recorded for the years 1759-1762 inclusive.[28] Some of these vessels found profitable employment in the shipment of stores and war materials from Boston and Philadelphia to the Saint Lawrence, for high

---

[26] W. Stewart Wallace, *The Pedlars from Quebec and Other papers on the Nor' Westers*, (Toronto), p. 21.

[27] *Glasgow Journal*, June 4, 1759.

[28] *Glasgow Journal*, Shipping lists and "Plantation News," 1759-62.

freight-rates were paid for this service; but it was a risky route to ply, and the ship *Hunter* of Greenock, which was taken by a small French privateer operating out of the Gut of Canso, was only one of the six Scottish vessels engaged on the Philadelphia-Quebec route to be lost to privateers in 1759-1761.

With the fall of Quebec, a strong body of opinion developed in Glasgow and Greenock in favour of retaining Canada. A letter from "Britannicus" to the editor of the *Glasgow Journal* in January, 1760 stated: "of all our acquisitions the conquest of Quebec, and, consequently, of the country of Canada, is the most important and most beneficial to this Kingdom, for by the reduction of that place and country, the British Empire in America will be perfectly secured from all future attempts of our enemies; and also such a source of trade and commerce opened to us here, as will be fully sufficient, had we no other, to employ all our trading and commercial people; and find a vent or constant consumption for all our goods, products and manufactures. It is therefore above all things to be wished that the country of Canada may never be relinquished."[29] This was only the first of a long series of letters which show the high hopes of the local business interests for a new and profitable outlet. The Editor of the *Journal* echoed the views of his contributors, urging the completion of the conquest, regardless of expense, as "the most thrifty disbursement ever made," expatiating on the benefits, "An exclusive fishery! A boundless territory! The fur trade engrossed! and innumerable tribes of savages contributing to the consumption of our staple! – These are sources of exhaustless wealth! Ignorant and designing men have called this a quarrel for a few dirty lands or acres of snow, but the British public will soon have feeling (sic) proofs that Great Britain must sink or swim with her colonies."[30]

Agitation in Glasgow and Greenock for the retention of Canada "regardless of our outlay in moneys and blood" continued through 1760. Groups of interested merchants besought the Provost, the baillies, and local nobility and gentry to use their influence with members of Parliament to ensure that "the French should be totally cleared out of North America," and, with the imminent fall of Montreal, the *Glasgow Journal* demanded the "complete expulsion" of the French from the Province. Accounts from Montreal, soon after it was taken, were published in the *Journal* and throw interesting light on the reactions of Scottish "mercantile men" to the French community in Canada. A letter from a Scottish trader published in January, 1761, deplored the distress among the French due to the fact that their bills or remittances for furs "drawn on the French king" were now "not worth a farthing." The total amount of these "useless paper scraps" in circulation was in the region of three million pounds sterling, according to the writer, and "many of those

[29] *Ibid.*, January 14, 1760.
[30] *Ibid*, January 28, 1760.

who had with great danger and labour acquired estates worth £ 20,000 by the fur trade or otherwise, can scarce procure a dinner."

The Scots were certainly impressed by the standards of living which they found in this French colonial town, but mingled with their admiration was a deprecation which boded ill for the future relations between Scottish mercantile settlers and French residents. The "elegant churches" were noted with surprise, but the style of living was obviously resented.

"The people here are extremely fond of dress. A stranger would take Montreal to be inhabited by none but the rich and idle. They are all finely powdered, walk with their hats under their arms and wear fine long coats embroidered with tinsel lace, and buttoned down to the extremity. Since I came here I have not seen one man dressed as a tradesman. The ladies in general are handsome, gay, and well-bred."[31]

By this date the famous controversy as to the relative merits of retaining Caribbean or Canadian conquests was under way, and the general consensus of opinion in Scotland, judged by the views expressed in the Glasgow and Edinburgh press, was that Canada should be preferred. This was possibly due to the fact that Glasgow merchants had already secured interests in the West Indies which they felt might be injured by the acquisition of further islands and competitive sugar plantations.[32] Some believed that the powerful "London and Bristol sugar interest" desired to obtain Guadeloupe and the other French islands so as to oust the Scots from the trade through "a hurtful monopoly," and that these "guileful artificers" had concocted the rumour that the French in Canada, by articles 26, 37 and 48 of the capitulation, were to have the right to export peltries to France, "by which they will engross all the fur trade, and even import goods of the manufacture of France, by the way of Guernsey and Jersey, by which they will always be enabled . . . to laugh at all the efforts of the British merchants to share the fur trade with them."[33] The controversy is of interest in that it reveals the intense suspicions of English or London "monopoly" interests that prevailed in Scotland at the time.

The enthusiasm for Canada as a field for commercial enterprise continued to run high in 1763-1764, encouraged by letters in the Scottish press from Scots merchants who had won a foothold in Quebec and Montreal, and who signed their missives, unfortunately for the historian, by such *noms-de-plume* as "Mercator" and "Caledonicus." One of these, written from Quebec, stated that the writer had recently acquired the papers of "a deceased merchant of La Rochelle" containing an account of a most profitable cargo of furs shipped to France in 1758, and asserted that "the trade of this land of Canada will turn out superior in importance to Martinico or Guadeloupe, *or*

[31] *Ibid*, September 18, 1760; January 8, 1761.
[32] *Ibid.*, March 12, 1761; Broadside Pamphlet, *Sugar Enough, or no Sustenance to Planters*, Clerk of Penicuik Collection, Scottish Record Office, Edinburgh.
[33] *Glasgow Journal*, May 14 and 21, 1761.

even both put together."[34] The direct commercial connection between Scotland and Canada had now begun, and Robert Finlay of Glasgow, agent for his brother James, in Quebec, was advertising the first direct peacetime sailings for the province, the snow *Apthorp*, to leave Greenock in February, 1764, and the schooner *Bonny Lass of Livingston* to sail for freights. He also sought skilled craftsmen for his brother and his brother's mercantile friends in Quebec, who had begun to acquire land, and sought to build warehouses and stores: "Masons skilled in building, gardeners, quarriers and millers, fabricators of dry stone dykes, and good and sober men skilled in the management of flour mills and saw mills" were asked to come forward for free passage and well-paid employment.[35] The two vessels owned by the Finlays were the first "regular traders" to operate between the Clyde and Quebec, and their services were supplemented temporarily later in 1764 by the full-rigged ships *Africa* and *Maria* (owners unknown) which were usually engaged in the West African slave trade. Other vessels engaged in the Quebec trade in 1764 were the Greenock brig *Fair Canadian* which arrived home with furs, timber and potash for an unspecified owner, and the Greenock ship *Jean* which reached Quebec with a full cargo of wines from Lisbon.[36]

From perusal of the shipping lists in the Scottish press, it is apparent that the Clyde shipping interest, centred on Greenock, and acting on behalf of Glasgow owners' agency, had secured by 1776 a share of the shipping trade to Canada out of all proportion to Scotland's relative strength in shipping. The expectations of the Glasgow-Greenock mercantile interest were in fact fulfilled, and the founding of a consortium such as the North West Company of fur traders in Montreal in 1779 must be viewed as the natural outcome of fifteen years of successful commercial operations by Scots in the conquered province, who were already well-established as general traders and men of business. By 1770 at least eleven reputable firms in Glasgow, Greenock, and the surrounding area were engaged either fully or partly in the Quebec trade. Colin Dunlop and Son of Glasgow as agents, and James Wilson of Kilmarnock as owner were jointly advertising the fine ship *Diana*, not only for freight (she was a vessel of 400 tons – large for that time by Scottish standards) but also for passengers, "the highest class of cabin accommodation being available." Clearly, the Scottish "debut" in the Canadian shipping field was not made by the timber-ships of dubious quality which dominated the Miramichi and Saint John timber trade in the early 1800's but by superior vessels, sailing to the new-won province of Quebec in the 1760's and 1770's.[37] Regular traders, Greenock vessels, were in fact plying between the Clyde and Canada from 1764, between the Clyde and Nova Scotia from 1768, and between the

---

[34] *Ibid.*, January 26, 1764.
[35] *Ibid.*, February 2, 1764.
[36] *Glasgow Journal*, Shipping lists, 1764.
[37] *Ibid.*, March 8, 1770. See also shipping lists, 1765-1770.

Clyde and New Brunswick from 1768 – long before Captain Alexander Allan of Saltcoats, founder of the Allan line, sailed from Greenock for Quebec in June, 1819. Yet Allan's voyage has often been described as the beginning of regular sailings between Scotland and British North America.

Ironically, it was not Scotland, but London, which benefited from the steady "engrossment" of the Montreal fur trade between 1763 and 1821. This was for two reasons, the first being the undisputed primacy of London as the British market for furs, with its long-established manufactures of hats and other fur products, its specialist buyers and handlers, and all the other appurtenances of the trade that had developed since the beginning of success-ful activities by the Hudson's Bay Company in the 1680's.[38] Another was the fact that the leading Scots firm in the British-Canadian fur trade, that of Phyn, Ellice and Co., composed of scions of the gentry of North-East Scotland, was itself centred in London. The partners of their Canadian subsidi-ary, Forsyth, Richardson and Co. of Montreal, had a similar background. It was with this thriving firm that the North West Company and its predecessors dealt, and it was trade goods from London rather than from Glasgow or Greenock that sustained the fur trade.

In London the friends and agents of the Company used their not inconsi-derable political influence to maintain the copartnery's position against the Hudson's Bay Company and its claim to have monopoly in the North. David Macpherson, the Scottish commentator on trade, stressed the "free enter-prise" character of the North West Company in his *Annals of Commerce* (1805, vol. 4, p. 129): "without any exclusive privilege, or any advantages, but what they derive from their capital, credit and knowledge of the business, their prudent regulations, and judicious liberality to their clerks and servants of all kinds, they have carried their branch of commerce to a height never before attained." Ironically Nor'Westers themselves were to become virtual monopolists in their own sphere of influence in the 1790's, but of course, they viewed this control in a very different light from that of the "English" monopolists. Their commanding position over the wide area they controlled seemed the natural reward of enterprise. As W. Stewart Wallace showed conclusively in his *Documents Relating to the North West Company*, (Champlain Society, Toronto, 1934), the Company was composed almost entirely of Scots, very largely drawn from Aberdeenshire, Banffshire and Inverness-shire, many of them with military, farming or small landholding backgrounds. Of the 255 persons listed in Wallace's "Biographical Dictionary of the Nor'Westers" (Appendix A, pp. 425-505 of the *Documents*), 126 were Scots born, 33 were of Scots descent, and others were possibly Scots. No fewer than eleven were established and operating in Quebec as early as 1763-5.

The London firms with which they principally dealt were invariably Scots –

---

[38] For the development of this trade see E. R. Rich, *The History of the Hudson's Bay Company*, 1670-1870, (London, 1958-9).

Phyn, Ellice and Co., and Robert Grant and Co. – operated largely out of Schenectady in New York before the American Revolutionary War, and between 1783 and 1790 when they set up in Montreal, the five Forsyth brothers conducted general and fur-trading activities out of Niagara and Kingston.[39]

Between 1764 and 1778 only four mentions were made in the Glasgow press of the arrival of furs in the Clyde, and these were small consignments. According to David Macpherson's *Annals of Commerce, Fisheries and Navigation*, (Edinburgh, 1805, vol. 3), 346,794 skins were shipped to London in 1766, and the total value of English imports from the province was almost £47,000, as against Scotland's imports of £700. English exports to Quebec for the same year were valued at £366,573, as against Scotland's exports of £5,417. Of 152 ships recorded in Colonial Office and Board of Trade lists as sailing from Montreal and Quebec for the United Kingdom with full cargoes of furs between June, 1786 and January, 1814, only seven sailed for Scottish ports – one for Queensferry in 1786, one for Ayr in 1802, two for Greenock in 1802 and 1809, two for Aberdeen in 1811 and one for Kirkcaldy in 1811. Scotland was alive at this time with new manufactures, but there is no record of any significant development of fur-using industries.[40]

It was in the field of general trade, and, after 1805, in the timber trade, that the province of Canada was to bring most advantage to Scotland, and Montreal, Halifax and St. John, and to a lesser degree St. Andrews in New Brunswick, were to become the principal centres of Scottish enterprise in North America after 1776. But the 1760's and early 1770's were comparatively lean years for the connection, and the few Scottish merchants in Quebec appear to have had a thin time of it until the War of 1776 brought extended opportunities for trade, and a further influx of enterprising fellow countrymen of the Loyalist persuasion from centres in the colonies which had declared their independence. By 1768 Scottish merchants were numerous enough in Halifax, Nova Scotia, for sixteen of them to form a North British Society, which thrived and grew lustily from the time of its inception, but it was otherwise in Quebec and Montreal until the fur-trade magnates and the Loyalist merchants came in. Many of the first Scottish merchants, who came in with the conquering army, or on its heels, like the Finlays of Glasgow, had their fingers badly burned by dealings in the "Cards and Billets of Ordonnance" to which reference has already been made. These were accepted in exchange for goods by the Finlays and others, and it is also likely that these merchants were speculating in the paper. Bigot had made heavy issues of this currency in 1759 for war purposes, and the French government

---

[39] W. Stewart Wallace, *op. cit.*, pp. 40-50 and R. Harvey Fleming, "Phyn Ellice and Co. of Schenectady," in *Contributions to Canadian Economics*, Vol. IV (Toronto, 1932).

[40] Compiled from Colonial Office Records, Series 47, Vols. 80-83, and Board of Trade Records, Series 5, Vol. 8, P.R.O.

declared on several occasions in 1763-4 that it was unable to redeem the paper.[41]

At the instigation of the British merchants in Quebec and Montreal, and especially of the Scots, the British government requested the lawyer – philosopher David Hume of Edinburgh – to make proposals to the French authorities for the settlement of the matter. Hume submitted in September, 1765, that the merchants insist that the payment of fifty per cent for the Bills of Exchange was too low, as well as twenty-five per cent for the Cards and Billets of Ordonnance "because there never was so considerable a difference made between Paper and Money in Canada." He also contended that the merchants had suffered "great hardship and injustice," but in the circumstances of 1765, with the French treasury badly depleted, Hume's submission, and all the eloquence of ambassadors, was of no avail. The Scottish merchants never recouped their losses on the Canada paper currency.[42]

After 1776, with the influx of Scottish fur-traders and general merchants, the Scottish faith in Canada as an outlet for their energies was largely justified. War, as always in the period, gave further stimulus to the nation's commercial and industrial development. In the colony it also stimulated economic development by providing, in the armed forces, not only a market for colonial agricultural produce, but also an increased flow of currency, in the form of soldiers' and sailors' pay in coin, officers' pay in Treasury bills, payment for supplies in Commissary and Artillery Bills and other useful media of finance. Scottish officers in the colonies, in this and in the Revolutionary and Napoleonic Wars, had a particular proclivity for lending money to merchants among their countrymen, and occasionally even used them as "fronts" or agents in trading, privateering or prize buying activities.[43]

These transactions were usually highly successful, but occasionally they misfired, as in the case of the "Cochrane scandal." In 1780-2 the Honourable John Cochrane, son of the Earl of Dundonald, and agent-general for "The Remitters of the Public Money" advanced large sums in bills of exchange sold on credit from his chest to a group of Montreal merchants. Governor Haldimand took exception to these transactions, in which the merchants involved were mostly Scots, and included such Montreal worthies as Messrs. Scott and Burn, Buchanan and Shannon, Simon Fraser senior, John McCord, John Pagan, John Reid, Hugh Ritchie, David Ross, Murdoch Stuart, and many others, whose names read like a Scottish census list. Through his powerful family connections, especially his uncle Andrew Stuart, a member of Parliament who had the ear of the all-powerful Dundas,

[41] *Glasgow Journal*, Letter of "Mercator," January 5, 1764.
[42] David Hume's Memorandum to the Court of France, September, 1765, National Library of Scotland, MS. No. 2618.
[43] See especially below, in the discussion of the Scottish commercial circle in Halifax in 1794-1815.

Pitt's political manager for Scotland, Cochrane was able to escape unscathed, but the affair is interesting because it shows how high government officials of Scottish origin could and did use their funds to promote their own and their countrymen's interests. In defence of his financial transactions, which Haldimand had tried to check by withdrawing authority for the sale of the bills on credit, Cochrane maintained that Haldimand was antagonistic to the merchants, especially the Scots, and that since no specie had arrived in Canada in 1780 or 1781, his sale of the Bills had "kept up the rate of exchange and other public advantages." The incident also throws light on the attitudes of the Scots mercantile class in Montreal at the time, for these Cochrane certainly shared. In his opinion, expressed to Stuart, for relay to Dundas, Haldimand was "the curse and ruin of the Province" and the Province itself was being wrecked by deference to the French.

Ten years later, in 1794, Cochrane, still in communication with his Montreal associates, continued to relay their views to Pitt's government, that the province was "utterly disaffected," but by this time his own attitude to the country he had long ago left behind had changed. He suggested that, rather than go to war with the United States, it would be "better to make them a present of the province altogether, since the more extensive their territory, the sooner they will separate into distinct states." In his view "trade with the United States is the only reason for keeping Canada, since it runs at the back of America and will prevent America from laying any very heavy duty on British manufactures, since should they attempt it, wholesale smuggling will be encouraged."[44] In this last prognosis at least, Cochrane was to be a true prophet.

The link between the Scots merchants in Quebec and Montreal and the Pitt and Liverpool governments through Dundas and his son, the second Viscount Melville, who succeeded to the political "managership" in Scotland, was a strong one. Henry Caldwell, naval officer in 1759 and merchant in Quebec thereafter, was influential in persuading Dundas, who headed the Admiralty, to develop Canadian timber resources for the Navy in 1804. As early as 1775 Caldwell had surveyed the timber resources of what was later to become Upper Canada, and in 1777 in conjunction with Sir Arnold Nesbit and Lord Heniker, he made a conditional contract with the Navy Commissioners for masts. Due to the "uninhabited nature of the region, and the reason that it was not yet opened up" the scheme had failed, but Caldwell, through Dundas influence, had better fortune in 1804-5.[45] A similar use of Scottish political influence was made in 1787 by George Buchan Hepburn

---

[44] Stuart-Stevenson Dundonald Papers, National Library of Scotland MSS 5376, 5496, 5497. Cochrane to Stuart, May 3, 1784, October 19, 1794, with "Memoir on the Frontier and the Fur Trade."

[45] Melville Papers, National Library of Scotland MS. 3847. Caldwell to Dundas, October 27, 1804.

of Montreal who asked Dundas's assistance in securing an estate "with exclusive rights of trading with the Northern Indians of the King's Post on the Tadusac and Chicotimi Rivers."[46]

JAMES DUNLOP, ENTREPRENEUR IN CANADA, 1776-1815

The years 1774-80 saw the arrival of Scottish merchants in Montreal to augment the struggling Finlays and others of the first "Conquest" wave. Simon McTavish, known to his familiars as "The Marquis", uncrowned king of the Montreal fur-trade, arrived in Montreal in 1775 after operating successfully out of Albany and Detroit.[47] James McGill appeared in 1774, after experience as a trader in several American colonies, and James Dunlop transferred his capital North from Virginia in 1776.[48] These three were to dominate the Scottish mercantile circle in the town, just as that circle domi-nated the trade of the town and province. It is unfortunate that the personal papers of McTavish and McGill have not survived, and that we have so few insights through what remains into their outlooks and their activities.[49] In the case of Dunlop, who is in many ways the most interesting of the three, since he was not involved directly in the well-documented fur trade, such materials do exist, in the series of letters which he wrote to his brother, sister and brother-in-law in Glasgow in 1796-1815, and which is preserved in the Scottish Record Office.[50]

Dunlop, as befitted a Glasgow-trained merchant, had strong free-trade ideas. He was ebullient, even boastful (at least in his letters home) but he was undoubtedly successful, and when the scale of his ship-owning, land-holding, property-owning, general trading and other diverse operations is considered there seems little reason to doubt the claim he made in 1814, that he was wealthiest man in the province. He was convivial, enterprising and bold, and the impression he made in the community was strong enough for the Rever-end Robert Campbell, seventy years after Dunlop's death, to record with satisfaction, that this early parishioner of St. Gabriel Street Presbyterian Church "remitted to Britain, shortly before his death in 1815, the sum of £ 30,000, the largest bill of exchange ever sent from the colony up to this date."[51] Between 1776 and 1796 Dunlop steadily built up a general trading business, dealing largely in imported textiles, liquors and groceries, and centred on his large warehouse in St. Paul Street. The War with Revolution-

[46] *Ibid.*, Hepburn to Dundas, September 12, 1787.
[47] W. Stewart Wallace, *op. cit.*, pp. 485-6.
[48] *Glasgow Burgh Court Records*, October, 1777; *The Macmillan Dictionary of Canadian Biography* (Toronto, 1963).
[49] The surviving McGill Papers are quite fragmentary, another instance of the dearth of record material pertaining to key figures in the history of Canadian business.
[50] Letters of James Dunlop, G.D. 1/151, Scottish Record Office, H. M. General Register House, Edinburgh.
[51] The Reverend Robert Campbell, *A History of the Scotch Presbyterian Church, St. Gabriel Street, Montreal* (Montreal 1887), pp. 96-8.

ary France, as for so many other Scots merchants in this and other colonial centres, provided new opportunities, and Dunlop launched out in several new lines of activity, with boldness and verve, travelling frequently between Montreal and Quebec to promote his new ventures. Unlike the fur-traders, he and his Quebec friend and agent, John Pagan, dealt largely with Scotland, through the agency of the important Greenock firm of Alan Ker and Co. The increase in the scale of trading operations between the province and Scotland at the time is indicated by the following table, abbreviated from the Glasgow Chamber of Commerce Abstracts.

Table 2. Scottish Trade with Canada, 1785-1801

Year	Scottish Imports from the Province of Canada (in pounds sterling)	Scottish Exports to The Province of Canada (in pounds sterling)
1785	344	3670
1790	392	21724
1795	2564	21055
1797	7364	26457
1798	9920	63136
1799	17774	35504
1801	49800	63157

Those figures are reinforced by David Macpherson's figures for Scottish trade with the North American colonies generally between 1794 and 1799. These, from his *Annals of Commerce* (1805), are as follows:

Year	Exports to the Colonies (in pounds sterling)
1794	102946
1798	236310
1799	225508

Dunlop and his friends benefited greatly from the Act of Parliament of 1788, which permitted vessels carrying lumber, provisions and livestock from the province of Quebec to trade to the West Indies and to bring back thence sugars, rum, and other commodities, to the value of the outward cargo, free of duty. Even before the War of 1793 increased the demand for high-quality colonial timber, Dunlop was also exporting cargoes of choice Canadian oak to the important Leith timber firm of Allan, Stewart and Co., the first commercial concern on the East Coast of Scotland to show any interest in Canada. In October, 1789, the Leith Customs Quarterly Accounts recorded the arrival of an entire shipload of oak pieces and oak planks in the ship *Brothers* from Quebec for the firm, consigned by Dunlop. Almost certainly this cargo was destined for the shipyards of the Firth of Forth.

By 1797 Dunlop was writing to his sister in Scotland that "the variety and multiplicity" of his business made it necessary for him to recruit more clerks, in Scotland. One of the new activities in which he was engaged was the wholesale purchase of grain in the country areas – an increasingly profitable business, in view of the growing demand for flour in the colonies, the West Indies, and Britain, where scarcity was beginning to cause occasional disturbances, such as the Scottish "meal mobs." Fernand Ouellet, in his recent writings on the economy of the province has stressed the importance of grain production at this time, and it is interesting to see, from this Scottish merchant's angle, just how much could be made from dealings in this commodity. In the fall of 1797 Dunlop remitted to his brother Alexander, a bookseller and stationer in Glasgow, bills to the value of over £17,000 derived largely from the sale of grain.[52] By this date he was importing consignments of rum – as many as seven hundred barrels at a time, from Glasgow, but he considered that the export of Canadian grain and potash was his most promising "line," though he had also developed a trade in gunpowder, which he re-exported from Canada to New York, and in Osnaburgh linens and Russian linen shirtings of which he held a very large speculative stock. Very large consignments of Madeira wines, Scottish woollens, teas, and olive oils were also being imported by him, and he showed considerable expertise in gauging the state of the market to avoid "flooding."

The potash trade was particularly lucrative, a consignment of 951 barrels dispatched to the Clyde in 1798 selling in Glasgow for the high price of almost £63 per barrel, bringing in the handsome profit of £2,000. The scale of Dunlop's transactions in wheat and potash continued to increase as the War went on – no fewer than twenty thousand bushels of wheat being exported to Halifax in 1798. From being essentially a large-scale importer, Dunlop was changing to an exporting magnate, and it was only natural that he should develop shipping interests. The new Quebec-built ship of 250 tons, the *Caledonia*, of which he was part-owner with others of the Scottish mercantile clique, sailed for Port Glasgow early in 1799 with 12,000 bushels of Canadian wheat, and later in the year Dunlop purchased an extensive lot on the Saint Lawrence River with a good wharf, houses and stores, which he planned to be "largest mercantile establishment in the colony."[53]

An interest in shipowning was natural enough for a Glasgow man with Greenock contacts, for this was the period of Scotland's remarkable maritime expansion. According to Macpherson's *Annals of Commerce*, one seventh of the total number of vessels registered in the United Kingdom by

---

[52] Dunlop Letters, Dunlop to Alexander Dunlop, April 15, 1798.
[53] *Ibid.*, same to same, December 29, 1799.

1800 were owned in Scotland. In the same year, the Scottish population stood at just over one and a half million, as against a total of sixteen millions for the entire United Kingdom. The country, in truth, was beginning to possess a disproportionately large share of Britain's mercantile marine, a fact which drove its shipowners to seek new trade routes. War stimulated this expansion, for it kept freight rates high until about 1807, and to Dunlop and others in the province, the building and owning of their own vessels seemed an obvious avenue to greater profits. Scottish shipbuilders were already active in the province by 1798, when John Munn launched his first sizeable vessel at Quebec.

The bargaining and negotiating for grain with the growers and landowners were done by Dunlop himself, travelling with a pair of Scots clerks through the country areas while other Scots subordinates manned the Montreal establishment. As the finances at his command grew, the merchant found increasing opportunities for profit in the discounting of bills, a business in which he showed considerable acumen. In June 1800, to give only one example of how he worked, he purchased £21,000 of Bills drawn on the Paymaster General at a discount of two per cent, selling them in New York, at a premium of almost two per cent for specie. By July of the same year, he stated that "for several years I have been a loser by my great importations," but admitted to his brother that he was rapidly accumulating a large fortune in other ways.[54]

By 1800 whole cargoes of potash and grain were being dispatched by Dunlop for the Clyde and the Thames, and he was chartering sizeable ships and seeking to purchase other vessels. This trade particularly interested him, since he estimated that relations between Britain and the United States must inevitably deteriorate, and that this in turn would lead to a stoppage in supplies of the much needed potash to Britain from that quarter. If this came about, the Canadian product would be at a premium, and, gambling on the outcome, Dunlop began in 1801 to "stockpile" large quantities of potash and wheat. In 1801-1802 his wheat and flour exports rose to a new peak, making up a sizeable part (though the exact proportion is difficult to assess in view of the lack of his accounts) of the amazing total of wheat exports from the province in 1802, as calculated by Fernand Ouellet, of 1,151,530 "minots." The short peace that followed the Treaty of Amiens upset his calculations and brought about a serious glut of British imports in Canada, but the set-back was only temporary, and the resumption of hostilities enabled Dunlop to enter his most creative and profitable phase as entrepreneur and pioneer of new trades.

The export of grain, to Britain, Nova Scotia and the West Indies, and of potash to the Clyde, with shipowning and bill discounting, were the four principal bases of Dunlop's later success, and the War of 1812 added other

---

[54] *Ibid.*, same to same, and to Mrs. Janet McNair, July 1, 7 and 24, 1800.

profitable sidelines. By 1810 he owned three vessels and was building two more for his fleet in Montreal, using a dozen ship carpenters brought in from New York, and fifty local workmen. The new ships, named in honour of members of the Dunlop family, were sizeable craft of over 400 tons, and they plied regularly between the Saint Lawrence and the Clyde with wheat, potash, pine staves and pine boards, occasionally sailing for Jamaica with flour, pork, fish and lumber to load rum and molasses for the Clyde. The Collector of Customs' Report of Exports from the port of Quebec for the year 1807 shows that 231,543 bushels of wheat, 20,442 barrels of flour and 28,047 quintals of biscuit were exported in that year, making up, with other grain-stuffs, the principal item on the list. A proportion of this was sent out by Dunlop, for by 1806 he had established a branch and a shipyard in Quebec, and was spending a good deal of time travelling between the two ports, incidentally arranging grain and potash deliveries *en route*. Dealings in locally-produced hemp and flax were on a small scale, and Dunlop deplored the quality of the specimens offered. In view of his experience, and that of others before him with these products it is rather surprising to find the Scottish trade expert, Patrick Colquhoun, still contending hopefully, in his great *Treatise on the Wealth Power and Resources of the British Empire* (1814), that the Canadas would become vitally important to Britain as suppliers of hemp, flax and flax-seed. Yet the pathetic fallacy of the North American colonies' potential in this regard was to persist well into the 1820's, probably because of wishful thinking on the part of the home authorities, and because of the misguided enthusiasm of some in the colonies, such as the Quebec Agricultural Society, which had advocated the wholesale cultivation of hemp in 1791, urging the British government to direct Scottish settlers to Canada for the purpose.

On the launching of a third new ship, the *James Dunlop* in May, 1811, a ball was provided for the workmen and guests, and some five thousand persons attended. Living now in a large mansion, with a retinue of servants, Dunlop was regarded as the town's most prominent shipowner, and his exports of wheat and timber were, on his own admission, bringing him great profits – sufficient for him to be able to weather the loss of £10,000 in 1811, when the London firm of Howard and Bell, which handled his potash in England, suddenly collapsed.[55] Domestic servants for the mansion, clerks and storemen for the business headquarters, and entire crews for the new ships were recruited in Scotland through Alan Ker and Co. of Greenock, and from passing references in the Dunlop correspondence it is obvious that Dunlop's Scottish friends and associates in Montreal and Quebec followed the same policy of bringing in their countrymen wherever possible. The Scottish circle was growing increasingly anti-American and anti-French Canadian at this time, and Dunlop claimed to be expressing the general view of

---

[55] *Ibid.*, Dunlop to Mrs. Janet McNair, Glasgow.

the group when he wrote that "our government is too passive regarding the politicks of the United States. It is my opinion that we should long since either have made them to enter into a treaty with us, offensive and defensive, or made them open enemies."[56] Sir James Craig's dislike of the French made him popular among the "circle," and Dunlop was deputed by the "gentlemen inhabitants" of Montreal to present a farewell address to the Governor on his departure.

As war with the States appeared more imminent, Dunlop calculated, and correctly, that he stood to profit greatly by it. His two newest and largest ships would be suitable for service as privateers against American merchant shipping; there would be possibilities of a lucrative business in the discounting of Treasury, Army and Navy Bills; the rum trade from Jamaica and the wheat trade would benefit greatly from an increase in the armed forces in the North American colonies; the potash and flour trades to the Clyde would not suffer from the withdrawal of American competition, and the demand for oak and pine for British shipyards would increase even further. There is more than one suggestion in the correspondence that Dunlop and other members of the Montreal circle had formed a "ring" to hold down the prices of Canadian wheat, and to form a sort of "corner" in it. With three ships engaged in the Montreal-Jamaican trade by November, 1811, returning on an average some £1,500 clear profit per voyage, Dunlop was in a good position to speculate in wheat, potash and timber, with a view to wartime profits.[57] Some of his purchases at this time were large – including 14,000 *minots* of wheat for the Clyde, in March 1812, and he was laying down the keels of three new vessels.

This growth in the business – remarkable when one considers the average scale of operations in the colony at the time – was financed partly through dealings in bills. The discount on bills on Britain was 17½ per cent on Government Bills, and twenty per cent on private bills. The Montreal headquarters of James Dunlop and Co. was a centre of frenzied activity – and new "lines" were constantly opening up. Numerous wheat cargoes were arranged for Glasgow and Greenock importers and shipowners. A new commercial link with Scotland was forged by the arrangement of timber cargoes for the prominent Leith firm of Allan and Co., and an even more profitable venture than these was undertaken in June, 1812 – the supplying of the armies in the Peninsula. The *James Dunlop* was despatched for Lisbon with 350 barrels of beef and 3350 barrels of Canadian flour, the first of several profitable shipments. The newest vessel in the Dunlop fleet, the *George Canning* of over seven hundred tons, was meanwhile being freighted for the Clyde with oak and pine logs and all of the firm's ships were accorded "letters of Marque" as privateers.

---

[56] *Ibid.*, same to same, June 1, 1811.
[57] *Ibid.*, same to same, November 9 and 30, 1811.

In the mood of patriotic fervour that swept the town, the Scottish circle assumed a martial as well as a mercantile air. Dunlop became a major of Volunteer Artillery, boasting when he heard of American plans against Montreal, that "my great guns will make thousands of them sleep with their fathers."[58] The *Dunlop* took an American vessel prize off Newfoundland, and the merchant's calculations regarding potash and timber and flour prices in the United Kingdom proved correct, though the scarcity of grain in Canada in 1813 reduced the supplies available for this profitable export trade. Yet by April, 1814, Dunlop could declare: "I have done more good business since the War began than ever I did in the same space of time, but I also have been more bold in my speculations than any other person or Company in this province." Even the import trade, marginally profitable since 1800, repaid Dunlop handsomely, and in May, 1814, he stated that he had never gained more in any year than in 1813-14. Cases of import goods, mostly textiles, which he had wisely held during the "glut" period, rather than sell them at heavy losses in the "public vendue," fetched remarkably high prices, and there were still large stocks on hand – valued at £40,000. Dunlop calculated in 1814 that his annual profit would be more than £20,000.[59]

This account of Dunlop's activities is given in some detail, because it is rare for such personal notes by a colonial merchant of the time to survive. The key to the man's success was obviously the combination of commercial steadiness – (refusal to panic over the import "glut" for instance, in 1807 – 1812) and calculated boldness – (large-scale operations, willingness to enter new fields, and shipbuilding on his own account which some of his friends in the "circle" reckoned to be extremely hazardous.) The *James Dunlop* for example, of 440 tons, was built at a cost of almost £10,000 – a very high figure, much greater than a comparable vessel would have cost on the Clyde. Though colonial timber costs were low, labour costs were high. Yet the shipowning ventures paid well, and Dunlop received offers for the *George Canning* as soon as the vessel was built which, had he accepted, would have shown him a handsome profit on the outlay.[60]

The Dunlop correspondence is also important as showing the considerable profits to be made from potash and wheat exports in the period, 1794-1815, and sufficient data is contained in the letters for a comparative table to be drawn of prices paid in Canada as against prices realised in Greenock and Glasgow. The trades had downturns due to fluctuations in prices, but were generally profitable.

Dunlop certainly stands out as one of the most colourful and imaginative of the early Scottish merchants in Canada. Here was a man who dealt not in

---

[58] *Ibid.*, same to same, November 14, 1812.
[59] *Ibid.*, same to same, May 17, 1814.
[60] *Ibid.*, same to same, August 9, 1811.

consignments, but in full cargoes; who aimed, albeit in collusion with others, at "cornering" the production of a whole province; who built and operated his own merchant fleet, and pioneered new trades. His importations in one cargo in November, 1813 alone, consisted of eight hundred tons of goods, valued at £50,000, including the duties. It is interesting to consider what he might have gone on to do, had he not died suddenly in August, 1815, for he had embarked on a massive speculation in importing Irish flour – thousands of tons of it, and had purchased the fine East Indiaman *Earl St. Vincent* of almost nine hundred tons for his fleet, and was on the look-out for similar vessels. One of his last acts was to write to Canning in London and to the Members of Parliament for Glasgow and its environs urging the continuation of the War against the United States since "we will never again have the same good opportunity of bringing them to our own terms,"[61] and another was to import a large quantity of Tennent's Glasgow beer, for which he hoped to build up a market in the colony. At his death his inventory of imported goods in hand stood at one hundred thousand pounds. Having no partners, and no heirs, the house of "Dunlop and Co." vanished at his decease. Canadian historians have tended to be so preoccupied with the stirring events, political and military, of the period 1794-1815 that they have been inclined to ignore the obvious fact that this, for the colonies, as for Scotland and the rising industrial areas in England, was a period of intense, unprecedented economic, and hence, social development. Never did the opportunities for trade, for selling, for exchanging, for dealing, loom so large for the inhabitants of the Canadas, of Nova Scotia and New Brunswick. When the Peace of Ghent and the Vienna Treaty settled the clouds of war, a very different society emerged from the mists to that which had heard with some apprehension the declaration of hostilities against Revolutionary France twenty years before. Under the new dispensation, the merchants in the trading centres had an even greater influence, politically and socially as well as economically. In Lower Canada, as the events of 1815-1837 were to show, the almost total control of trade by British (largely Scottish) merchants had serious political consequences.

THE HALIFAX AND NEW BRUNSWICK CIRCLES

Many similarities with the Montreal circle are to be found in the Scottish mercantile groups in Halifax and Saint John, though they lacked the flamboyance of the fur trade magnates and the ebullient, calculating grandeur in concept that marked James Dunlop. As with Dunlop and the Newfoundland firms their closest links were with Greenock and Glasgow, for as a commentator noted in *The Scots Magazine* in 1805, Greenock had long been a centre, not only for the Newfoundland fisheries, but also for those of Nova

[61] *Ibid.*, same to same, March 27, 1815.

Scotia.[62] As in so many other areas wartime opportunities figured largely in attracting Scots merchants to Halifax, already an important naval base by 1756. The Seven Years' War saw the arrival of John Gillespie and John Taylor, Aberdeen men who had been traders in New York, and of Alexander Brymer, an enterprising and influential merchant, who had been in business in Glasgow, and brought over a capital of four thousand pounds sterling. A handful of Scots merchants were already established in the town when these three arrived, notably Peter McNab, of Inverness, merchant and organiser of salmon fishing ventures, and John Geddes of Glasgow, who came out in 1754 and 1755 respectively, but Brymer was to prove a key figure as "Father of the Scottish Community of Merchants," for here too the Scots were to form a close-knit body, interdependent and often acting in concert in large-scale ventures. They formed the core of what Harold Innis called "the little commercial group which dominated Nova Scotian behaviour." According to the chronicler of the North British Society of Halifax, Brymer "by his advice brought out several Edinburgh and Glasgow men, some of them with means, who, entering into trade, rapidly made their fortunes."[63] By all accounts, he was prosperous, and lived in a handsome residence known as "Brymer's Palace." By 1768 the North British Society was formed and its "Annals" leave little doubt that this was essentially a mercantile club, though it had benevolent and charitable aims as well.

As in all colonial communities, the wars brought a rapid increase in trade with Scotland:

Table 3. Trade between Nova Scotia and Scotland, 1779-1800 (figures in pounds sterling: based on the Glasgow Chamber of Commerce Abstracts)

Year	Scottish Imports from Nova Scotia	Scottish Exports to Nova Scotia
1779	1751	16629
1785	1443	19653
1790	836	23037
1795	2015	29938
1796	5893	39863
1800	7863	37857

The Newfoundland trade, the West India trade, and, after 1805, the timber trade to Britain were the chief areas of activity of these merchants, but a distinctive feature of the Halifax group (shared by that in Saint John from

---

[62] "View of the Situation and Trade of Greenock" in *The Scots Magazine*, vol. LXVII, 1805, p. 10.

[63] James S. MacDonald, *Annals of the North British Society, 1768-1903* (Halifax, 1905), p. 27.

the 1780's) was the manner in which many combined general mercantile and shipping enterprises with a specialised trade or calling. James Thomson, for example, who arrived in 1768, was a cabinet maker and a skilled mason as well as a merchant. John Rider, in addition to being a trader, and an organiser of fishing enterprises, kept an inn, "the best in Halifax." It is interesting to note that, as the North British Society increased in membership (to more than one hundred by 1777), it became necessary for a full-time messenger to be employed to maintain communication among the members. This "caddie" as he would have been termed in Scottish parlance, was no doubt indispensable in the conveyance of tidings among the members, pertaining to arrivals, departures, cargoes and other confidential matters. (He was, of course, a Scotsman).

Another distinctive feature of the Society was the large number of professional men, physicians, ministers of religion, military, naval officers and officials who were members, and participated in all types of mercantile enterprise, in co-operation with the merchants. Dr. Duncan Clark, a Scots born Loyalist from New York and the town's leading physician, speculated successfully in privateering ventures as well as forming a literary "coterie" in the Pontac tavern, where the North British Society held its regular meetings. Clark also superintended the Naval Hospital, and introduced many useful naval contacts to the "circle" in the 1780's and 1790's.

The merchants brought out by Brymer, like other members of the North British Society, speculated successfully in the purchases of prizes and cargoes condemned by the Admiralty Court – a Halifax specialty which was to prove increasingly lucrative.[64] The ships were sold to the highest bidder, and, according to James S. MacDonald, "after perhaps a slight inspection" so that full knowledge of a cargo could obviously mean the securing of a "bonanza" profit. According to MacDonald, "it was not unusual at this date to clear £5,000 on a single capture" (i.e. after paying for the ship and re-selling it and/or the cargo). It is difficult to avoid the conclusion that the close relations between the merchants and the naval officers and officials must have often proved most profitable to all concerned. The Honourable Henry Duncan, cousin of Admiral Duncan of Camperdown fame, was a Commander in the Royal Navy, and Commissioner of Halifax Dockyard. He became a member of the North British Society in 1786. In his thirty years in the town, which covered the period of the Wars of 1793-1815, Duncan, according to MacDonald, "engaged in various large-scale speculations with Alexander Brymer and others." The actual records of the prize speculations are slight, but MacDonald's words are worth quoting: "The world was in a continual state of war. Many prizes were captured by the great fleet of men-of-war and privateers on this station; brought into Halifax, condemned in Admiralty Court and sold at auction. Many of these prizes were first-class ships, well

[64] *Ibid., passim.*

built and equipped for long service. Syndicates or Companies of our merchants would purchase these vessels and cargoes sometimes at a low rate, and being all ready for sea they would at once be dispatched to foreign markets. The result of these speculations would at times ensure tremendous returns. These vessels would take return cargoes, and when trading in the East at times would not return to Halifax for years after. Meanwhile their business results would be transmitted to Halifax and invested in further speculations; so that, although Halifax had a small population at this time, the enterprise of her Scottish merchants was known to all mercantile centres of the trading world."[65]

Officers of the highest rank participated in this business, and looked upon it with favour. At the Saint Andrew's Day Dinner of the North British Society in November, 1813, Admiral Sir John Borlase Warren, guest of honour, spoke complimenting the Scottish merchants upon their sagacity and the rapid fortunes they were realizing from the prizes brought into Halifax. He referred to one sale which had taken place on March 19, 1813, when twelve full-rigged ships, eight brigs and nineteen schooners were sold to the highest bidders.[66]

WILLIAM FORSYTH AND HIS COMPLEX OF TRADE

Not all of the Scots merchants regarded the traffic in prizes as entirely beneficial to their interests. William Forsyth, a key figure in Nova Scotian commerce, whose vitally-important letter book for the period August, 1796-October, 1798, is preserved in the Nova Scotian Archives, saw the dislocation which captures brought to business. In a letter to his Scots correspondent, the merchant James Crawford in Philadelphia, in September 1796, Forsyth wrote: "We cannot help thinking that the British cruisers are drawing the cord too close at the present juncture, and that the Vice Admiralty Courts are too much disposed to gratify them, contrary to the intention of the Government. But . . . we shall upon all occasions afford American citizens every protection and assistance in our power to obtain justice, it being no more than we should expect of others were our property in the like situation."

Almost half of the hundreds of letters entered in the Forsyth letter book in 1796-1798 deal, in fact, with matters pertaining to prizes, for Forsyth built up a new branch of business in assisting American, German and Dutch shipowners to save their vessels from condemnation by the Vice Admiralty Courts. He was not always successful in this, but his charges for helping in this regard must have brought in a considerable income at this period. Forsyth himself dabbled occasionally in speculation in prizes, bidding successfully for a particularly fine French privateer, a schooner, which he added

[65] MacDonald, op. cit., p. 63.
[66] MacDonald, op. cit., p. 122.

to his fleet of nine vessels. With his other smaller vessels this ship was engaged in the West India trade, the larger ships being used in the mast and general transatlantic traffic.

So little primary source material has survived relating to the important Halifax commercial circle, that the main features of Forsyth's activities are worth indicating, for they throw considerable light on how the Scottish merchant worked in this colonial setting. By 1796 Forsyth was rising to a position of pre-eminence in the town, with his fleet growing steadily and his Nova Scotian, Quebec, West India, Newfoundland and mast-supplying branches of business developing rapidly. According to Innis, in his *Cod Fisheries*, there was a steep rise in prices offered for dried and salt cod, as much as twenty-five per cent in the period 1782-3, even before the French War of 1793 drove prices up further. Forsyth benefited greatly from this, and fish were, in fact, the basic stock of all his trade.[67]

He had home partners in Greenock, that hub of Scottish overseas enterprise, in the persons of Messrs. Hunter, Robertson and Co., who ranked next to Alan Ker and Co. in the scale of their business with the North American colonies. The web of communication which he maintained with agents and firms in all his areas of operation was entirely Scottish. His Newfoundland agents were the Greenock based firm of Andrew Thomson and Co., which maintained several branches in the island colony, and supplied Forsyth with the fish he required as trading stock for his trade to Jamaica, Grenada, Barbados, and Martinique. In Grenada his agents were Cruden, Pollard and Stewart, a Scottish firm. In Saint Andrews, New Brunswick, there was Robert Pagan, in Saint John the Scottish family of Black. In Martinique he had Alexander Brymer, also a Scot. In Jamaica there were Bogle and Jopps, a Scottish house of good repute; in Charleston, Boston, and New York he dealt with Scottish firms, and through all these connections, Forsyth was able to develop some interesting, profitable and novel lines of trade such as sending his smaller vessels with codfish to Madeira for wine, which was then sold in Jamaica, the proceeds going into cargoes of rum and sugar for Halifax. Much of this West India produce was then reshipped, as recent research by David Sutherland in this important field suggests, into the firm's larger vessels which plied to Greenock.[68] The vital importance of Halifax as an entrepot for many trades at this time clearly emerges from Forsyth's records, and perusal of the *Greenock Advertiser* for the year 1805 shows that no fewer than fifty eight firms in Greenock, Glasgow, Port Glasgow and Saltcoats were dispatching vessels to that port, or importing consignments from it.

[67] Forsyth to Crawford, September 16, 1796, Letter Book of William Forsyth and Co., 1796-8, Archives of Nova Scotia. Harold Innis, *The Cod Fisheries* (Toronto, 1954), pp. 288-9.
[68] Forsyth Letter Book, *passim*, Archives of Nova Scotia.

Forsyth had vision, and realised as early as 1796 the tremendous potential of New Brunswick timber in the West India trade, as well as for masting. In November of that year he wrote at length to Messrs. J. Petrie Campbell and Co., and other Scottish firms in London, that in view of the loss of shipping in the War, "it might be an object, . . . as lumber in quantity will be required in the West Indies after the War . . . for those with connections in the West Indies, to have vessels built in New Brunswick and sent thither with lumber, there taking on freights for Britain."[69] Forsyth proceeded to order a series of large vessels in New Brunswick, additions to his fleet that made it the largest in the province.

Another specialty of the firm was the handling of entire cargoes of the prime Liverpool or Cheshire salt that was required in great quantities in the Arichat and Newfoundland fisheries. His large vessels of some six hundred tons brought in such amounts that Forsyth virtually controlled the entire supply. His wartime losses were considerable. He lost his brig *Halifax* to a French privateer in 1797 and his fine ship *Brunswick* fell to a French frigate soon after. His ship *Earl of Mansfield* was taken off the Western Isles of Scotland by another French privateer in 1798, but he appears to have had the knack of insuring his vessels cleverly and fully. In 1797, the *Halifax* was so well covered that the loss was negligible. The ships were insured in Halifax, the cargoes in Boston and New York. This was probably facilitated by Forsyth's helpfulness to American owners whose ships had been seized. As he wrote to Joseph Maryatt in London, in February, 1798, "I have never withheld protection from any American shipmaster brought in as a prize when they have applied to me for advice and assistance." The wide range of close and useful contacts, most of them Scots, which Forsyth had in American ports at this time is clearly indicated in his letter book, and an increasing business in the Eastern Seaboard of the United States supplemented his thriving business. Also useful were his own relatives, the London Forsyths, who had a strong connection with the North West Company and, after 1802, with the British Naval Contractors for colonial timber. In addition there were other Forsyths established in Montreal from 1790 – prominent traders in furs, timber and corn.

It is difficult to estimate the precise relationship between William Forsyth of Halifax and his Greenock "partners" Hunter and Robertson, because the records are lacking, but large sums to Forsyth's credit were remitted to Greenock. Greenock was also his principal and preferred source of supply for many items, including cordage, gunpowder, linens and other Scottish specialties. Forsyth not only used these items in his own business operations; he also supplied other firms, mostly Scots, such as Hannay and Co. of St. John's Newfoundland. Almost invariably, the agency or large-scale trading business he did was with Scots, such as James Hunter and Co. of Greenock,

[69] *Ibid.*, November 12, 1796.

whom he supplied with large consignments and entire shiploads of "marketable fish" for their thriving Lisbon trade, or Nathaniel G. Ingraham of New York, obviously of Scots blood. In the Miramichi area he dealt, naturally enough, with the Scottish house of Fraser and Thom, the leading firm in the area.

Fraser and Thom came out as partners from Scotland in 1786, and established a trading base on Beaubair's Island, from which they rapidly built up an overseas trade to the West Indies in fish and timber. Backed by the powerful Greenock firms of Alan Ker and Co. and Hunter Robertson and Co., (in which Forsyth was a partner) they were in a good position to avail themselves of the wartime opportunities of the 1790's. Among the first to realise the potential of New Brunswick as a shipbuilding centre they brought out shipwrights from the Clyde and built vessels for their own trade and for sale in Halifax, Boston and Kingston, Jamaica. The disappearance of their records is one of the tragedies of Canadian business history, for their establishments on the Gulf of Saint Lawrence and the Northumberland Strait provided, eventually, settlers and craftsmen for Pictou, New Glasgow, and Antigonish, soon to be thriving centres of the Nova Scotian shipbuilding industry. With that Captain Lowden, from the South of Scotland who founded the flourishing shipbuilding trade in Pictou County in 1788-92, Fraser and Thom are dim figures in the canon of Canadian history, while many a petty official, of no great import, has been immortalized in its pages. Lowden was obviously more than an amateur builder, for in 1798 he launched the ship *Harriet* of six hundred tons, by far the largest vessel built in the province to that date. According to Murdoch's *History*, the vessel, built largely of oak and black birch, was pierced for twenty four guns. In size alone, this was an achievement which rivalled the product of the best British yards of the time.

It is interesting to note that the Halifax merchant shared the interest of James Dunlop in the potash and pearl ashes trade. With textile industries thriving in both England and Scotland, there was a growing demand for this commodity on the Thames and the Clyde. Unlike Dunlop, Forsyth had no readily available source of supply, but he used his good Scots Boston contacts to obtain American ashes in quantity. Other goods that figured largely in his transactions in 1796-8 were Quebec flour for local Nova Scotian and West Indian consumption, and Cape Breton coal for Newfoundland, cod and dog-fish oil for Britain, British cottons and stoneware for the colonial market. It is apparent from the Forsyth letter book's references that transactions in West India produce, especially rum, sugar, mahogany and coffee, were among the most profitable lines pursued. Good strokes of business were done in such dealings as the import of pork and beef from Quebec to Halifax in times of local scarcity, but the basic, profitable business of the firm was carried on in fish, madeira wines, dry goods from Britain, and colonial produce.

Shipbuilding in the firm's own New Brunswick yard was conducted on a considerable scale – vessels of over six hundred tons being constructed for the Forsyth fleet. This activity may have sparked off the interest of the Scotts of Greenock in establishing a yard at Saint John in 1798, a topic that will be considered below.[70] Shipping matters certainly played an important part in the lives of the Halifax mercantile community, so dependent as they were on sea-routes for their trade. Many merchants in the town became experts on the subject of prizes and Vice Admiralty Courts, and through his agency activities on behalf of foreign owners, Forsyth became particularly well versed in the intricacies of these matters. British vessels which had been taken by the enemy, and subsequently re-taken, could lose their registration as British vessels, meaning under the Navigation Acts that they might not be permitted to sail in British or colonial trades. This often led to re-taken prizes being sold at very low prices, if registration had been lost. It might sometimes be possible, however, to secure re-registration which could mean a large profit on re-sale. On such questions as these Forsyth and his Halifax confreres spent much time.[71] In this wartime ploy and in the increasing needs of the British navy for masts, there was profit to be made, and William Forsyth was well to the fore.

According to R. G. Albion, in his study of *Forests and Sea Power* (Hamden, Connecticut, 1965, pp. 348-9), the firm of Hunter Robertson and Forsyth, of Greenock and Halifax, made a contract with the British Admiralty in 1788 for the supply of masts from New Brunswick for six years, and this was renewed in 1795 by a seven-year contract to supply no fewer than thirty full cargoes of masts to the naval bases in Halifax, Antigua, Jamaica and England. In the spring of 1798 Forsyth dispatched no fewer than five full cargoes of masts "as fine sticks as were ever sent out of this country" to another London agent, the Scot Robert Livie.[72] There is no record of his actual profit on this mass of timber, but it was sufficient for him to decide to broaden these mast and yard-shipping operations, to supply the builders of merchant ships in Britain as well as the Naval yards.

These successes attracted investment from the ranks of the local serving officers and according to MacDonald, Lieutenant General James Ogilvie, Commander of the forces in Nova Scotia, invested £20,000 as a "silent partner" in Forsyth's firm. Ogilvie's son joined the firm and as MacDonald described it, "the young man retired after several years with £40,000."[73] The Earl of Dalhousie, while in the colony, is also reputed to have engaged in large-scale speculations with Matthew Richardson, a prominent Scottish trad-

---

[70] *Ibid.*, to Robert Livie and Co., London, November 10, 1796.

[71] *Ibid.*, f. 173.

[72] *Ibid.*, Forsyth to Livie, June 21, 1798.

[73] MacDonald, *op. cit.*, entries of 1784.

er in Halifax. The close connection between the mercantile and service officers elements of the large Scottish community in the town can be gathered too from the case of John Grant, a merchant, who secured the victualling contracts to the Navy for several years and prospered exceedingly, becoming prominent in local politics.

This was a tight group, and it grew as more Scots arrived. It would possibly be going too far to accept MacDonald's statement that "the (North British) Society had by then (1789) enrolled all the leading citizens of the city, they being nearly all Scotsmen," but the new Scots arrivals of the period 1790-1812 did include some men of high ability in mercantile affairs, notably John Black, who came over from Saint John, New Brunswick, possibly attracted by the wartime activity in Halifax.[74]

The North British Society was not simply a commercial club and a social organisation. It was also giving aid to numerous impoverished Scots immigrants in 1785-6. When increasing numbers of their distressed countrymen in the Northern States besought aid in the 1790's to enable them to return home to Scotland, the Society provided assistance. William Forsyth's ships, on their voyages to the Clyde, usually took back several of these poor Scots. Distressed emigrants were also assisted, for there is evidence that some of the Halifax merchants resented the misrepresentations which caused many of their poorer fellow countrymen to cross the Atlantic. In the Appendix to the November issue of *The Scots Magazine* of 1784 appeared a letter "from a gentleman at Halifax" (it may have been William Forsyth) to his friend in Aberdeen, which stated that:

> ... thousands of emigrants from Scotland to this province make them as great a glut as dry goods, which will hardly sell at any price ... I am given to understand that the spirit of emigration rages greatly at home. I wish those who had come over to this province would give their friends a faithful account ... I had an opportunity of seeing the most flattering accounts sent to their friends in Scotland by people who were relieved from distress by myself. This is a wantonness which deserves to be checked. In what manner many of those who come over here may be able to subsist during the ensuing winter, He only can tell who feeds the young ravens when they call to Him.

As in Lower Canada, and in Scotland, the War of 1793 was a great stimulus to trade and local production, and the emigrant flow from Scotland to the North American colonies, which had developed so strongly in the 1770's and 1780's continued to increase, swollen by merchants who heard from their countrymen in Montreal, Quebec, Halifax, Saint John, and Saint Andrews, of the good prospects in the new area, and by growing numbers of Highlanders, feeling the pressures of "Clearance," the falling in of tacksmen's leases

[74] *Ibid.*, p. 62.

and the stagnation of agriculture in their home areas.[75] By 1800 the emigration from the Highlands began to reach flood proportions, and Colin S. MacDonald has estimated that in the first six years of the nineteenth century no fewer than ten thousand people emigrated from the islands, the glens and the Highland seacoast, mostly settling in the Maritime provinces.[76] Sir John Sinclair, author of the *First Statistical Account of Scotland*, estimated that "between 1771 and 1790, no fewer than eight large transports sailed from the Island of Skye alone, with more than 2,400 emigrants to seek settlements, taking with them £24,000, ship freights included." For the most part they sailed out in vessels owned in Greenock, Glasgow and Port Glasgow, the ports which had most dealings and traffic with the Highlands and the Hebrides. Greenock, in fact, was the customs and ship registration centre for the West Highlands. A few Aberdeen vessels participated in this trade, and there were, very occasionally, English contractors involved. In August, 1802, twelve vessels, nine of them Greenock ships, were "engaged" for this emigrant traffic, to carry what *The Scots Magazine* described as "these deluded people" to North America. The *Magazine* was bitterly opposed to the emigration, but the editor was possibly not exaggerating when he described how, "before they have been three hours at sea, some of the poor creatures come next morning and ask the sailors if the land they see is America."[77]

Most of the contractors for the Highland traffic were either Greenock merchants and shipowners, or Highland tacksmen, men of some substance who purchased vessels for the purpose. This is obvious from the tables printed in Brown's "Answer to the Earl of Selkirk," published in *The Scots Magazine* in 1806. Some of these tacksmen were colonial proprietors, including several of the sixty-seven men, some of them Scots, who had received the disposal of Prince Edward Island as early as 1767.[78] There were, it is true, a few English "proprietors" who took part in the North American traffic, an outstanding example being James Hodges, of the firm of Bouches, Hodges and Co. of London, who sold many thousands of acres in the Island to Highlanders in Mull and Skye at a rate of five hundred per cent above the wholesale prices, providing passages for £6 per head for adults. But as *The Scots Magazine* of 1806 makes clear, Hodges chartered vessels for this purpose from Scottish firms, notably Messrs. James Strong and Co. of Leith. This was probably done because Scottish freight rates tended to be lower than

[75] For the best studies of the emigration movement from Scotland at this time, see Helen I. Cowan, *British Emigration to North America: The First Hundred Years*, (Toronto reprint 1961), and D. F. Macdonald, *Scotland's Shifting Population, 1770-1850* (Glasgow 1937).

[76] Colin S. MacDonald, "Early Highland Emigration to Nova Scotia and Prince Edward Island from 1770-1853" *Collections of the Nova Scotia Historical Society*, vol. 23, 1936, p. 48.

[77] *The Scots Magazine*, vol. 64, 1802, pp. 705-6.

[78] J. D. Rogers *Historical Geography of the British Colonies*, (London, 1913) vol. 5 part B, p. 81.

English ones, and because the West Highland water and sea approaches were better known to Scots master mariners. At any rate, it was the Scottish shipping interest which benefited from the traffic, whether conducted through English or Scottish contractors.

The growing Scottish interest in Canada was reflected, not only among mercantile men and Highland emigrants, but also among writers and journalists. Young John Galt, recently a merchant in London, penned a "Statistical Account of Upper Canada" for *The Philosophical Magazine* in 1807. Galt had never been across the Atlantic, and he based his surveys on material given to him by one Gilkison who was in business in "Amherstburgh" (sic) in that province. The "Account" was glowingly optimistic, like so many other early nineteenth century Scottish views of British North America. Galt saw Upper Canada as a future important supplier of hemp, wool, tobacco and wines, and his essay was sanguine in the extreme. Characteristically, he repeated earlier Scots views of the French Canadians as "an indolent and thoughtless race . . . their attention only turned towards amusement." Galt's essay is chiefly important as one of the few extant expressions of opinion by a Scottish "commercialist" at the time.[79] A few years later, in 1814, another Scot, a true expert on commerce, Patrick Colquhoun, was to lead in the advocacy of wholesale emigration to the North American colonies, in the same sanguine hopes of hemp, flax and potash at cheap rates for Britain.

Among the hundreds of mercantile Scots who took up residence in Halifax in the 1790's and early 1800's – traders, shipowners, master mariners and skilled craftsmen, and dissenting secessionist Presbyterian divines – the most outstanding in his contribution to the community's commercial development was John Black, who came on from Saint John, New Brunswick, in 1808. He had arrived in New Brunswick in 1786, as an agent of the Admiralty, and as representative of the London (Scottish) firm of Blair and Glenie, entrusted with the shipment of masts and yards. He was quick to sense the importance of Saint John and the Passamaquoddy Bay as an entrepot for trade between the West Indies and the United States, as well as for the timber trade, and invited several of his relations to join him in a trading venture in the colony. The Blacks, originally from Aberdeenshire, were prominent in the trade of Saint John, which they dominated, in conjunction with another of these Scottish mercantile circles, remarkably similar to the one in Halifax, with its own Scottish Society, known as the Saint Andrew's Society, formed in 1796. Black rapidly built up a fleet with which he traded to the West Indies and Scottish ports, especially Greenock and the old family home of Aberdeen. Black had thriving branches in Fredericton, Saint Andrews, Miramichi, and Montreal, and even a full-time representative in Aberdeen, Scotland, who handled his timber sales there.[80] He built a fine

---

[79] *The Philosophical Magazine*, London, vol. 29, No. 113, October, 1807, pp. 3-10.

[80] James S. MacDonald, *op. cit.*, p. 114; *The Judges of New Brunswick and Their Times*, St. John, 1912, pp. 223-4.

mansion near Government House in Halifax, reputedly of granite shipped out in his vessels from Aberdeen, but more important was the significant part he played in organising co-ordination, not only among the Halifax merchants, but of those in several of the scattered colonial centres. In 1804 he was instrumental in the formation of "the Halifax Committee of Trade" to meet the threat to the town's commerce, due to the U.S. Government's bounties on fish, which were attracting many fishermen south to American ports from the British colonial fishing centres. The flush wartime days of prosperity, privateering and dealing in prizes had been temporarily brought to a close by the Amiens Peace, and the merchants had been forced back on their West India trade in fish for survival. According to G. F. Butler, "most of the fish caught in the province were being sold to the Americans (due to the bounties in the States) or exchanged for smuggled goods and then exported from Boston to the West Indies."[81] In this crisis a "Committee of Trade" with an elected executive of five prominent merchants was formed, four of them Scots, and submissions were made to the British Government, asking for a monopoly of the West India fish trade for British subjects, and pointing to the U.S. bounties and the lower freight and insurance charges, which combined to give the Americans a competitive advantage. The submission was entirely successful – a remarkably early example of effective mercantile pressure in a British colonial society. Instructions were given to the governors of West Indian islands that articles from the United States should only be admitted in cases of "great and urgent necessity," and bounties were declared for imports of fish to the islands in British vessels. When the new short-lived Whig administration in 1806 refrained from enforcing the restrictions on the Americans, the Halifax Committee at once renewed its activity, setting up a London Committee with Nathaniel Atcheson, prominent Scottish Newfoundland merchant as Secretary, and concessions for Halifax as a "port open to neutral (i.e. American) shipping" were won, to counter the effects of Jefferson's embargo.[82]

An even more interesting feature of the Committee's methods at this time was John Black's action in 1808, as Secretary, in organising support for the Halifax merchants in Quebec through his agents there, the prominent Scottish firm of Irvine, McNaught and Co. In his approaches, the interests of all the colonies and their commercial centres were stressed – showing that narrow localism did not always prevail among the Scottish merchants, especially when abroad. In 1809, his agitation led to the foundation of the "Quebec Board of Trade." As might be expected, Black was prominent in the North British Society (President in 1808) and it is obvious from the Saint John, Montreal and Halifax press that he possessed exactly the same type of "connecting web" of Scottish agencies, correspondents and contacts that

---

[81] G. F. Butler, "The Early Organisation and Influence of the Halifax Merchants," in *Collections of the Nova Scotia Historical Society,* vol. 25, 1942.

[82] *Ibid.,* pp. 7-8.

enabled William Forsyth to carry on such an extensive business with so much success. Good use was made of Scottish political contacts and influence in securing these results. Black and the Quebec Scots brought pressure to bear on Viscount Melville, head of the Tory interest in Scotland, President of the Board of Control, and, from 1812, First Lord of the Admiralty. A further example of the way in which the powerful Scottish "interest" in the Government was solicited on behalf of the colonial merchants' aims may be seen in the memorial submitted to Melville in 1813 by the Newfoundland merchants, under the Chairmanship of J. McBraire, asking that no concessions be given to either France or the United States in the island fisheries in any peace settlement. Like his father before him, Melville at the Admiralty maintained a steady correspondence with Scots merchants in Canada on the subjects of timber and shipbuilding, and he was instrumental in awarding substantial contracts to several of them, including that "Mr. Gillespie, an astute and intelligent merchant of Quebec" who laid down two vessels each of some eight hundred tons in his own yards, in 1810. The Melville Papers in the National Library of Scotland show the statesman's keen interest in these subjects, and also his desire to encourage the enterprises of his fellow countrymen. This may have been done partly to ensure the votes of their friends, relations and business contacts in the Melville "electoral appanage" of Scotland, but it undoubtedly was a great advantage to the mercantile Scots abroad to have such a powerful friend at home. The "Dundas System," for all its drawbacks, did give Scots, for the first time since the Union, some chance of expressing their views effectively in London.

The Halifax circle was so numerous, influential and prosperous, so daring in its new ventures, that another of its worthies should be mentioned as revealing a further aspect of contemporary enterprise. This was John Young, later known by his *nom de plume* of "Agricola," who left off trading in Glasgow in 1814, hearing of the boom that Halifax had enjoyed since the outbreak of the American War in 1812. Young was a graduate of Glasgow College. In his own words, he had "laboured in vain" in Scottish commerce for ten years. On his arrival in 1814, with a large stock of dry goods, he set up at once as "John Young and Co.," operating in the captured port of Castine. There he conducted both legal and illegal operations, the latter being undoubtedly the most lucrative. This was the practice of "trading on the Line" that was bringing so much wealth to Nova Scotia and New Brunswick in the War of 1812, and Young's graphic letters give a fascinating account of the ruses that were involved in an illicit trade with the enemy.[83]

Skilfully using "covers" (i.e. small amounts of goods shipped from Halifax), Young purchased large quantities of American flour, tobacco and cotton at reasonable rates of barter for his textiles, West India molasses and rum, hardware and crockery. He had well-considered plans for the develop-

---

[83] See D. C. Harvey, "Pre-Agricola John Young," in *Collections of the Nova Scotia Historical Society*, pp. 125-139.

ment of this business, and would doubtless have made a fortune had not, as he wrote in 1815, "this peace blasted all our prospects."[84] Young's later fame as an exponent of agricultural improvement on the Scottish "high farming principle" might have brought him some satisfaction, but continued operations at Castine would have brought him more profit.

It is perhaps difficult to agree with all of James S. MacDonald's rather sententious statement of 1905, regarding the Scots merchants of Halifax that "at a time in Halifax of great demoralisation and profligacy, they set an example for uprightness and virtue which was a very bulwark of strength to our community," but his stress on the Scottish domination in commerce is certainly valid.[85] As late as 1829, John MacTaggart, Clerk of Works on the Rideau Canal, selected for that post by John Rennie himself, personal friend of Colonel By and of Philemon Wright of Hull, noted in his *Three Years in Canada* that the recent importation of "red sandstone, and all the ironwork for the beautiful inland navigation from Dartmouth Lake near Halifax to the Bay of Fundy," had been made in Scotland. The Halifax mercantile community met with his approval, for MacTaggart believed strongly in homogeneous settlements. As he put it elsewhere in his book: "Settlers come on better by planting themselves down in large communities from one and the same country than by any other plan . . . The Irish about the Rice Lake in Monaghan . . . and the Glasgow weavers revel in Lanark, along the banks and lakes of the Massapi."

THE NEW BRUNSWICK CIRCLE

The third and final centre in the mainland of British North America where Scottish merchants established a rapid dominance in the period of their home country's dramatic surge forward in commerce was Saint John, New Brunswick, with the neighbouring settlement of Saint Andrews, in many ways its outlier and subsidiary. The Loyalist influx of 1784 brought many Scots, but even before this, Scots were active in the fields of fisheries and timber-getting. There is evidence that development of New Brunswick fisheries was an extension of Scottish interest in the Newfoundland fisheries. William Davidson and his partner, John Cort, who hailed from Inverness and Aberdeen, secured a large grant of 100,000 acres on the Miramichi River in the 1770's and appear to have been chiefly interested in the export of barrelled salmon to the West Indies and the Mediterranean, but they rapidly developed an interest in the timber trade as well.[86] Davidson and Cort, according to Rattray, were established on the Miramichi as early as 1765, in an area abandoned by the French, from which they were able to export from 1400 to 1800 tierces of salmon (about 1000-1200 barrels) annually in the mid 1760's.

[84] *Ibid.*, p. 137.
[85] James S. MacDonald, *op. cit.*, p. 93; J. MacTaggart, *Three Years in Canada, 1826-28*, (London, 1829), vol. II, p. 192-337.
[86] George MacBeath and Dorothy Chamberlin, *New Brunswick*, (Toronto, 1965).

It is probable that they both had experience of large-scale salmon fishing operations on the Don or the Dee in their home country, and of the salting and pickling methods followed there. Yet another Scot, Alexander Walker, who settled at Alston, on the North side of Bathurst Harbour in the 1760's, traded extensively in fish, furs, walrus tusks and hides, oil and other local products. Tragically little is known about these early enterpreneurs, who were the true pioneers of commerce in that area, or of Edward Mortimer, from Keith in the shire of Banff, the "King of Pictou" who made Pictou the business centre of the Gulf of Saint Lawrence in the 1780's. Mortimer's partner, George Smith, another Scot, who was Pictou's leading businessman in the early 1800's, is also an obscure figure, and the Patterson brothers, from Greenock, who traded on a large-scale from Pictou to Jamaica and built hundreds of fishing vessels and small merchant ships, are also lost in the mists, for none of their records have survived. Yet these were key people in the economic development of the Maritime Provinces. The rapid development of Scottish interest in the timber trade and in the promotion of colonial hemp and flax-growing was natural enough, for in the last thirty years of the eighteenth century, Scottish traders were experiencing increasing difficulties in carrying on profitable commerce with Russia, a major supplier of timber, and the chief supplier of hemp and flax.[87]

Long before Tsar Alexander I entered Napoleon's Continental System at Tilsit in 1807, the pressing need to seek out timber, flax and hemp led the Commissioners for Trade to look favourably to British North America as a source of these materials. As early as the 1760's Nova Scotia was being viewed by London as a potential centre for the growing of flax, so necessary for the manufacture of sailcloth, and after 1784, New Brunswick and Canada were both regarded as possible suppliers of hemp, for cordage and of timber, for ships.[88] The Russian rulers, their civil servants, and the nobility were becoming increasingly reluctant to supply these goods to the predominantly English or Scots buyers at what they considered to be "give-away" prices or at what the British purchasers considered to be "reasonable prices." In 1762 the Empress Catherine herself contrived to establish a profitable "corner" in hemp, and the records of the London-based Russia Company for the second half of the century contain numerous complaints of high Russian prices, of poor quality, and deliberate foisting-off of inferior produce, sometimes with the connivance of Russian officials. There was also the growth of strong "protectionist" attitudes among trade officials and the educated nobility, which found expression in the writings of Mikhail Chulkov, secretary of the College of Commerce, in the new Russian tariff of 1782, which imposed higher duties on both imports and exports, and in

---

[87] For this question, see David S. Macmillan, "Scottish Trade with Russia, 1750-1796, Profits and Problems," *Canadian Review of Slavic Studies*, Fall, 1970.

[88] Duncan Campbell, *Nova Scotia, Historical Mercantile and Industrial Relations* (Montreal 1863), p. 161.

Catherine's prohibitions against the importations of a wide range of British manufactures in 1793. Ukases of 1794, ordering that all import and export duties be paid by British merchants, in rix-dollars, instead of Russian currency (a special concession enjoyed up to this date), further antagonized British traders for their charges were increased, according to David Macpherson, by seventy per cent. These moves caused consternation and dismay in Greenock and other Scottish ports.[89]

Relations between the countries were, in fact, deteriorating rapidly after 1770, passing through the worsening stages of the "Ochakov incident" of 1790, and Pitt's "Russian armament" scheme, to the almost open warfare of the Tsar Paul's 1798 Ukase prohibiting timber exports, and his seizure of hundreds of British vessels in Russian ports in 1800-1801. This situation alarmed the Scottish merchants, whose high hopes after 1776 for the development of an increased trade with Russia had led by 1790 to the completion of the expensive Forth-Clyde Canal, to link Glasgow and the industrial area, and Greenock and its West India produce with the Baltic. It had been hoped that Scotland's trade with Russia would increase, and by 1790 it had done so – imports had risen from £132,000 in value in 1772 to £310,000 in 1790. By 1794 imports from Russia were valued at £395,000, and in 1799 they reached a value of £645,000, according to the Glasgow Chamber of Commerce Abstracts. These high figures were partly accounted for by rises in the prices charged by the Russians, but they also show a considerable increase in the volume of the trade. But, disturbingly for the Scottish merchants, there was only a slight increase in Scottish exports to Russia. These were valued at £21,000 in 1772 and £25,000 in 1794. Even in 1799, that year of great importations from the Tsar's domains, Scottish exports to Russia were valued at only £32,000. Of particular concern to many Scots was the fact that their country, proportionately to its population and resources, was importing far more from Russia than was imported into England. Yet England's exports thither were far greater than those of Scotland. During the 1790's the difficulties of carrying on the trade increased, and the shocks of the 1798 Ukase and the seizures and confiscations inclined many timber merchants and shipbuilders in Scotland to turn their attention to the North American timber trade long before the first large contracts for colonial timber were awarded in 1804-5. These firms were centred chiefly in the Glasgow, Greenock and Port Glasgow area, but several Grangemouth and Leith firms on the east coast also began to seek North American contacts in the 1780's, for the gradual completion of the Forth and Clyde enabled timber cargoes to be shipped to them after being landed in the Clyde. As early as 1785 the

---

[89] See M. S. Anderson, *Britain's Discovery of Russia 1553-1815* (London, 1958), pp. 132-183; Walter Kirchner, *Commercial Relations between Russia and Europe, 1400 to 1800* (Bloomington, 1962); John Ehrmann, *The British Government and Commercial Negotiations with Europe, 1783-1793* (Cambridge, 1962), pp. 92-136; and D. B. Horn, *Great Britain and Europe in the Nineteenth Century* (Oxford, 1967), pp. 203-233.

press of Saint John recorded two departures of vessels with loads of timber for Glasgow, and by the following year, Scots were obviously the most numerous element among the town's mercantile men, their centre of operations being "Scotch Row" and their principal rendezvous "McPhail's Tavern."[90]

It should be noted that while these earliest lumber shipments recorded from Saint John to the Clyde were composed, not of masts and spars, but largely of square timber, staves, and other workaday materials, a few shipbuilding items appeared in the manifests, notably oaken knees, spars, and oaring.

Again, in this New Brunswick port, as in Halifax, the list of thriving commercial houses in the later 1780's reads like a Scottish census list: James Stewart and Co., importers on a grand scale of rice and molasses from the United States; Campbell Stewart and Co., importers of books, rum and foodstuffs from the Clyde; McGeorge, Elliot and Co., importing textiles of all types; McCall and Co., importing British textiles and India goods; and John Colville and Co., David Blair's Co., Hector Scott and the brothers William and Thomas Pagan, formerly of Greenock, all exporting timber and bringing in rum, bibles and gunpowder, often in Scottish vessels, mostly from the Clyde. There were a few non-Scottish merchants but they were sorely outnumbered.[91] Another similarity between Saint John and Halifax was the large number of shopkeepers and tradesmen in the town – tailors, clock-makers, bakers, gold and silversmiths, cabinet-makers, hair-dressers and coffee-house keepers. It is not surprising that a flourishing Saint Andrew's Society should have been in existence by 1798.

Here again, the dependence on a web of Scots connections and contacts, not only in the homeland, but in foreign ports, is strikingly obvious. Saint John traders dealt with Scots firms in American, West Indian, English, and even Spanish and French colonial ports. Many vessels from the Clyde unloaded part of their cargoes in Halifax, passing through the hands of Blacks, Bremners, Brymer, Forsyth and other Scots houses there as agents, before proceeding to Saint John for their timber cargoes. Lesser centres like Shelburne and Saint Andrews also had Scottish houses which acted for Saint John, Halifax and, on occasion, for Montreal merchants of the Scots connection. In the first decade of the town's existence, the number of Scots merchants increased, swollen by new arrivals, mainly from Glasgow and Greenock, lured by the timber trade, and by 1797 the houses of Pagan and Co., Hugh Johnston and Co., John Black and Co., and Andrew Crookshank and Co., stood out as pre-eminent among the twenty-five Scottish firms which, essentially, controlled the trade of the new province's major port.

The variety, not so much of lines of trade as of function, was a notable

---

[90] *Royal Gazette and New Brunswick Advertiser*, October 11, 1785.
[91] *Ibid.*, Advertisements, 1785-6.

feature of these firms, – due perhaps to the newness of the country and the settlement and the demand for services – in a smaller, newer community than Montreal, or even Halifax. Crookshank acted as an administrator of estates, a land agent, an auctioneer of furniture and personal effects, an appraiser of damages for insurance and judicial purposes, as well as purveying vast quantities of rum, porter, and sugar. As in Halifax, supply of the fisheries was a vitally important line of trade, and Blacks, Johnstons and the rest shipped in from Greenock "large and small" salt in copious amounts, as well as shiploads of Scotch goods which comprised whisky and textiles. By 1799, it was obvious to many, in Saint John and Greenock, as well as to William Forsyth, in Halifax, that a most profitable trade might be opened up by sending vessels from New Brunswick to the West Indies with lumber, loading them there with sugar, rum and molasses, and shipping these to Greenock. There the sugar and molasses could be unloaded for refining and distilling, and the vessels loaded with "Scotch goods," which would duly be shipped back across the Atlantic to New Brunswick with the rum, the most valuable of all colonial commodities. The potent beverage that resulted from the "travelling" was apparently much prized, for John Black, advertising in May 1799, described a large consignment as "of superior quality and flavour, having been twice across the Atlantic."[92] Hugh Johnston, who had come out from Morayshire in 1784 in his own ship, with a cargo of Scots trade goods, appears to have specialised in the supply of unmarketable or refuse fish (i.e. not suitable for the European market) to the Caribbean plantations as food for the slaves. He had eleven small ships, brigs and schooners, in the West India trade by 1796, and, because of his "specialty" probably did not suffer so much as other New Brunswick merchants from the increasing competition of United States' traders in the Caribbean after 1794, well described by W. S. MacNutt in his definitive study of the colony (Toronto, 1963). In 1794, according to MacNutt, American vessels were allowed entry to the trade as a wartime expedient, which led to New Brunswick becoming a "feeder" of fish and lumber to the United States, for re-shipment to the Caribbean: "The Americans set the prices and took high profits from the industry of the New Brunswickers," and the coastal trade with the States replaced the deep-sea trade with the West Indies.

A few Scots merchants, such as Johnston and Crookshank, appear, however, to have kept on in the trade, though they also increasingly shipped their fish and lumber to Boston. Johnston was keenly interested in steam navigation, being one of the consortium which owned the *General Smythe*, the province's first steamboat, plying on the Saint John River, and half-owner of the *Saint John*, the first steam vessel to cross the Bay of Fundy. He took the lead among the New Brunswick merchants in this exciting field, and the New

[92] *Ibid.*, May 14, 1799.

Brunswick Museum's archives contain correspondence which shows that he was in close touch with Henry Fulton in New York in 1812 to obtain designs, advice and engineers.

(As the need for shipbuilding materials grew desperate on the Clyde, due to Russian difficulties and the exhaustion of home resources, and as the premium on ships, of any quality, rose due to war losses to privateers, it was natural that Scottish builders should hear of the possibilities of establishing yards in the new timber-rich area of New Brunswick.) Through his agents in Greenock, Alan Ker and Co., Andrew Crookshank encouraged the already famous firm of Scott and Co., shipbuilders at Greenock, to build new vessels on the Saint John River.

Remarkably, while the entire early eighteenth century records of Scotts Ltd. were destroyed in the Greenock "Blitz" of 1941, the letter-book covering the years 1798-1800 has survived, and it contains a full acount of the transfer of Scottish shipbuilding techniques, men and *materiel*, to the distant shores of New Brunswick.) In this the volume ranks equally with the Forsyth letter-book in the Halifax archives, which also provides a new insight into the operations of a colonial merchant in the classic post-French period of Canadian economic development. It is interesting to note, as an example of the close-meshed web of Scottish commercial connections at the time, that the Scott firm shared with Forsyth the same Liverpool, London and Jamaican agents.[93]

The firm of Scott dated back to the very beginning of the eighteenth century. One of its founders had worked in the preparation of the ill-fated Scottish Darien expedition in 1698, and by 1790 the firm was noted for the production of high-quality West Indiamen. It already had a connection with the Maritimes, for in the early 1790's it had constructed the superb mastships *Brunswick* and *Caledonia*, vessels which had a carrying capacity of about one thousand tons, and were by far the largest to be built in Scotland up to that time. As well as building vessels, the Scotts were shipowners on a considerable scale, and the galling experience of seeing vessels which had passed through their hands fetch three times their original cost as new ships apparently made them decide to attempt this venture, which was a novel one for a Scottish, indeed for a British shipbuilding firm. By October, 1798, much-prized customers, including Glasgow West India merchants, were being turned down when they asked for new ships, due to the Baltic timber situation, another reason for the New Brunswick decision, for the timber there might supply the Greenock yards, and enable such orders to be filled. The plan which the Scotts obviously wished to follow was to build a series of vessels on the Saint John, loading them with timber for the Clyde on com-

---

[93] Letter book of Scotts Ltd. Greenock, September, 1798-August, 1800, Archives of the Scotts, Cartsburn Dockyard, Greenock.

pletion. On arrival at Greenock the vessels would be unloaded, and sold for high prices on the British market.[94]

It was a sound scheme, involving the shipment of craftsmen and such materials as nails, iron spikes, jobbing iron, anchors, and copper spikes, (all manufactured in the Muirkirk Ironworks) and the nucleus of the crews for the first vessels. Heading the "expedition" was Christopher Scott, younger brother of James and William Scott, the firm's principals, an experienced supervisor of ship construction, and a master mariner in his own right, who sailed in March 1799. By mid-April he had two vessels under construction, and further shiploads of materials, including Archangel tar, Russian cordage and Scottish sailcloth, were being shipped to him. Furthermore, with the continued shortage of shipping in British ports, Christopher Scott was instructed to purchase any colonial-built "vessels of quality" that might be available, even if they were only "half or quarter built" and even although he was required to pay in advance.[95]

Shipbuilding was already an established industry on the Saint John when Scott arrived. Men such as Adonijah Colby, William Olive, and the others described by Esther Clark Wright in her fine study of the Saint John River (Toronto, 1949), had been active for some years, but the appearance of the Greenock firm in the town helped to speed up that activity, and also to develop more fully the strong trading links with the Clyde which already existed. In December, 1798, John Black (inevitably, the Scotts' agent, as well as acting for Forsyth in Halifax and Dunlop in Montreal) imported a cargo of Scotch woollens, cordage, iron, gunpowder, Canada stoves and liquor from Greenock in the Scotts' vessel *William* which was bringing out shipbuilding supplies, further craftsmen and crews for the ships a-building.[96] Black was keenly interested in promoting hemp-growing in the province, and Scott was instructed to follow developments in this field by his older brother at Greenock. Probably the Scotts saw New Brunswick as a future supplier of this vital raw-material for cordage as well as of timber. Certainly, their difficulties with Baltic suppliers were reaching crisis-point at this time.

The increase in the scale of shipbuilding operations affected more than the merchants. In June, 1799, the shipwrights of Saint John held a meeting "for the purpose of regulating working hours agreeable to the rules established in Great Britain and in the neighbouring provinces." It was resolved that there should be a ten hour working day (from 6 a.m. to 6 p.m.) with three quarters of an hour at breakfast and one and a quarter hours at dinner; that when the short days did not admit, wages would be reduced accordingly; that in graving and similar work every tide would be considered a full day's work.[97]

[94] John Scott to Messrs. Robert Livie, London, February 1, 1799, Letter book. *Two Centuries of Shipbuilding by the Scotts at Greenock* (London, 1906), p. 4.

[95] *Ibid.*, John Scott to Christopher Scott, May 25, 1799.

[96] *Royal Gazette*, December 4, 1798.

[97] *Ibid.*, June 4, 1799.

This set of regulations was laid down before the passing of the British Combination laws, and it is interesting to speculate as to the part that Scottish shipwrights imported by the Scotts from the Clyde may have played in framing them. Unfortunately, no names were mentioned in the press notice of the occasion.

The vessels which the Scotts were building were sizeable craft of three hundred tons or more – considered large by the standard of the time, and progress was good. Also, a highly profitable sideline was found in the export of black birch from New Brunswick to Greenock for the growing furniture industries of Paisley and Beith. The Scottish cabinet makers rapidly developed a taste for this fine material, and it became a regular part of the cargoes of the Scotts' vessels.[98] An indication of New Brunswick's wealth in this fine timber was the fact that William Forsyth in Halifax ordered his new five hundred ton vessel, built in New Brunswick in 1797, to be constructed almost entirely of it.

Saint John, like Montreal, Quebec, and Halifax, benefited considerably from the growth of trade with Britain in wartime. The shipping lists and advertisements in the *Royal Gazette and New Brunswick Advertiser* indicate this increase quite clearly. In June, 1799, for example, Hugh Johnston advertised two cargoes from the Clyde, consisting of Scottish manufactures, and cordage, rigging and anchors to supply the area's growing shipbuilding industry. The presence of troops in the area provided "Artillery," commissary and treasury bills, which facilitated commerce at all levels, and increased the flow of imports from Scotland. There was also a noticeable increase in the West India trade, and Saint John was becoming just as Halifax had become earlier, a point of transhipment of rum, sugar and molasses, and a collecting place for fish and lumber for the Caribbean trade.

Shipbuilding was also thriving, through the activities of Christopher Scott and other entrepreneurs. As with the merchants, local shipwrights and shipbuilders often combined other occupations with their calling. Timothy Perry, for example, who laid out and supervised vessels for the Scotts, kept an inn at Kingston.[99] In December, 1800, the *Royal Gazette*, announcing the departure of the newly built ship *Diana* for the Clyde with "ton timber," stated that "there are now fitting for sea six new ships, which will compleat (*sic*) thirty one new vessels from this port from January last, from 80 to 380 tons. . . . If we are able to effect this under all the disadvantages of War, what may we not expect in peace"? The statement, of course, ignored the fact that wartime requirements had largely stimulated the demand for New Brunswick vessels.

The Scotts certainly realised this for, seeing no imminent end to hostilities, they ordered more and more vessels to be laid down, and even made plans to

[98] Letter book of Scotts Ltd., John Scott to Messrs. Hunter and Walkinshaw, Paisley, August 23, 1793.
[99] *Royal Gazette*, December 2, 1800.

smuggle large quantities of copper bolts and fittings out of Scotland, in defiance of Orders in Council, for these new vessels. The experienced Scots builders' reaction to their first New Brunswick-built vessels, when they reached the Clyde, was mixed. They approved generally, but considered that too many copper spikes were used needlessly by the local workmen and that the ships were poorly masted and badly rigged. The profits to be made by selling ships, not only in Britain but in the colonies, had become so great by September, 1799, that Christopher Scott was instructed to push on with even more construction. If cordage was not available the hulls should be sold "as they stand." If copper bolts could not be obtained, iron ones should be used as a makeshift, taking care only to "let no iron heads appear anywhere."[100]

Skilled shipwrights, carpenters, blacksmiths and caulkers were being sent out continuously by the Scotts to their new yards during this period, often in small groups in vessels sailing from the Clyde, but occasionally in larger numbers in the Scotts' own vessels. It is interesting to speculate on the impact of these men, and the techniques they brought from Scotland, on shipbuilding generally in the Maritimes. Entire crews for new vessels, from commanders to cabin boys were also shipped out for the new vessels.

Inevitably, in the Saint John community, Christopher Scott became involved in trading and shipping ventures, purchasing maple, beech and pine, all in strong demand in Scotland, and dealing in pot ashes, planking, staves, turpentine and tar. In securing these for export he had the co-operation of local Scots merchants, who also used available space in the firm's ships for speculative consignments to and from Scotland. Scott also engaged in the West India trade, using new vessels which were loaded with lumber and sent off to Jamaica for sale of both ships and cargoes. These vessels, which were claimed to be "superior to most vessels from that quarter" (i.e. New Brunswick), fetched prices as high as £17 per ton register in the West Indies, and the firm made considerable profit on this side of the business.[101] By April, 1801, the Scotts had built, commissioned, purchased or otherwise acquired the surprising total of twenty-seven vessels constructed on or around the Saint John River – a remarkable total, and it does not include eleven other vessels in various stages of construction which they also owned. The achievement was possible only because of Christopher Scott's contacts in the dominant Scots mercantile community and the co-operation of local builders, timber suppliers and workmen which this ensured as well as the backing of the powerful home firm on the Clyde. It was an outstanding example of the projection of early industrial Scotland into the colonial scene, an amazingly large-scale operation for the time, involving the transfer of hundreds of artisans, hundreds of sailors for crews, and thousands of tons of cordage, copper, iron-work, sheathing paper and "chandlery" across the Atlantic

---

[100] Letter book of Scotts, Ltd., to Christopher Scott, September 12 and 14, 1799.
[101] *Ibid.*, to same, March 23, 1800.

from the Clyde to service the new vessels. The smuggled copper, which the home firm was in a position to obtain through Liverpool business contacts, undoubtedly put its New Brunswick vessels in a higher category than locally-built vessels which lacked copper bolts and sheathing, and enabled handsome prices to be asked, and obtained, for the ships.[102]

The building of ships as a speculation was a practice that had begun early on the Clyde, in times of slack demand. The Scotts of Greenock were engaged in it in the late 1780's. There is little evidence that colonial builders, in New Brunswick, Canada or Nova Scotia were prepared to take such risks until Christopher Scott appeared on the scene at Saint John in 1798. Yet within ten years of his arrival, the export of ships, packed with lumber cargoes, had become a mainstay of branches of colonial commerce that extended to Greenock, Liverpool, Bristol, Boston, Kingston in Jamaica and even to London itself, where brokers clamoured for "colonial vessels, of a good and secure build, highest prices to be paid for New Brunswick vessels, if they are well found and put together under able and craftsmanly supervision, after the manner of Saint John." The evidence produced by Lord Liverpool's Ship Registration Act of 1786, so important for students of trade and commerce in this period, shows that most colonial-built vessels met with ready sale in British ports, for the quality of the materials used in them was usually high, especially before 1825. Certainly, the arrival of numerous new vessels of this type, destined for sale in British ports, acted as a stimulus to the rapidly growing class of ship-brokers who were to form an integral part of the British commercial maritime scene in the nineteenth century. In Greenock and Glasgow, as well as Liverpool, the new profession grew apace, fostered by the influx of colonial-built vessels, and by 1825 there were four brokers in Greenock who specialised in buying and selling colonial-built ships. By this date Saint John, New Brunswick, had twenty-five shipyards, and there were scores of yards in Nova Scotia.

Most of the Saint John merchants, with the Scots to the fore, were augmenting their fleets during this boom period, buying more vessels, and larger ones at that, extending their operations to Turks Island for salt, to Madeira for wines, and to newly-conquered Trinidad. In all of these places they found Scottish merchants and agents to handle their cargoes. Some engaged in new local industries such as lime-burning, but most limited themselves to the three principal lines of business in the province – importing, shipbuilding, and securing timber for export by contract and barter operations.

The short peace that followed the Amiens Treaty brought a temporary slowdown in shipbuilding, and Christopher Scott returned to his native land for a time; but the desperate need for ship-building timber brought on another boom in the Maritimes and the Scotts of Greenock opened up new contacts with shipbuilders at Pictou, supplying them with copper and iron

---

[102] *Ibid.*, to same, March 29, April 12, May 11 and 17, 1800.

fittings. They also engaged in the Highland emigrant traffic and maintained their Saint John and colonial connections. Here again there is evidence of the tightly intermeshing Scottish commercial world in the Atlantic area, for the Scotts imported seal-oil for use in lighthouses from William Forsyth in Halifax, and despatched shiploads of rum to James Dunlop in Montreal, importing wheat from that merchant, and offering him "special preferences" (i.e. cut freight rates) for such Clyde-bound cargoes.[103]

The resumption of War gave further stimulus to trade in the North American colonies and particularly, to the New Brunswick timber-boom. Christopher Scott, having lost the brig *Mary* which he commanded to a French privateer off the Hebridean island of Barra, purchased the full-rigged ship *Wilson* and set up as a merchant at Saint Andrews, near the American border, where he prospered as a dealer in timber, a "trader on the Line," and a speculator in "bargains" among the prize ships auctioned off at Halifax in the War of 1812.[104] At Saint Andrews in 1812 he built a strong blockhouse to defend the town, almost entirely at his own expense. The most striking memorial to his wealth, and his local Scots patriotism, is the magnificent wooden church, designed in Scotland, and, characteristically, known as the Greenock church which he built for his fellow countrymen and Presbyterians. It still adorns the town of Saint Andrews, and is among the finest examples of "colonial" architecture in New Brunswick. Though exact details of his gains are lacking in the Scott correspondence, it is clear that his gains from the "Line" traffic were very substantial, as he was able to set up as a country gentleman in both New Brunswick and Scotland on the estates of Blackhouse and Quarter, near Largs, purchasing a fine landed estate in the colony, as his testament in the New Brunswick Museum shows, and possessing town property, silver plate and shares in vessels and banks.

The years after 1804 saw the beginning of the "golden age" of the New Brunswick timber trade, and the apogee of Scottish mercantile influence in the colony. In 1807, 156 ships sailed from the colony's ports, with 27,430 tons of timber. The Free Ports Act of 1807, passed to counter the American policy of non-intercourse, gave a further stimulus to the area's commerce.

Many Scots settlers, almost all from the Lowlands, Renfrewshire, Ayrshire, Dumfriesshire and Galloway came out, bringing valuable experience of "improved" farming methods. By 1825 Peter Fisher, in his *Sketches of New Brunswick* was reporting that more than three hundred vessels were loading annually at Miramichi alone. The existent Scottish houses at Saint John, Saint Andrews, Fredericton and Miramichi were strengthened, and dozens of other new Scots firms joined them. Greenock remained the principal port through which New Brunswick maintained its British trading connection,

---

[103] *Ibid.*, to William McIver, Liverpool, August 6, 1802; to Captain Ninian Thomson, May 5, 1804.
[104] *Ibid.*, John to William Scott, Bristol, February, 1813.

though occasional vessels arrived from Aberdeen, Liverpool and London. The spring of 1808 witnessed the arrival of Scottish vessels in Saint John at an unprecedented rate, as the need for timber drove vessels which normally operated in the Baltic trade across the Atlantic in search of cargoes. In the last week of April five such vessels came in, and by the following year even greater numbers were arriving weekly, many from Scotland's east-coast timber trading ports of Aberdeen, Leith, Banff, Kincardine and Alloa. The booming timber trade from 1808 thus opened up the North American colonies to a far greater degree of contact with eastern Scotland than they had experienced previously. Greenock and Port Glasgow remained the chief centre of Scottish Canadian trade, but Aberdeen, Banff and the ports of the Forth now almost rivalled the Clyde in it.[105]

Many of the Scottish ships which entered Saint John for timber cargoes were in ballast, having disembarked emigrants or unloaded cargoes of Scottish wares in Halifax and other Maritimes ports; but there was also among them an increasing number of "regular traders," such as the sizeable full-rigged ships, *Rosina* and *Northern Friends*, both of Greenock, which had made the voyage several times by January, 1810. The bulk of the import cargoes by these "regular traders" consisted of textiles and hardware, and was obviously much greater in quantity than the amount required for colonial consumption. It is interesting to speculate as to the proportion of these goods that was shipped to the United States borders from Saint John and Saint Andrews for import into the United States during this "Embargo" period and, later in the "trading on the Line" operations during the War of 1812. The overloading of timber ships on their homeward voyages led to numerous losses during the timber boom, but another cause of such disasters was the fact that many of the Scottish vessels employed in the trade had been engaged in the Baltic timber carrying traffic for many years before they encountered the more exacting weather conditions of the North Atlantic. Robert Hamilton, influential Scottish shipowner in Liverpool, wrote to his friend John Gladstone in May, 1812, that "the ships' owners resort to Canada because they have no other trade to go into . . . but the freights are not very good ones."[106] Unhappily, few fragments of the New Brunswick commercial correspondence of these years have survived, but the Crookshank letters in the Saint John Museum are among them. A letter from Harry Crookshank, of Stromness, Orkney, Scotland, to his cousin Andrew Crookshank of Saint John, in this collection, shows clearly the predicament faced by a Scottish shipowner and timber importer in the treeless island of Orkney in April, 1808. Complaining that trade was at a standstill in the Baltic, he an-

---

[105] *Royal Gazette*, Shipping lists, 1800-1812; W. S. MacNutt, *New Brunswick, 1784-1867*, (Toronto 1963), p. 150 *et. seq.*

[106] Hamilton to Gladstone, May 12, 1812. (I am indebted for this reference to Professor S. G. Checkland, of the Department of Economic History in the University of Glasgow.)

nounced his intention of sending two small brigs to New Brunswick for timber "tho' far too small for lumber cargoes." He also stated that he would send specimens of Orkney knitted stockings and the Stromness straw bonnets, a new manufacture of his area, in an attempt to boost his district's trade. The Orkney merchant complained bitterly that American ships were "making fortunes" in the Russian trade, by smuggling Baltic goods into Britain, and asked his cousin if he could suggest contacts for the securing of foreign West Indian salt, say at St. Ubes, which the Scots could then smuggle over to Russia. In addition to these agency services, and the specialised advice, the Orkney man also sought to place some relations, including a bankrupt, in his kinsman's service as clerks.

Official government archives of the period make few allusions of value to business matters, and such glimpses of the workings of the commercial mind as can be gleaned from the Dunlop and Crookshank correspondence and the Scott and Forsyth letter books are rarely available. Yet the *Royal Gazette* in its advertisements and shipping notices for the period 1808-1825 does show clearly the quickening tempo of Scottish participation in the timber trade. Invariably, Scottish ships were consigned to Scottish agents for loading. Almost invariably, except when in ballast, they brought over consignments, probably at "special preference rates of freight" for Scottish merchants. At a time when over-production and the Continental Blockade were posing serious problems for Scottish manufacturers and traders, the Canadian trade and the "intercourse" with the United States through New Brunswick must have provided a most useful outlet. Certainly, the sheer quantity of goods shipped into Saint John in Scots vessels could not possibly have been consumed locally. A characteristic cargo of the wares in question, brought by the brig *James and Anne* from the Clyde for James Hendricks in May, 1810, included:

Dry goods in large quantity	Swedish steel
slops ditto	Carpenters' jointers, and coopers' tools
loaf-sugar (a Greenock specialty)	glass and glassware
iron	paints
ironmongery	swords and pistols
	japanned and tinware

Similar complete cargoes from the Clyde, consigned to Hendricks, included large quantities of writing desks, backgammon tables, choice furniture, silver and gold epaulettes, and other wares for which the colony's demand would obviously be slight at that time.[107]

By 1812 the powerful Pagan family, of Greenock origin, with agencies at Quebec and in the West Indies, was advertising its services as Lloyd's agents

---

[107] *Royal Gazette*, June 11, 1810, August 5, 1811.

in Saint John, and many of the larger "regular traders" such as the *Rosina* of Greenock were sailing under letters of marque, so that they might engage in privateering against the Americans. Crookshanks, Pagans, Johnstons and other locals joined in ventures of this kind, just as their countrymen in Halifax were doing. They were staunchly in favour of the War against the States, as long as it did not injure their trade, quite prepared to "trade on the Line," (obviously differentiating between their New England neighbours and the "War Hawks" of the West who threatened Upper Canada) and they had a high regard for George Canning's commercial and political attitudes, as the local newspaper, the *Royal Gazette* showed clearly in its reports of his speeches in favour of greater freedom of trade and related matters.[108]

In the area of local politics and government, in the House of Assembly in this province and in the legislatures of Nova Scotia and Lower Canada at the same period, the Scottish merchants were well represented, in accordance with their wealth, social position and value to their communities. This is not the place to trace their contributions in the political field, their attitudes or their influence on governments, both at home and in the colonies, but a study of their role would probably be rewarding. Many of them must have found the wartime situation confusing and perplexing, even though wholesale "Trading on the Line" made it profitable, and accorded well with their Free Trade notions, for American privateers, ironically, often intercepted cargoes which were intended for this trade. This was possibly the case with the brig *Anne*, which regularly traded between Glasgow and Saint John, bringing entire cargoes of Scottish textiles of the more expensive kinds (shawls, printed cambrics, fine cottons and gauzes) for James Bremner, one of Saint John's Scots merchants. When the vessel was taken in August, 1813, her cargo was held to be worth half a million dollars, and it was almost certainly intended for the American market. The arrival of shiploads of such value, including large consignments of silks, fine mattresses and choice furniture indicates the profitability of this trade, and there are also indications in the local press that American merchants were employing Saint John traders as agents, and chartering (unofficially) British colonial vessels to transport imported goods from Saint John and other ports to points of transshipment near the Border.[109]

Even before the Peace of 1815, industrial over-production and a glut of tonnage were causing difficulties for Scottish manufacturers, merchants and shipowners. To many owners, after 1814, the New Brunswick timber trade seemed a feasible employment for their vessels, even if it involved, as it usually did, sending them out in ballast. At least they could be sure of finding dependable Scottish agents at Saint John, Saint Andrews and Miramichi, who could be relied upon to find suitable cargoes at reasonable

---

[108] *Ibid.*, January, 1813.
[109] *Ibid.*, August 20 and December 21, 1813, December 12, 1814.

Port	1785	1786	1795	1798	1799	1800	1801	1802	1803	1804	1805	1806	1807
Greenock				2	3	3	5	4	5	5	6		7
Aberdeen													
Glasgow	2	4			2	3							
Port Glasgow			1										
Peterhead													
Dumfries													
Leith										1			
Dundee													
Grangemouth													
Ayr													
Banff													
Irvine													
Bo'ness													
Berwick													1
Kirkcaldy													
Lerwick													
Montrose													
Perth													
Saltcoats													
Stranraer													
Stromness													
Thurso													
Totals for years	2	4	1	2	5	6	5	4	5	6	6		8

Table 4. Participation of Scottish Ports in the trade to and from St. John, New Brunswick, October 1785 to June 1822. Arrivals and Departures of vessels from and to Scottish Ports, are noted by year, the ports are listed in order, headed by those from which most vessels cleared for St. John in the period. (From figures based on available issues of *The Royal Gazette and New Brunswick Advertiser*, 1785-1822). It should be noted that there are sizeable gaps in the extant file of this newspaper, in some cases for several months in various years in the period.

charges, for the New Brunswick trade, from its earliest days, had provided profitable employment for Scottish vessels.

Many of the New Brunswick merchants, with no wartime ventures to distract them, applied themselves to becoming agents for the supply of timber, and to exploring new shipping possibilities, like the largely Scottish combine which began to operate the first steamboat on the river between Saint John and Fredericton in 1816. Christpher Scott, as the letterbooks at Greenock show, became an expert in the securing of the finer grades of timber for the Clyde shipyards and for the furniture-making industry, and a

1808	1809	1810	1811	1812	1813	1814	1815	1816	1817	1818	1819	1820	1821	1822	total
10	10	12	8	6	8	4	5	5	20	21	36	2	16	5	208
7	9	5	4	3		2	9	18	27	8	5	2	3		102
	1	5	2	1	1	1	1		2	4	2	1			32
		1	2	1	2				6			4	5	6	28
	3	5	1	4			2	3					3		21
	1		1						3	2	3	4	6		18
		2		1					5	3	2		4		17
	2	1	1	1					2	1		2	3		11
	2	1	1	1					1						6
									1	1			2		4
	1	1	1	1											4
		2										1			3
				1											1
													1		1
		1													1
				1											1
	1														1
		1													1
												1			1
												1			1
													1		1
												1			1
17	27	36	19	21	11	7	17	26	67	40	48	19	44	11	464

specialist in the loading of timber ships. A typical example of loading instructions for a vessel owned by the Scotts, and sent out for a cargo in 1817 runs:

> In the bottom, 40 or 50 tons black birch of good lengths and squares, to be fit for keels and plank, (small, ill-squared timber will not answer for our work). Then 300 tons of choice well-squared fir timber of good lengths, not over-large in the square. Also 100 to 150 small spars about 5-7 inches fit for steering sail booms and boats' masts and 100 large spars from 6-9 inches, 20 large spars 12-14 inches. They must be all clean straight and freshly cut, with 4 to 6 masts 60-70 feet long and 18-20 inches diameter. The deck cargo to be of ash and fir staves and deals, as much as possible.[110]

Further instructions were given to the ship's master to check the quality of each item of the cargo – a sign of the increasing competitiveness within the trade.

The number of vessels engaged in the trade made it impossible for many to

[110] Scotts Letter book, No. 777, April 2, 1817.

obtain outward freights, especially as more and more owners in outports on the Solway, in Ayrshire, and on the Moray Firth turned desperately to the timber trade for employment for their vessels. Some found a solution in shipping emigrants not only from Scotland but from Ireland as well. There were better prospects for larger ships in this line of business, and full-rigged, sizeable vessels such as the ship *Favorite* of Greenock, which arrived at Saint John with 126 settlers for the colony in December, 1816, and the ship *Elizabeth*, of Dumfries, which brought 130 artisans and farmers in May, 1817, were obviously more attractive to the intending emigrant than the plethora of small brigs, brigantines and snows which frequented the New Brunswick ports. Yet even those who were fortunate enough to obtain such passengers found like the Scotts of Greenock that profit margins on round voyages were becoming slighter between 1815 and 1820. In the Scottish ports, as well as in Saint John, there were dissolutions of partnerships, bankruptcies, and a mounting degree of distress.

From a study of previous employments of the numerous vessels in the trade (almost one third of the 230 which arrived at Miramichi in August-September, 1818, were Scots vessels) it appears that participation in the timber trade was often a remedy of desperation, regarded as an expedient to keep vessels at sea until times could improve and they could resume their normal trades. By September-October, 1818, nineteen out of thirty-six vessels clearing from the Miramichi were Scots, mostly smallish vessels, and practically all had arrived in ballast. The poor condition of many was attested by the loss of three brigs from Aberdeen alone on their Spring voyages to New Brunswick in 1819. By that year, a particularly distressed one in the shipping trade, no fewer than half of the first arrivals on the Miramichi were from ports on the Clyde and the Forth.

Scotland was paying the price for its rapid wartime expansion in shipping and industry, and Christopher Scott at Saint Andrews was not the only merchant who found his stocks of "tartan plaid, Scotch homespun, linens, glassware and Paisley cottons" almost unsaleable. He reported to his relatives in Greenock that many of his fellow countrymen who were dispatching timber cargoes home were finding that their exported lumber, as well as their imported manufactures, simply could not find markets. Large-scale emigration from Scotland and from Ulster did provide some business for shipowners at this time, but razor-keen competition sliced the passenger rates down, as Alan Ker and Co. of Greenock complained when their ship *Ben Lomond* sailed from Londonderry in June 1819, with "near three hundred persons at a low rate, many destitute, not all paying, and numerous requireing to be sustained from the ship's stores."

Even old-established firms in the North American colonial trade like Alan Ker and Co. were experiencing fierce competition for this emigrant traffic from outsiders who were desperate for employment for their larger and superior vessels. In June, 1821, for example, the wealthy Glasgow firm of

Table 5. Miramichi – arrivals from and clearances for Scottish ports, 26th August to 31st December, 1818, entire year 1819, and 1820, and January to June inclusive 1822. Arrivals from these ports are recorded first, followed by clearances for them.

	1818		1819		1820		1st half 1822		totals	
	Arrivals from	Clearances for	Arrivals from	Clearances for	Arrivals from	Clearances for	Arrivals from	Clearances for	Arrivals from	Clearances for
Aberdeen	2	4	10	7	3	1	—	3	15	15
Alloa	—	—	6	2	4	1	—	—	10	3
Ayr	2	1	2	5	—	—	—	2	4	2
Bo'ness	—	—	—	4	—	1	—	—	—	5
Dumfries	—	2	2	2	1	—	—	—	3	5
Dundee	1	—	—	2	1	—	—	—	1	2
Girvan	—	—	—	1	—	1	—	—	—	2
Glasgow	1	—	—	2	—	1	—	—	—	3
Grangemouth	1	5	8	12	2	—	—	1	11	18
Greenock	2	—	7	4	7	—	—	—	16	5
Irvine	—	—	1	1	1	1	—	—	2	2
Kirkcaldy	—	—	1	—	1	—	—	—	2	1
Kirkcudbright	—	—	—	2	—	—	—	—	—	3
Leith	—	—	—	7	—	4	—	4	—	15
Montrose	—	—	—	1	2	3	—	—	2	4
Perth	—	—	1	1	—	—	—	—	1	1
Peterhead	—	—	1	1	—	—	—	—	1	—
Port Glasgow	—	—	—	—	—	—	3	—	3	1
Saltcoats	—	—	—	—	1	1	—	—	1	—
Stranraer	—	—	—	2	—	1	—	—	—	3
Troon	—	—	—	1	—	1	—	—	—	2
Wigtown	—	—	—	—	—	1	—	—	—	2
Totals for years	8	12	38	59	23	18	—	11	72	100

In addition to the sailings above, two vessels sailed, in 1819 and 1820 respectively, for the port of Berwick-upon-Tweed. (Figures based on available copies of *The Royal Gazette and New Brunswick Advertiser*, 1785-1822).

Finlay and Co., prominent in textile manufacture and in the East India trade, dispatched their first class vessel the *Earl of Buckinghamshire*, possibly the finest ship then owned in Scotland, to Quebec with six hundred would-be settlers, described in the *Royal Gazette* as "mostly of respectable appearance." This, and successive operations of the kind, were carried out under the noses of the clique of Greenock firms which had controlled the Scottish trade to the Saint Lawrence, and which would gladly have benefited from the conveyance of passengers on such a scale. In 1820-23, a large proportion of the Scottish emigrants to Canada was drawn from the distressed weaving population of Lanarkshire and Renfrewshire, – the hinterland of Glasgow and Greenock. This, as the percipient Robert Rintoul, editor of the *Dundee, Perth and Cupar Advertiser* noted in June, 1821, gave "an additional advantage to the shipowners and agents of Greenock, Port Glasgow and Glasgow, who already, by their position to the West, can cut their freights and passage moneys, and thus attract the intending emigrants from all parts of Scotland."

The Scotts of Greenock too, that well-established firm, found "a great dullness in all shipping concerns, and particularly in the building of ships. This has caused all our active young men to push out to Canada and the States in quest of employment." The only advantage to the Scotts from the glut in colonial lumber and the general depression was that, having adopted "Sepping's system of construction," involving the use of much larger quantities of timber to strengthen their ships, they were now able to do this more cheaply because prime timber could be purchased at lower prices.

Scotland's economic crisis, and the need to clear the country of the unemployed, led to some amazing statements at this time. The new Dundee *Caledonian*, a literary quarterly, expatiated on the glories of Canada and the Maritimes, and went so far as to compare Montreal with Dundee itself, except for the fact that the roofs of the former were of tin, while those of the latter were of slate. It may be significant, too, of competition that among numerous Miramichi arrivals recorded in the *Royal Gazette* of these distressed years, 1818-1821, Scots vessels tended to form a larger proportion of the "first arrivals" in April to May than of later. Possibly their owners hoped to do slightly better by reaching the home markets before they were saturated.

CONCLUSION

What are the conclusions to which this brief survey of certain aspects of Scottish commercial activity in the area brings us? The first is that, with the loss of the tobacco trade, a large number of the rapidly growing mercantile class found a ready, congenial and profitable field of operations in the older of the provinces of what is now Canada. There they functioned as traders in an environment in which "monopoly" or privileged rivals had not had a chance to become established, or were too weak to resist them. By dint of strong home connections and support, backed by a growing strength in Scottish industry and shipping, they were themselves able to assume a position, if not of monopoly, of predominance in the commercial sphere. That established and wealthy shipowner in the trade, in the first rank of British merchants, Robert Hamilton of Liverpool, might write to John Gladstone, another Scot, in London in May, 1812, that he had a poor opinion of the initiative shown by men of business in the North American colonies, and that for a "revival of the spirit of speculation" British merchants "must depend on the Yankees" – but from the surviving evidence of the enterprising activities of Dunlop, Forsyth and Scott this would appear a harsh judgement. These men were hampered by occasional need of operating capital, by the periodic gluts of imports which caused them loss, and by the constant need to alter their trading patterns to meet the changing circumstances of war, embargo and "Non-Intercourse"_restrictions, but they certainly showed no hesitancy in launching out in new ventures, and diversifying their businesses. Tenacity was a well-recognised national characteristic, and that astute observer, James MacGregor, was not merely being patriotic when he wrote in his description of the Maritimes in the 1820's: "The lessons of early life infuse among the lower and middle classes in Scotland, a spirit which will endure the greatest hardships without repining, whenever a manifest utility is to be attained."[111] The leading Scottish role in the founding of banks and insurance companies, in Montreal, Saint John, Halifax, Toronto and lesser centres does not come within the scope of this survey. It is recorded elsewhere, but it is explained by the position that Scots had already won in the colonial economy by 1817-1835.

At the foundation of the Bank of Montreal in 1817, five of the directors were Scots, including John Forsyth of the Montreal-Quebec branch of that family. In the following year, three more Scots or first-generation Canadians of Scots blood joined the board. Of the twenty original board members of the Bank of New Brunswick, established in 1820, at Saint John, no fewer than ten were Scots, or of Scots descent, including Christopher Scott, the shipbuilding entrepreneur whose colonial career has been surveyed above. In the Charlotte County Bank, set up in Saint Andrews in 1825, there were fourteen Scots in a total directorate of twenty-five. These are typical, and not outstanding examples of Scottish participation in the formation of the early Canadian banks. In the circumstances it was natural that these banks should follow the design of the "new Scotch institutions" which had revolutionized the whole concept of banking in Britain, if not in Europe. These were the Commercial Bank (1810) and the National Bank of Scotland (1825), both founded in Edinburgh, with their novel systems of "cash-credits" and

[111] J. MacGregor *Historical and Descriptive Speeches of the Maritime Colonies of British North America* (1828) (Toronto, 1968), p. 72.

"branch banking," and with the even more novel feature that they had large numbers of shareholders drawn from the lower middle class.

The adoption of such models is clearly seen in William Jarvis's manuscript account of 1869, now in the New Brunswick Museum, of the launching of the Commercial Bank in Saint John in 1832-4. Emphasizing the progressive character of this bank, Jarvis described how its founders intended that it "would give increased facilities for trade, and was rendered necessary by the inability of the existent institutions to afford sufficient accommodation." The Commercial Bank's capital was large for the period – one hundred thousand pounds – and it was divided into small shares of twenty-five pounds each, so that "persons of the most moderate means might share its benefits." This feature it shared with its namesake and model, the Commercial Bank of Scotland, which the "Commercial Whigs" had founded in 1810, and no doubt was left as to the intentions of the organisers, for they declared at a public meeting in Saint John, held to launch the new project, that "in establishing this new bank, the Scotch System of Banking should be brought into operation in the Province."[112] By this, specified Jarvis, was meant the system of cash credits, by which customers could obtain advances to certain definite amounts, on entering into bonds, with sureties, to repay on demand, with interest. This principle came to be widely applied in Canadian banking.

Many of the men who prospered in such centres as Montreal, Halifax, Saint John and Saint Andrews returned to their native land to enjoy the fruits of the fur trade, of shipowning, and other ventures. Christopher Scott, with his New Brunswick lands, James Keith, with his shares in the Hudson's Bay Company, the Lachine Railway, and the Bank of Montreal, and his extensive property holdings in Quebec City and Toronto, were typical examples, and John Forsyth of Montreal was another. All maintained a steady interest in colonial business developments, even increasing their holdings though they lived in Britain. But many more of the successful men stayed on in the land where they had made their homes, and continued to participate directly, or through their sons or imported nephews, in its economic life. T. W. Acheson's chapter in this volume on the social origins of the Canadian industrial elite at the end of the nineteenth century shows clearly how their influence was exercised well beyond their own generation.

If the theory of the "metropolitan focus" of Canadian history is a valid one, as suggested by some historians – the "foci" comprising London as well as the cities of the Saint Lawrence System, – then Glasgow and its Clyde port of Greenock should surely be included in the list of urban centres from which Canadian economic development was planned, organised and effected.

The sheer preponderance of the Scots in business, their wholesale pervasion of commerce in the area would, perhaps, have received more attention

---

112 Second Letter of William Jarvis to the Shareholders of the Commercial Bank, 1869. Jarvis Papers, 16/19, New Brunswick Museum, Saint John.

had it not been for two decisive developments. The first was their rapid assimilation. Even James Keith, who had commanded on the Columbia River in 1814 for the North West Company, living in retirement in Aberdeen, Scotland in the early 1850's, often wrote nostalgically to his friends in Lachine and described himself as "in some sort . . . a Canadian." Those who did not go back must have assimilated even more easily than this particularly patriotic and stiff-necked man from the heart of Scotland's North East. The other reason was the fate of Scotland itself, in the later nineteenth century, when the country became materially absorbed in the affairs of Great Britain, when "Hungry London," as Lord Cockburn put it, attracted the best of Scottish talent, as well as the most profitable of Scottish companies.

In their transactions in the North American colonies between 1760 and 1825, the Scots had their best opportunity of making their impact on a new, largely unsettled territory, and as a nation rising in industrial, financial and shipping strength, they were in the best position in their entire history to make such an impact. The means they used in making this, apart from their initiative, energy, and industry, their capital and their web of home and overseas connection, were often dubious, sometimes downright illegal – but they had been raised in a system where defiance of regulation was, more often than not, the only ready method to break the stranglehold of entrenched and inimical "interests." It has been argued that Scotland exhausted itself in its rapid social and economic transformation, and there are grounds for holding the argument a valid one; but if it is valid the main beneficiary, in people, initiatives, and economic strength gained by investment, trade and enterprise, was undoubtedly the group of colonies which were eventually to confederate.

The Business Community in the Early Development of Victoria, British Columbia

J. M. S. Careless, Professor of History, University of Toronto

The rise of Victoria from the Hudson's Bay fort of the 1850's to the substantial commercial city of the later nineteenth century may be readily associated with striking events like the Fraser and Cariboo gold rushes, the political course of able Governor Douglas and the somewhat colourful officialdom about him – or the still more colourful doings of Amor de Cosmos, a kind of dedicated opportunist in politics, working toward the crucial decision of federal union with Canada. Far less likely is Victoria's growth to be associated with the more prosaic, lower-keyed activities of the city's businessmen. None the less, their quieter, continuing operations played an essential part in making the Vancouver Island community the chief entrepot of young British Columbia. Nor was the process lacking in colour or in noteworthy figures of its own. To trace that process, the development of the business community in conjunction with Victoria itself, is thus the object of the present study.[1]

Before 1858, and the onset of the gold rush to the Fraser on the neighbouring mainland, Victoria was a tranquil little hamlet of some three hundred inhabitants clustered about a fur trade depot. For Victoria, founded in 1843, did have the distinction, of course, of being the Hudson's Bay headquarters on the coast, as well as seat of government for the colony of Vancouver Island that had been erected in 1849, still in the keeping of the fur trade company. As a part of a great British commercial and imperial enterprise, and on the open Pacific within the world reach of British seapower, Victoria was by no means wholly isolated or unchanging. Parties of colonists had arrived from the United Kingdom to settle among the Company's officers and employees. The mild climate and fertile soil of the adjacent districts produced good crops. The Company had opened valuable coal mines up the coast at Nanaimo in the early fifties, and the timber wealth of the Island's heavy forests was initially being tapped. Finally, there was an increasing trade southward in coal, lumber, and sometimes fish or potatoes to San Francisco, the bustling Californian gold metropolis, from where most of the colony's necessary imports were derived.

Nevertheless, Victoria had remained an outpost community of small endeavours and limited opportunities. It was not one to invite much business enterprise when the fur company dominated the major economic activities –

---

[1] On the general significance of this theme, see D. T. Gallagher, "Bureaucrats or Businessmen? Historians and the problem of leadership in Colonial British Columbia," *Syesis*, Vol. 3, 1970, pp. 173-186.

not to mention political – and when markets were either local and scanty or far off and uncertain. True, the Hudson's Bay interests had worked at developing farms, mines or sawmills, and had diversified their trading operations on the coast well beyond the traffic in furs. Yet problems of access to market and to sufficient shipping plagued them too, while the established, hierarchical ways of the old fur monopoly inevitably made new adjustments harder. Outside of the quasi-bureaucratic world of the Bay Company, moreover, there scarcely was a business community, other than well-to-do tavern-keepers like James Yates (a former Company employee), some artisans, and a few independent settlers engaged in trade.

John Muir, formerly a Company coal-miner, sent spars, piles and lumber to Victoria from his small mill at Sooke, for shipment to the California market. Captain William Brotchie had pioneered in opening the spar trade, but found it hard to get adequate transport, and subsequently became Victoria's Harbourmaster. And Captain James Cooper, who had commanded Hudson's Bay supply vessels, had set up as an independent trader, bringing the little iron schooner, *Alice*, out from England in sections, then shipping cargoes like coal, cranberries and spars to San Francisco and the Hawaiian Islands. The role of sea captains in early business development on Vancouver Island was notable, in fact. But shipmasters then had long been roving businessmen, used to trading where they could, seeking cargoes, and commissions in their own or others' service. They were particularly prominent in early lumbering on the Island. Of fourteen subscribers to the Vancouver Steam Saw Mill Company five were ship captains, the rest Hudson's Bay officials or associates.[2] The Company itself introduced the first steam saw mill machinery to Victoria in 1853, but the venture failed from lack of sufficient capital, and the mill did little before it was destroyed by fire in 1859.

This, then, was the restrictive climate for business enterprise in early Victoria: lack of funds outside the Company for any but the smallest scale of operations, and lack of stimulating demands generally. The San Francisco market itself was far from satisfactory, when the products of Washington or Oregon were competitive and closer, and also did not face duties there. During the California boom that reached a peak in 1853, demands had been high enough to make the Vancouver Island lumber trade important; and of the nineteen lumber ships that left Victoria that year eighteen were bound for San Francisco.[3] When the boom faded, however, so did much of the Island's wood trade. Coal did better, earning a place in the California market as good steamer fuel; but again it could suffer from price fluctuations and the competition of coal from Britain, Australia or the eastern United States. In short, down to 1858, Victoria had not yet found a trade pattern that could

---

[2] W. K. Lamb, "Early Lumbering on Vancouver Island," I, *British Columbia Historical Quarterly*, January, 1938, p. 43.

[3] *Ibid.*, p. 46.

encourage much business growth. Then came gold, to change the picture almost overnight.

In the spring of 1858, news of gold strikes in British territory along the lower Thompson and Fraser valleys reached San Francisco. The mass hysteria that makes gold rushes surged within the city, and thousands prepared to leave for a new El Dorado. Some might make their way to Puget Sound or by rough overland trails up through the mountainous interior, but most chose the quickest, surest route by sea, the four-day passage to Victoria. For here was a port of entry to the British far western domains, the one place of settlement in all that wilderness. It offered a base of supply and a point of transhipment for the river journey up the treacherous Fraser, unnavigable by large ocean-going vessels. The importance of already existing patterns of transport in focussing this flow of traffic is fully evident here. The mass of shipping that was now swept into highly profitable runs to Victoria was simply following a recognized lane to an established harbour that lay beside the entrance to the Gulf of Georgia, from where the fur trade had long maintained contact with the mainland posts of the interior by way of the Fraser route.

For Victoria, however, the flow of ships brought golden inundation by waves of eager miners, who needed food and shelter, transport to the interior, supplies beyond what they had carried with them, and had money to spend for it all. The first four hundred and fifty arrived in April on the American steamer *Commodore*. They came in ever-mounting numbers through the summer, until, it was estimated, the town's population had climbed to seven thousand.[4] Most of the newcomers soon had to be housed under canvas; Victoria became a veritable tent city. But construction proceeded rapidly, brick as well as wooden buildings going up, while land values soared – rising for choice lots from an initial fifty dollars to three thousand dollars and more.[5] For with the miners had come entrepreneurs with capital, store and hotel keepers, commission merchants and real estate buyers, who were ready to invest in the business which they envisaged would acrue to Victoria from its services to the gold fields.

Some, of course, were essentially speculators, planning to grab a quick return and move on. Others were agents of established San Francisco firms, seeking profitable new branches, and still others were more vaguely attracted by the thought of commercial opportunities in another California-like boom. Many would leave, especially after the initial enthusiasm of the rush ran out in disillusionment by the winter, and contraction and depression followed. But enough of the new commercial element remained, along with miners in the hinterland, to bring an enduring change to Victoria. And when the next year sufficient finds further up the Fraser kept the mining frontier going, then its main outlet continued to grow also as a town. Though Victoria's

[4] *Gazette* (Victoria), December 25, 1858.
[5] Alfred Waddington, *The Fraser Mines Vindicated* (Victoria, 1858), p. 19.

population had fallen back under three thousand by 1860,[6] it had indeed become an urban centre with a trading pattern of its own, supplying a considerable market on the mainland and exporting quantities of gold to San Francisco.

The pattern was strengthened in 1860, when Governor Douglas declared the town a free port. New Westminster, established near the mouth of the Fraser in 1858 as capital of the new mainland province of British Columbia, faced the burden of customs duties as well as the problems of Fraser navigation. It became little more than a river-steamboat halt, while Victoria remained the terminus for ocean shipping. The Vancouver Island town, indeed, had the best of both worlds: free external contact with an international, maritime traffic system, customs and licenses on the mainland to check encroachments on its inland trade from over the American border. Accordingly, although Victoria's business life, like its population, ebbed and flowed with the fortunes of gold mining, it nevertheless acquired substance and solidity as an entrepot, building a merchant group alongside the older Hudson's Bay and official elements that would steadily gain in stature.

Its business community grew particularly with the new rush to the Cariboo goldfields in 1862. Over the next two years, as Barkerville and other mining towns grew up far in the interior, as the Cariboo Road was opened to serve the fields, and as their deeper-driven mines increasingly needed capital and a greater volume of supplies, Victoria once more grew apace. But this time its business operations were necessarily on a bigger scale, in provisioning, transporting and financing for the larger enterprises of the Cariboo – where, moreover, farming and ranching were soon widening the bases of hinterland activities. It was good evidence of growth when Victoria was incorporated as a city in 1862, and its Chamber of Commerce was organized in 1863. That year, indeed, *The British Columbian and Victoria Guide and Directory* could say of the new city, "Her true position as the center and headquarters of commerce north of the Columbia has been placed beyond a doubt."[7]

In these early years of growth, Victoria's business community of several hundreds had acquired some significant characteristics, as well as many individuals worthy of note. One frequently remarked feature was the high proportion of Americans in the rising merchant group; another, its strongly marked cosmopolitan flavour as well. The former was to be expected from the commercial ties that made Victoria an outpost of San Francisco. The latter reflected the multi-national nature of gold rush society, whether among miners or those who would mine the miners, and whether in California or the British possessions to the north. But if Victoria had become "in effect,

---

[6] *British Colonist* (Victoria), June 12, 1860.
[7] *The British Columbian and Victoria Guide and Directory for 1863* (Victoria, 1863), p. 49.

San Francisco in miniature,"[8] it none the less had features of its own. There were the continuing elements of the older settler society and the Hudson's Bay-official elite. Some of their members did quite well by the Victoria boom, in hotels, stores and real estate; James Yates, for instance, piling up sufficient fortune to retire. Besides, other businessmen of British or British North American background arrived to share in the town's expansion, and later more generally stayed on, when Americans tended to withdraw. Finally, some of the "American" business migrants were better included in the multi-national category, since a number of them had earlier been immigrants to the United States; and, having moved on temporarily to San Francisco, had now moved on again.

In this regard, it has been noted that of the first 450 newcomers who arrived in 1858 aboard the *Commodore* from San Francisco, only about 120 were either British or Americans (about equally divided), the rest being mainly German, French or Italian.[9] There was also a notable Jewish admixture in the cosmopolitan influx of the gold-rush era, not to mention a significant contingent of American Negroes, and additional numbers of Slavs, Hawaiians and Chinese. The commercial community that took shape in Victoria was more Anglo-American in its upper ranks, more varied on the level of small shopkeepers or skilled tradesmen. Yet French, German and Jewish names figured prominently on the higher levels, while two Negroes, Mifflin Gibbs and Peter Lester, set up the first large general store to compete effectively with that of the Hudson's Bay Company.[10]

Adolph Sutro, a cultivated German Jew, arrived in 1858 to extend the wholesale and retail tobacco business he and his brothers had established in San Francisco. The Sutro warehouse in Victoria continued under brothers Gustav and Emil, though Adolph shortly afterward returned to San Francisco, to make a fortune in the Comstock Lode and became one of the Californian city's most lavish benefactors.[11] In similar fashion David and Isaac Oppenheimer, also German Jews, arrived from California to develop a wholesale dry goods business in Victoria. After flourishing for years, they were to move to the newly founded town of Vancouver, where they became two of its wealthiest citizens and David a celebrated mayor.[12]

And in the days of the rising Victoria business community there were, besides Sutros and Oppenheimers, men like Selim and Lumley Franklin, English-born Jews, who again came in the early wave from San Francisco. They were two of Victoria's first auctioneers, prospered in real estate and as

[8] W. Ireland, "British Columbia's American Heritage," *Canadian Historical Association Annual Report for 1948*, p. 68.

[9] *Ibid.*, p. 69.

[10] M. Ormsby, *British Columbia: A History* (Toronto, 1958), p. 141.

[11] R. E. and M. F. Stewart, *Adolph Sutro* (Berkeley, 1962), *passim*.

[12] "The Oppenheimers of Vancouver," typescript, British Columbia Archives (hereafter BCA).

commission agents, promoted shipping and cattle sales. Selim, moreover, sat for Victoria in the Vancouver Island legislature from 1860 to 1866, while Lumley was mayor of the city in 1865.[13] Still further, there were names like Ghiradelli and Antonovich, commission merchants, Jacob Sehl, furniture dealer from Coblentz, and P. Manciet, who kept the Hotel de France (a leading establishment in the sixties), all to demonstrate the variety of this new little urban business world.[14]

As for Americans, almost the most significant for the future was William Parsons Sayward, of New England origin. In 1858 he came up from a lumber business in San Francisco to found a similar one in Victoria. His wharf and yards grew over the years; but, more important, he went into sawmilling at Mill Bay in 1861, and ultimately became one of the chief figures in lumbering on the North Pacific coast.[15] Then, there was C. C. Pendergast who opened an office for Wells Fargo in Victoria in 1858. From the start, Wells Fargo played a major part in banking, in exporting gold to San Francisco, and for some time in handling mail for the business community: all of which made "Colonel" Pendergast a man of wide regard.[16] Equally well regarded was T. N. Hibben, a South Carolinian whose stationery and bookselling firm, begun in 1858, would have a long existence in Victoria. Still others prominent in the American segment of the community were Edgar Marvin, hardware and farm machinery importer (an 1862 arrival who became United States consul), and J. A. McCrea and P. M. Backus, both auctioneers.[17] Theirs was an important occupation at the time, when so many cargoes as well as properties inland were disposed of through auction sales.

There were also agents of San Francisco shipping lines, wholesalers and forwarding houses in the Victoria trade; for example, Samuel Price and Company, Dickson, De Wolf and Company, or Green Brothers. Sometimes their local representatives were Americans, but often instead they were Victorians of British background, serving as local partners in their firm – which itself might reach back far beyond San Francisco in a chain of interlocking partnerships to New York, Liverpool and London. Dickson De Wolf, for example (locally Dickson and Campbell), was based on H. N. Dickson's of London, and also had houses or correspondents in Liverpool, Boston and Halifax.[18] Yet from the time of the Fraser gold rush, a good deal of Victo-

---

[13] British Columbia Archives, Vertical Files (hereafter, BCAVF).

[14] Edgar Fawcett, *Some Reminiscences of Old Victoria* (Toronto, 1912) p. 60; British Columbia Miscellany, Bancroft Library, Berkeley.

[15] W. K. Lamb, *op. cit.*, II, *British Columbia Historical Quarterly*, April 1938, p. 114.

[16] Fawcett, *op.cit.*, p. 64.

[17] BCAVF.

[18] *Prices Current* (San Francisco). See advertisements from 1853 onward; also E. Mallandaine, *First Victoria Directory* (Victoria 1860), p. 42. For Samuel Price, Gazette, January 25, 1858 – J. N. Thain was the local representative.

ria's expanding wholesale trade was handled by local commission agents and general merchants, who of course had San Francisco correspondents. And in this field it seems evident that the British segment of the business community became particularly important.

The relative prominence of British wholesale merchants in the basic import trades no doubt related to the fact of operating in British territory, and the likelihood of their securing better contacts with colonial authorities or the still influential Hudson's Bay Company – not to mention the possibility of their having useful business ties back to Great Britain herself, where some of them returned to visit. A good illustration is that of J. J. Southgate, an Englishman who had been a commission merchant and ship-handler in San Francisco, but moved to Victoria in 1858 with a letter of introduction to Governor Douglas. Southgate soon prospered there, gaining, for example, a contract to provision His Majesty's warships lying in nearby Esquimalt harbour.[19] He built a fine brick store (still standing), with financial backing from Commander H. D. Lascelles, R.N., dealt in real estate, took the lead in organizing a Masonic Lodge, and was elected to the legislature in 1860.[20] Another example is that of the Lowe brothers, Thomas and James, two Scots commission merchants in San Francisco, who similarly transferred their business to Victoria in 1861-2. Thomas was an old Hudson's Bay man who had close links with the Company trading network along the coast, and in the fifties had pioneered in selling coal from the Company's Vancouver Island mines in the San Francisco market.[21] It was notable, incidentally, that the Lowe firm wrote the letter of introduction that Southgate carried to Douglas.[22] Subsequently the brothers took over the latter's wholesale business when he was absent in England; and James Lowe became President of the Chamber of Commerce in 1866, though he failed to win election to parliament in 1869.

Among many other leading early British businessmen one may mention R. C. Janion, with Liverpool and Honolulu connections, J. Robertson Stewart, Robert Burnaby and G. M. Sproat - President of the local St. Andrew's Society in 1863. Born in Kirkcudbrightshire, Gilbert Sproat had come to Vancouver Island in 1860 in the service of Anderson and Company, a big London firm of shipowners and shipbrokers who were developing a large steam sawmill at Alberni on the west coast of the Island. He became manager of the mill himself when its initiator, Captain Edward Stamp, resigned; but he also built up his own importing and insurance business in Victoria.[23]

---

[19] *Colonist*, February 2, 1865.

[20] Fawcett, *op. cit.*, p. 62; *British Columbian and Victoria Guide*, p. 137.

[21] On the Lowes, see J. M. S. Careless, "The Lowe Brothers, 1852-70: A Study in Business Relations on the North Pacific Coast," *B.C. Studies*, No. 2, 1968-9, pp. 1-18.

[22] *Ibid.*, p. 10.

[23] I. M. Richard, "Gilbert Norman Sproat," *British Colonial History Quarterly*, January, 1937, pp. 22-3.

Another Anderson employee was to become Sproat's partner, Andrew Welch, an Englishman with a distinguished business career ahead of him. And Thomas Harris, also from England, Victoria's first butcher, grew to be a well-to-do provisioner and the city's mayor in 1862.

The British element was also found in banking, for the wealthy London-based and chartered Bank of British North America had opened a Victoria branch in 1859. A few months previous, however, the town's first private bank had already been established by Alexander Macdonald, an enterprising Scotsman who had come up from California with the gold rush in hopes of living by it. He did well at first, making advances in gold dust for sale in San Francisco. But in 1864 his bank was burgled (through the roof) of well over $25,000, which ruined him, and sent him fleeing back to California.[24] The Bank of British Columbia, again London-based with a royal charter of 1862, proved more substantial and reliable, helping to finance wholesale operations, and soon, indeed, the government itself.

"British" at this period quite properly could cover subjects of the Queen who came to Victoria from the eastern colonies of British North America. It is of interest to note that there was some (prospective) Canadian content in contemporary Victoria business and professional circles, as evidenced by Thomas Earle, wholesale grocer and later member of parliament, an Upper Canadian who arrived in 1862.[25] Gradually more eastern British Americans did appear, usually still by way of California; but one of the earliest significant indications of their coming was in journalism. The first newspaper, the *Victoria Gazette*, established in June, 1858, may have been an extension of American press enterprise, but it is worth observing that its publisher, James W. Towne of California, was born in Nova Scotia.[26] And the far more important David Higgins, who arrived in 1860 and subsequently would edit Victoria's enduring *Colonist* for many years, was similarly of Nova Scotian birth, if American upbringing.[27] Above all, there was the founder and first editor of the *British Colonist* (begun late in 1858), Amor de Cosmos, also a native Nova Scotian, who also came via California. His vehement and erratic career in press and politics may not suggest too close an analogy with Joseph Howe; but at least there was some Nova Scotian ingredient added to early Victoria, through this transplanting of Bluenoses from one coast to another.

The character of this business community, strongly associated with the American Pacific metropolis but also with the older British metropolis of the Atlantic, did not greatly change for years the stamp it had received in the gold boom era of the early 1860's. New men were to come forward, addi-

---

[24] BCAVF.
[25] British Columbia Miscellany, Bancroft.
[26] BCAVF.
[27] *Ibid.*

tional interests to develop; but the men largely emerged out of older firms and partnerships, and the broader economic developments did not alter Victoria's basic role as a maritime commercial entrepot serving a simple extractive hinterland. Of course, declining gold production from the mid-sixties onward, the coming of Confederation with Canada in 1871, and the mounting influence of Canadian metropolitan power thereafter – signalized by the National Policy of 1878 and the building of the Canadian Pacific in the next decade – all brought significant changes that inevitably affected Victoria business more and more. Yet well into the 1880's, and perhaps even to the nineties, the patterns of Victorian commercial society set between 1858 and 1864 continued as a basis; even while American or continental European elements within it decreased or were assimilated, and British and Canadian elements were enlarged. This, then, is the general framework for the next two decades. It remains to discuss the newer activities and the newer men that did emerge inside it.

The falling output of the gold mines after 1864, and the failure to find rich, easily workable new fields, did not seriously harm Victoria at first, still living on the momentum, so to speak, of the expectations of more finds, and with some stimulus to trade derived from the American Civil War. Falling gold revenues and heavy colonial debt burdens, however, did lead in 1866 to the union of Vancouver Island and British Columbia as an urgent move of retrenchment. And this union sharply affected Victoria by removing its privileges as a free port. It was almost the hand-writing on the wall; continental costs of development and need for customs duties had defeated the interests of maritime free trade. At the public proclamation in Victoria of the new united province of British Columbia, so the *Colonist* noted, members of the crowd variously informed the sheriff that he was reading his death-warrant, warned a red-nosed bystander that port was no longer duty-free, and urged "a seedy-looking individual" to hurry up Government Street and buy a suit while he could still save fifteen per cent.[28] At least there was the consolation that Victoria remained provincial capital – to New Westminster's chagrin.

Activity in lumbering had offset in some degree the lessening role of gold. At Alberni, Gilbert Sproat's steam saw mill had reached a splendid peak in 1863, producing over eleven million feet of lumber, until the rapid exhaustion of timber close to water, accessible to the hand or ox-logging of those days, forced its closing by 1865.[29] However, the saw mill that W. P. Sayward had opened in 1863 up the Island's east coast near Cowichan thrived on a more accessible timber supply. In 1864 his mill alone brought two million feet to Victoria, and by the close of the decade put him into the export trade.[30] At the time of the union of 1866, moreover, there were six Van-

[28] *Colonist*, November 20, 1866.
[29] W. K. Lamb, *loc. cit.*, II, p. 105.
[30] *Ibid.*, p. 114.

couver Island saw mills in operation, much of their produce being marketed by way of Victoria. Furthermore, during the depression of the later sixties, they and the Burrard Inlet mills, that had now appeared on the mainland at Moodyville and Hastings, ended the former dominance of American Puget Sound mills over the import market.[31] While for some years following, Island lumbering failed to grow markedly, an important productive basis had been laid for future development, in which the Sayward milling and lumbering interests would play full part.

Then there was coal. In 1858 the Hudson's Bay Company had returned control of Vancouver Island to the Crown, and the next year its trading rights on the mainland had ended. Thereafter the Company had sought to concentrate on its original concern, the fur trade, divesting itself of other complicating ventures, such as its coal mines in the Nanaimo area. Thus in 1862 it sold these holdings to the Vancouver Island Coal Mining and Land Company, which was based in England and backed by British capital. (It also seems to have had an oddly literary connection, since T. C. Haliburton was its first chairman and among its investors were Agnes Strickland and the father of John Galsworthy).[32] In Victoria, the thriving firm of Dickson, Campbell and Company served as its agents, George Campbell being made a director. Much of the Vancouver Coal Company's output went directly from Nanaimo to market, to San Francisco or the Royal Navy based at Esquimalt. But some as well went via Victoria, where Charles Wallace, also of Dickson and Campbell, managed the two ships that the Company bought for its trade in 1864.[33] The next year coal production rose to 32,000 tons; and to 44,000 in 1868.[34] But by 1870 it seemed to have reached a plateau, and in the following decade the Company ran into trouble, owing to lack of further capital to develop new mines, and competition not only in the American market but within Vancouver Island itself.

The latter competition came from Robert Dunsmuir, the son of a Scottish coal master, who had first been employed at Nanaimo in the Hudson's Bay Company mines, but had been engaged in his own independent workings there since 1855. In 1864 another English coal mining venture, the Harewood Company, was launched, backed by the Hon. H. D. Lascelles, commanding H.M.S. *Forward*, and Dunsmuir became its resident manager.[35] Though he drove his miners rigorously (which did not stop them entertaining him to a public tea that year),[36] he could not overcome the fact that the Harewood Mine, after starting well, began to peter out. Dunsmuir withdrew.

[31] *Ibid.*, p. 121.

[32] BCAVF.

[33] P. A. Phillips, "Confederation and the Economy of British Columbia," W. G. Shelton, ed., *British Columbia and Confederation* (Victoria, 1967), p. 51, BCAVF.

[34] Phillips, *loc. cit.*, p. 51.

[35] Ormsby, *op. cit.*, p. 215.

[36] J. Audain, *From Coal Mine to Castle* (New York, 1955), p. 36.

In 1869, however, he discovered the truly rich Wellington Mine, and set up a company to work it, with financial aid from another naval officer, Lieutenant W. N. Diggle of the *Grappler*.[37] The Dunsmuir Company soon flourished, having one of the best coal seams on the coast and thus well able to stand the competition in the San Francisco market. Moreover, it undertook dock and railway developments at Nanaimo that ministered to that town's growth. And some of the benefit would redound to Victoria, since it kept much of the supply trade of the area. Hence, by the seventies, at least, growth in this coal hinterland could help balance decline in the older one of gold.

And then there was shipping. During the 1860's Victoria became the centre of shipping and shipbuilding interests of its own. It started, of course, with the rush of mining traffic to the Fraser. At the outset the Hudson's Bay Company had commanded the transport service; its pioneer steamers, the *Beaver* and *Otter*, would long be famous around the coasts and up the lower reaches of the river. But because of the demands for transport during the gold rush, Governor Douglas had recognized the need to allow American steamboat captains to enter the river navigation. A number of veterans of Puget Sound or Columbia River steamboating thus came in, and largely found it practicable to make Victoria their base of operations, as the main terminus of the Fraser trade. Captain William Irving became the most prominent and enduring of them – but here again the description of "American" is misleading, since he was a Scot, with much seagoing experience behind him before he pioneered with the first steamboat in Oregon.[38]

Irving joined with another Scottish steamboat pioneer from the Columbia, Alexander Murray, to build the stern-wheeler *Governor Douglas* at Victoria in 1858, her engine being brought from San Francisco.[39] This "first steamer built in the province for the inland trade" was soon joined by a sister ship, the *Colonel Moody*.[40] The previously mentioned merchants, Thomas and James Lowe, invested in the vessels; James for a time was an agent for the line, as were the also-mentioned Samuel Price and Company.[41] Irving built still more ships at Frahey's yard in Victoria, the *Reliance* in 1862 and the *Onward* in 1865.[42] The Hudson's Bay Company also acquired new craft to meet their competition and that from American steamboats. But the fall in gold-mining activity after 1864 led American captains to leave the Fraser, so that for the rest of the decade Irving's and the Bay Company's ships between them controlled the river.[43] Indeed, this situation virtually continued until

[37] *Ibid.*, p. 51.

[38] M. A. Cox, *Saga of a Seafarer* (New Westminster, 1966), p. 8.

[39] E. W. Wright, ed., *Marine History of the Pacific North West* by Lewis and Dryden (New York, 1961), p. 81.

[40] *Ibid.*

[41] Careless, *loc. cit.*, p. 10. Lowe Papers, BCA, T. Lowe to A. C. Anderson, July 2, 1859.

[42] Lewis and Dryden, *op. cit.*, p. 140.

[43] *Ibid.*, p. 82.

Captain Irving's death in 1872, and afterwards his son, John Irving, built a still larger shipping domain.

Joseph Spratt was significant also, because the Albion Iron Works, the foundry and marine machinery works he established in Victoria in 1862, became central to the subsequent growth of the city's shipping activities. After having had some training as a marine engineer in England, Spratt had gone to San Francisco, where he had opened a foundry and reputedly built the first steam locomotive on the Pacific coast.[44] As well as running his iron works, he went into shipbuilding, later salmon-canning and whaling, and organized a shipping line up the island's east coast. In any case, by the end of the 1860's he had added the beginnings of industrial enterprise to Victoria. And by that time, too, nine of the seventeen steamers trading to British Columbia and eighteen of the twenty-eight schooners were Victoria-built.[45]

As the sixties drew to a close, however, the city was in a state of depression. The newer activities in lumber, coal or shipbuilding had not yet hit full stride, and what was still far more apparent was the passing of the gold frontier, with its consequent effects on the wholesale trade, real estate and financial interests of the Victoria entrepot. Business in the city in 1869 was so slow, in fact, that thistles grew in the gutters along Government Street, while the population was falling back again to little more than three thousand.[46] In this condition, it is not surprising that the business community was considerably despondent, or that, in the midst of continuing discussions on joining the new and far-off Canadian Confederation, some of its members might look to the simpler, sharper release of annexation to the United States. At any rate, the Annexation Petition of 1869 appeared in Victoria in November, signed with 104 names in all.

It is true that this was a limited number; that many of the signers were small men, not leading merchants; and that they included a large element of foreign born who had no strong political positions, either anti-British or pro-American, but voiced what was indeed "primarily an expression of economic discontent."[47] It is also true that the essential issue in Victoria was union with Canada or no union; that annexation was never a real alternative. Yet it is possible, besides, that doubts and fears expressed in anti-unionism among Victorians found a sharper focus in some of those businessmen who did subscribe to annexation: a matter of choosing the devil you knew at San Francisco to the distant unknown one at Ottawa, especially when the former so obviously commanded power and fortune. And certainly one might see concern for the wholesale trade or property values in such substantial signatories as Isaac Oppenheimer and David Shirpser, dry goods merchants, W.

[44] BCAVF.

[45] Phillips, *loc. cit.*, p. 57.

[46] S. Higgins, "British Columbia and the Confederation Era," *British Columbia and Confederation*, p. 28.

[47] Ireland, *loc. cit.*, p. 71.

H. Oliver and W. Farron, heavy investors in Victoria real estate, or Emil Sutro, tobacco merchant, and T. N. Hibben, the prominent stationer.[48]

At all events, the flurry passed with little consequence; and within a few months Confederation was settled policy. By the time it took place in July, 1871, a brighter Victoria was ready to welcome it, hopeful indeed of the terms that had been agreed upon, including a railway to link East and West. For it well might be expected that a Pacific railway would have its terminus in or near Victoria, crossing to Vancouver Island over the narrows at its northern tip. Certainly the fact that a survey party for the projected Canadian Pacific were present in Victoria for the celebrations that accompanied the proclamation of British Columbia's entry into Confederation did not lessen the festivity.[49] And Victoria's businessmen could thus anticipate that change would also mean improvement for their community.

As the 1870's opened, it was a good thing that Victorians did have expectations from Confederation, for times continued slow in many respects: their city's population only passed 4,600 by 1874.[50] However, they could look to some federal relief from the provincial debt burden, some aid from a broader union in meeting the high costs of developing transport in the rugged hinterland. And there was the prospect of the railway, which raised new visions of Victoria as the San Francisco of the North, with its own transcontinental rail link like the newly opened Union Pacific, and its own Pacific oceanic empire of trade. Politically, at least, the city had been connected into a new continental system. Now it looked for the necessary communication network to be constructed also, to put it on the highroads of world development.

Gradually, moreover, its basic hinterland trades improved. Gold production, after reaching a low point in 1870, went up in 1871, and up still further in 1874-5, although it never came near the scale of the early sixties.[51] Coal output also began a steady climb from 1873 to 1879, though bigger years of growth would come in the next decade.[52] And if lumbering on the Island experienced no great advance yet, a new hinterland enterprise of considerable export potential made its appearance: salmon-canning. The salmon-canning industry had reached the American Pacific coast in the 1860's, from earlier beginnings in Maine and New Brunswick; but it was first established on the lower Fraser in 1870, independent of any American connection.[53] Victoria commission merchants effectively financed the Fraser river canneries and acted as agents in exporting their product directly to Great Britain.[54] For the

[48] BCAVF.

[49] *British Colonist*, July 20, 1871.

[50] *City of Victoria Directory for 1890* (Victoria, 1890), p. 122.

[51] *Annual Report of the Minister of Mines* (Victoria, 1900), chart, n.p.

[52] *Ibid.*

[53] Phillips, *op. cit.*, p. 55.

[54] K. Ralston, "Patterns of Trade and Investment on the Pacific Coast, 1867-1892: the Case of the British Columbia Salmon Canning Industry," *B.C. Studies*, No. 1, 1968-9, p. 42.

canning process offered a means of overcoming the barrier of distance between a rich North Pacific food resource and a hungry industrial market. Furthermore, it produced a valuable trade that did not face the impediment of ever-rising American tariff barriers.

British Columbian salmon-canning grew slowly at first in the seventies, faster in the eighties, by which time the industry had spread northward to the Skeena (in 1877) and to the Nass and beyond. Victoria businessmen continued to play a major role in the enterprise: J. H. Todd provides a good example. Born in Brampton, Upper Canada, he had gone to Barkerville in 1863, speculated in mines and operated a successful merchandising business before moving to Victoria in 1872 to undertake another. Through profits from mining properties, and through acting as agent for canners on the Fraser, the Todd wholesaling firm was able to acquire two canneries there and another at Esquimalt. Subsequently it added a much larger one on the Skeena obtained from another prominent Victoria house of the day, Turner, Beeton and Company. Todd and Sons, in fact, continued to operate from Victoria as late as 1954, its fishing interests ultimately going to B. C. Packers.[55]

Furthermore, the redoubtable Joseph Spratt of the Albion Iron Works early entered the business. He developed the oilery (for pressing out herring oil)that he had opened on Burrard Inlet in 1868, at the site of the present city of Vancouver, into a floating salmon cannery.[56] Popularly termed "Spratt's Ark," it was a pioneer in the area's canning industry. More important in the long run, however, was R. P. Rithet, a Victoria wholesale merchant of widespread interests and enterprises. After acting as an agent for local Fraser river canners, he organized a number of them into the Victoria Canning Company in 1891, to meet the competition of two British-backed companies, British Columbia Canning and Anglo-British Columbia Packing, who had acquired virtually all the other canneries on the river.[57] That story, however, runs beyond this study, and it is more important here to examine the advancing career of Robert Paterson Rithet as an exemplification of Victoria business in itself.

Born in Scotland in 1844, he was in the Cariboo in 1862; but after a few years came to Victoria, still in his early twenties, to find employment in the wholesale trade. In 1868 he was working for Sproat and Company; indeed, was running its Victoria office, since Gilbert Sproat, a man of many parts – merchant, insurance agent, sawmill manager, lobbyist, author and ethnologist – was then mainly in London, directing the Committee on the Affairs of British Columbia that he had organized.[58] The next year Rithet moved to

[55] BCAVF.
[56] J. M. Grant, "British Columbia in Early Times," *British Columbia Magazine*, June, 1911, p. 494.
[57] Ralston, *loc. cit.*, pp. 42-3.
[58] Richard, *loc. cit.*, pp. 22-9.

San Francisco, to deal with the firm's interests there; evidently a promotion, for Sproat had sent him "kind words of confidence" by letter.[59] And here he came in close contact with Sproat's San Francisco partner, Andrew Welch. Welch, who had begun as a bookkeeper from England and worked with Sproat in the Alberni sawmill before entering into partnership in his wholesale business, was already emerging as a wealthy and prominent member of the San Francisco commercial elite. Before his death in 1889 he was to become a millionaire several times over, do much to develop the shipping trade between Victoria and that city, gain control of the Burrard Inlet mills at Moodyville, and thus build up a large-scale lumber export business.[60] Rithet could hardly have made a better connection. It resulted, eventually, in his own partnership with Welch.

Before that transpired, he returned to Victoria, still in Sproat's service; and there in 1870 had a stiff little encounter with a Mrs. Sutton, who did not approve of his attentions to her daughter. In fact, he broke his engagement to Miss Sutton by formal note to her mama – a Victorian touch in the wider sense of the term.[61] That year, moreover, Rithet left Sproat's firm to join that of J. Robertson Stewart, one of the old original British merchants in Victoria, who carried on insurance business for British and American companies, and helped direct the British Columbian Investment and Loan Society, as well as operating a large wholesale warehouse.[62] In May of 1871, Rithet was "at present managing his business" because of Stewart's illness.[63] The latter soon decided to dispose of his interests and retire to Scotland. Andrew Welch bought him out, with Rithet's cordial approval.[64] In fact, that August a new firm was announced in the press, Welch, Rithet and Company, successors to J. Robertson Stewart. "We began," wrote Rithet, "under very favorable auspices, when the colony seems to be about to enter an era of improvement and progress. . . . with houses in San Francisco and Liverpool we should be able to make a business, and our outside connections are also tip-top."[65]

Thereafter through the seventies, and on into the eighties, Rithet's interests continued to grow: in wholesaling, shipping, insurance, lumbering, canning, grocery importing, and generally financial investment in a wide range of enterprises. With Welch, he became engaged in the sugar trade of the Hawaiian Islands; they acquired control of plantations there.[66] He invested in the mills at Moodyville, the Albion Iron Works, in sealing, whaling and in

[59] BCA, *R. P. Rithet Letterbook*, I, Rithet to G. Sproat, December 11, 1868.
[60] BCAVF.
[61] *Rithet Letterbook*, Rithet to Mrs. Sutton, April 16, 1870.
[62] *British Colonist*, November 11, 1869.
[63] *Rithet Letterbook*, Rithet to R. P. D. Duff, May 9, 1871.
[64] *Ibid.*, Rithet to A. Welch, August 24, 1871.
[65] *Ibid.*, August 25, 1871.
[66] *Colonist*, July 26, 1889.

farming. He became president of the Board of Trade and a justice of the peace in the 1870's, mayor of Victoria in 1885, then was elected to the legislature in the 1890's.[67] And on Welch's death he took over as head of both Welch and Company, San Francisco, and R. P. Rithet and Company, Victoria.[68] There is no space to deal with his later ventures in the mining and railway development of the British Columbia interior, nor in the building of deepwater dock facilities at Victoria through his Victoria Wharf and Warehouse Company. All that can be noted is his connection with the continued growth of the city's shipping interests through the founding of the Canadian Pacific Navigation Company in 1883. And this brings in another of the leading Victorian entrepreneurs of the era, John Irving.

Irving had assumed control of his father's steamship company in 1872, although only eighteen years of age. Gold discoveries in the Stikeen and Cassiar districts in the seventies revived the coastal shipping trade, and Irving moved vigorously into competition, adding new boats to his fleet. At the same time growing settlement on the mainland and its expanding needs produced more traffic to the Fraser, while soon plans for the Pacific railway's construction brought a further stimulus. In 1878 Irving obtained a contract to carry the first shipment of rails from Esquimalt to Yale, and from then on increasingly left all rivals behind.[69] His chief competitor was still the Hudson's Bay Company's fleet. In 1883 he successfully arranged to merge it with his own.

It might not be without significance that a year earlier John Irving had married the daughter of Alexander Munro, Chief Factor of the Company in Victoria – nor that two of the bride's brothers worked for R. P. Rithet, who himself had married one of the Munro girls in 1875.[70] At any rate, the Canadian Pacific Navigation Company that now emerged to combine the lines under his management had Rithet as one of its directors and chief shareholders, along with Munro and that other noted business figure, Robert Dunsmuir of colliery fame.[71] Understandably, one of the line's fast ships was the *R. P. Rithet.* Irving's shipping empire (a far cry from Captain Cooper's little schooner, *Alice*) took over minor companies at the end of the eighties, and increasingly went into inland navigation on the lakes of the interior. It was ultimately bought out by the Canadian Pacific Railway as its coastal service in 1900. That, in itself, marked the passing of Victoria's as well as Irving's steamboat hegemony; but it had been a very good run indeed.

Meanwhile Robert Dunsmuir's coal operations had grown steadily. In 1873 his one mine, the Wellington, had turned out 16,000 tons (just entering full production) to 45,000 for all those of the Vancouver Island Coal Com-

---

[67] BCAVF. See also *Victoria Illustrated* (Victoria, 1891) pp. 77-8.
[68] *Ibid.*
[69] BCAVF.
[70] *Colonist*, April 17, 1889.
[71] Lewis and Dryden, *op. cit.*, p. 303.

pany's.[72] In 1880, his holdings alone produced 189,000 tons, and three years later he bought out his partner for $600,000.[73] He was well on his way to being the province's outstanding industrial capitalist, with a fleet of cargo vessels, a mine railway and a large part of the Albion Iron Works besides.[74] As if to fit the classic picture of the nineteenth-century capitalist, he had a hard reputation with labour. He faced strikes at the mines in 1877 and 1883, brought in strikebreakers, and on the former violent occasion, a gunboat and the militia also. Apart from this, Dunsmuir now settled in Victoria, was also moving into railway promotions and construction. In 1883, the Esquimalt Railway Company of which he was president (it included the powerful figures, Leland Stanford and Charles Crocker of San Francisco, and C. P. Huntington of New York) obtained a contract from the federal government to build the Esquimalt and Nanaimo line, on terms that included a lavish grant of land.[75] Begun in 1884 under Dunsmuir's direction, it was finished in 1886, for the first time giving Victoria overland access to the coal hinterland.

Yet the seventy-mile Esquimalt and Nanaimo was a rather small consolation prize for Victoria not securing the Canadian Pacific – which was essentially what it had turned out to be. Through much of the seventies the city had envisioned and urged the transcontinental line by way of Bute Inlet and Seymour Narrows to Vancouver Island, and hotly protested proposals for a Fraser valley route to tidewater instead. In 1874 the railway on the Island was at least promised anew by the Mackenzie federal government, but the bill for it was defeated in the Senate, leaving Victoria bitterly disappointed, and much angry talk of secession in political and business circles. But though the dispute rose and fell in the ensuing years, with recurrent swells of separatism again, the fact was that the capital or the Island did not necessarily speak for the province as a whole; and the British Columbian mainland communities saw far more benefit to be gained from a Fraser valley rail route. Here was, indeed, still further indication that the island community of Victoria had been brought into a continental system, and now had little weight to bear against the whole thrust of Canadian metropolitan designs. The best that could be done was look for consolation prizes.

The Esquimalt dry dock and the E. and N. itself were two of these. And by the time that Dunsmuir undertook to build the latter (seeking truly magnificent consolation for himself and friends in terms for subsidies, coal fields and lands), Victoria interests were ready to make the best of the inevitable. Hence, in 1884, when the C.P.R. was already well advanced in its building, both up the Fraser and into the Rockies from the east, a final settlement of terms was harmoniously achieved. Victoria still had a sizeable

---

[72] Audain, *op. cit.*, p. 52.
[73] *Ibid.*, pp. 65, 73.
[74] *Colonist*, April 13, 1889.
[75] Audain, *op. cit.*, p. 79.

and prosperous maritime trading domain; its population stood at twelve thousand that year,[76] and the city was thriving and hopeful. For at least it would have its own Island railway now.

Not only was the Island railway opened in 1886, but the C.P.R. that year also carried its first through trains to the Pacific – to Burrard Inlet. And this really marked the ending of an era for Victoria, for now Vancouver's meteoric rise was under way, as the true beneficiary of the transcontinental railway, the National Policy, and the forces of Canadian metropolitanism in general. The little lumber settlement on the Inlet had been launched into its role as Canada's chief western outlet and Pacific port of entry. Not till 1898 did the import trade of the upstart city pass that of Victoria's; yet the trend was there before that was to make Vancouver the new British Columbian entrepot and distributing centre.[77] In the later eighties and nineties Victoria would further develop its coal, salmon and lumber trades, along with new growth in deep-sea fishing, scaling and also in grain exports. But a reorientation of commercial patterns from sea to land was in process, in which Victoria could not hope to dominate great new hinterlands of deep-rock mining in the interior ranges or of agriculture on the prairies. A phase was over for the maritime city; and the completion of the transcontinental railway signalized it better than anything else.

There had not been want of energy or initiative in the Victorian business community. Men like Rithet, Dunsmuir and Irving demonstrated that fact, as did W. P. Sayward, who had built a large new lumber mill at Victoria in 1878 – which by 1890, was cutting nearly eleven million feet a year itself, while Sayward's logging camps were scattered up the Island, feeding his large-scale export trade.[78] Others, perhaps, in the community had showed less enterprise, being more content with things as they were, in a pleasantly civilized little world readily open to greater worlds in San Francisco or London, but remote from the harder, cruder surroundings of the continental interior. Yet it would be difficult to prove such a point; and in any case it was not so much lack of enterprise as lack of situation and economic leverage that had placed it beyond the power of Victoria's businessmen to deal with changing patterns of trade. They had responded successfully to various favourable factors in the climate of enterprise; there was not much that could be done when the unfavorable overtook them.

There are many other names that could be singled out in the period of the seventies and eighties that would show the general stability and substance of this business community. Many firms from gold rush days continued in being, carrying on names like Southgate, Hibben, Dickson and Campbell, Sehl, Pendergast, Heisterman and others. Some early merchants indeed had

[76] *City of Victoria Directory for 1890*, p. 122.
[77] *Annual Reports of the British Columbia Board of Trade*, 1887-1900 (Victoria, 1900), tables, n.p.
[78] *Victoria Illustrated*, p. 50.

died, retired or left, the Lowes going, one to Scotland, one to San Francisco, in the seventies; David Oppenheimer shrewdly moving to Vancouver in 1886, to become "the father of Vancouver's jobbing trade."[79] Yet there were still others who had known Victoria's earlier days actively on hand, like William Ward, manager of the Bank of British Columbia since 1867 and clerk before that, or A. H. Green of Garesche and Green, whose large private bank had taken over from Wells Fargo in 1873 but who had worked for that agency previously.[80] A notable feature of the Victoria commercial community, in short, was still its continuity; new leaders largely rose from within its own ranks. But no doubt this was a result of there having been no spectacular advances since the gold rush to bring new groups of entrepreneurs. Victoria was already an "old," settled, quietly-growing town, after less than three decades of urban existence.

Its ties with San Francisco and Britain remained fully evident. In 1886, the bulk of its external trade was still directed to the former, though British goods continued to be of much significance as imports, and exports of salmon to Britain (and eastern Canada) were fast rising. Offsetting San Francisco influence, of course, was British influence through politics, capital investment, business personnel, and the very dealings with major firms in San Francisco that were themselves part of a London-Liverpool and Glasgow metropolitan network; like Welch and Company, Dickson, De Wolf, Falkner Bell, and several others.[81] Noticeable, too, was the growth of eastern Canadian agencies and imports in Victoria by this time, behind the national tariff wall; but nothing comparable to the change effected in a few years through the C.P.R. – to which one might ascribe the fact that advertisements for Canadian firms and products clearly began to displace those of San Francisco in Victoria directories by about 1890.

And thus, in a sense, passed the San Francisco of the North, gradually to be replaced with today's centre of tourism and retirement enterprises, and of that truly big modern growth-industry, provincial government. Yet the businessmen who had seen Victoria rise from a fort or a gold rush tent town to a

---

[79] L. Makovski, "Rise of the Merchant Princes," *British Columbia Magazine,* June, 1911, p. 57.

[80] BCAVF. Francis Garesche was drowned in 1874, but the firm continued in both names.

[81] See directory and newspaper advertisements of period for indications of operations of these firms. On all three, for example, see *San Francisco Directory for 1873,* M. G. Langley (San Francisco, 1873), and on Falkner, Bell specifically, W. T. Jackson, *The Enterprising Scot* (Edinburgh, 1968), pp. 222, 374, *passim.* Falkner, Bell also appear in the Lowe and Rithet letters – and Jackson's work notes that the Scottish American Investment Company, for and with which they dealt, bought extensive California ranch property on the recommendation of John Clay (who had been George Brown's estate manager in Ontario), as well as involving Thomas Nelson, the leading Edinburgh publisher in its investments. Nelson was Brown's brother-in-law, who with Clay succeeded in restoring Brown's Bow Park estate to financial health after the latter's death. One can see many ramifications here worth tracing out!

flourishing port city in well under thirty years, had no cause to minimize the comfortable affluence they had acquired, and done much to give to their adopted home.

What had the business community done for Victoria? In the first place – without at all forgetting other factors, the role of politicians and bureaucrats, of the labour force, or simply, the citizenry of consumers – they had essentially shaped its economic functions, furnished the bulk of jobs and services that made it an operative centre of urban population. In the second place, they had considerably influenced its political, social and cultural life, businessmen having widely entered into provincial and municipal politics, benevolent and religious societies, educational movements, literary, musical organizations and the like. To deal with this would be to write another chapter. All that can be said here is that the record of early Victoria's business community in participating in primarily non-economic activities in their society seems as good as, or better than, the record of similar groups in comparable Canadian cities at similar stages of development. And this, again, is not to see this very human collectivity of fallible, self-interested individuals as peerless visionaries and altruists. It may have been more a result of Victoria's relative isolation, insularity and small size, whereby the entrepreneurial element readily came to know, and feel committed to a fairly compact local society that did not soon become heterogeneous and amorphous through continued rapid growth.

In the third place, the business community marked Victoria's character in the broadest sense: in its identity, to use a not-unheard of term. The city's affiliations with California that still exist surely relate not just to sea and sunshine (unlike the humidity of Vancouver and the northwest American coast) but to the historic communications and exchange that its merchants sustained with San Francisco. Victoria's oft-noted "British" attributes, also, may well be derived less from an obsolete Bay Company officialdom or a small emigrant English gentry than from the strongly British element in the dominant wholesale trades, which easily maintained the outlook and behaviour of the old gentry elite as it rose in wealth and social position. And finally, even the faint continuing touch of cosmopolitanism in an otherwise provincial city – which seems to give it a more mature ambiance than many an older Canadian town – assuredly may come from the original non-British, non-American component of the business community that largely persisted through Victoria's first formative decades. There is, then, much more in the early development of Victoria than the affairs of provincial governments or the vicissitudes of public men.

2/The Social and Political Significance of Business Groupings

The Montreal Business Community, 1837-1853

Gerald Tulchinsky, Assistant Professor of History, Queen's University

The years between 1837 and 1853 were a highly important period in the economic development of the metropolis on the St. Lawrence river. Most outstanding were the great improvements in transportation and the dramatic expansion of industrial activity in the city. At the same time there was a significant growth of new insurance, banking and telegraph companies, as well as capital expansion amongst the older banks, established by Montrealers who were keenly aware of the potentialities in these ventures, and in enterprises designed to profit from the expansion of the city's population during this era.

Companies engaged in shipping from Montreal to ports along the Ottawa and Richelieu, as well as on the St. Lawrence above and below the city expanded while a small but flourishing ocean-going merchant marine was founded during the late 1830's, to follow on the pioneering activities of merchant ship owners such as James Dunlop. With the deepening of the St. Lawrence shipping channel in the early 1850's and the beginnings of regular steamship connections to Britain in 1853, Montreal was provided with important new facilities to augment the upper St. Lawrence canal system built to draw western trade to her port. Railways, too, among them Canada's first line, the Champlain and St. Lawrence, were constructed throughout this decade and a half. Running south from villages on the St. Lawrence river opposite Montreal to Atlantic ports, these railways provided a vital winter outlet for the city's trade. By 1853, Montreal entrepreneurs built three such lines – linked by United States railroads – to the sea. At the same time, these Montreal argonauts, with expectations characteristic of most at the dawn of the railway age, were planning to build still other lines west and north in order to secure Montreal's commercial ties with her restless hinterlands and to acquire, at last, the elusive trade from the American mid-West. By 1853, these hopes seemed to be very close to realization; out of the competition of various groups for the charter to build the Grand Trunk line, there emerged one company which began that very year to construct the Victoria bridge at Montreal to connect the western line with the Atlantic railway.

Commerce, with finance, shipping and many other attendant activities, were outstanding features of Montreal's economic life during this era. But by the end of the 1840's, manufacturing was clearly emerging as a vitally important sector. The water power of the enlarged Lachine canal, now available, induced several established Montreal industrialists and many new men to erect large factories on the banks of the waterway. These workshops, with a total labour force of more than two thousand, were a novel and striking feature of the Montreal economic and social landscape by the early 1850's; they were impressive evidence of increasing economic diversity in the metropolis of the St. Lawrence. The rise of Montreal as a manufacturing centre took place despite the unwillingness or inability of all but a few of the city's merchants to exploit this new industrial frontier.

By 1853 Montreal was at the threshold of an era of even more rapid and extensive railway and industrial development.[1] In the space of only fifteen years the city's merchant-entrepreneurs wrought great changes in the pace of Montreal's economy while another group, composed largely of newcomers, added a whole new dimension to the life of the city.

Although a handful of leaders all but dominated developments in transportation, the pattern of participation in these years reveals that many other members of the Montreal business community, and some professional men besides, were recruited to back these and various other joint stock or private ventures. Their participation may be described as consisting either of the investment of at least £500, or the holding of a directorship in any one of the many joint stock enterprises which were established in this period. Indeed their business activities might well have been much more extensive and have included other investments – for example, in real estate,[2] personal loans, or in trade – but evidence of this sort is extremely difficult to discover.

Nevertheless, though the measurable participation in the widening of economic activity in Montreal clearly demonstrates that a great many merchants were promoters or directors of at least one company, it is also clear that they were only a minority of the city's total business community, which besides wholesalers and general merchants included shipowners, industrialists and lesser manufacturers, commission merchants and agents, auctioneers and brokers, and retailers in all branches of trade.

For example, among approximately thirty local boot, shoe and leather

[1] See John I. Cooper, *Montreal: A Brief History* (Montreal, 1969), chapter 5; and his "The Social Structure of Montreal in the 1850's," *Canadian Historical Association, Report*, (1956), *passim*.

[2] The City of Montreal property assessment records from 1852 are available in the Montreal City Archives at City Hall.

store owners operating between 1845 and 1852[3] – many of them manufacturers and wholesalers as well as retailers – not one fits our particular category. Excluded are not only a large number of very small shoemakers but also owners of large establishments such as Brown and Childs (which catered to the wholesale trade) or J. and T. Bell, and W. Smyth and Co., each of whom might well have employed a significant proportion of the many local shoemakers.[4] And among the eight firms of brewers, only William Dow and William Molson shared in these transport and industrial ventures. But, of the members of approximately thirty-five hardware firms in existence between 1845 and 1852, a larger proportion did participate – including Benjamin Brewster, John Frothingham, William Workman, Joseph Barret, James Ferrier, Henry Mulholland, and Charles Wilson.

Among brokers, general merchants, auctioneers and commission merchants there was only slightly greater enthusiasm for railway and shipping companies. Out of more than fifty commission merchants and agents in Montreal during this period only four figured as promoters, directors or large shareholders in transportation and industrial undertakings. Among general merchants, however, there was a much higher proportion of participants as directors and leading shareholders of the companies established during this period. Of the forty-four firms of this sort existing in Montreal in 1843, twenty-two partners were active, including Adam Ferrie, George Moffatt, Peter McGill, John Torrance, and John Young.

One of the problems associated with accurate description and measurement of the Montreal business community arises from the mutability of some of the categories of commerce. One group described as general merchants included some who acted as importers, wholesalers and retailers of imported goods as well as brokers, commission agents, auctioneers or – in a few instances – as specialists in dry goods. Another difficulty lies in the high turnover of individuals and the frequent changes within firms during these years of shifting business conditions. For example, of the twenty-three commission merchants and agents, some of whom are also included among general merchants in 1845, ten were no longer in business in 1852.[5] This represents a decline of 43.5 per cent in six years. Over ten years the decline was greater; out of twenty firms in this category in 1843,[6] only six remained in business by 1852.[7] Of twelve auctioneers and commission merchants (a single category) in 1843, six survived until 1852.[8] But of fifteen boot, shoe and leather dealers, both wholesale and retail, only five continued to 1852, and of nineteen hard-

---

[3] *Montreal Directory* (1845-6), pp. 224-228; (1852), pp. 270-1.
[4] *Census of Canada* (1851-2), I, p. 406.
[5] *Montreal Directory* (1845-6), pp. 244-246; (1852), p. 290.
[6] *Ibid.*, (1843-4), pp. 269-271.
[7] *Ibid.*, (1852), p. 262.
[8] *Ibid.*, (1843-4), p. 239; (1852), p. 262.

ware firms eight had survived.[9] The severe attrition, however, was even more pronounced in the dry goods trade; out of twenty-nine wholesalers in 1843, only eleven lasted until 1852 and of forty retailers, only one seems to have survived the decade.[10]

Individuals or firms sometimes moved to another branch of commerce, so that the attrition was more apparent than real. In the overwhelming majority of cases, however, those who did not remain appear to have left the business community altogether, though some stayed in Montreal probably in retirement or as employees of others. Still, it is clear that there were comparatively few instances of commercial longevity in the city's business community during the period. This is demonstrated by the fact that such a small percentage of the firms in hardware, dry goods, general merchandising, auctioneering or the commission trade lasted from 1843 through to 1852.

The numbers of firms – many of which had two or more partners – also fluctuated during the decade and the amount of change varied with the branch of trade. The number of general merchandising houses varied from thirty-nine in 1843 to fifty-five in 1845, to forty-five in 1849 and thirty-five in 1852.[11] In hardware the variation in numbers was not as great, but the same general tendency to fewer firms was in evidence at the end of the 1840's; firms numbered nineteen in 1843, twenty-three in 1845, twelve in 1848 and nineteen in 1852.[12] And the number of dry goods merchants also fluctuated throughout the decade, showing a decline in the late 1840's. There were twenty-nine wholesalers and forty-one retailers in 1843; forty-five in both branches in 1845; twenty-four wholesalers and thirty-three retailers in 1848 and thirty-one and forty-two respectively in 1852.[13] Much the same pattern was in evidence among commission merchants, as their number changed from sixteen in 1843 to fifteen in 1845, to ten in 1848, and up sharply to approximately twenty-one or twenty-two in 1852.[14] In these four branches of Montreal commerce fluctuations in the number of firms were very likely related to alterations in general business conditions in the port. The expansion in these lines early in the 1840's matched the increase in the city's trade, the growth of its own population and the general prosperity in Western Canada, while the contraction at the end of the decade reflected the reduction of commerce. Many marginal firms with limited capital and small turnover were forced out of business in these years of stringency, while most of the larger and stronger houses – whose partners supported the new transportation ventures – endured throughout the period.

These figures have been compiled only for 1843, 1845, 1848 and 1852,

9 *Ibid.*, (1843-4), pp. 244-6; (1852), pp. 270-1.
10 *Ibid.*, (1843-4), pp. 264-7; (1852), pp. 281-4.
11 *Ibid.*, (1843-4), pp. 269-71; (1845-6), pp. 244-6; (1852), pp. 290.
12 *Ibid.*, (1843-4), pp. 274-8; (1845-6), pp. 250-3; (1852), pp. 293-5.
13 *Ibid.*, (1843-4), pp. 264-7; (1845-6), pp. 240-2; (1852), 281-4.
14 *Ibid.*, (1843-4), pp. 256-7; (1845-6), pp. 236-7; (1852), pp. 276-7.

and do not fully account for the brief entrance and exit of probably many other merchants into these fields in intervening years. Nor do the statistics take account of the entry of firms after 1843, some of which remained in existence until 1852 and probably beyond. What is provided, however, is a glimpse of the rapidity of change and of the size and flexibility of the business community in Montreal during the 1840's and early 1850's. It is also noteworthy that even from the commercial groups most intimately connected with trade there was, at best, only a moderate participation in shipping, railway and industrial enterprise.

Among more than one hundred leading Montrealers who were prominent as shipowners, railway and other company directors, there were members of all the city's ethnic, religious and commercial groups along with a small number of Montreal's professional men. The scale of their investments and evidence of the size of their commercial activities indicate that most were highly successful and wealthy merchants many of whose careers long preceded the 1837-1853 period. Some of the most prominent merchants, like Hugh Allan, John Young and William Workman, were just beginning lengthy careers as businessmen – entrepreneurs who dabbled occasionally in provincial and municipal politics. Yet the fifteen years from the late 1830's to the early 1850's, though only a stage, was for them a highly productive and profitable era, when they broadened their interests extensively from commerce to a wide range of enterprises that dealt in insurance, banking, mining and gas works, besides the various shipping, railway and industrial firms.

The absence of sufficient information makes it all but impossible to determine the financial worth of most Montreal merchants in this period. It is clear, however, that some of the city's wealthiest mercantile leaders refrained from putting substantial sums in railway and shipping companies and limited themselves to investing in either the City Bank or La Banque du Peuple, and in one or more of the gas, telegraph and insurance companies. But they still constituted only a handful of exceptions to the general pattern of the established Montreal mercantile group supporting and directing the new shipping and railway ventures.

This group, in short, tended to concentrate its directorial activity and local corporate investments in railway companies and shipping, and in one of the commercial banks, usually the Bank of Montreal. The amount invested need not have been very large for some of these merchants to be elected to the boards of directors. Commercial prominence, reputed wealth, service in organizations like the Board of Trade or in provincial or municipal politics, seem to have been other important criteria for directorships in the companies. Some of the most active and successful leaders were men such as Peter McGill or the Molsons and the Torrances, among others, who had managed substantial shipping firms and had probably the keenest understanding of the profit potentials in innovations in the field of transportation. The experience and enthusiasm they provided helped to elevate them quickly to positions of leadership in the railway companies. Along with those who came mostly from older trading firms, they understood better than others the necessity to improve Montreal's transportation network.

This cadre of leaders were not men of poor or modest beginnings. Late nineteenth-century eulogists' accounts (usually containing all that is known of the origins of these men) indicate that most prominent members of the Montreal commercial fraternity were favoured with considerable advantages. Family business connections in Montreal combined with some experience, and often backed by grammar school (or collège classique) education, paved the way for their easy entry and accelerated advancement to positions of leadership in the city's commercial affairs. In most cases, too, it seems that they were in command of or had access to substantial capital. Their recruitment to the largest or best established firms was not, then, a result of "upward mobility" – though this was true of a few – but the result of transference of wealth and advantage within Montreal families, or the transmigration of capital and skills, entrepreneurial and technical, from Britain or the United States.

There was also a correlation between the involvement in new transportation enterprises and various kinds of commercial businesses. As general or commission merchants, most directors and heavy investors in railways and in shipping were dealers in imported goods or in exported commodities, or both. Others specialized in certain kinds of items, hardware predominating. These were the branches of Montreal commerce most amenable to improvement by more efficient transportation and that expectation provides one additional explanation of their practitioners' active and keen pursuit of improvements of this sort.

Although many of the most prominent Montreal businessmen were of Scottish birth or family background, this was by no means characteristic of the whole business community, or of any one of its branches. Besides the Scots, the Montreal business community was also composed of significant numbers of American, English, or Irish-born and a sizeable Canadian group from both the English and French-speaking communities. Although national, ethnic, and religious divisions kept Montreal socially and politically divided to some extent, there was considerable integration in the realm of business, especially among members of the English-speaking groups. Even apart from the joint-stock companies, there were a number of co-partnerships in which for limited terms sons of the heather joined up with Vermonters or French-Canadians.

American-born merchants came to be among the most eminent men in their special branches of Montreal business affairs. They included the Wards, in the construction of steam engines, and John Frothingham, Benjamin Brewster, J.T. Barrett, Samuel Hedge, Jacob De Witt and Samuel Bonner in the hardware trade – described by Senator Edward Murphy in 1882 as a business sector "...in which Americans largely preponderated."[15] Among staples dealers, Massachussetts-born Horatio Gates had been the recognized Montreal leader until his death in 1834;[16] but following him were several others, such as Harrison Stephens, who was of immense importance in this trade, Stanley Bagg, Jedediah H. Dorwin and Orlin Bostwick, all of whom were active until the mid-1840's. In chemical and drug-manufacturing and wholesaling there was the Lyman family, in private banking John E. Mills, in flour milling Ira Gould, in rope manufacturing John Converse: all American-born Montreal businessmen of significance. So, too, were Charles Seymour, an active commission merchant throughout the late 1840's and early 1850's, Caufield Dorwin, an exchange and money broker, D.W. Eager and Charles L. Ogden provision inspectors, Norman Froste, a general merchant, William F. Hagar, a hardware merchant, J.A. Perkins, a commission merchant, William Phillips, a wealthy grocer, George Warner, an exchange broker and commission merchant,[17] and Hannibal and N.S. Whitney, who operated a wholesale drygoods house in these years. There were many other members of the Montreal American community, which was strong both in the number of men engaged and their prominence in commercial and industrial pursuits.

Though it would be difficult to determine the exact number of American-born merchants or to quantify their prominence,[18] they were probably the second most significant national group in the economic life of Montreal in the period from 1837 to 1853. Although they mixed with others somewhat more freely than in the days when steamboat builder John Ward had first arrived in 1818, the Americans, like the Montreal Irish, the Scotch, and the Jews, maintained national bonds in their own American Presbyterian Church[19] and in the New England Society,[20] keeping alive, perhaps like Ward,[21] fond hopes of returning home from their "exile" in Canada.

Other immigrants who had become commercially prominent in Montreal

[15] P.A.C., M.G. 27, I, E 10A, Edward Murphy Papers, II.

[16] McGill University, McCord Museum, Jedediah Hubbell Dorwin, Antiquarian Autographs. This is a collection of signatures of various businessmen with whom Dorwin was associated in the Canadas, United States, Maritime provinces and Britain. Most autographs – many followed by Dorwin's brief but very valuable comments – are numbered. The Gates entry, however, is not numbered.

[17] *Montreal Directory* (1845-7), pp. 64, 71, 80, 93, 161, 166, 211. These men are known to be of U.S. birth either by membership in the American Presbyterian Church, by a notation to that effect in Dorwin's "Antiquarian Autographs," or by their signing a statement proclaiming loyalty to Britain by Montrealers of U.S. birth. This statement was published in the *Montreal Transcript* on November 28, 1838.

[18] But see David C. Knowles, "The American Presbyterian Church of Montreal," 1822-1866 (M.A. Thesis, McGill University, 1957), p. 156.

[19] *Ibid., passim.* See also Elizabeth Ann McDougall, "The American Element in the Early Presbyterian Church in Montreal, 1786-1824" (M.A. Thesis, McGill University, 1965).

[20] Knowles, *op. cit.,* p. 238.

[21] Americans living in Montreal experienced social discrimination, according to Ward, Public Archives of Canada, MG 24, D19, Ward Papers. See letters John to Silas Ward,

by the 1840's were small numbers of Irish, including the Workman brothers, William and Thomas, Edward Murphy, a drygoods merchant, and Henry Mulholland who owned a large hardware firm. John and Thomas Ryan, who were general commission merchants, also operated their own ships between Montreal and Quebec. These businessmen, along with a few others such as tavern owners, artisans, or operators of small shops of various types ,[22] were the sole representatives in the business world of Montreal's huge Irish population – by 1851 some 11,736[23] – most of whom were working-class and many of them common labourers.[24]

The small number of Jewish merchants in Montreal, however, were drawn from a community numbering less than two hundred.[25] Theodore Hart, Jesse Joseph and Alexander Levy were in commerce, while the Moss family, as well as selling clothing, manufactured some of its own merchandise. Of these, only Theodore Hart had any connection with the shipping or railway companies.

There were some English-born among Montreal's prominent businessmen, but apparently fewer than either Scots, Americans or French-Canadians. Among the English were Joseph Shuter who, as well as serving on the board of the Champlain and St. Lawrence, was also a director of the Bank of Montreal from 1831 to 1847. Steamboat builder William Parkyn and engineer John Bennett were leading English-born businessmen of Montreal; as was William Lunn, a director of the Bank of Montreal from 1828 to 1849, of the Provident Savings Bank, the Montreal Insurance Company from 1839 to 1849, and a promoter of the New City Gas Company. So, too, was brewer John Molson, whose sons, John, William and Thomas (the former two in particular) were both directors of the Bank of Montreal, and partook of other joint-stock ventures besides their railway and shipping interests.

While French-Canadians were not numerous as directors of, or large investors in many joint-stock companies, they were nevertheless a significant element in the business community, though not all were themselves in com-

---

Oct. 30, 1821 and February 1, 1829. Among the reasons for this discrimination was the belief that many American criminals were taking refuge in Canada: [Auto] Biography of Harrison Stephens, (typescript), p. 5, Mr. Murray Ballantyne, Montreal. One indication of the contempt (or fear) felt by some Montrealers towards Americans in local business was expressed by R. H. Bonnycastle in his *The Canadas in 1841* (London, 1842), pp. 76-7, quoted in W. H. Parker, "The Towns of Lower Canada in the 1830's," R. P. Beckinsale and J. M. Houston, eds., *Urbanization and Its Problems* (Oxford, 1968), p. 396.

[22] D. C. Lynne, "The Irish in the Province of Canada," (M.A. Thesis, McGill University-1960), p. 79. See also John Irwin Cooper, *Montreal, the Story of Three Hundred Years* (Montreal, 1942), chapt. 14.

[23] *Census of Canada* (1871), IV, p. 206.

[24] See *Montreal Directory* (1842-53), *passim*; H. C. Pentland, "The Lachine Strike of 1843," *C.H.R.*, XXVIII (1948), pp. 255-277.

[25] *Census of Canada* (1851-2), I, p. 40.

merce. Pierre Beaubien, a medical doctor, was a director of La Banque du Peuple, the Mutual Insurance Company, a promoter of the Montreal Mining Company, and the owner of considerable real estate in Outremont. Alexandre Maurice Delisle, a lawyer, was a director and large investor in both the Champlain and St. Lawrence and the Montreal and Bytown, besides owning valuable local property. Most French-Canadian businessmen, even the wealthiest, however, kept aloof from extensive involvement in railway ventures, though not from other joint-stock companies. Yet, Olivier Berthelet, who held extensive real estate, was a backer of only the abortive Banque des Marchands, while Jean-Baptiste Bruyère was a director of the Montreal Gas Company from 1842 to 1849. Augustin and Maurice Cuvillier took active roles, respectively, in the Committee of Trade and the Bank of Montreal. Édouard Raymond Fabre, publisher of *La Minerve* and a local bookseller, was active briefly as a director of La Banque du Peuple. Jacques Grenier, a dry goods merchant and an officer in the Montreal Board of Trade, was also a director of La Banque du Peuple, another director of which, Pierre Jodoin, held a £300 investment in the Montreal and Lachine railway.

Then, in addition to his political activities, Augustin Norbert Morin was active in the St. Lawrence and Atlantic Railway Company and was a director of the Montreal Mining Company. Joseph Vallée, a wholesale provisions merchant, was a director of the City Bank, La Banque du Peuple and of the City and District Savings Bank. Amable Prevost and Jean Bruneau (both drygoods merchants) and Frédéric-Auguste Quesnel were all directors of La Banque du Peuple.[26] Louis Comte, a builder, and Joseph Bourret, a barrister, were directors of the Mutual Insurance Company of Montreal while the latter was also a director of the Montreal Mining Company.

Hence, while few French-Canadians were directors or heavy investors in railways, some were active in the City Bank, (besides dominating La Banque du Peuple), the Montreal Mining Company and the Mutual Insurance Company. Besides these concerns, a few French-Canadians were active also in shipping and shipbuilding. Many of them followed various branches of commerce throughout the 1840's and early 1850's. In some sectors they were less prominent than in others. Among commission merchants and agents, for example, there were practically no French-Canadians. None were listed in a directory of 1845 and only one in 1852. This was true also of the hardware trade, wholesale and retail, while there was one French firm of brewers out of eight during these years. There were no French-Canadian brokers nor one firm of boot, shoe or leather dealers that lasted for more than a few years. And out of seventeen auctioneers operating between 1845 and 1852, only three were French-Canadian, while one firm lasted only a few years.[27]

[26] *Montreal Directory, passim.*
[27] *Ibid.,* (1845-6), p. 221; (1852), p. 262.

But in the dry goods trade, both wholesale and retail, and especially the latter, there were many French-Canadians. Of approximately twenty-five wholesalers operating between 1845 and 1852, four firms, or sixteen per cent, were French-Canadian; but of thirty-two retail firms (some of which also dealt in wholesale), eighteen or fifty-five per cent, were French-Canadian.[28] From this group came some of the most active French-Canadians who participated in joint-stock ventures including the Hudons (shipping), Jean-Louis Beaudry, Jean-Baptiste Bruyère, Amable Prevost, Jean Bruneau, the Cuvilliers (also in auctioneering) and the Massons.

This was, nevertheless, a small degree of participation from a French-speaking community which in 1851 was forty-six per cent of the city's total population.[29] Though these joint-stock ventures and others were not the only channels of participation in Montreal's economy in this period, they were the newest and in some ways the most dramatic. But they all required acceptance of the structure of joint-stock companies as well as agreement with the purpose for which these companies were established. With the latter probably most French-Canadian businessmen would have agreed, but not with the requirement that they relinquish control of their funds to an impersonal company. French-Canadians might have been less attracted to these ventures, which were beyond their direct control, than they were to investments in enterprises directly under their own management[30] from which a quicker and more predictable return was forthcoming. Nevertheless, though their businesses were small and short-lived in many instances, some of Montreal's most important traders and investors were drawn from the French-Canadian community.[31]

The Scots, finally, comprised the dominant group in most forms of commerce and were the most active in the enterprises examined in this study.

[28] *Ibid.*, (1845-6), pp. 240-2; (1852), pp. 280-4.

[29] *Census of Canada* (1871), IV, p. 206.

[30] Norman Taylor has recently demonstrated that this was one important consideration governing the unwillingness of certain French-Canadian industrialists to expand their factories: Norman W. Taylor, "The French-Canadian Industrial Entrepreneur and His Social Environment," Marcel Rioux and Yves Martin, eds., *French Canadian Society* (Toronto, 1967), pp. 271-95.

[31] Jean Bruchési's assertion that "ce n'est qu' à partir de 1840 ou 1850 que les Canadiens français sortiront de l'ombre, qu'ils envahiront notamment pour y occuper la première place, le commerce des épiceries en gros" – is open to serious doubt. See Jean Bruchési, "Histoire Economique," Esdras Minville, ed., *Montreal Economique* (Montreal, 1943), p. 29. An examination of McKay's Montreal directories for 1845-6, 1852 and 1854, reveals that very few French-Canadian firms were listed either as "Grocers, Tea and Spice Dealers," or as "Grocers, Wine and Spirit Dealers": *Montreal Directory* (1845-6), pp. 247-9; (1852) pp. 291-2; (1854), pp. 341-3. One contemporary noted, however, that "the rise of the French element in wealth, business importance and influence in trade in the city, since the establishment of the Banque du Peuple in 1834, and the change produced by the events of 1837, are wonderful to those who can remember their depression up to that time": Thomas Storrow Brown, "Montreal Fifty Years Ago," *New Dominion Monthly* (1870), March, 25.

Among brewers, there was William Dow; among brokers, John and Robert Esdaile; and Robert Anderson owned a glass and china firm. All of these were leading firms in their fields. In the dry goods trade during the 1840's and early 1850's Scottish-dominated firms were the most prominent, especially in the wholesale branch. Among these firms were those of the Gillespies, the Gilmours, of J. G. Mackenzie, Joseph Mackay, Henry Morgan and Dougald Stewart, while in the retail trade there was William Stephen. John Young was prominent as a commission merchant. The Gilmours and the Allans owned the chief ocean shipping establishments, while the Redpaths, prominent contractors, became leading industrialists during the 1850's.

These were the most famous of the Montreal Scottish merchants, whose biographies – written for the late nineteenth century biographical dictionaries – – included details about birthplace and early education in Scotland. But there were many others with Scottish names among the mercantile community about whom there is very little biographical information. Since they were not members of the American community, from which they might conceivably have come, and were almost certainly not French-Canadian or Irish, it is reasonable to assume that they were Scots in origin. And they were legion. In the dry goods trade alone Scottish names abounded: Campbell, Douglas, Fraser, Reid, Galbraith, MacFarlane, Morrison; in brokerage, Gairbairn, Geddes, and Macdougall; and among commission merchants and agents, Dougall, McTavish, McGill, Anderson, Bell, Auld, Campbell, McDonald, McKay, McNaught, and Redpath.

Scots were the single most active group in the company ventures examined here. The exploits of William Dow, James Ferrier, William Edmonstone, John Gordon Mackenzie, David Macpherson, Peter McGill, Hugh Allan and John Young in shipping and in railways – as well as in telegraph, gas, mining and insurance – were of outstanding importance in these enterprises. Others participated at lesser levels. Robert Anderson was a promoter of the Montreal and Bytown railway and a director of the New City Gas Company, while Robert Armour, a bookseller, had directorships in the City Bank, the Montreal Insurance Company, the Montreal Gas Company, and the Montreal Provident and Savings Bank. Adam Ferrie an Ayrshireman who emigrated to Canada in 1829 after a successful commercial career,[32] helped to establish the City Bank[33] to compete with the Bank of Montreal, was also a director of the Montreal Insurance Company and the Montreal Gas Company, as well as of the Gore Bank in Hamilton. John Jamieson, a director of the Bank of Montreal (1835-1839), was a merchant who operated his ship *Douglas* in Montreal's ocean trade. James Leslie, a general merchant who had retired by the mid-1840's, was nevertheless among the promoters of

---

[32] See *Life Hon. Adam Ferrie* (n.p., n.d.).

[33] P. R. Austin, "Two Mayors of Hamilton: Colin C. Ferrie and George E. Tuckett," A Speech before the Head-of-the-Lake Historical Society, March 11, 1855 (Typescript), p. 8.

John Young's abortive scheme of 1849 to build a canal from the St. Lawrence at Caughnawaga to Lake Champlain. Andrew Shaw, a general merchant, was an extensive ship owner with three large ocean-going barques, and one of the founders and early presidents of the Montreal Telegraph Company. John Smith, like Shaw, was a promoter of the Montreal Steamship Company, the Montreal Insurance Company and a director of the Montreal Mining Company. William Watson, the flour inspector whose estate helped to establish the Ogilvie milling company, was a founder of the Montreal Insurance Company, and the owner of real estate in the city. And William Macdonald served as a director of both the St. Lawrence and Atlantic, and the Montreal and New York.

Besides these interests, many of the same businessmen of Montreal were prominent shareholders and directors of the insurance, telegraphs, mining and gas companies established in Montreal during these years. Moreover, these same individuals were connected with well-established business institutions such as the commercial banks – most of them with branches throughout the Canadas[34] – which also increased their capitalization during the 1840's; the Bank of Montreal to £750,000[35] in 1842 from £500,000, and a further £250,000 in 1853. The capital of the City Bank was raised to £500,000 from £300,000 in 1847,[36] La Banque du Peuple was chartered in 1844 at £200,000.[37] As for new ventures, the Montreal Mining Company was incorporated in 1847 at a capital of £200,000,[38] the Montreal Fire, Life and Inland Navigation Assurance Company (later the Montreal Insurance Company) at £200,000 in 1843,[39] the New City Gas Company in 1847 at £25,000.[40] The older Montreal Gas Light Company increased its capital the same year to £50,000,[41] while the Montreal Telegraph Company,[42] and the

---

[34] Out of five banks operating in Toronto in 1851, two were branches of Montreal banks: Donald C. Masters, *The Rise of Toronto, 1850-1890* (Toronto, 1947), p. 18. This was only one aspect of Toronto's subordination to Montreal at this time; *ibid.*, p. 19.

[35] Merrill Denison, *Canada's First Bank, A History of the Bank of Montreal* (Toronto and Montreal, 1966-7, 2 vols.), II, pp. 9, 67.

[36] *Stats. Prov. Can.* (1847), 10 and 11 Vic., c. 116. The City Bank's capital, however, was reduced two years later to £375,000 as a result of heavy losses; *ibid.*, (1849), 12 Vic. c. 185.

[37] *Stats, Prov. Can.* (1843), 7 Vic., c. 66. La Banque du Peuple was established in 1835 by Viger, De Witt and Company with a capital of $300,000: Adrien Leblond de Brumath, *Histoire Populaire de Montréal Depuis Son Origine Jusqu'à Nos Jours* (Montréal, 1890), p. 367. See prospectus of the bank; Chateau de Ramézy, Montreal, p. 827.

[38] *Stats. Prov. Can.*, 10 and 11 Vic., c. 63.

[39] *Ordinances of the Special Council of Lower Canada* (1841), 3 and 4 Vic., c. 37; *Stats. Prov. Can.* (1843), 6 Vic., c. 22. The company was renamed the Montreal Assurance Company in 1850; *ibid.* (1850), 13 and 14 Vic., c. 121.

[40] *Ibid.*, (1847) 10 and 11 Vic., c. 79.

[41] *Ibid.*, (1847) 10 and 11 Vic., c. 80.

[42] *Ibid.*, (1847) 10 and 11 Vic., c. 83.

Montreal and Troy Telegraph Company were capitalized at £ 15,000 and £ 5,000 respectively. Though not all of the capital was raised at once, these new companies are evidence of faith in the strength of the city's economy felt by contemporary Montrealers, who supplied most of the capital and direction for these enterprises.

Thus shipping, railway and industrial activities were only aspects of the larger setting of business development in Montreal during the period from the late thirties to the early fifties. In the former enterprises, as well as in all the new ventures being established during this period, a segment of the Montreal business community demonstrated impressive talent for mobilizing the capital resources of the community to broaden the city's economic capacity. Yet their interest was, with few exceptions, limited mainly to endeavours that would enhance the commercial power and extend the metropolitan reach of Montreal. Shipping, railways, insurance, banking and even telegraphs were all enterprises which served this end. Fewer men were prepared to move into industrial ventures with the same degree of alacrity. Most of those who did, participated in concerns the same as, or similar to, the ones in which they were already involved, even though (in most of these instances) it was on a modest scale. Conversely, extremely few of the leading industrialists participated actively in promoting railways or shipping enterprises – except for a few steamboat builders who briefly owned shares in the vessels they built.

The portion of the Montreal business community that first took up the challenge of railways and of ocean-going steamships was above all attempting to solve the problems created by the inadequacies of lower St. Lawrence river transportation, just as their predecessors had earlier tried to overcome similar difficulties in the upper section of the river by advocating the construction of the Lachine and other canals. There was hard economic reasoning behind their promotion of railways south to the north-eastern United States, which they viewed as a short land bridge to the Atlantic. Supplemented by steamships, the railways, they hoped, would reduce transportation costs to a level that would make Montreal a greater entrepot of trade. In short, these Montrealers were attempting to complete the last links in the transportation chain which they saw as vital to the city's continuity as a metropolitan centre. It is worth emphasizing that there was in this little economic nationalism – there was no hesitation in linking their own railways to American sister lines being eagerly thrust northward by New England entrepreneurs. Nor were all of these Montrealers entirely convinced that railways, after all, provided the best solution to the city's transportation problems. Some were prepared to support John Young's dubious scheme of building a new canal between the St. Lawrence river and Lake Champlain. But the main aim was still to improve transport to the sea.

Soon, however, many Montreal businessmen became convinced of the utility of railways as tools of opening up new hinterlands and of ensuring the city's hegemony over its traditional ones. Other entrepreneurs were prepared to build railways that would rival already existing or soon-to-be-completed lines from Montreal. The abortive St. Lawrence and Ottawa Grand Junction scheme provides an example of such ambitious enterprise on the part of a small but influential group which attempted to use the railway to develop a new hinterland. These new ventures were also evidence of optimism, both for the future of Montreal's commerce and for the availability of sufficient capital in the city.

Thus, between 1837 and 1853 the city's business community experienced not only general enlargement, consolidation in its various branches of commerce, and the addition of significant groups of manufacturers, but also witnessed the rise of a group of aggressive entrepreneurs in transportation and industrial ventures. Gaining experience in these and other local joint-stock companies, they were able to generate wealth and self-confidence for similar ventures during the later 1850's and well beyond.

Though notably united throughout the period in many joint-stock companies in which they were shareholders, directors or customers, most Montreal businessmen would have considered themselves as a community long before. Whether importer or exporter or, more often, both; whether wholesaler or retailer in hardware, clothing or dry-goods, there were strong bonds of unity between the members of Montreal's commercial houses notwithstanding their business competition. The very imprecision of business categorization – the term general merchant including specialists in hardware, or drygoods who also dealt in wheat – suggests the flexibility which characterized many businessmen as they crossed and recrossed each other's business lines. Moreover, they signed for each other's notes and loans and they formed numerous co-partnerships and acted as assignees for bankruptcies among them.[43]

Symbolizing this unity were several institutions that flourished in the period. Associations of businessmen like the Montreal Board of Trade brought together virtually all the city's merchants in an active association which eagerly, often stridently, asserted commercial interests before provincial and imperial governments and, when necessary, before the rest of the Montreal community. Changes in the usury and bankruptcy laws, navigation on the St. Lawrence by vessels of United States registry, improvements to the navigation on Lake St. Peter and the Ottawa river, enlargement of the Lachine canal's locks and basin, and uniform postage rates, were among the many requests addressed to the provincial and imperial governments in a series of Montreal petitions throughout the period. Numerous memoranda were despatched to government on a host of matters affecting business conditions, conveying complaints, suggestions, accusations. Characterized by a minimum of obsequiousness, flourishes and circumlocutions, these statements from the Board of Trade are indicative of the sense of power and habitual authority

___

[43] See *Morning Courier*, Feb. 27, 1849.

possessed by the Montreal business group, which believed itself the equal of politicians and officials, and believed also that the satisfaction of its interests would benefit the whole province.

The Board of Trade was established in 1842 to succeed the Committee of Trade, " ... a standing committee of Merchants to be authorized by their constituents to watch over the general interests of trade of the country," formed twenty years earlier by Montreal merchants who realized the inadequacy of " ... the solitary exertions of individuals or ... occasional hasty and inadequate deliberations of public meetings. ... "[44] Horatio Gates, George Auldjo, George Moffatt, François Antoine Larocque, Peter McGill, John Forsyth, Charles L. Ogden, James Leslie, John Flemming, Henry McKenzie, Campbell Sweeny and Samuel Gerrard[45] had been elected to the Committee to defend Montreal's trading interests by making representations to those in authority, to assist members, to decide disputes between members and to put down illicit trade. Fifty-four merchants,[46] virtually the whole commercial community, had subscribed to this early association, which soon busied itself with petitions to the Lower Canadian legislature for aid in deepening the channel of the St. Lawrence and other matters which merchants brought to their attention.[47]

For nine of the Committee's seventeen year existence – it ceased to function after June, 1839 – George Auldjo was its president, serving from 1825 to 1833 and from 1835 to 1836.[48] With his brother, Alexander, a partner in the firm of Auldjo and Maitland, George Auldjo personified the transitional entrepreneurship of Montreal in that era of the rapid decline of one Canadian staple and the rise of others. Though connected by marriage to John Richardson, a leading partner in one of the firms dominant in the North West Company, and though his own firm (in operation as early as 1785 under John Auldjo,[49] another brother) had undoubtedly participated in the fur trade, George was deeply involved in Montreal's newer commercial affairs. He and George Garden, another partner, were both directors of the Bank of Montreal during the 1820's and, as a sideline to their general merchandising business, (specializing in wines, spirits and drygoods) they acted as Montreal agents for two foreign insurance companies.[50] George Auldjo was the owner of considerable real estate in Montreal besides.[51] The careers of other original members on the

[44] "Origins of the Montreal Board of Trade," *Journal of Commerce*, Series II, LV (1927), p. 28.

[45] Montreal Board of Trade, *One Hundred and Twenty-Fifth Anniversary Volume* (Montreal, 1947), n.p.

[46] "Origins of the Montreal Board of Trade," p. 29.

[47] *Montreal Transcript*, Apr. 21, 1838.

[48] *125th Anniversary Volume*, n.p.

[49] Robert Campbell, *History of the Scotch Presbyterian Church, St. Gabriel Street, Montreal* (Montreal, 1897), p. 99.

[50] *Ibid.*, *Phoenix Assurance Company, First in the Field* (Montreal, 1954), pp. 8-10.

[51] Archives of the Superior Court, Montreal, V. H. Griffin, Dec. 11, 1838, pp. 16, 382; *Montreal Transcript*, Apr. 13, 1839.

executive of the Committee of Trade, McGill, Gerrard, Moffat, Larocque and McKenzie,[52] testified to the shift away from the fur trade to a new commercial orientation and to greater diversity.

In 1842 the Montreal Board of Trade received a charter from the legislature of the new United Province of Canada.[53] Like its parent, the organization was primarily concerned with the health of Montreal's trade and specific matters which affected the business climate.[54] These concerns were reflected in the membership, which was drawn almost entirely from the commercial community, and in the issues deliberated at general and council meetings. The leading officers of the board and the members of its subcommittees were the very élite of the trading fraternity.[55]

The years 1845 and 1846 were especially busy and anxious ones for the Board. Besides its usual concerns that year about improvements to the city's commerce, including the St. Lawrence and Atlantic railway, enlarging the port of Montreal, deepening Lake St. Peter, improvements to the navigation of the Richelieu[56] and the establishment of uniform postal rates,[57] the Board was faced with serious external threats to Montreal's established trade pattern. The American drawback legislation of 1845, allowing goods to pass duty free through the United States by inland navigation to Canada,[58] would increase the preference for importing via United States ports. Thomas Cringan, the Board's Vice-President, wrote gloomily that unless extra duties were placed on goods imported through the U.S. this trade " . . . will . . . stop a most important trade, that of the direct trade to Cuba and Porto Rico; will injure the carrying trade, that of the direct trade to Cuba and Porto Rico; will injure the carrying trade both by sea, and the canals in Canada; will tend to divert a considerable amount of the Canada trade from Great Britain, to the United States, and by depriving vessels of their outward freights, raise the freight upon exports; as also by diminishing the upward freights of the Canal boats very much enhance the downward freights."[59]

[52] Campbell, *op. cit.*, pp. 366-8.

[53] *Stats. Prov. Can.* (1841), 4 and 5 Vic., c. 90.

[54] An organization akin to a Junior Board of Trade was formed in January, 1841 for the " . . . mental improvement of the numerous and highly respectable body of young men engaged in counting houses and stores, and who are to become the future merchants in the city"; *Montreal Transcript*, Jan. 30, 1841.

[55] The presidents from 1836 to 1871 included Jules Quesnel, Austin Cuvillier, J. T. Brondgeest, George Moffat, Thomas Cringan, Peter McGill, Thomas Ryan, Hugh Allan, John Young, Luther Holton, Thomas Kay, Edwin Atwater, Thomas Cramp and Peter Redpath; *125th Anniversary Volume*, n.p.

[56] P.A.C., R.G. 4, C1, Provincial Secretary's Correspondence, CLI (1846), p. 1027, hereafter cited as "Prov. Sec. Corres."

[57] *Montreal Gazette*, Apr. 15, 1845.

[58] Prov. Sec. Corres., CXXVII (1845), p. 1386.

[59] *Ibid.*, (enclosure). These views were echoed by submissions from the Quebec Board of Trade and by Thomas Ryan, a Montreal ship-owner. See also *ibid.*, CSLIX (1846), p. 781.

The Board's reaction to an even more serious threat posed by the withdrawal of imperial protection for Canadian wheat and flour was stronger and more protracted, and immediately took the form of recommendations for repeal of Imperial duties on American wheat imported into Canada,[60] and for repeal of the Navigation laws.[61] Some Montreal merchants, led by John Young, however, found the Board's policy still too cautious and established the Free Trade Association to seek the adoption in the Province " . . . of Free Trade principles . . . in all their comprehensiveness . . . ."[62]

Throughout the 1840's and the early 1850's, the Montreal Board of Trade remained pragmatic, defensive and cautious. Though its council meetings and annual general sessions occasionally considered grand schemes like John Young's proposed St. Lawrence and Lake Champlain canal to sharply increase Montreal's trade,[63] the members devoted their main attention to more mundane concerns such as those previously mentioned. The Board never did support Young's proposal, and only mildly endorsed railway projects, even during the latter part of this period when several such schemes were under way with many leading businessmen as backers. Restrained in endorsing new fangled transportation schemes, the Board worked actively to improve the river systems that had traditionally carried Montreal's trade and to change specific laws, provincial and municipal, in order to improve the climate of business enterprise in the city.

While the Montreal Board of Trade was the largest and most broadly representative of all sectors of the local business community, there were also other organizations of businessmen. Some were informal and small groupings, such as the Board of Brokers, an association of produce dealers through whom a large proportion of Montreal's export trade of staples was conducted by 1850.[64] After meeting each week to exchange information, the brokers published a circular listing prices and quantities of commodities, shares bought and sold at Montreal as well as news of ship arrivals from sea, from inland ports, and ocean freight rates.[65] This publication helped to systematize commercial news for merchants in Montreal, upcountry centres and Britain.[66] A reorganization of the Board of Brokers took place in 1862, perhaps because of increasing specialization in the brokerage business. The Montreal Corn Exchange, which was formed in 1863, included several of the men previously prominent in the earlier association.[67] A number of Montreal merchants who traded shares and securities had been meeting regularly

[60] *Ibid.*, p. 884.
[61] *Ibid.*, CLXVIII (1846), p. 2895.
[62] *Ibid.*, CLVI (1846), p. 1595.
[63] *Morning Courier*, Apr. 5, 1849.
[64] *Ibid.*, Apr. 3, 1850.
[65] Montreal Board of Trade Archives, J. and R. Esdaile Circulars, 1848-1851.
[66] Montreal Stock Exchange, "One Hundred and Thirty-two Years of Progress" (typescript), 1.
[67] O.R. Evans, *Montreal Corn Exchange Association*, 1863-1963.

since 1854,[68] and were probably the same group which had come together in 1849 to seek incorporation as the Merchant's Exchange and Reading Room of Montreal.[69]

Another organization, the Mercantile Library Association formed in 1841,[70] was more than just a club for the city's commercial fraternity and more than just a library and reading room with trade news publications from abroad.[71] The association was a kind of Mechanic's Institute for merchants, and it is noteworthy that in the early Victorian "age of improvement" there was a search for self-improvement among many Montreal merchants who attended the annual winter series of lectures offered through the 1840's in search of deeper understanding of the complexities of their commercial world. These included discourses by John Dougall on "The Principles and Objects of Commerce,"[72] by Augustin Norbert Morin on "the importance to the inhabitants of cities to encourage the production in the country of articles for importation,"[73] by W. H. Sherwood on the usury laws,[74] by Henry Driscoll, Q.C., on commercial law, and on "joint-stock companies and the law of principal and agent,"[75] by T. S. Hunt on the discoveries of modern science,[76] or by the Rev. Mr. Cordner on the importance of shoes in history.[77] The well attended lectures provided the listeners with ideas and information through the long Montreal winters while commerce lagged, awaiting the spring cargoes of ships from sea and the vessels from upriver with produce from the West. Montreal's merchants were fortified also by assurances from Lord Elgin himself, who, in introducing the 1848-9 lecture series, spoke of " . . . the useful and honourable career of the British merchant, . . . which, when [followed] with diligence and circumspection, leads always to respectability, not unfrequently to high honour and distinction."[78]

[68] John S. Johnson, History and Organization of the Montreal Stock Exchange (M.A. Thesis, McGill University, 1934), p. 14.

[69] *Stats. Prov. Can.* (1849), 12 Vic., c. 194.

[70] *Montreal Transcript*, May 18, 1841.

[71] The association prided itself on the number and value of the books in its collection. Members were occasionally urged to contribute to the Library's book fund: *Montreal Gazette*, Mar. 14, 1849. There was keen interest in the library and in the type of periodicals placed in the reading room. See *Report of the Speeches and Proceedings at a Special Meeting of the Mercantile Library Association of Montreal, Held on Monday Evening, April 8, 1850, to take into consideration the action of the Board of Direction in respect to the expulsion of the "Christian Inquirer" from the News Room* (Montreal, 1850).

[72] *Montreal Gazette*, Mar. 6, 1845.

[73] *Ibid.*, Apr. 15, 1845.

[74] *Ibid.*, Mar. 17, 1847.

[75] *Ibid.*, Jan, 3, 5, Feb. 23, 1849.

[76] *Ibid.*, Feb. 11, 1850.

[77] *Ibid.*, Jan. 16, 1852. Lectures on topics of interest to businessmen, or those who aspired to be, were the type most commonly offered. Some were published. See Edward L. Montizambert, *A Lecture on the Mercantile Law of Lower Canada* (Montreal, 1848).

[78] T. Walrond, ed., *Letters and Journals of James, Earl of Elgin* (London, 1873), p. 68.

Though characterized by heterogeneity in racial composition, religion and business affiliation, as well as by a constantly changing personnel, the Montreal business community had an obvious unity of purpose – the pursuit of maximum profits – for which viceregal blessings provided comforting, but unnecessary justification. Yet most of its members already realized the need for voluntary association in societies to lend collective strength to these private aims which they all shared. The 1840's, therefore, was a period of transition not in the reshaping of their purposes but in the pursuit of them during the concurrent series of crises caused by external forces and the challenges and opportunities of the North American transportation revolution.

In the period from 1837 to 1853 Montreal's successes and failures in meeting these circumstances were largely the result of the conjuncture of strengths and weaknesses arising from its location on the major artery of navigation, which, however – despite the construction of canals – could not match the advantages provided by alternative United States routes for the interior trade. Though it was the metropolis of the St. Lawrence, its businessmen came to learn that this was not an advantage on which they could rely for success in the competition for commercial hegemony. The experiences of the city's merchant-entrepreneurs in shipping and railway enterprises would reveal both the vestiges of the old dreams and belief in the possibility of a master-stroke, along with a growing belief that limited objectives involving some continental integration were more realistic for the business interests of Montreal.

The Social Origins of the Canadian Industrial Elite, 1880-1885

T. W. Acheson, Assistant Professor of History, University of
New Brunswick

The Canadian industrial record of the 1880's presents the picture of a small
agricultural economy rapidly developing a sophisticated manufacturing base.
In part this growth represented the continued expansion of an industrial
sector which had emerged in the preceding three decades. In part, too, the
expansion of these traditional elements and the development of specific new
forms of industry were initiated largely under the aegis of the new experiment
in economic nationalism which had begun in 1879. The record of growth
was impressive. Throughout the decade industrial output expanded at a
compound annual rate of 4.8 per cent, one of the highest at any period in the
nation's history, and the highest of any decade marred by prolonged economic depression.[1]

The expansion depicted by the figures on output provides only one measure of the speed at which the process of industrialization was occurring in
the period. In fact, the growth of manufacturing facilities in many industries
occurred at a much more rapid rate, particularly during the halcyon years
between 1880 and 1884. In political, if not economic, terms the policy of
economic nationalism expressed in the tariff structure of the decade was
entirely successful. As early as 1885 the expansion of the means of production in a wide variety of manufactures had proceeded to the point where the
nation had the capacity to provide for all domestic needs in these areas. For
example, the 125 per cent increase in the value of cotton cloth output between the two ends of the decade[2] scarcely demonstrates the amazing growth
of the manufacturing potential of the industry, a development which more
than tripled the number of mills, spindles, looms and capital investment in
half a decade.[3]

The industrial experience of the period was directed, in a greater or lesser
way, from hundreds of traditional commercial and agricultural communities
by thousands of entrepreneurs. From among this multitude a few hundred
individuals appear to have largely dominated the industrial life of the period
and to have initiated most new developments. It is with this elite of 168
industrialists that this paper is concerned.[4]

[1] Gordon W. Bertram, "Historical Statistics on Growth and Structure of Manufacturing
in Canada 1870-1957," Canadian Political Science Association Conferences on Statistics
Papers (1962 and 1963), p. 103. Bertram estimates that the rate of real manufacturing
output increased from 4.4 per cent in the decade 1870-80 to 4.8 per cent in the decade
1880-90, then declined to 3.2 per cent in the 1890's. Only in the decades 1900-1910 and
1919-1929 did the rate of growth surpass that of 1880-90.
[2] Canada, *Census* (1881), III, 485; (1891), III, p. 120.
[3] *Monetary Times*, Oct. 5, 1888 – "Canadian Cotton Mills."
[4] The selection of the members of this group was made qualitatively. Emphasis was placed

Although the family firm was still the dominant business form in the early part of the decade, there were already sufficient joint-stock firms developing in the nation for the elite to contain two identifiable functional groups: those who were manufacturers by vocation – about five-sixths of the total – and those by avocation, mostly composed of policy-making wholesalers who

Table 1. Primary Occupation of the Industrialist

	% of Group
Shipper	1
Wholesaler	9
Finance Executive	1
Transportation Executive	2
Manufacturer	85
Other	2
Total	100
Total Cases: 168	

Table 2. Principal Manufacturing Interests

	% of Group
Leather Products[1]	5
Food Products[2]	13
Musical Instruments	3
Wood Products[3]	24
Paper Products	4
Textiles[4]	21
Iron & Steel Products[5]	23
Other[6]	7
Total	100
Total Cases: 168	

[1] Includes leather, shoes, boots.
[2] Includes liquor, tobacco, flour, meat, confectionery, sugar, spices.
[3] Includes lumber, pulp, furniture, building materials.
[4] Includes hosiery, woollens, cottons, silk, clothing, hats.
[5] Includes agricultural implements, castings, machinery, stoves, nails, screws, cast & bar iron, steel.
[6] Includes rubber, oil, cement, glass, paint, chemicals, jewellery.

on the importance of the individual to the industry rather than simply including all persons of a particular rank throughout a number of firms. The choice of individuals was made on the basis of 3 criteria: 1) those who were regarded by contemporaries as the major industrial leaders of the period – accounted so by their inclusion in one or more of the numerous biographical dictionaries which became so popular at the end of the nineteenth century; 2) those who were consistently referred to in trade journals as being significant to companies; 3) those active in positions of leadership in trade organizations such as the Canadian Manufacturers Association and in major concerns.

dominated the firm through the medium of the corporate directorate.[5] The following tables will serve to present a broad characterization of this powerful socio-economic element.

Table 3. Regional Distribution

	% of the Group	% of the General Population
Maritimes	19	20
St. Lawrence[1]	40	38
Lake Peninsula[2]	37	38
The West[3]	4	4
Total	100	100

Total Cases: 168

[1] Includes Quebec and eastern Ontario to the Kingston area.
[2] Kingston to the Lakehead
[3] Lakehead to the Pacific – the latter "region" is actually several regions lumped together because of the minuteness of the sample.

This study will attempt to present a collective social portrait of this influential group, to examine the degree of social mobility and migration which it represented, and to assess the relative influence of "inherited" social tradition and environmental factors on the behaviour patterns of its members.

Social mobility in the elite of the 1880's could not be divorced from the question of immigration. In striking contrast to the American experience of the period,[6] the upper levels of the Canadian social system were almost entirely dominated by immigrants or children of immigrants. About half of

[5] The group of course varied slightly in composition. Several members died during the course of the period; others were added.
[6] Considerable work on this subject has been done in the United States largely under the auspices of the Research Centre of Entrepreneurial Studies at Harvard. C. Wright Mills attempted a generational study of American business leaders from 1600 to 1919 in 1945. Four years later, using much the same technique, William Miller undertook an examination of the social characteristics of the business elite of the first decade of the twentieth century. For comparative purpose Frances Gregory and Irene Neu examined the origins of selected industrial leaders of the 1870's in 1952. It is this latter study which is the source of most of the comparative American data used in this article. Gregory and Neu drew their sample of 247 leaders in about equal proportions from two manufacturing industries – textiles and steel – and from railroad companies. See: C. Wright Mills "The Business Elite: A Collective Portrait," *Journal of Economic History*, V (supplement), (1945), pp. 20-44; William Miller, "American Historians and the Business Elite," *Journal of Economic History*, IX, (1949), pp. 184-204; William Miller, "The Recruitment of the American Business Elite," *Quarterly Journal of Economics*, LXIV (1950), pp. 242-53; Gregory and Neu, "American Industrial Elite in the 1870's," in William Miller, *Men in Business* (Cambridge, Mass., 1952), pp. 193-212.

its industrial leaders were foreign-born,[7] although this proportion varied radically from region to region. Virtually all of the successful Maritime entrepreneurs were native-born, as were nearly half of those of the St. Lawrence region. By contrast, more than three-fifths of the Lake Peninsula leaders were foreign-born, a proportion which significantly exceeded the proportion of immigrants in the population of Ontario at any time in the nineteenth century.[8]

Table 4. Birthplace of the Industrial Elite

United States *Elite* %		*Canada* *Elite* %	*General Pop.* %
	Maritimes	18	18
	Quebec	16	31
	Ontario	16	34
	West	0	2
90	Native Born 51%		85%
	Scotland	20	3
	Ireland (Ulster)	.5	4
	Ireland (South)	2	
	England	6	4
	United States	12	2
	Germany	4	1
10	Foreign Born 49%		14%
100	Total	100	99
247	Total Cases	164	4,324,000

Coupled with this immigrant strength among the elite was the almost total absence of any inter-regional migration in eastern and central Canada: Scots, Americans, Irishmen, Englishmen, and even Germans were far more significant elements in the industrial life of these regions than were Canadians from any other region.

[7] Since Canada was a colony of Great Britain, no British subject in Canada could be legally classified as "foreign-born." The term is applied here to *all* individuals not born in Canada solely for the purpose of comparison with the American situation.

[8] It is tempting to hypothesize that the elite of the 1880's tended to reflect the demographic characteristics of the population of the 1830's and '40's. This is untrue, as can be demonstrated by reference to the Lake Peninsula. The earliest census of birth place, taken in Upper Canada in 1842, indicated that 48 per cent of the population was foreign-born. (Canada, *Census of 1871*, IV, 136).

Table 5. Migration and Industrial Opportunity by Region

Region of Success	Mari-times %	St. Lawrence %	Lake Pen. %	Birthplace Scot. %	Eng. %	Irish %	Amer. %	Germ. %	Total %	Number %
Maritimes	85	3	–	3	3	3	3	–	100	31
St. Lawrence	2	42	2	23	3	10	15	3	100	63
Lake Peninsula	–	2	35	28	8	7	13	7	100	63
The West	29	13	29	–	29	–	–	–	100	7

The diverse social traditions of the group were further emphasized in the birthplace of the fathers of the elite members. Nearly four-fifths of the latter were foreign-born, a proportion which would rise to nine out of ten if the Maritimes were excluded from the sample. The dominant element, expectedly, was Scottish, but the relative equality of size of the other major groups –

Table 6. Father's Birthplace

United States Elite %		Canada Elite %	General Pop. Male[1] %
	The Canadas	9[2]	
	The Maritimes	13	
89	Native born:	22	62
	Scotland	28	
	Ireland (Prot.)	14	
	Ireland (Catholic)	4	
	England	13	
	United States	15	
	Germany/Switzer.	5	
	Foreign born:	78	38
	Total	100	100
	Total Cases: 151		

[1] Canada *Census of 1891*, II, pp. 228-30. Unfortunately information showing the birthplaces of males over 40 is not available.

[2] A proportion which drops to only 4 per cent if the French-Canadians are removed from the group.

American, Irish and English – gave confirmation to the hypothesis that not only, did no common "Canadian" social tradition exist, but that the diversity of the immediate background of the members of the group severely retarded its development.

Table 7. Father's Birthplace by Region

Father's Birthplace	Region			
	Maritimes	St. Lawrence	Lake Peninsula	The West
	%	%	%	%
The Canadas	–	16	8	–
The Maritimes	64	2	–	–
The United States	3	18	19	–
Ireland (South)	7	5	5	20
Ireland (North)	13	13	5	20
Scotland	10	31	37	40
England	3	12	17	20
Germany	–	3	9	
Total	100	100	100	100
Total Cases	30	58	58	5

Table 8. Father's Occupation

American Elite %		Canadian Elite %
13	Professional	8
	Businessman [1]	23
54	Manufacturer	32
	Manager [2]	5
25	Farmer	26
8	Craftsman	6
	Labourer	–
100	Total	100
167	Total Cases: 105	

[1] Includes shippers, construction executives, and a few retailers, but largely composed of wholesalers.

[2] Includes most civil servants, sea captains, plant managers

Yet, if the nativity of the Canadian manufacturer and his father presented a picture which was the antithesis of the American experience, the occupations of the fathers of the two national elites coincided to a remarkable degree. At first glance it would appear that most Canadian industrialists inherited rather than acquired their status in society: nearly one-third were sons of manufacturers, more than a fifth were raised as children of men engaged in a variety of other business occupations.

Nonetheless, it is dangerous to generalize that a relatively closed social system thus operated. Although it was true that the Alger-like popular conceptions of the rise of the poor boy to the great industrialist were false – not a single member of the elite identified himself as the son of either an industrial or an agricultural labourer – it is equally true that a far higher status was attached, on the whole, to the fathers of the non-manufacturing entrepreneurs, to those merchants and other businessmen who had just begun to enter the manufacturing field as promoters and directors of the new joint stock companies. The leading Montreal dry goods wholesalers, Matthew and Andrew Gault, who dominated several major textile manufactories, were sons of a Tyrone merchant and ship owner who had married into the Donegal gentry.[9] Their Halifax equivalent, John F. Stairs, who controlled most Canadian rope output, was the son and grandson of major Nova Scotian shippers.[10]

By contrast the manufacturers had traditionally been the proletarians of the business community, usually having emerged out of a system of skilled labour.[11]

Table 9. Occupations of the Fathers of Manufacturers and Other Entrepreneurs

Father's Occup.	Manufacturers	Other Mfg. Entrepreneurs
	%	%
Labourer	–	–
Farmer	30	13
Craftsman	8	–
Manager	3	13
Manufacturer	38	6
Business	16	50
Professional	5	18
Total	100	100
Total Cases	89	16

9 *Cyclopedia of Canadian Biography* (CCB), pp. 431-2.

10 W. J. Stairs, *History of Stairs-Morrow* (Halifax, 1906), pp. 5-6.

11 The President of the Canadian Manufacturers Association, W. H. Storey, made this point quite clearly in his opening address to the Association's 15th annual meeting: "In this meeting we are all workers. Most of us have risen from workingmen and are workers yet . . ."

Many of the complaints against organized labour voiced by manufacturers in the 1880's were not so much the class reaction of the liberal capitalist, as that of successful craftsmen vehemently denying the principle that all should be rewarded equally regardless of ability or contribution to output. The concept held by many Ontario manufacturers of their status and role in society was reflected in the ease and frequency with which the editor of the *Canadian Manufacturer* fulminated against the "rich" and their privileged institutions, the universities and other professions. As late as 1893 the editor was able to postulate a social theory which lumped the manufacturer and the labourer into a common exploited working class:

> It has become painfully obvious that society is divided into a privileged class and a class who not only have to bear their own burden, but are outrageously taxed to help support the others . . . The colleges are not accessible to the poor man's son, but the poor man is forced to contribute to the education of the rich man's son!

He went on to add that many who became "professionals" could have made some significant contribution to society had they engaged in a useful occupation such as farming, the crafts, or even manual labour."[12]

In large measure the attitudes of the industrial trade journals reflected the training and life style of most manufacturers. Even those who were sons of manufacturers rarely had been raised in the traditional manner of gentlemen. While there were manufacturers such as John Barber, who was able to assume the management of his father's Streetsville woollen mills at the age of twenty and to succeed to the latter's Georgetown paper mills at thirty-nine,[13] most followed the pattern of Charles Raymond, whose father, a Massachusetts carriage manufacturer, apprenticed him as a machinist in the Lowell Cotton Mills Co. at the age of seventeen. Raymond worked in several ventures as a practical machinist before successfully establishing his own small sewing machine firm at Guelph at the age of thirty-six.[14]

Aside from the broad range of experiences undergone by those who had been sons of a variety of "manufacturers" the degree of social mobility evident in the elite varied widely from region to region and from birthplace to birthplace. The Maritimes, where two-thirds of the fathers of manufacturers were also manufacturers, represented the region of most limited mobility; the Lake Peninsula, where the proportion of native born manufacturers was least, was that of the greatest. For Englishmen, Irishmen, and Americans, the move from Europe usually represented a case of horizontal mobility; in effect, an unpenalized status transfer into the new society. Herbert Ives, son of a Connecticut hardware manufacturer, moved to Montreal in 1859 and immediately established the first hardware manufactory in the colony;[15]

---

12 *The Canadian Manufacturer*, Nov. 17, 1893, "Student Pranks."

13 *CCB*, p. 438; *Canadian Manufacturer*, (CM), July 6, 1888; *Canadian Men and Women of the Time* (1898) [CMWT], p. 48.

14 *Canadian Biographical Dictionary* (CBD), I, pp. 378-80; *CM* July 20, 1888.

15 *CCB*, II, 629; *CMWT* (1912), p. 571.

George Burland, scion of a wealthy Anglo-Irish family, after the period of service with his publisher-uncle, established the British American Bank Note Company in Montreal;[16] Thomas Daniel, son of a Bedfordshire gentleman, succeeded to his uncle's St. John wholesale dry goods firm, the largest clothing manufactory in the maritime colonies.[17]

Most upward mobility within the elite involved a movement from the farm to the workshop, a not surprising phenomenon since more than half of those classified as gainfully occupied males in Canada were considered to have been members of the "agricultural class" in 1851.[18] While members of this agrarian group were drawn from several ethnic origins and geographical areas, a clear majority, regardless of whether they themselves were British or Canadian born, were sons of Scottish farmers.

The most characteristic Canadian success stories were those of the large group of young sons of Scottish farmers who, armed with little more than a traditional craftsman's training, descended upon the Canadas in the 1840's and '50's, and by dint of industry and frugal living rose in middle age to the proprietorships of substantial manufacturing establishments.

In part, the unusual success gained by the Scottish members of the elite in the field of manufacturing was due to the emphasis which this form of enterprise placed upon technical skill and workmanship in the middle nineteenth century. Capital and commercial aptitude were ultimately necessary to the development of the manufactory, but the principal asset of such a firm was the outstanding skill which could produce a superior product. To the ambitious lad with a thorough training, vocational success was more easily gained in manufacturing than in any other form of business endeavour, a fact reflected in the tendency of most farmers' and tradesmen's children to enter the industrial elite as manufacturers rather than by any other avenue. While Calvinist values and cold oatmeal porridge undoubtedly played a formative role in the development of certain qualities in the character of most young Scots, the more immediate cause for their industrial success seems to have stemmed from their superior preparation for the industrial life.

This had little to do with the traditional education process. As a group the Scots were probably the most poorly educated element in the elite – and the best trained. By comparison, the native born were the best educated – particularly those from Nova Scotia – and the most poorly trained. The apprenticeship system had been a common feature in the early lives of most of the manufacturers' sons who had been raised in Lake Peninsula, the St. Lawrence, the United States, England, Ireland and Germany, a fact which seemed to bear out the hypothesis that most manufacturers tended to think of themselves as the highest of the lower orders of society. What distin-

---

[16] *CCB*, II, 441-2; *CMWT* (1898), p. 321.
[17] *CCB*, II, pp. 610-1.
[18] Canada, *Census of 1871*, IV, p. 193.

Table 10. Ethnicity and Social Origins

Father's Occupation

	Can	Mar	US	Ire(S)	Ire(N)	Scot	Eng	Germ	Total	Total Cases
					Father's Birthplace					
Farmer %	4	0	20	0	12	52	12	0	100	25
Craftsman %	0	0	0	0	17	66	0	17	100	6
Management %	0	0	25	0	0	60	40	0	100	5
Manufacturing %	13	22	19	0	15	19	6	6	100	33
Business %	8	25	13	8	13	4	29	0	100	23
Professional %	0	0	34	0	11	11	22	22	100	9

Table 11. Comparative Ethnic/Economic Origins

Father's Occupation

	Can	Mar	US	Ire(C)	Ire(P)	Scot	Eng	Switz/Germ
					Father's Birthplace			
Farmer %	14	0	29	0	23	46	19	0
Craftsman %	0	0	0	0	8	14	0	20
Management %	0	0	0	0	0	11	12	0
Manufacturing %	0	54	35	100	38	21	12	40
Business %	29	46	18	0	23	4	45	0
Professional %	57	0	18	0	8	4	12	40
Total %	100	100	100	100	100	100	100	100
Total Cases %	7	13	17	2	13	28	16	5

guished the Scots from all other groups was that most farmers' sons had also undertaken this arduous training and, because they had started earlier than most others – usually at thirteen or fourteen years of age – they were able to compete for positions of responsibility at a comparatively young age. Trained in a variety of skills – providing vocations as dissimilar as those of foundry-man, baker, cabinet maker, engineer, dry goods merchant, woollens maker – the young Scots learned their lesson sufficiently well that by the 1880's the clan dominated most manufacturing fields. This was exemplified by David Morrice, Andrew Elliott, Andrew Paton, James Cantlie, George Stephen in textiles, James Thomson in paper, William Christie in bakery products, George A. Drummond in sugar, John Walker in oil, Robert Hay in furni-ture, James Goldie in flour, William Bell in musical instruments,[19] and by John Haggart, Alexander Gartshore, John Bertram, Thomas Wilson, Rob-ert McKechnie, James Smart, John McDougall and John Milne in iron and steel products. The Scots, moreover, had acquired a virtual monopoly of the St. Lawrence textile industry and the Lake Peninsula iron and steel indus-tries.

For the poorer members of this group, success had come as the result of diligence and persistence. Robert Hay had worked as a journey man cabinet-maker for several years following his apprenticeship. At the age of twenty-seven, with a partner, $400 capital, and two apprentices, he established a furniture-making shop in Toronto which developed into the largest firm of its kind in the country.[20] Andrew Elliott struggled his way from farm labour-er to store clerk to retail grocer until, at the age of forty-four, he had sufficient capital to erect a small woollen mill.[21]

In the final analysis, it was the transfer of technology from the more sophisticated Scottish industrial economy to the more primitive Canadian, coupled with the traditional practice of providing some form of training for those sons who would not inherit, that gave the Scots their advantage. They came from an industrializing society in the mid-nineteenth century and came prepared, on the whole, to function in and to give leadership to the fledgling Canadian industries. Moreover, because of the Scottish-Canadians' tendency to perpetuate this system of "providing a trade" for the sons, and because of the intense ethnic loyalties which characterized the outlook of most Scottish migrants, the group managed to preserve this technical superiority over members of most other ethnic groups even into the second generation.

Thus, through ties of ethnicity, John Gartshore, a pioneer saw and grist mill manufacturer who had come from Scotland and established the Gart-shore Foundry and Machine Works at Dundas in 1838, succeeded in father-ing virtually every major foundry in the south-western Lake Peninsula. At

---

[19] Although his primacy was seriously challenged by the Germans Theodore Heinzeman and Samuel Nordheimer.
[20] *CBD*, I, pp. 192-96.
[21] *CBD*, I, pp. 476-7; *CCB*, II, p. 92.

the height of the railway movement of the 1850's, Gartshore employed more than three hundred men and trained a number of apprentices. One of these, Thomas Wilson, came with his Scottish farmer father to Dundas in 1843 and began his apprenticeship as a machine founder. Following this he worked for Gartshore for twenty-five years, and finally purchased the works from his employer in 1870, reconstituting it as the Dundas Foundry and Engine Works.[22] A second apprentice, Robert McKechnie, came with his family from Glasgow, and in 1847 was apprenticed as a pattern maker in Gartshore Foundry. From there he went on to found the Canadian Tool Works, to become the largest machinery manufacturer in Canada by 1880.[23] His partner in the latter concern was John Bertram, a native of Peebleshire who was brought to Canada in 1852 as an engineer with the Gartshore Foundry, and who left in 1865 to assist in the creation of the Canada Tool Works.[24] Gartshore's eldest son, Alexander, after a common school education, was sent to New York for a four-years' apprenticeship in the foundry trade, and returned to enter his father's firm in 1858. Twelve years later, on the latter's retirement, they sold the firm, and the younger Gartshore moved to Hamilton, where he established a major new foundry manufacturing castings and iron pipe.[25] Gartshore's second son, William, worked with the Toronto Wheel Foundry before marrying the daughter of John McClary and assuming the general managership of the McClary Manufacturing Company of London.[26]

Social mobility on a more modest scale was also evident among the number of the native-born members of the elite. Hart Massey persuaded his prosperous farmer father to finance a small foundry at Newcastle in 1847. From this developed the principal agricultural implements firm in the country.[27] The most notable example was that of Alexander Gibson, New Brunswick's lumber king. The son of an immigrant Ulster farmer, Gibson began his career as an axeman in the St. Stephen lumber industry. By heroic efforts, which made him a legend in his own lifetime, he succeeded in creating one of the largest industrial complexes in Canada by 1890, an empire based on lumber, cottons and railroads.[28]

The apprenticeship system of the 1840's and '50's had provided a basic training for much of the industrial elite of the 1880's. By the latter date, however, with the increasing development of mass production factory tech-

---

[22] *CBD*, I, pp. 529-30.

[23] *Prominent Men*, p. 278.

[24] *Prom. Men*, p. 122; *Industrial Canada*, March, 1905; *CM*, July 6, 1888.

[25] *Men of Can.* I, 170; *CM*, July 20, 1880; *Prom. Men*, p. 131.

[26] *IC*, Jan., 1914, *CMWT* (1912), p. 434.

[27] *Encyclopedia of Canadian Biography*, I, p. 8; *CM*, Aug. 17, 1888; *Prom. Men*, pp. 774-6; *CCB*, pp. 774-6.

[28] *Our Dominion. Historical and Other Sketches of the Mercantile Interests of Fredericton, Marysville, Woodstock, Moncton, N.B., Yarmouth, N.S., etc.* (Toronto, 1889), pp. 48-53.

niques, the whole system was gradually being abandoned in most manufacturing trades. It had disappeared entirely in the boot and shoe, textile, and clothing industries, and even the iron and steel trades, traditionally the most demanding crafts, were being given over. Because of the traditional role of these crafts as a vehicle for social mobility – through the ladder pattern of apprentice-journeyman-master – it is difficult not to sympathize with the often-heard lament of craftsmen that they were being demeaned to factory hands, and that the new factory managers were deliberately conspiring to destroy this traditional avenue of promotion.[29]

Table 12. Paternal Ethnic Origins

American Sample %		%	*General Pop.* %
7	Scottish	32	16
(Can) 2	American[1]	22	-
11	Irish Protestant	14	22
	Irish Catholic	3	–
71	English	13	20
–	French	7	30
–	Loyalist	5	–
4	German/Swiss	4	6
100	Total	100	100
175	Total Cases	155	4,234,000

[1] In the case of the American Sample this includes those of Canadian origins. In the Canadian Sample this includes those of American birth. The census, however, made no such distinction and the American born were considered as belonging to some European tradition.

Aside from the factors of birthplace, occupation, social mobility and training, the social ethos which shaped the members of the elite was compounded of a cultural milieu centered on the factors of ethnicity, education, religion, community and region.

In a period when four-fifths of the group were either immigrants or the sons of immigrants, the question of ethnicity was deeply significant, ethnic loyalty frequently acting as the primary focus of identification. The most notable feature in this respect was the dominant place of the Celtic fringe within the elite: Scottish and Irish Protestant elements alone comprised near-

[29] Royal Commission on the Relations of Labour and Capital in Canada (1889) *Evidence*, II, pp. 20-30, 46, 296-302; IV, pp. 308, 364, 456-69. Canada, *Sessional Papers* (1896), No. 61, "Report upon the Sweating System in Canada."

ly an absolute majority of the group; and Protestant and Catholic Irish, peculiarly drawing from a common tradition, together outnumbered those of English origins.

The demographic changes of the previous fifty years were also evident in the birthplace of the elite by ethnic groups. Those of Irish, English, French, and Loyalist origins were largely native born; Scots, Germans, and Americans were mostly not.

Because the mingling of newer and older groups injected both a fluidity and a lack of cohesion to the societies comprising the Canadian state, it tended to add to the appeal of ethnic loyalty, and permitted the individual to view himself as an extension of his cultural metropolis. The Scots were notorious for this self-image. John Gartshore was perhaps the most obvious example of this form of identification, but others were as common in the Montreal Scottish community. Similar traditions were maintained by both varieties of Irishmen. Matthew Gault founded the Irish Protestant Benevolent Society of Montreal, and most Irish Protestant industrialists, including George Burland of the British American Bank Note Co.[30] and the paper manufacturer, J. C. Wilson,[31] actually supported this ethnic welfare organization. Irish Catholics maintained their own ethnic charities in which the Halifax Sugar manufacturer, Thomas Kenny, played a major role.[32] Many, too, played an active role in the Irish Home Rule movement. It was, as the New Brunswick lumber baron and Conservative member for Gloucester, Kennedy Burns, observed, an issue which:

> should be dealt with and spoken of by every Irishman and descendent of Irishmen and every lover of Ireland and freedom the world over. Especially do I think it the province of Irishmen occupying representative positions to speak out boldly on an occasion of this kind.[33]

Thomas Long, the Collingwood flour and cottons entrepreneur and Conservative member of the Ontario Legislature actually served as a delegate to the Irish National Convention of 1896.[34]

The tradition and ideology of ethnicity was usually institutionalized in one of the existing denominational structures. The correlation between Scottish, English, native Irish, and German immigrants and the traditional religious denominations in Canada was extremely high. For example, eleven of the fourteen Scottish-born members of the elite in the Lake Peninsula were Presbyterians. The three non-conformists in the group consisted of a Scottish Congregationalist – scarcely a doctrinal radical – and two Anglicans, both of whom had left their native Presbyterian faith in middle age.

[30] *CCB*, II, pp. 441-2; *CMWT* (1898), p. 132.
[31] *CCB*, pp. 149-50; *CMWT* (1898), p. 1091.
[32] *CCB*, II, pp. 729-31; *MT*, Nov. 7, 1908.
[33] Canada, *Commons Debates* (1887), pp. 67-9.
[34] *CMWT* (1898), p. 588.

Above all, the manufacturers as a group were religious men, devoted in varying degrees to this symbol of their traditional culture, a fact reflected in the alacrity with which most of them disclosed their religious allegiances.[35] In some, perhaps, it was a perfunctory duty performed out of a sense of tradition or conformity to a religious norm demanded by their community. For most it was a matter of conviction, and a number of the more prominent members of the elite actively participated in the most significant religious functions of their denominations.

Table 13. Religion

United States Elite %		Canada Elite %	General Pop. %
14	Presbyterian	36	16
25	Anglican	19	15
6	Methodist	19	18
–	Roman Catholic	12	42
4	Baptist	6	6
22	Congregationalist	4	1
11	Protestant	4	2
100	Total	100	100
144	Total Cases	138	4,234,000

The cotton kings, Matthew and David Morrice[36] were respectively a warden of Christ Church Cathedral in Montreal, and a Presbyterian elder. The New Brunswick lumber king, Alexander Gibson, imposed his puritan Methodist ethic upon the entire town of Marysville by prohibiting the sale and consumption of all alcoholic beverages. The Hamilton clothing manufacturer, Senator William Sanford, was a Methodist steward, trustee and member of General Conference,[37] while the Brantford agricultural implement manufacturer, Alanson Harris, occupied every position in the Baptist denomination open to a layman.[38] David Morrice, the St. Stephen ship builder, Zechariah Chipman,[39] the Montreal broom manufacturer, Horatio Nelson,[40]

[35] A common practice was that of describing oneself as a "Strong Presbyterian" (or other denomination). 138 out of 168 voluntarily disclosed this affiliation. Equally important, at least that number *had* a known specific traditional affiliation. Only one declared himself to be a "liberal agnostic."

[36] *CCB*, p. 325; *Men of Canada*, II, p. 23; *CMWT* (1898), p. 652.

[37] *CCB*, pp. 30-31; *CCB*, II, pp. 753-5; *CBD*, I, pp. 434-46; *MT*, July 14, 1899; *Men of Canada*, I, p. 74.

[38] *Men of Canada*, I, p. 154.

[39] *MT*, Oct. 26, 1883; *CBD*, II, pp. 657-8.

[40] *CBD*, II, pp. 71-2.

Table 14. Religion by Region and Birthplace

	Maritimes		St. Lawrence		Lake Peninsula		West	
	Native %	Foreign %	Native %	Foreign %	Native %	Foreign %	Native %	Foreign %
Presbyterian	33	25	19	53	15	42	20	50
Anglican	21	25	19	14	5	27	40	50
Methodist	30	—	4	14	55	6	20	—
Roman Catholic	4	25	46	3	—	3	20	—
Baptist	4	—	4	3	15	10	—	—
Congregationalist	8	—	4	3	5	3	—	—
Lutheran	—	25	4	7	5	3	—	—
Total	100	100	100	100	100	100	100	100
Total Cases	24	4	26	30	21	6	5	2

Table 15. Religious Offices by Region

	Maritimes		St. Lawrence		Lake Peninsula		West		Total	
	Mfs.	Offices	Mfs.	Offices	Mfs.	Offices	Mfrs.	Offices	Mfrs.	Offices
Methodist	4	6	1	1	7	13	—	—	12	20
Presbyterian	2	2	5	7	6	9	—	—	13	18
Anglican	3	3	2	2	2	2	—	—	7	7
Baptist	—	—	—	—	4	8	—	—	4	8
Congregationalist	2	2	2	2	1	2	—	—	5	6
Lutheran	—	—	—	—	1	1	—	—	1	1
Total	11	13	10	12	21	35	0	0	42	60

and the Toronto hat manufacturer, John Gillespie,[41] all shared a common office – that of sabbath school superintendent. Guelph had its two principal manufacturers in this office: the woollens manufacturer, Thomas McCrae, at the Presbyterian Sunday School,[42] and the sewing machine manufacturer, Charles Reymond, at the Baptist.[43] In all, thirty-nine manufacturers, about one quarter of the group, held fifty-six major religious offices.

The importance of religion was further characterized in the gifts and bequests of the elite. Canadian manufacturers were far more likely to contribute to religious than to secular causes. While few could match the generosity of the Massey family which heavily endowed a variety of Toronto Methodist institutions,[44] Senator James Ross of Quebec left $135,000 to various Presbyterian organizations at his death in 1894, and another $120,000 to several Protestant educational and charitable organizations.[45] Others, such as Alanson Harris, William Buck, David Morrice and A. F. Gault, made numerous more modest contributions. In describing A. F. Gault, *The Canadian Magazine* asked, "Is he better known as a captain of industry or as fairy godfather to the Church of England?"[46] Only in the largest centres, among the most cosmopolitan individuals, was the practice of secular contributions beginning to gain ground. Hart Massey endowed a music hall, but his efforts were overshadowed by the gifts of the Montreal industrialists, W. C. MacDonald and G. A. Drummond, to secular, educational, and health causes.[47]

Yet, although ethnic traditions frequently persisted into the second and third generations, and while the traditions and training of the foreign-born was always crucial to the career and outlook of the first generation Canadian, the social ethics of even the immigrant was altered and shaped by the traditions of the community in which they settled and achieved their success.

[41] *CBD*, I, p. 514.

[42] *CCB*, pp. 677-9.

[43] *CM*, July 20, 1888; *CBD*, pp. 318-20.

[44] Hart Massey contributed heavily to Metropolitan Church, established the Massey Music Hall and the Fred Victor Mission, and at his death left most of his fortune in trust, the revenues to be used to provide for the Methodist Colleges at Sackville, Toronto, Winnipeg, and St. Thomas; the American University, the YMCA, Salvation Army, Sick Children's Hospital and the Upper Canada Bible Society. One son, Walter, left approximately $100,000 to church and charity at his death in 1896; another son, Chester, contributed $205,000 to seven Methodist Churches, $200,000 to Victoria College, $100,000 to Toronto General Hospital, $150,000 to the YMCA, $25,000 to Methodist Social Action. See: *MT*, Dec. 31, 1901; *CMWT*, p. 738; *ECB*, II, p. 8; *CCB*, pp. 774-6; *Prom. Men* pp. 326-30; *CM*, Aug. 17, 1888; Merrill Denison, *Harvest Triumphant* (Toronto, 1948), pp. 141-2.

[45] *MT*, July 6, 1894, "Bequests of Sen. J. G. Ross,"

[46] *The Canadian Magazine*, XXI, p. 201.

[47] MacDonald gave more than $5,400,000 to McGill University, most of it for the establishment of an agricultural college. Drummond founded St. Margaret's Home for Incurables at Montreal. *Montreal*, III, pp. 304-10; *ECB*, II, p. 1; *CMWT*, p. 684.

The attitudes of the communities in turn were partially shaped by the regional experiences of the immediate colonial past. At some point in this contin-
uum, inherited and environmental traditions either met and co-existed to
create a pluralistic society, or met and melded to create a new community
consensus.

The most obvious consequence of the latter development was the inability
of ethnic groups in the elite to sustain their cultural homogeneity within the
context of the national society – a phenomenon most evident in the religious
affiliations of the second and third generation Canadian.

Table 16. Religion of the Native Born and Foreign Born

	Foreign Born	*Native Born*
	%	%
Presbyterian	46	23
Anglican	21	17
Methodist	9	28
Roman Catholic	5	18
Baptist	5	6
Congregationalist	3	5
Other Prot.	11	3
Total	100	100
Total Cases	65	76

In the Lake Peninsula the Methodist Church had firmly established itself in
many communities as the institution which embodied the ideology and aspirations of the native British American society. Methodism tended to replace
ethnicity and ethnic loyalties with a secularized religious tradition as a "free"
church, free from the taints of both Establishment and Americanism; it
could well claim to represent homogeneous indigenous nativism. It counted
among its supporters and converts most of the second generation members of
the industrial elite who were of English or American origins, as well as a
number of second generation Scottish Canadians. Voluntaryist, prohibition-
ist, Arminian, offering a clearly defined social philosophy particularly adapted to the region,[48] the Methodist Church brought together families of such
diverse origins as the Masseys, second generation Vermonters; the Fleurys,
the only French-Canadian member of the elite in the region;[49] the Scotts,

[48] A hypothesis confirmed by the rapid growth of the Methodist Church in the Lake
Peninsula in the last third of the nineteenth century. Between 1851 and 1901, at a time
when the immigrant population of Ontario was in decline, Methodists increased from 22
per cent to 31 per cent of the region's population. Only with the advent of the wheat-
boom migration in the first decade of the twentieth century did this proportional influence decline.

[49] *CBD*, II, pp. 422-3.

second generation Scottish paper makers;[50] and the Fitzgeralds, Canadian-born offspring of Ireland, and the leading force in the Imperial Oil syndicate.[51]

In both the St. Lawrence and the Maritimes regions the ethnic factors remained, on the whole, the basis of identification for most manufacturers. The entente achieved among competing groups in these areas was rather one of a group of societies co-existing within a single state, a situation described somewhat over-enthusiastically by Thomas Kenny, Conservative member for Halifax, in the Commons debates on the Orange Incorporation Bill in 1890 and the Manitoba Remedial Act of 1896:

> The Orange Order was incorporated in Nova Scotia in 1857 – since that time it has given no trouble. But ours is a model province, and the city from which I come is a model community. We may differ politically in that community, but I am happy to say that a great spirit of tolerance exists there. We boast that our civilization comes from the east, and I think it would be well for the western provinces in this Dominion occasionally to look to the east for a lesson in that particular . . . . The Nova Scotia School Law is good . . . its administration is a matter of compromise, and it is creditable to the people of Nova Scotia that such a settlement and adjustment of the question has been made . . . (Cartwright told us) that we Nova Scotians were the greatest boodlers in the universe . . . I have to say to him that in matters of religious liberty and toleration we set a good example to the other provinces of the Dominion.[52]

The industrialist of the 1880's, whether native or foreign born, tended to be the product of a rural or small town environment. The manufacturers of Montreal and Toronto, on the whole, were migrants from smaller centres. In the smaller communities – over half the manufacturing industry of the 1880's was centered in communities of under 10,000 population[53] – the native born industrialists came in about equal numbers from the town itself and from surrounding villages and rural areas.

Even among the immigrant members of the elite, few had come from any major urban centre, a fact reflected in the birthplaces of the Scottish entrepreneurs: Glasgow (6), Ayrshire (4), Edinburgh (2), Banff (2), Perthshire (2), Aberdeen, Stirling, Kells, Argyllshire, Huntly, Renfrew, Prestonpans, Berwick, Roxburgh, Fife, Leith, Lanarkshire, Peebleshire, Dumfries, Inverary, Paisley, Dunbartonshire. Among the native industrialists, there was

---

[50] *CCB*, pp. 695-7.
[51] *CCB*, pp. 708-9.
[52] Canada, *Commons Debates* (1890), p. 1299; *Ibid* (1896), p. 3394.
[53] The nine cities over 10,000 – Montreal, Toronto, Quebec, St. John, Halifax, Hamilton, Ottawa, London, Kingston – produced 43 per cent of Canadian manufacturing output in 1880: See Canada *Census of 1891*, IV, pp. 252, 368-9.

Table 17. Career Patterns: Geographic Structure

	Maritimes %	Halifax	St. John	St. Lawrence %	Quebec	Montreal	Ottawa	Lake Peninsula %	Toronto	Hamilton	The West %	Winnipeg
Outside Metro — Remained[1]	48											
Outside Metro — Moved Outside[2]	13											
Entered Region — Outside Metro[3]	3											
In Metro — Moved Out[4]	3											
Outside Metro — To Metro[5]		0	10		9	9	6		10	8		0
Entered Region — To Metro[6]		0	3		1	30	8		13	12		71
In Metro — Remained[7]		10	10		3	10	0		0	0		0
Total	100%			100%				100%			100%	

Total Cases: 164

[1] Began his career in a community outside a major centre, remained in that community throughout his career. For purposes of this study the term "metro" indicates any one of the eight Canadian cities listed in the table.

[2] Began a career outside a major centre and later moved to another community within the region. At no time did he settle in a metro.

[3] Entered the region usually from another country in the pursuit of a career. Settled in a community outside a metro.

[4] Moved from a metro to another community in the region.

[5] Moved from a smaller regional community to a metro in the pursuit of a career.

[6] Entered the region, usually from another country, in the pursuit of a career. Settled in a metro.

[7] Usually a native of a metro. Began and continued career here.

surprisingly little movement over the course of their careers. In fact, aside from the Nova Scotians, who as a group were singularly well travelled, most English-speaking natives appear to have had few contacts outside their own region.

In sharp contrast to this was the experience of the French-Canadian industrialists, most of whom had spent at least several years in the United States. Theophile Girouard acquired sufficient capital during four years in the California gold fields to enable him to establish a successful lumber firm in the Eastern Townships;[54] the Hon. Guillaume Bresse and Louis Coté had worked together in the New England shoe factories before returning to establish factories at Quebec and St. Hyacinthe;[55] Senator Louis Senecal lived two years in Vermont before establishing his Vercheres business.[56]

Members of the elite, were, in general, marginally better educated than their fellow townspeople, although even here there was considerable variation from region to region. The native born had attained a higher level of education than had any immigrant group with the exception of the Irish Protestants and Americans. College graduates were rare but most natives had spent some time in local grammar schools. Following school and training, the sons of the more well-to-do frequently acquired managerial appointments in one concern or another. The less fortunate began their careers as craftsmen, clerks, or salesmen while in their late teens and spent a number of years at menial or supervisory work before acquiring sufficient capital to establish their own firms.

Although they were prosperous and productive members of their communities, few Canadian manufacturers of the 1880's could have been described as wealthy by comparison with other Canadian businessmen. In a survey of Canadian wealth conducted in 1892, the *Canadian Journal of Commerce* gave pride of place to the transportation entrepreneurs whose personal resources frequently exceeded several millions of dollars.[57] The remaining Canadian millionaires were all "merchant princes" – wholesalers and shippers. In addition, it estimated that a number of businessmen of whom several were probably manufacturers, commanded resources of between $500,000 and $1,000,000.

The *Journal* article probably did not do justice to the industrialist. In point of fact several of the leading members of the elite almost certainly were millionaires: Alexander Gibson's several enterprises were amalgamated into a $3,000,000 joint-stock company in 1888, almost all held by members of the family; Hart Massey received shares to a value of $1,678,000 in the Massey-

[54] *CCB*, II, p. 558.
[55] *CCB*, II, pp. 588-90, 583-4; *CM*, Oct. 19, 1888.
[56] *CCB*, II, pp. 452-5.
[57] *The Canadian Journal of Commerce*, March 17, 1893, "Millionaires."

Table 18. Education

American Elite %		Canadian Elite %
–	None	4
30	Common School	55
33	High School	36
37	College	5
100	Total	100
183	Total Cases	122

Table 19. Birthplace and Education

Birthplace	*Educational Level Attained*					
	None	Common Sch.	High Sch.	College	Total	Total Cases
Maritimes %	4	48	40	8	100	26
St. Lawrence %	5	43	43	9	100	21
Lake Peninsula %	5	50	40	5	100	20
United States %	0	43	57	0	100	14
England %	0	56	29	15	100	7
Scotland %	5	75	15	5	100	20
Irèland (Prot.) %	0	43	57	0	100	7
Ireland (Cath.) %	0	66	34	0	100	3
Germany %	0	75	0	25	100	4

Harris amalgamation of 1891,[58] and left assets valued at $2,000,000 at his death five years later. Yet these individuals were the exception which proved the rule: leading merchants easily outdistanced leading manufacturers in the scale of their resources. Randolph Hersey, a leading Montreal iron and steel products manufacturer, shared with the Pillow family the $600,000 paid-up stock in the Pillow-Hersey firm, on which they realized about fifteen per cent profit per year.[59] The output of the firms of twenty-two members of the elite

[58] W. G. Phillips, *The Agricultural Implements Industry in Canada: A Study in Competition* (Toronto, 1956), p. 52; *ECB*, II, p. 8.
[59] William Kilbourne, *The Elements Combined* (Toronto, 1960), p. 15.

averaged about $300,000 in the early 1880's, and the net profits of these concerns would probably have amounted to about ten per cent of this gross.[60]

Some manufacturers had private investments outside their firms. The Ottawa lumber baron, Allan Gilmour, for example, held Bank of Commerce stock to the value of $443,000 in 1884 and the Toronto piano manufacturer, Samuel Nordheimer, possessed $270,000 in Federal Bank stock.[61] But the "typical" industrialist of the period was a man whose personal fortune, largely invested in his physical plant, probably amounted to $100,000 to $300,000 – a modest sum when measured in either international or national business terms.

Most industrial leaders were products of small communities and modest educations, and retained the marks of these conditions throughout their lives. Their social interests and activities centered on their churches, ethnic societies, fraternal lodges and occupational organizations – notably the mechanics, institutes, the boards of trade and, in Ontario, the Canadian Manufacturer's Association. Ethnic societies ran a poor second to the fraternal orders, the principal of which, the Masonic, brought together members of almost all groups, particularly those of Scottish and American origins, and those living in the Maritimes and the Lake Peninsula. In Montreal and Ottawa, a few manufacturers were joining the fledgling elite clubs, but even in Montreal most more closely resembled John McDougall who designated his only non-business activities as St. Andrew's Presbyterian Church and his five children.[62]

Most industrialists in the smaller communities participated actively in municipal government as magistrates, school commissioners, aldermen and mayors. With their obvious local influence they were usually leaders in the riding associations of both major parties, and were frequently sought as candidates for provincial and federal office.

---

[60] The firms examined were those of Alexander Gibson (Cottons & lumber, N.B., $600,-000), Mathew Cochrane (shoes, Quebec, $500,000), D. M. MacPherson (Cheese, Ont., $350,000), Alfred Watts (Soap, Ont., $500,000), Stephen Noxon (Ont., Ag. Imp., $250,000), Reuben Hamlin (Ag. Imp., Ont., $130,000), Billa Flint (Lumber, Ont., $200,000), John Elliott (Ag. Imp. Ont., $150,000), Francis Frost (Ag. Imp., Ont. $150,000), Evans Ames (shoes, Que., $400,000), Hubert Ives (Castings, Quebec, $200,000), Andrew Elliott (Woollens, Ont., $120,000) Robert Hay (Furniture, Ont., $350,000), John Milne (Iron Works, Ont., $200,000), Charles Raymond (Sewing machines, Ont., $200,000), Andrew Paton (Woollens, Que., $600,000), Louis Breithaupt (Leather, Ont., $120,000), Thomas Wilson (Machinery, Ont., $125,000), James Harris (Machinery, N.B., $200,000), William Buck (Ag. Imp., Ont., $175,000), Hart Massey (Ag. Imp., Ont., $1,000,000), Joseph Fleury (Ag. Imp., Ont., $120,000). The figures are estimates, usually given by the entrepreneur himself, at various times throughout the 1880's.

[61] Canada, *Sessional Papers* (1885), #17.

[62] *CBD*, II, pp. 319-20.

Table 20. Political Offices by Region[1]

	Maritimes	St. Lawrence	Lake Peninsula	West	Total
Lt. Gov.	1	–	1	–	2
Senator	4	8	4	–	16
M.P.	7	10	3	3	23
Cabinet	1	–	–	–	1
MLC	3	3	–	–	6
MLA	10	10	5	3	28
MEC	1	1	1	–	3
Municipal	8	20	16	2	46
School Comm.	3	4	3	–	10
Magistrate	6	5	3	–	14
Total	44	61	36	8	149
No. of Individuals	28	29	22	5	84

[1] These include all offices held during the lifetimes of members of the elite.

Half of them held some public office during their careers, about one in three occupying a major political office at the provincial or federal level, although there were sharp regional distinctions in the practice. Virtually all Maritime members of the elite held public office at some time in their lives, a ratio that declined to one in three among those from the Lake Peninsula. On the whole they appeared to be effective spokesmen for their communities; only rarely did they act as a class in an effort to secure legislation favourable to their group. The single issue which could do this in the 1880's was the tariff policy. Yet at no time did this temporary allegiance to a "foreign" political party to obtain these class ends imply any weakening of their traditional political faith. Most manufacturers who had been Liberals before 1878 considered themselves members of that party throughout the following decade and usually publicly declared that allegiance.

Table 21. Political Allegiance 1879-1887

	%
Conservative	55
Lib. turned Cons.	3
Liberal	40
Independent	1
CNC[1]	1
Total	100
Total Cases	121

[1] Conservative turned liberal nationalist (1885-87)

Table 22. Political Affiliation by Region, Birthplace, Religion, and Industrial Interests

Birthplace	Faith	Maritimes Cons.	Maritimes Lib.	St. Lawrence Cons.	St. Lawrence Lib.	Lake Peninsula Cons.	Lake Peninsula Lib.	West Cons.	West Lib.
Canada	Catholic	U		C					W
	Methodist	WC©U		[W]C(W)HP	BLLC	ASP	PSSWWW		
	Presbyterian	USSS	SHH	BB	B	S	S		
	Anglican	SSSCCU		WWWCC	W	CA	PS	W	W
	Bapt./Cong.	C				M	S		
	Quaker			L(B)	F	SD			
	Unknown	S	W						
Scotland	Presbyterian		U	CCC(C)U	W	CM(P)S	CSSBBAWP		
	Anglican					S			
	Bapt./Cong.					B	S		
	Unknown					S	S		
Ireland	Catholic	W		S		B			
	Methodist			BP					
	Presbyterian			CC			C		
	Anglican			B			C		
	Unknown					S			

Birthplace	Faith	Region							
		Maritimes Cons.	Maritimes Lib.	St. Lawrence Cons.	St. Lawrence Lib.	Lake Peninsula Cons.	Lake Peninsula Lib.	West Cons.	West Lib.
England	Methodist				C				
	Anglican					G	R	Y	W
	Presbyterian								
United States	Methodist					C			
	Presbyterian			S W	R W W				
	Anglican					A B			
	Baptist						S S		
	Unknown								
	Agnostic								
Germany	Lutheran				U	M	L L		
	Unknown								
Totals		17	5	32	13	23	27	2	3

Legend:

A-oil
B-flour, food
C-textiles
D-drugs
E-Rubber
F-furniture
G-soap
H-ships
L-leather
M-music
P-paper
R-broom
S-iron & steel
U-sugar
W-wood
Y-beer

○-shifted political allegiance: Lib-Cons.; Cons.-Lib.
□-shifted political allegiance: Cons.-Nationalist

While most Liberals were prepared to support Macdonald on the single issue of tariff policy, they would, as Frederic Nicholls explicitly stated, do so only so long as the Conservatives maintained a high tariff and the Liberals did not: at any sign of change in this equation, they would revert to their traditional voting patterns.

" . . . Canadian manufacturers are not necessarily members of the Conservative Party merely because they vote for Conservatives in preference to Reformers in Dominion elections . . . quite a large portion . . . are regular and staunch adherents of Reform Party in all things and at all times except when the National Policy is a question. In local politics they are unswerving Reformers and because of this the governments of about all the Provinces of the Dominion are in the hands of Reform statesmen . . . There is nothing else in common between these pro-tariff Reformers and the Conservative Party . . . This situation accentuates the fact that the National Policy is the key-stone of political success. . . . If the Conservatives expect to retain power it must be by a faithful observance of the National Policy. The manufacturers would be the arbiters if the Reformers were smart enough to catch onto a good thing when it comes within their reach.[63]

Fundamentally the manufacturers were products of both inherited and acquired environmental traditions, a combination vividly portrayed in their political preferences. Given several areas of loyalty – region, ethnicity, religion, occupation – the weakest valence proved to be occupational class groupings; the strongest were factors of region and, within the regional colonial tradition, religion. Thus within the relatively sophisticated political structure of the Lake Peninsula, the marked party traditions of the colonial period were still clearly evident among the elite of the 1880's. These in turn had become structured in large measure around denominational systems, the native Methodist and Scottish Free Presbyterian traditions providing the basic ideological foundations for the perpetuation of the old Reform tradition. The ethnic tradition here had largely been replaced by the religious: the Scottish-born Anglicans, for example, usually converts, were also Tories.

In the St. Lawrence and Maritime regions, MacDonald had succeeded in overcoming the weaker party traditions and in almost re-establishing a compact conservatism among the industrialists of these areas. Certainly the striking difference in the political reactions of the Lake Peninsula and Montreal Scottish Presbyterians was an eloquent tribute to the impact of geography both in overcoming inherited tradition and in moulding the viewpoint of its inhabitants.

Yet, within the region, religion was significant as an ancillary to political views. The Church of England well merited the sobriquet, "the Tory party at

---

[63] *Canadian Manufacturer*, Sept. 2, 1892, "The Key-Stone of Political Success."

prayer." Regardless of region or occupation, almost every Anglican in the elite was a Conservative. More significant is the fact that many of the most ardent Anglican Tories, including the Scottish-born iron manufacturer, Robert McKechnie, the Scottish-born textile manufacturer, Senator Donald MacInnes, the American-born hardware manufacturer, Hubert Ives, and possibly the Scottish-born sugar magnate, Sir George A. Drummond, had left their native Presbyterian faith – and often their Liberal political faith.

Three distinct social streams nourished the industrial elite of the 1880's. The smallest consisted of a group of old Canadian industrial and commercial families often of several generations standing in British North America. The largest contained a number of individuals of British, American and German backgrounds, scions of industrial or commercial families in their native lands who succeeded in transferring their status to the new society through a form of horizontal mobility. Finally, a third group, largely of Scottish or native-Canadian farm or minor industrial origins, succeeded over a lifetime in achieving a significant degree of vertical mobility.

In the final analysis, the industrialist of the 1880's tended to be essentially a community entrepreneur of rather narrow horizons; a product of mid-nineteenth century colonial society with an essentially regional bias; a man, frequently of modest origins, who on most issues tended to side with his community rather than his class.

Appendix

Subjects mentioned in the *Study of the Industrial Elite*

Name	*Centre*
Allan, Andrew	Montreal
Allan Sir Hugh	Montreal
Ames, Evan F.	Montreal
Baker, Hon. Loran E.	Yarmouth
Balcer, Henry M.	Three Rivers (NS)
Barber, John R.	Georgetown (Ont)
Baumgarten, Alfred F. M.	Montreal
Bell, William	Guelph (Ont)
Bertram, John	Dundas (Ont)
Beveridge, William B.	Andover (NB)
Bickerdike, Robert	Montreal
Birge, Cyrus A.	Hamilton
Boak, Hon. Robert	Halifax
Booth, John R.	Ottawa
Bresse, Hon. Guillaume	Quebec
Breithaupt, Louis J.	Berlin (Ont)
Breithaupt, Louis	Berlin (Ont)

Brock, William R.	Toronto
Bronson, Erskine H.	Ottawa
Bronson, Henry F.	Ottawa
Buck, William	Brantford
Burland, George B.	Montreal
Burns, Adam	Halifax
Burns, Kennedy F.	Bathurst (NB)
Burpee, Hon. Isaac	St. John
Cantlie, James A.	Montreal
Carmichael, James W.	New Glasgow (NS)
Cassils, John	Montreal
Chesley, John A.	St. John
Chipman, Zechariah	St. Stephen (NB)
Christie, William A.	Toronto
Cochrane, Hon. Matthew H.	Compton (Que)
Cook, Hermon H.	Toronto
Cooper, James	Toronto
Conmee, James	Port Arthur (Ont)
Côté, Louis	St. Hyacinthe
Cowan, Thomas	Galt (Ont)
Crossen, James	Cobourg (Ont)
Cunningham, Henry	Kingston
Daniel, Thomas W.	St. John
Davison, Edward	Bridgewater (NS)
Dessaulles, Hon. George C.	St. Hyacinthe (Que)
Doolittle, Charles E.	Hamilton
Drewery, Edward L.	Winnipeg
Drummond, Sir George A.	Montreal
Eddy, Ezra B.	Ottawa
Edwards, Hon. William C.	Ottawa
Elliott, Andrew	Almonte (Ont)
Elliott, John	Toronto
Elliott, R. W.	Toronto
Ellis, John R.	Toronto
Englehart, Jacob L.	Petrolea (Ont)
Ewing, Samuel H.	Montreal
Fitz-gerald, Frederick A.	London
Fleury, Joseph	Aurora (Ont)
Flint, Hon. Billa	Belleville (Ont)
Fraser, Alexander	Ottawa
Fraser, Graham	New Glasgow (NS)
Frost, Francis T.	Smith Falls (Ont)
Gartshore, Alexander	Hamilton
Gault, Matthew H.	Montreal
Gault, Andrew F.	Montreal
Gibson, Alexander	Marysville (NB)
Gillespie, John	Toronto
Gilmour, Allan	Ottawa
Girouard, Theophile	Stanstead (Que)
Goldie, James	Guelph (Ont)
Gurney, Edward	Toronto
Hadley, Sylvester	Chatham (Ont)

Haggert, John	Brampton (Ont)
Hamilton, Hon. John	Hawkesbury (Ont)
Hamlin, Reuben S.	Oshawa (Ont)
Harris, Alanson	Brantford
Harris, Christopher P.	Moncton
Harris, James	St. John
Harris, John L.	Moncton
Hay, Robert	Toronto
Heinzeman, Theodore	Toronto
Hendrie, William	Hamilton
Hendry, John	Vancouver
Herring, John	Napanee (Ont)
Hersey, Randolph	Montreal
Howland, Sir Wm. P.	Toronto
Hudon, Victor	Montreal
Humphrey, John Albert	Moncton
Ives, Hubert R.	Montreal
Jones, Hon. Thomas R.	St. John
Karn, Dennis W.	Woodstock (Ont)
Kenny, Thomas E.	Halifax
Kilgour, Robert	Toronto
King, James	Quebec
Le Mesurier, John	Quebec
Leonard, Hon. Elijah	London
Long, Thomas	Collingwood
Lovitt, John W.	Yarmouth (NS)
McClary, John	London
McCrae, Thomas	Guelph (Ont)
MacDonald, Sir Wm. C.	Montreal
McDougall, John	Montreal
McGregor, Hon. James D.	New Glasgow (NS)
MacInnes, Hon. Donald	Hamilton
McKechnie, Robert	Dundas (Ont)
McLennan, Hugh	Montreal
MacLaren, James	Ottawa
MacPherson, D. M.	Glengarry (Ont)
McShane, James	Montreal
Massey, Hart A.	Toronto
Meighen, Robert	Montreal
Milne, John	Hamilton
Miner, Stephen H.	Granby (Ont)
Minnes, James	Kingston
Mitchell, Robert	Montreal
Mitchell, Thomas	Bransford
Moore, Dennis	Hamilton
Moore, Samuel J.	Toronto
Morrice, David	Montreal
Murchie, James	St. Stephen (NB)
Nairn, Alexander	Toronto
Nelson, Horatio A.	Montreal
Nordheimer, Samuel	Toronto
Nozon, Stephen	Ingersoll (Ont)
Ogilvie, William W.	Montreal

Ogilvie, Hon. Alexander W.	Montreal
Parks, John H.	St. John
Paton, Andrew	Sherbrooke (Que)
Paul, Frank	Montreal
Pickard, John	Fredericton
Pillow, John A.	Montreal
Price, Evan J.	Quebec
Raymond, Charles	Guelph (Ont)
Robb, Alexander	Amherst (NS)
Robb, David W.	Amherst (NS)
Robinson, William	Winnipeg
Rolland, Hon. Jean D.	Montreal
Rosamund, Bennett	Almote
Ross, Arthur W.	Winnipeg
Ross, Hon. James G.	Quebec
Rourke, James	St. John
Sanford, Hon. William E.	Hamilton
Scott, John K.	Napanee (Ont)
Senecal, Hon. Louis A.	Vercheres
Shorey, Hollis	Montreal
Smart, James	Brockville (Ont)
Smith, Bennett	Windsor (NS)
Sprague, Daniel E.	Winnipeg
Stairs, John W.	Halifax
Stephen, Sir George	Montreal
Sutherland, Hugh M.	Winnipeg
Thomson, James	Newburgh (Ont)
Thomson, Robert	Woodstock (Ont)
Thorne, Hon. William H.	St. John
Thornton, John	Coaticook (Que)
Todd, Freeman H.	St. Stephen (NB)
Tuckett, George E.	Hamilton
Valin, Pierre V.	Quebec
Valliere, Philippe	Quebec
Villeneuve, Hon. J. D.	Montreal
Ward, Hon. James K.	Montreal
Walker, John	London
Waterous, Charles H.	Brantford
Waterson, Isaac	London
Watts, Alfred	Brantford
Wilson, J. C.	Montreal
Wilson, Thomas	Dundas
Withall, William J.	Quebec
Wood, Andrew T.	Hamilton
Wood, Josiah	Sackville (NB)
Young, Levi	Ottawa

"Dyspepsia of the Mind": The Canadian Businessman and His Enemies, 1880-1914

Michael Bliss, Lecturer in History, University of Toronto

The late nineteenth and early twentieth centuries were the Golden Age of Canadian business enterprise. Or, for those not impressed with unrestrained capitalism, they were the years of the Great Barbecue in Canada. The close class linkages between businessmen and politicians, the numerical insignificance of the Canadian labour movement, the subsidization of entrepreneurship in Canadian national tariff and transport policies, miniscule taxation and the eagerness with which Canadian resources were doled out to capitalists native and foreign, all suggest an environment promoting the maximum business opportunity while providing minimum social regulation of profit-making. It was the age of the Canadian Captain of Industry, the age when businessmen seemed to be the national class in Canadian life and an enthusiastic editor could put everyone in his place with the following:

> The development of the last few years has been magnificent; the development of the next few years depends on our having confidence. The country is rich, immigration is proceeding apace, the Government is doing its duty, and the rest lies with the people – the capitalists, the bankers, the businessmen, and the other classes.[1]

But one of the more unexpected conclusions that emerges from a study of business rhetoric and action during this period is that the business class on the whole perceived itself to be operating in a hostile environment. In many instances businessmen felt themselves to be under severe pressure from competing social groups, sometimes at the mercy of these groups. More important, they also felt at the mercy of one another because of the competitiveness of the Canadian economy, so much so that doing business at times seemed an almost unbearable strain. The Captains of Industry, it turns out, often thought their ships were sailing through exceedingly stormy seas.

From a contemporary perspective the relations between businessmen and Canadian governments after Confederation seem almost idyllic. To take the two most obvious examples, the tariff seemed to exist in large part as the repayment of subsidies given by the manufacturing interest to the Conservative Party. Similarly the Canadian Pacific Railway was what John A. Macdonald called the "sleeping partner" of the Conservative government in the 1880's (though it could be remarkably awake and active at election time). Actually neither the manufacturers nor the C.P.R. were ever particularly satisfied with this apparently happy political relationship. At the best of times

[1] *Canadian Magazine*, March, 1905, p. 487.

their spokesmen were haunted by doubt and uncertainty as to the reliability of their political allies.

Even in the heydays of the National Policy in the 1880's the federal government appears to have made clear to the Canadian Manufacturers' Association that it would not accept manufacturers' demands for Chinese Wall protectionism[2]. Then in the later years of the Conservative regime manufacturers had first grudgingly to accept tariff readjustments to mollify public opinion, and almost immediately afterward watched and fretted helplessly as racial and religious issues wrecked "the only party which is prepared to protect the manufacturer."[3] Actually the Liberal party turned out to be sound on the broad principle of protection by 1896 (though the C.M.A. officially panicked at the thought of a Liberal victory), but the Laurier Government's introduction of preferential tariff schedules, its refusal to bow to the heavily financed protectionist campaign of 1902-6*, above all its reversion to reciprocity in 1911, all frustrated manufacturers who found that the government was by no means in their pocket. The members of the C.M.A.'s important Tariff Committee satisfied themselves in December 1910 that reciprocity was a dead issue;[4] the agreement with the United States was announced a month later. Such were the uncertainties of mixing business with politics. It cost an annoying amount of money and time to help overthrow the government and preserve the *status quo.*

The alliance between the Canadian Pacific Railway and the Canadian Government, personified respectively by George Stephen and Sir John A. Macdonald, was one of the closest political-business friendships in North American history. Nevertheless it had ups and downs. A great many of the eight hundred or so letters Stephen wrote to Macdonald contain bitter complaints about the failure of the government to safeguard properly the interests of the railroad. "The Company has never had a transaction with the Government to which there was not, in the end, some mischievous condition attached, which largely lessened the benefit which would otherwise have come to the Company,"[5] Stephen wrote in 1889 in a fairly typical letter. The next year he summed up a decade of frustration in a remarkable outburst:

[2] Canadian Manufacturers' Association, *Scrapbook, 1883-1888*; General letter to members of the Ontario Manufacturers' and Industrial Association, signed by A. W. Wright (Secretary), Nov. 14, 1883; General letter to members of the O.M.A. signed by Frederic Nicholls (Secretary), Nov. 1885.

[3] *Canadian Manufacturer*, Jan. 17, 1896, "The Fiscal Outlook." The article continues, "It is an unpleasant thing to say but it is one which every thinking man knows – we cannot, dare not, trust the Liberal party."

[4] C.M.A. Tariff Committee, *Minutebook*, Dec. 5, 1910.

[5] Public Archives of Canada, *Macdonald Papers*, Stephen to Macdonald, Sept. 3, 1889.

* It is significant for the general argument of this essay that the C.M.A. launched its campaign for more tariff protection at the peak of the first round of Laurier prosperity, arguing that depression would soon come again and Americans would breach our industrial fortresses. So much for the infant industries developing the confidence of adolescence.

It is positively heartbreaking the way we are treated and I am tired of beseeching & begging for fair treatment, & have resolved on giving up all further efforts to secure it, as useless, . . . in almost every transaction we have had with the Govt arising out of the contract we have been taken advantage of and duped and deceived in the most cruel manner. Had I been the worst enemy of the Govt politically I could not have been worse treated than I have been by the Dept of Railways.[6]

The government's disregard of his railway so depressed Stephen that for the only time in the entire correspondence he reminded Macdonald in this letter of his contribution of one million dollars to the Conservative cause since 1882, adding that he would not ask anything of the government "but what is right and fair, and which ought to be granted even had I never done a thing or spent a dollar for it politically." Macdonald's replies to these and similar criticisms involved chastising the C.P.R. for asking too much ("You C.P.R. folk are forgetful and I fear rather too ungrateful"), arguing that the Government had to respond to other pressures ("We are closely watched by the opposition who are lying in wait for us at every turn"), and urging the Company to involve itself still more deeply in political manipulation ("The C.P.R. might get control of the legislature of Manitoba for the next four years if it chose, and those would be four years of comfort").[7] This was very far from an alliance of two equal colleagues smoothly dividing the reins of power – the alliance that contemporary Liberals as well as later critics have thought existed, the alliance that George Stephen always hoped would exist.

In addition to having to worry about the refusal of governments to bend totally to their will, businessmen could not help but be anxious about any question that was an issue of partisan politics. What happened when the other side won? Both the C.P.R. and the Canadian Manufacturers' Association had to intervene directly in politics in the 1880's because they were convinced a Liberal victory would have had a catastrophic effect on their interests. In their ideal world both political parties would have recognized that high tariffs and railways were always and utterly in the national interest, thereby removing the issues from politics entirely and relieving interested businessmen from the need to go electioneering. A typical protectionist editorial in 1882 was entitled "Let Us Have Peace" and read in part:

It is for the country's interest that the trade question should be taken out of politics. . . . as long as it continues to be a political issue there continues also the element of doubt and uncertainty as to the future, which is a prime hindrance to the country's development. . . . For want of complete assurance as to the permanence of the National Policy the country is losing millions annually. . . . . Capitalists require certainty,

[6] *Ibid.*, Stephen to Macdonald, July 29, 1890.
[7] P.A.C., *Stephen Papers*, Macdonald to Stephen, April 28, 1889; Oct. 6, 1887; June 15, 1888.

they want the assurance that the conditions upon which they embark their capital will be permanent. Something hinders this assurance from being as complete and as satisfactory as it ought to be, and what is it? Everyone knows that it is the interference of *political* contingencies with the question whether the investment of capital in this or the other industry would be safe.[8]

Of course the trade question was not taken out of politics, and throughout the last quarter of the century there were frequent complaints that almost no business was done during election campaigns while everyone waited until the settlement of "political contingencies" also settled the future course of business.[9]

(Complaints about political interference with business may have been more justified in the late nineteenth century than they are now. From about 1911 a combination of shifting public concerns, Parliament's devolution of responsibility for many areas of government-business contact into the hands of administrative bodies, and the professionalization of the civil service seem to have made many issues such as transport regulation and tariffs less politically volatile. Certainly neither of Canada's two major political parties has recently frightened leading business interests as much as the Liberal Party did in the 1880's and 1890's. Except for the somewhat shadowy presence of the C.C.F.-N.D.P. the Canadian political system seems to have provided a much more certain environment for business activities than it did in what is thought to have been the period of greatest business-government cooperation. Alternatively it may be that private business has simply learned to expect less from government and roll with the political punches with rather more good grace than formerly. Still, the only election since the depression that has frightened the Canadian business community as much as those of 1878, 1882, 1887, 1891, 1896, and 1911 was the Quebec provincial election of 1970.)

Provincial governments during the period were also acting with less docility than we would expect from John Porter's model of them as guardians of vested business interests.[10] The corporation tax, for example, came to Canada in 1882 in the Province of Quebec. When companies refused *en masse* to pay the new imposition, the government coolly laid four hundred charges for non-payment of taxes, causing the organ of Montreal's business community to doubt "if any similar instance of oppression can be cited in modern history."[11] A test case carried to the Privy Council was finally decided in

---

[8] *Canadian Manufacturer*, May 12, 1882, p. 169. The C.M.A. would later advocate a Tariff Commission for the same reason.

[9] *Canadian Manufacturer*, May 26, 1882, p. 192; "The Elections," *Canadian Journal of Commerce*, Jan. 21, 1887, p. 152; "The Coming Election," *Ibid.*, March 6, 1891, p. 454; "The Results of the Elections," *Monetary Times*, June 5, 1896, p. 1560.

[10] John Porter, *The Vertical Mosaic*, pp. 379-485.

[11] *Canadian Journal of Commerce*, Dec. 29, 1882, pp. 621-2, "The Business Tax."

favour of the Quebec government in 1887; the Mercier administration, ignoring deputations of the leading businessmen of the province, proceeded to collect five years' back taxes. This was a government which the same year had been hailed as one that would give the "skillful protection and encouragement" to the business community "which their importance warrants."[12]

Almost simultaneously the citizens of Manitoba were winning their great struggle against the monopoly clause of the C.P.R. charter, a remarkable victory over both the greatest corporation in the Dominion and the federal government. Later the private telephone interests and the grain elevator owners in western Canada would be unable to prevent the growth of government ownership and regulation in their industries. In general, for all their complaints against eastern business oppression, Western Canadians were remarkably successful in passing legislation to limit the powers of private corporations.[13]

The most sensational struggle of the period in the provinces was the Whitney-Beck crusade to create Ontario Hydro against the determined opposition of the private power interests. The turning point in an otherwise typical conflict between the "people" of Ontario and a few large power corporations came with Whitney's Power Commission Amendment Act of 1909 by which all municipal contracts with the Ontario Hydro Commission were declared valid by act of the legislature and all pending and future court actions testing that validity were void.[14] The investment community exploded in anger over what the *Financial Post* called "one of the most tyrannous acts that has ever been committed", an Act which violated all basic declarations of right from the Mosaic Code to Magna Carta. Such legislation, accompanied by judicial decisions upholding a province's absolute constitutional power to override civil and property rights (as the federal Minister of Justice admitted, proved provincial legislatures really could repeal Magna Carta), brought home to businessmen for the first time the fragility of property rights in a British parliamentary system. Disallowance petitions and political pressure flowed to Ottawa to stop the renegade province, more court cases were launched, amendments to the B.N.A. Act were suggested, and concerted efforts were made at home and abroad to ruin Ontario's credit. All failed. For the *Financial Post* Whitney became "the Socialist Premier now masquerading under the title of a Conservative"[15] and the public ownership movement marched on. Indeed the hydro fight was only the most spectacular instance of the nation-wide expansion of municipal ownership of utilities from about 1890 to 1914, always carried out against the opposition of private companies.

[12] *Ibid.,* Feb. 4, 1887, pp. 272-3, "The Quebec Cabinet." See also J. H. Parry, *Taxes, Tariffs and Subsidies,* (Toronto, 1955) V. 1, pp. 77-8.

[13] V. K. Fowke, *The National Policy and the Wheat Economy* (Toronto, 1957) pp. 93, 153 ff.

[14] Merrill Denison, *The People's Power* (Toronto, 1960), Ch. 9; *Canadian Annual Review,* 1909, pp. 371-383.

[15] *Financial Post,* June 5, 1909; July 31, 1909.

These political frustrations of the business classes – and there were many more of them – were simply the consequence of the Canadian political system's responsiveness to the desires of a plurality of interest groups. In the early years the most powerful group opposing businessmen was the agricultural interest – permeated with free trade ideas, stoutly opposed to insolvency laws that would limit the freedom of debtors (commercial interests failed for twenty years to have a federal insolvency law passed), anti-railroad, anti-corporation, and often anti-urban. The Quebec corporation tax was a clear instance of the use of agrarian power against companies – what the *Journal of Commerce* alternately called "hayseed" and "class" legislation foisted upon the province by rural assemblymen of "bovine" simplicity.[16] Similarly the agrarians provided the voting base for anti-protectionist campaigns and it was the revival of agrarian power with the opening of the West in the Laurier years that swung the Liberal party back to reciprocity in 1911. The manufacturers fully realized this; the C.M.A.'s closed strategy sessions – when businessmen were talking to themselves and not for public consumption – resounded with denunciations of a government that sacrificed manufacturing interests for farmers. Significantly, the manufacturers thought that the best way to apply political pressure to the government against reciprocity would be to sponsor delegations of farmers and workingmen to protest the agreement.[17]

But by 1911 delegations of workingmen were used to going to Ottawa for distinctly different purposes than supporting the political aims of the C.M.A. The direct power that organized labour could mobilize for either industrial disputes or independent political action was still comparatively insignificant; the indirect influence it exercised on politics and business was not. This influence was not sufficiently hostile to the interests of employers that the business community already had a healthy sense of being harassed by organized labour.

For one thing the agitations of the unions seemed to bear political fruit. From the initial legalization of trade unions in 1872 through the Factory Act legislation of the 1880's and 1890's, down to Ontario's model revision of workmen's compensation legislation in 1915, the advances in labour legislation in Canada were surprisingly rapid in the context of both the late development of Canadian industrialism and what the business community would have liked to concede.[18] In terms of what organized labour thought it

16 *Canadian Journal of Commerce*, July 9, 1887, p. 20; "The Tax on Corporations," July 13, 1888, pp. 67-8, "The Tax on Corporations."

17 C.M.A. Tariff Committee, *Minutebook*, Dec. 5, 1910; C.M.A. Executive Council, *Minutebooks*, May 5, 1910; Feb. 16, 1911.

18 Margaret Evans, "Oliver Mowat and Ontario, 1872-1896: A Study in Political Success" (unpublished Ph.D. Thesis, University of Toronto, 1967), ch. III. For the integration of the early labour movement into the existing political system see Martin Robin, *Radical Politics and Canadian Labour, 1880-1930* (Kingston, 1968), pp. 1-18 (esp. pp. 17-18: "The spread of trade unionism in Canada testified to the ability of the organized skilled stratum of artisans to win concessions under the prevailing system; its very success

should get, of course, the pace of legislation was agonizingly slow. But business organizations made exactly the same complaints about the reluctance of government to legislate in their interests. In fact, promoters of associational activities by businessmen consciously and enviously took trade unions as their model. "Labor, in particular, is becoming so effectively organized that it wields a power and influence that is astonishing," the C.M.A.'s Secretary told the annual meeting in 1887, going on to add, "the manner in which they have perfected their organization affords a lesson, not without significance to those to whom this paper is addressed."[19] Businessmen thought it particularly unjust in 1888 that business combinations designed to achieve a "living profit" should be the subject of a Parliamentary inquiry, while labour combinations for the same purpose were being ignored.[20] The 1889 legislation following the combines inquiry did not, as some historians have believed, place all combinations in restraint of trade on the same footing. Trade unions were guaranteed exemption from the laws governing business "unions," a fact that caused bitter complaints about "class legislation" from big businessmen in the Senate.[21] The further clarification of labour's right to strike in 1890 seems to have been a deliberate reaction against prosecutions sponsored by the C.M.A.[22] And Sir John Thompson's amendment to the Criminal Code in the same year protecting female factory employees from seduction by their employers was considered a pernicious and humiliating example of the "Minister of Injustice" courting the "beslobber-

---

guaranteed that drastic solutions would not be sought"). For the striking success of the Provincial Workingman's Association in achieving legislative concessions in Nova Scotia in the 1880's and 1890's see H. A. Logan, *Trade Unions in Canada* (Toronto, 1948), pp. 172-3: "In 1896 the grand secretary declared that the miners of Nova Scotia were in advance of those of any English-speaking country with regard to legislation."

[19] From a paper on "Organization" read at the 1887 annual meeting of the C.M.A. by its Secretary, Frederic Nicholls, *Canadian Manufacturer*, March 18, 1887, p. 176. See also the call for a "union" by a small jeweller in *The Trader*, June 1884; also *Canadian Grocer*, April 12, 1895, p. 8, "Where Do We Come In"?

[20] *Report of the Select Committee to Investigate and Report Upon Alleged Combinations in Manufactures, Trade and Insurance in Canada* (Ottawa, 1888), pp. 516-7, 519; *Canadian Manufacturer*, March 16, 1888, p. 184, "The Trades Union 'Combine'".

[21] The Liberals claimed that the new statute took away the right to strike that had been granted to labour in 1872. This interpretation was accepted and popularized by Bernard Ostry in "Conservatives, Liberals and Labour in the 1880's," *Canadian Journal of Economics and Political Science*, XXVII, p. 2, (May, 1961). In fact the Government assured unions that the bill did not apply to combinations of workingmen, promised to appeal any successful action against unions under the Act to the highest court, and, as is noted in the text, strengthened the right to strike in the following year. See Thompson's speech to the House of Commons, April 30, 1889, *Debates*, p. 1690, and the report of his promise to Montreal printers in the Toronto *Mail*, Sept. 4, 1890. See also the exchange on the subject between Senators Power and Sanford, Senate *Debates*, April 29, 1889, p. 650. Also the speech of Senator Ogilvie, *Ibid.*, p. 643.

[22] House of Commons, *Debates*, April 10, 1890, pp. 3163, 3372-9; *Canadian Manufacturer*, June 21, 1889, p. 392, "Justice Versus Trade Unions."

ment of the Knights of Labor."[23] In the Laurier years businessmen called repeatedly for measures to force unions to become legally responsible corporate bodies in the same way that business organizations were. They did not succeed, and always resented the special status labor organizations seemed to them to enjoy in law and practice.[24]

Secondly, even though serious industrial disputes in Canada were comparatively rare – though by no means non-existent – the spectre of open industrial or class warfare began to haunt Canadian business from at least the 1880's. There was the United States – the country of Haymarket, Homestead, Pullman, *et al* – providing the model of what real industrial strife in a society could mean. There were the socialists – Anarchists, Nihilists, Communists, Single Taxers, *et al* – causing trouble in all the other countries of the world and posing the ultimate threat of social cataclysm. Canada was virgin land still; but these things had a way of spreading, say through the organizers of international unions. Businessmen were not sure whether repression or concession would be the most appropriate response to large scale labour troubles when they finally came to Canada. The significant point is that they perceived foreign social unrest as a model of what could be in store for Canada, and they worried about it.[25] In the 1960's, one of the happiest decades in their history, Canadians did exactly the same thing.

The business community's sense of weakness in the face of labour was reflected in any number of ways. Editors of business journals marvelled at political, public, and newspaper pandering to the prejudices of labour leaders from the mid-1880's. They worried incessantly about the "Labour Question" as the great issue of the day, and used an endless stock of arguments to convince the "fair-minded" worker that his "interests lay with his employer" rather than with the "walking delegates" and "jawsmiths" of the union.[26] In a more positive way business journals discussed such schemes for industrial reconciliation as profit-sharing from the 1880's and always encouraged the firm picnics, dances and excursions that were commonplace in the period. By the Laurier years there was a significant industrial welfare movement in

---

[23] *Canadian Manufacturer*, May 2, 1890, p. 292, "Pernicious Legislation."

[24] *Industrial Canada*, Oct. 1907, p. 211 (Report of Parliamentary Committee to C.M.A. annual Convention).

[25] One of many examples of this perception is "Undesirable Emigrants," *Canadian Journal of Commerce*, Aug. 6, 1886, p. 385: "The United States is already suffering from the Bohemian and other foreign Anarchists who have chosen it for their temporary home, and though as yet, the solid common sense and sturdy industry of the Canadian has swamped their incendiary efforts on this side of the line, the increasing number of idle and unemployed of the vicious classes in our cities must eventually form a fruitful ground for their mischievous and vicious doctrines."

[26] For example, *Canadian Journal of Commerce*, June 3, 1881, "The Labor Question"; April 28, 1882, p. 335, "The Labor Question," May 22, 1886, p. 1342, "The Labor Question"; *Canadian Manufacturer*, Feb. 5, 1886, p. 80, "The Relations of Capital to Labor," Feb. 18, 1887, p. 115, "The Labor Candidate."

Canada, urging concessions to labour for both humanitarian and strategic reasons.[27] The Canadian Manufacturers' Association was much less eager to engage in all-out struggles against organized labour than its American counterpart, the National Association of Manufacturers. Its minutebooks show a surprising caution and regard for public opinion on such issues as recruiting skilled labour, engaging in strike-breaking, and overt resistance to the more reasonable legislative requests of unions.[28] In addition, the *cris de coeur* that rang out against unions in private meetings of C.M.A. committees ("Mr. Harris . . . quoted from his own experience with the unions to show that the union leader had no soul, that the union man had to do what he was told and that generosity and fair treatment counted for nothing"),[29] belie the supposition that public anti-unionism was merely a cynical tactical ploy. There was something almost pathetic about the 1910 decision of the Executive of the Toronto Branch of the C.M.A. to send an anti-labour journal, *The Square Deal*, for one year to two hundred prominent Canadians as a means of counteracting what they thought was labour's political strength.[30]

When political decisions were taken in the interests of labour or other groups in Canadian society, businessmen held legislators responsible for their actions. In their frustration they singled out and defined "professional politicians" as a distinct and disreputable social class. Most of them were lawyers or doctors, what J.B. Maclean called "the sediment of the learned professions," who went to Parliament because "it is the best paying job their mediocrity will allow them to obtain."[31] To preserve their comfortable incomes professional politicians became abject slaves of their political parties, the machines that existed solely to capture and divide the spoils of office. Concepts of patriotism, independent public service, and the national interest, were sacrificed to the whims of men "who care nothing for the country so long as . . . it affords for them a sure means of extorting from a long suffering people a living for which they never worked."[32]

The antidote to the professional politician was the businessman in politics – the practical, honest, patriotic man who knew that the business of Canada was business and was also wealthy enough not to be influenced by mere pecuniary considerations. Everyone who meditated on business matters called for more business representation in politics. No one knew how to encourage a

27 On profit-sharing see *Canadian Manufacturer*, Sept. 24, 1886, p. 549; for the industrial welfare movement see *Industrial Canada*, Nov. 1909, pp. 424-7, "Welfare Work in Factories"; Feb. 1910, pp. 693-6, "How Efficiency in Workmen is Improved."

28 For recruiting labour see C.M.A., British Office Committee, *Minutebook* (1906-08); on strike-breaking, C.M.A., Executive Council, *Minutebooks*, Sept. 18, 1902 (resolved "that no active part should be taken by the Association in organizing Employers' Protective Associations"); manufacturers' resistance to workmen's compensation was minimal.

29 C.M.A., Executive Council, *Minutebooks*, June 20, 1907.

30 C.M.A., Toronto Branch Executive, *Minutebooks*, July 14, 1910.

31 *Canadian Grocer*, June 19, 1896, p. 15.

32 *The Trader*, Oct. 1885, "Commercial Union."

most reluctant business community to dirty its hands with the muck of electioneering.[33] The trouble, explained the *Journal of Commerce*, was that the extension of the suffrage had confided the future of the country "to the hands of the poorest and most ignorant, and therefore most numerous" class of its population. It had set up "the rule of a brute majority over an educated and intelligent minority," resulting in that minority withdrawing from political life.[34] Control had been given over by default to the professional politician. This idea of an ignorant majority manipulated by an unprincipled, self-seeking elite was as dear to the hearts of Canadian businessmen in the 1880's and 1890's as it was to the Left in the 1960's. The businessmen may at least have had the virtue of originality.

Businessmen saw the Manitoba Schools issue as a prime example of how professional politicians neglected the real needs of the nation to pander to groups organized according to race and religion. By 1895 business interests found request after request ignored by a government totally preoccupied with education, religion and its own survival. Their frustration welled up in the columns of the *Canadian Grocer*, the country's largest trade journal:

... For three months the House has been in session; and what for? Merely to keep boiling the pot of race and creed; dividing race against race and creed against creed; creating food for sharpening the appetite of fanatics, who in the name of religion would tear each other to pieces.

While this is going on not only are the business interests of the country dying of neglect, but the Dominion is retrograding. ...

Goodness knows when this race and religious war in the hearts of the people will give place to peace. But one thing is certain: every year it continues it throws the country and the business interests of the country back a decade. If this thing goes on we shall ere long be back into the middle ages ...

Had the politicians at Ottawa – we cannot call them statesmen; we have no statesmen, or, at least, enough to act as pallbearers to a lightweight corpse – passed the three months in discussing ways and means of hoeing corn they would have done more good than they have done in discussing the question they have; they would not, at any rate, have done as much harm.[35]

---

[33] See, for example, the complaints expressed in the C.M.A., Toronto Branch Executive, *Minutebook*, Dec. 9, 1909.

[34] *Journal of Commerce*, May 23, 1890, pp. 978-9, "Political Morality"; *Industrial Canada*, Jan. 1908, p. 471, "Misleading the Masses."

[35] April 13, 1896. See also *Canadian Manufacturer*, Jan. 3, 1896: "Is it possible that the manufacturing industries of Canada are to be sacrificed to propitiate kickers who have no substantial grievances, or to enable the Government to hold to them those who would make the best interests of the country subservient to the demands of cranks who place religious prejudices above everything else?"

Complaints like these with their overtones of resentment at priority being given to the interests of religious groups reflected a more general business resentment at the role of the professional classes in Canadian society. In the early 1890's the *Canadian Manufacturer*, official organ of the C.M.A., carried on a prolonged campaign against the professional classes. It objected vigorously, for example, to the exemptions of religious institutions from taxation. Pointing out that the extra tax burden fell on manufacturers and workers alike, the journal assumed a common cause with labour against the power of organized religion:

> The lofty cathedral with its spire and bells, its expensive organ and its cushioned pews, costing thousands and thousands of dollars, and used almost exclusively by wealthy people, goes untaxed, while perhaps across the street, or within the shadows of its walls, is the small factory where the poor man works for his daily bread, and the humble cottage that shelters him and his family, and which are taxed, a part of the tax money going to support the rich man's church.[36]

The tax question opened up the whole issue of higher education, which at the post-primary level seemed directed almost solely towards producing more professional people – doctors, lawyers, and ministers. In an age before businessmen, their sons, or their employees felt they had any particular need for higher education, public subsidization of high schools and universities seemed to be an institutionalization of class privilege. As the *Canadian Manufacturer* put it:

> It has became (*sic*) painfully evident that society is divided into a privileged class, and a class who not only have to bear their own burdens, but are outrageously taxed to help support the others. As in days when the Israelites were in bondage in Egypt, there are taskmasters, and there are servants who labor for them. If a parent desires to give a son a collegiate education, let him pay for it out of his own resources, and not compel others to do it for him. The system that allows this to be done is inherently wrong.[37]

Moreover, businessmen complained that a social structure which gave the highest status to learned professionals led to an overcrowding of these professions at the expense of businessmen and farmers who suffered from labour shortages. "Hundreds of young men," the *Canadian Manufacturer* argued, "who might make good farmers, or blacksmiths, or coal heavers, or scaven-

---

[36] Dec. 2, 1887, p. 364. See also *Canadian Journal of Commerce*, Oct. 21, 1887, pp. 754-5, "The Civic Debt": "The existence of a law allowing exemption of property from taxation simply on the grounds of its belonging to a religious body is a relic of feudalism that is simply an anachronism in a civilized city in the nineteenth century."

[37] Nov. 17, 1893, pp. 402-3, "Student Pranks."

gers, or stablemen, are ruined for all useful purposes by a system which draws them away from the occupation for which they are best fitted, and at the expense of the public galvanized into professionals for which the country has no possible use."[38] The problem, it suggested, was the "glamour" with which the professional men artificially surrounded their occupations, "knowing that if this glamour is dispelled and their importance measured according to its true worth and intrinsic merit, a much larger percentage of them (*sic*) who are now unemployed would be forced to earn their bread by honest toil."[39] "Honest toil" was thought to characterize the businessman, the worker, and the farmer, but not the professional. He was too often "a caterpillar on the leaf of commerce."

By the twentieth century simple resistance to subsidizing education for professionals gave way in business circles to demands that the educational system be adjusted to include technical or vocational training; in other words that the state bear the expense of training workers just as it did the expense of training professionals. At the university level the transition came fairly easily because of the pressure that would-be philanthropists could apply, and also because the new scientific and technical courses could be tacked on to liberal arts programs without eliminating them.[40] The struggle to achieve technical education in the primary and secondary schools, though, was long and difficult. It took a decade of organized agitation by the Canadian Manufacturers' Association before the Dominion government appointed a Royal Commission on the subject and the provinces began making serious efforts in that direction. This was not the fault of a conservative, cautious business class – which in fact was more united and aggressive on this than any other single issue. Rather it was partly due to the rigidity of the constitution, partly to the conservatism of the professional elites in Canada who resisted challenges to their vested interest in an archaic educational establishment.[41]

It is unclear whether business distaste for professionals was objectively rooted in the Canadian class and power structure or whether many of the protests reflect business envy of the high social status accorded to professionals. In presenting a Board of Trade brief to the Royal Commission on Industrial Training and Technical Education in 1912, a Toronto manufacturer complained of the element growing up in Canadian universities "that looks down upon our commercial and industrial courses." Although the

[38] *Ibid.*

[39] March 26, 1891, p. 188, "Unemployed Churchmen." See also *Canadian Manufacturer*, Jan. 19, 1894, p. 51, "Over-Production of Professional Men"; July 17, 1891, p. 78, "The Education of Doctors"; *Canadian Journal of Commerce*, Dec. 12, 1890, p. 1125, "Our Boys."

[40] See *Report of the Royal Commission on the University of Toronto* (Toronto, 1906), *passim.*

[41] For technical education see the annual reports of the C.M.A. Technical Education Committee, reprinted in *Industrial Canada*; for professional resistance see *Canadian Annual Review*, 1904, pp. 579-80.

world had now become "a great arena for commerce," too much of the teaching in the schools emphasized the heroes of war, literature, art, and history. "Industry and commerce will never be put on its proper plane," he said, "until we have the idea from the beginning that the heroes and the great men and the industrious men in those two channels are just as great in the sight of Providence and in the sight of the nation as men in some of the professions."[42] Technical education would have improved the skills of this man's employees; honour to the heroes of industry would have uplifted his ego.

All the prestige-inflated professions, professional politicians, union agitators, and ignorant voters put together could not equal the threat to the businessman's well-being posed by members of his own class. Business disunity is the key factor explaining most of the problems bedevilling Canadian businessmen during the period. One main reason the C.P.R. could not feel secure in its partnership with the Conservative government was the Grand Trunk's active partnership with the Liberal Opposition. Then again, neither giant railway could be secure in its relations with any government after shippers began their campaign against soulless, irresponsible railway corporations in the 1880's.[43] The C.M.A. proudly took credit for the eventual establishment of formal public control over railways when the Board of Railway Commissioners was founded in 1902 and went on to sponsor many of the anti-railway charges brought before the Commission.[44] In turn, though, on the issue of protection the lumbering, mining, and importing interests formed a powerful Fifth Column in the business community working hand in glove with the farmer against the manufacturers (who always had great difficulty agreeing among themselves on desirable rates of duty). Businessmen also divided on questions of public ownership: Ontario's public power crusade was almost entirely a struggle within the business community, the nature of which was camouflaged only because for campaign purposes manufacturers equated their desire for cheap electricity with populist anti-corporation sentiment. Throughout the period honest businessmen who wanted to put business-government relations on a business-like basis were thwarted by the grafting and boodling section of the business community allied with the grafting and boodling section of the political community.[45] There was always an enterprizing businessman to break a common front against labour; alternatively the problem of competing with non-union firms stifled many prospects for mutual cooperation between well meaning employers and their

[42] Royal Commission on Industrial Training and Technical Education, *Report of the Commissioners*, (Toronto, 1913), Part IV, pp. 2102-3.
[43] See *The Trader, Canadian Manufacturer, Canadian Journal of Commerce*, pp. 1882-3, *passim*.
[44] *Industrial Canada*, Oct. 1903, p. 117.
[45] The problem greatly worried Joseph Flavelle. See Flavelle to J. Willison, Nov. 11, 1913, *Flavelle Papers*, Douglas Library, Queen's University.

unions. Small businessmen initiated most of the critique of big business usually identified with populism and progressivism in North America, largely because big business thrived on the wreckage of small business. Finally, organized in their local and regional Boards of Trade, businessmen engaged in endless struggles against one another for local and sectional profit, thus generating most of the sound and fury of Canadian regional disunity.

The associational activities of the business classes – usually organizations and combines to fix prices, control production, and limit access – were the clearest expression of a thrust towards class consciousness and unity. In most ways they were the exact analogues of labour unions, particularly in their vulnerability to that peculiar form of scabbing known in the business world as competition. Virtually every combine put together during the 1880's and 1890's was broken by business disunity. The government's fairly feeble anti-trust activities of the late 1880's were also directly sponsored by businessmen, though at this stage it was hardly necessary for the government to supplement the operations of the free market with legislation.[46] The very operation of the free market was both a symptom of the business disunity that existed and a guarantee that it would continue to exist.

The very real anxieties felt by businessmen operating in a harshly competitive environment were expressed in many ways. Dozens of articles in trade journals condemned unfair competitive methods, such as price-cutting, slaughter sales of bankrupt stocks, and the use of extended credits. There was even a wistful "Psalm for the Trade" printed in several trade journals of the 1880's:

> Shun this reckless competition.
> Look beyond the moment's gain,
> Learn that honest coalition
> Is far better in the main.[47]

"Demoralizing" was the standard word used to describe fierce competition in any trade. It carries endless connotations. Other writers condemned unrelenting business competition as a misapplication of the analogy of war to commerce, and blamed its practitioners for bringing the morality of war to business life.[48] Men who opposed any kind of limitation of competition were asked to consider "the heartbreaking anxiety of men who can only do business at a loss" and then they would appreciate the problem in a new light.[49] Images of business brotherhood and cooperation, the concept of strength

---

[46] *Report of the Select Committee to Investigate and Report Upon Alleged Combinations in Manufactures, Trade and Insurance in Canada* (Ottawa, 1888), *passim.* All of the witnesses against combines were businessmen. Chairman of the Committee and initiator of the first anti-combines bill, Clarke Wallace, was a small businessman.

[47] *The Trader*, Feb. 1885.

[48] *Canadian Grocer*, July 8, 1892, p. 1.

[49] *Monetary Times*, Feb. 22, 1895, p. 1091.

through unity, permeated the rhetoric of trade association banquets and journals.[50] The very idea of competition was dismissed as "too destructive to be permitted to exist," "too destructive to be tolerated"[51] (business historians, the worst "whig" historians of all, too often ignore the long failure lists published in every trade journal, mute evidence of the validity of the complaint). Businessmen frequently complained about too many men chasing too little business, suggesting now and then that a return to the farm would be the best thing that could happen to ease the crush of competition.[52] Looking into the future in 1894 a Canadian banker foresaw that competition was approaching the period of its old age, that individualism in material affairs would soon come to an end, and the "commissariat department of society" would soon be organized entirely "collectively." The insecurity of competitive business life would be banished forever, as the young man on leaving school or college "will be drafted into the service of one or other of the great industrial corporations of the country, which he will never leave during the period of his working life." That would be a wonderfully beneficial development.[53]

Feeling himself harassed and set upon by enemies and competitors, it is not surprising that the Canadian businessman worried about the state of his health. George Stephen constantly teetered on the brink of a nervous breakdown. Joseph Flavelle enjoyed good health himself, but repeatedly advised friends that they were making impossibly large drains on their stock of nervous force. A doctor advised businessmen through the *Monetary Times* that the constant overpressure they endured in modern business life was sure to lead to the destruction of the nervous system. And when Erastus Wiman was arrested on charges of embezzlement the same doctor argued that he had finally broken down under the strain and become completely insane.[54] The employee had a very easy time of life compared with his employer, claimed an article in the *Canadian Grocer*:

> His hours of labor are fixed, and his work is of a routine nature, requiring very little thought or care, except that necessary to the faithful performance of his duties. He knows just how much he is making, and when his day's work is done he can lay aside all care without fret or worry.

[50] *Canadian Grocer*, Jan. 29, 1892, p. 26; "Modern Industrialism," *Financial Post*, July 1, 1911.

[51] See any issue of the *Retail Merchant's Journal of Canada, 1903-07*.

[52] Speech of Geo. Hague at annual meeting of the Merchant's Bank, *Monetary Times*, June 18, 1886, p. 1447.

[53] Thomas Fyshe, "The Growth of Corporations," *Journal of the Canadian Bankers' Association*, II, 2, Dec. 1894, pp. 197-203.

[54] *Flavelle Papers*, Flavelle to J. S. Willison, Nov. 28, 1902; Jan. 22, 1903; *Monetary Times*, Dec. 23, 1887, "The Health of Businessmen," 790; June 29, 1894, 1651, "The Case of Erastus Wiman."

But with his employer it is quite different. With him it is constant, unceasing work, and his mind can never be entirely free from his business cares. He has to meet and overcome competition. He must watch the markets, both as a purchaser and a seller of goods. He must plan and devise, control and direct . . . Not for a moment can he rest.

The life of a successful business man is one constant round of work from morning till night, . . . [55]

Worry, it appeared, was the everyday state of mind of the man in business. It was a condition that the Winnipeg *Commercial* labelled "dyspepsia of the mind."[56]

This evidence should sustain the one proposition under examination: that in the formative years of Canadian industrialism the business class perceived itself to be operating in a hostile environment. Accepting that, many questions remain: Are these expressions of frustration and resentment, this basic business insecurity, simply self-pitying shudders at the approach of an imaginary wolf? Were these businessmen simply members of a simpering, paranoic elite, unaware of their overpoweringly dominant role in Canadian society – captains of industry raging through limpid pools? Or will future analyses of Canadian social structure in the late nineteenth and early twentieth centuries (at the moment of writing we have none) verify some of the business complaints? Perhaps Canadian politicians were an order unto themselves, juggling competing religious, racial, regional and economic interests to no purpose beyond being able to go on juggling. Possibly the liberal professions in Canada did enjoy a disproportionate share of social and political power. Similarly it may be that the Canadian working classes, benefiting from battles won abroad, in fact gained social and political influence in Canada relative to their employers more rapidly than workingmen had in other countries during the early years of industrialism.

Further, what are the entrepreneurial implications of this kind of insecurity on the part of a business community? Did we have in Canada a spiritually decapitated bourgeoisie, too timid and uncertain to provide us with the kind of solid national economic base that true Schumpeterian entrepreneurs would have created?[57] Does this in turn help to explain the ensuing decades of American takeovers of Canadian enterprises? Alternatively, it may well be that constant anxiety has always been the silent partner of businessmen operating in any society (when you have to rely on the future for returns on your investment how can you avoid anxiety?), particularly in fiercely competitive capitalist societies. Perhaps this very anxiety has in many cases driven

---

[55] *Canadian Grocer*, March 18, 1892, p. 8, "Attention to Business."

[56] *Ibid.*, July 31, 1883, p. 928, "Business Worry."

[57] As Melville Watkins has argued. See his "A New National Policy," in Trevor Lloyd and Jack McLeod, eds., *Agenda 70: Proposals for a Creative Politics* (Toronto, 1968).

entrepreneurs on to build great industrial empires, thus forestalling all future anxieties incident to competition (monopoly being the obvious answer to the parenthetical question).

Perhaps some variation of the Polanyi thesis applies to Canada: the social consequences of unrestrained capitalism were too much for actors in society to bear. They created an immediate and massive reaction against *laissez-faire* throughout the western world leading to social arrangements guaranteeing the individual a measure of relief from the strains of life in an unregulated, uncertain society.[58] Robert Wiebe and others have provided some evidence that this process did operate in late nineteenth century America, and that it was in part led by businessmen fleeing from the chaos of adolescent industrialism.[59] The simple generalization implied in this interpretation – that open competition in a dynamic society makes all its participants anxious – provides the broadest covering explanation of the evidence presented here. Further research will flesh out some of the details.

[58] Karl Polanyi, *The Great Transformation* (Boston, 1944).

[59] Robert Wiebe, *Businessmen and Reform*, (Cambridge, Mass., 1962); *The Search for Order* (New York, 1967); Thomas C. Cochran, *Railroad Leaders, 1845-1890* (Cambridge, Mass., 1953); Gabriel Kolko, *The Triumph of Conservatism* (New York, 1963); E. C. Kirkland, *Dream and Thought in the Business Community, 1868-1900* (Ithaca, 1956).

The Character of the Entrepreneur: The Case of George Stephen

J. Lorne MacDougall, formerly of the School of Business, Queen's University

The bare facts regarding George Stephen who died Lord Mount Stephen, full of years and honours in 1921, are soon told. He was born in Banffshire, Scotland, in June 1829, the son of a carpenter and grandson of a mason.[1] At the age of ten his father was ready to take him out of the parish school and relented only on pressure from the schoolmaster. From then on it is probable that he was out of school for as much as six months each summer. In the winter he certainly contributed to his own keep by acting as herd boy for the minister.

At the age of fourteen Stephen finally left school. His first job was as hostler at the local hotel. He was there for at least six months[2] and then he and the hotel-keeper's son went to Aberdeen and apprenticed themselves to a draper and silk-mercer.

In 1848, his apprenticeship finished, he went to Glasgow, found nothing in the way of employment because of the current depression, and went on to London. Here he found work, first with a draper and, later, with a wholesale dry goods house in St. Paul's Churchyard. Two years later his father's cousin, a wholesale dry goods merchant in Montreal, came into the establishment, was served by George Stephen, and ended by offering him a job. In a short while he was a junior partner and was making regular trips to England as buyer. From that point on he never looked back. His life was a steady progression up the ladder of success as wholesale merchant, entrepreneur in the organisation of manufacturing companies, financier, member of the groups which built what became the Great Northern Railway[3] in the northern United States and the Canadian Pacific Railway in Canada, and, finally, as an international capitalist, living in England.

The estimates of his personality are remarkably varied. Professor Donald C. Masters who had read his letters in the Macdonald papers speaks of him as a "big-hearted, generous impulsive man."[4] It is not a description which the present writer would have thought fitting, nor does it coincide with that

---

[1] *Heather Gilbert, Awakening Continent: the Life of Lord Mount Stephen*, I, chapter 1.

[2] Mrs. Gilbert says that he left school at the age of fourteen which would be before June 1843. He went to Aberdeen in 1844, but the month is not stated.

[3] Now a segment of the Burlington Northern. The merger of the Great Northern, the Northern Pacific and the Chicago, Burlington and Quincy in 1970 was merely the final step in an association which began in 1901.

[4] D. C. Masters, "Financing the C.P.R. 1880-85," *Canadian Historical Review*, 24 (1943), pp. 330-361.

of D. C. Coleman[5] who had the fullest opportunity to talk with those who had known Stephen in the C.P.R. The impression which both Coleman and Mrs. Gilbert give, and in which I concur, is that of a Scot who shared to the full in the shortcomings as well as in the positive qualities of his race – thin skinned, intensely proud, likely to draw back in hurt pride when under attack, and with an elephant's memory for past slights.

Of course he was generous. His gift of half a million dollars[6] to the Royal Victoria Hospital, made at a time (1886) when a dollar was a substantial sum of money, is the rough equivalent of some ten million dollars today; but it was the generosity of a man who could never be a hail-fellow-well-met. To read Van Horne's letters is to know exactly how he felt when he wrote. Stephen's letters, on the other hand, are those of a man who was, if anything, excessively controlled. He would keep every promise he ever made, but he could never reveal himself to others and, perhaps, not even to himself.[7]

This may appear critical of the man who, as much as any other single person, made Canada a coherent entity. It is rather to be viewed as a comment on the nature of political life in Canada. Anyone who expects gratitude for public service – and the linking of the country together by Canadian Pacific Railway was certainly a public service of a very high order – is perhaps naif. Stephen did expect that and withdrew from active direction of the C.P.R. in 1888 and from the country shortly after. There may be countries in which public service is rewarded with adulation and gratitude – but Canada is not one of them. The more likely public response is a period of intense questioning as to how much one has made out of it.

The really important question about George Stephen is how a man who was in effect a penniless immigrant at 1850 could become a prominent merchant in Montreal by 1860 and an entrepreneur of the first order by 1875.

To this question there are two answers; the first predominantly personal, the second, institutional.

George Stephen had come up in a house in which money was scarce and under the guidance of a mother who believed in whole-souled devotion to work. In his own words:

. . . It was impressed upon me from my earliest youth by one of the best

---

[5] D. C. Coleman, *Lord Mount Stephen: 1829-1921 and the Canadian Pacific Railway.* (New York, 1945). Mr. Coleman was Chairman and President of the C.P.R. in the early '40's, having spent his whole life in the service of the Company. He retired in 1945.

[6] *D.N.B.* 1912-1921, pp. 509-510. Donald Smith gave equal amounts. In his life Stephen gave a total of one million pounds sterling and left the residue of his estate to King Edward's Hospital Fund.

[7] Cf. the rather famous letter of 9th July, 1880, in which he withdrew from the early negotiations to build the C.P.R. It is reproduced most recently in J. Lorne McDougall, *Canadian Pacific: A Brief History* (Montreal, 1968), pp. 33-35.

mothers who ever lived that I must aim at being a thorough master of the work by which I had to get my living and to be that I must concentrate, I was told, my whole energies on my work, whatever it might be, to the exclusion of every other thing. . . .[8]

The message took root in his soul. Stephen was never one to shirk his duties. He would seem, also, to have been a man who had a nose for money, willingness to take risks to make it, and that sixth sense, which some have, which tells them when to take risks and when to draw back, when to say no, as the famous investment magnate Dundee Fleming put it when asked for the secret of his success.

Even as a young man in this twenties, Stephen seems to have been dominant in his cousin's dry-goods firm by sheer ability and not because of his capital contribution. The extent of the risks he assumed came close to terrifying the cousin; but he brought the ventures off profitably.[9] It is a reasonable guess that one of these ventures – heavy purchases of goods in England when the Crimean war was imminent but before prices rose – was an important contribution to his rise in financial power. It was before the first cable was established. He had to act on his own responsibility or let the opportunity go; but he bought and shipped the goods while vessels were still available; and when prices rose on account of shortages of both goods and shipping, and because a boom was developing in Canada, the Stephen firm was all set to take full advantage of it.

It is true that Stephen had the advice of an astute older man in these particular transactions; but this is normal in the rise of any young man of promise. Rising young men attract advisers because they show themselves quick learners.

Wholesale trade had much more generous profit margins at this time than it had after 1914, and Stephen used the strategic position of his firm to move out into industrial ventures. The firm had first established a good market for Canadian tweeds and then Stephen took the almost standard step of becoming a partner in a woollen mill. This occurred in 1866. A second woollen mill was added in 1868, and a cotton company in 1872. But Stephen stepped outside the standard pattern by refusing to confine himself to the textile field. In 1869 he was one of a group which took over the Montreal Rolling Mills. The Canada Rolling Stock Company followed in 1870. He also had an interest in the Canadian Locomotive and Engine Company of Kingston.

The final proof of Stephen's arrival as a leading business man came with his appointment as a director of the Bank of Montreal in 1871, Vice-President in 1873 and President in 1876. At the time, the Bank of Montreal was the dominant bank in Canada to a degree which has no modern parallel.

---

[8] Speech on receiving the freedom of Aberdeen in 1901. Quoted in Gilbert, *op. cit.*, p. 5.
[9] *Ibid.*, p.7.

By 1870 then, Stephen had demonstrated a capacity to run his own businesses profitably and a capacity for working as a member of small groups of entrepreneurs in running other businesses. In twenty years he had risen from penniless immigrant (or young man with prospects, but no tangible capital), to being a power in the land. How was it possible to rise so rapidly?

The first point that has to be made is that there was no income tax, personal or corporate. If a man was on the rise, he could accumulate capital very rapidly. As has been shown, *ad nauseam*, a high income tax weights the scales heavily against the new men. The rise of Henry Ford, for example, would certainly have been slowed down out of all recognition had income tax at current rates been in effect when he was getting started.[10]

This is, of course, just as important now as it was a century ago. A government which tries to encourage a higher level of capital investment than domestic saving will support, which keeps the income tax at a very high level, and which also deplores the growing foreign ownership of Canadian industry, may have its heart in the right place to win votes, but it cannot ask respect for its intellectual consistency. Great entrepreneurs must not only be venturesome, they must be able to accumulate the means to venture.

Secondly, the profits which Stephen made in Canada were probably[11] not adequate to support his largest and most important operation in Canada, the building of the C.P.R. The extraordinary success of the Hill-Stephen railway venture, which ultimately became the Great Northern, did two things. It put Stephen in funds so that he could undertake the C.P.R. and what is more important, it provided collateral against which he could borrow to support it.

James J. Hill's biographer reported the earnings of the St. Paul and Pacific in the year to June 30, 1878, as $474,000.[1] This figure is for the railway only, and does not include the land earnings. The combined railway and land earnings rose from $232,170 in 1877 to $680,582 in 1878[13] when the property was almost into the hands of the syndicate. Earnings of 1879 have not been traced but the years next following ran as follows on page 196.[14]

The syndicate received fifteen million dollars of common stock in the successor Company, the St. Paul, Minneapolis and Manitoba when it was formally organised at October 1879, and Stephen's share was at least twenty

---

[10] Cf. Butters and Lintner, *Effect of Federal Taxes on Growing Enterprises* (Boston, 1945).

[11] It would have been most valuable to have had a statement of his holdings at successive dates; but nothing of the kind seems to be available. Without such a statement, qualifications like this one are inevitable, and Stephen's case points the general prevalence of deplorable gaps in our knowledge concerning many key figures in Canadian business history. This tragic state of affairs is largely due to the destruction of business records over the last seventy years.

[12] J. G. Pyle, *The Life of James J. Hill* (New York, 1916), p. 353.

[13] See *ibid.*, p. 274.

[14] Poor's Manual, 1887, p. 836.

Year	Railway net earnings	Land Department, etc.
		in $000
1880	1,585	650
81	1,955	228
82	3,309	895
83	4,748	964
84	4,522	633
85	4,460	198
86	3,663	521

per cent of it. In the fall of 1881, a dividend of seven per cent was declared payable in February and August 1882. In 1883 the Company issued a new consolidated six per cent bond issue of which ten million dollars was at once sold to the stockholders at ten per cent of par value.

This was the cornucopia which made it possible for Stephen and his cousin Donald Smith, later Lord Strathcona, to stand under the C.P.R. and nurse it through to health.[15]

The legend that Stephen and Smith created the C.P.R. almost single-handedly, that they stood like rocks under it when it could not borrow on its own credit, is now very firmly established. In its main outlines it is true. But one can still wish that it was possible to know how they felt about the Company in the gruelling years of waiting which stretched out to 1896. Did they perhaps feel that they had been sucked into a bad speculation by the fantastic immediate success of the St. Paul, Minneapolis and Manitoba, and that the ease of building in the Red River valley was no preparation for Northern Ontario and the Rocky Mountains, or for those long dragging years when the Canadian Prairies failed to attract settlement?

For the writer, at least, it would add to their stature if it could be shown that they held on while being uncertain of the final outcome.

What a pity it is that all the interesting questions are nearly insoluble; but one still hopes that when the Hill papers are finally released,[16] Stephen's letters to Hill will at least permit some of those questions to be examined.

[15] One suspects that the inability of Van Horne to produce similar results from the C.P.R. was responsible for the coldness that developed between them. Still, sympathy goes to Van Horne; the growth of Minnesota and the Dakotas in the 1880's was paralleled in the Canadian west after 1896; but when Van Horne was heading the C.P.R. he could not counsel patience in the knowledge that growth would come. The entrepreneur hopes but cannot prove that it will come; and that is all.

[16] In 1957 the Hill family agreed to the formation of a committee to hold title to James J. Hill's papers and to administer them until December 31, 1981. On that date, the full legal title, the power to administer the papers, and the power to control their use, will be conveyed to the Hill Reference Library in Saint Paul, Minnesota.

3/Case Studies in North American Business

Peter Buchanan, London Agent for the Great Western Railway of Canada

Douglas McCalla, Assistant Professor of History, Trent University*

In 1845, a group of promoters in Hamilton revived the charter of the old London and Gore Railway and set out again to launch their city into the railroad age. Lacking capital, experience in corporate management and finance, and knowledge of the technology involved in construction and operation of a railway, they proposed nevertheless to build a line, to be known as the Great Western Railway of Canada, from Niagara Falls to Windsor via Hamilton. In this way they intended to connect Hamilton with its commercial hinterland in western Upper Canada while at the same time providing a part of the shortest rail route from New York to Chicago.

Historians have recorded only an outline of the complex process by which this inexperienced group, backing one among many Canadian railway schemes, most of which proved ephemeral, produced in a few years and with relatively limited government aid a heavily capitalized, profitable corporation.[1] There is, for example, no very convincing account of the financing of this company in London, where the bulk of the Great Western's capital had to be raised. To say this is not to slight the work of previous historians but to emphasize the amount of work still required before the history of even Canada's best known businesses can be said to have been written. This essay, then, focusses on the business history of the Great Western, especially its financing in London. Peter Buchanan, the central figure of this essay, is scarcely mentioned in the histories of the Great Western,[2] but he was impor-

* I should like to thank Professor Elwood Jones for his helpful advice and comments on a number of points. A grant from Trent University supported part of the research for this chapter.

[1] G. R. Stevens, *Canadian National Railways*, Vol. 1 (Toronto; 1960), pp. 90-150; and A. W. Currie, *The Grand Trunk Railway of Canada* (Toronto, 1957), pp. 161-219, remain the standard accounts despite R. D. Smith, "The Early Years of the Great Western Railway, 1833-1857," *Ontario History*, lx (1968), pp. 205-27.

[2] He is mentioned by Currie, p. 165, but identified, incorrectly, as a banker.

tant to the company in its early years, above all by helping it to launch itself in Britain.

In 1846, Peter Buchanan was forty years of age and for ten years had been senior partner in the mercantile firms of Peter Buchanan and Company, in Glasgow, and Buchanan, Harris and Company, in Hamilton. As his firm dominated the wholesale trade in Hamilton, he was the leading businessman resident in Britain with interests in Hamilton, but by the standards of the rich and diverse Glasgow and London financial and mercantile communities, his was a relatively small business. Even so, he was ideally placed to serve as a link between the Hamilton group of railway promoters and the British interests whose support the railway required.

Because the promoters of the Great Western needed capital above all, Sir Allan MacNab, their leading figure, travelled to England with J. B. Ewart in September, 1845, to seek funds. On arrival, they recruited Peter Buchanan in Glasgow and Malcolm Cowan, a London solicitor, to assist them. Buchanan readily agreed, for his wholesale house depended on the power of Hamilton over its commercial hinterland, and a railroad would therefore help his business.[3]

The four reached London at the height of the great 1845 railway share boom and quickly secured support from a syndicate of eleven powerful railway men. The famous George Hudson was much the most prominent of these, though it seems unlikely that he was the principal organizer;[4] in the long term, the two key figures were Samuel Laing, an emerging railway expert who had served on Lord Dalhousie's Railway Board, and John Masterman Jr., a London private banker with wide and growing railway interests. The eleven subscribed for all 55,000 shares to be issued in Britain, intending to manage their issue to the investing public in return for premiums on the shares. The syndicate began to issue scrip, which soon reached a premium of over five pounds. Peter Buchanan reported jubilantly that "there is no one more than another who can claim the credit of this masterstroke for the Interests of Canada. It has been the result of chance and good luck entirely."[5] Thinking the success of the project assured, he saw no reason not to join, with the Great Western's other three representatives, in the profits of

---

[3] Public Archives of Canada, *Buchanan Papers*, Peter Buchanan to Isaac Buchanan, Sept. 17, 1845; Allan MacNab and J. B. Ewart to Peter Buchanan, Sept. 13, 1845; Peter Buchanan to R. W. Harris, August 10, 1849 (copy). 13/11672, 46/37009-10, 67/52982. In subsequent footnotes, Peter Buchanan will be referred to as Buchanan. This chapter is based largely on the Buchanan Papers, a rich source as yet untapped by Canadian railway historians. Unless otherwise specified, all manuscript references are to these papers.

[4] Richard S. Lambert, *The Railway King, 1800-1871* (London, 1934), pp. 159-73. Henry G. Lewin, *The Railway Mania and Its Aftermath, 1845-1852* (New York, 1968), pp. 46, 77, 142. *Buchanan Papers*, Prospectus of the Great Western Railway of Canada, 1845, 93/65159.

[5] Buchanan to Isaac Buchanan, Oct. 3, 1845; also Oct. 10, 1845, 13/11680-3, pp. 6-7.

the London syndicate, and he urged his partners to watch for profits through contracts and patronage.

By November, 1845, however, the boom had collapsed and Great Western shares were at a discount. At once the differing perspectives of the Canadian and English groups in the company emerged: the Canadians sought their profit primarily through development of an area in which they were interested, while the English sought profit through short term speculation or dividends and capital gains. The Canadians hoped to force subscribers to pay on their shares. The scripholders and members of the London syndicate, which still held most of the shares, wanted no calls made. Some wished to wind up the company to recover deposits, some wished simply to escape any legal obligation to make further payments, even at cost of losing deposits paid, while a few wished to continue to develop the line.[6]

Negotiations between the groups in Hamilton and London concerning the company's future inevitably proved difficult. Peter Buchanan, among others, urged the appointment of an intermediary in whom both the English and Canadians had confidence, and volunteered for the position. Buchanan's credentials were sound. A permanent British resident, with real interests at stake in the Great Western project, he was a frequent visitor to Hamilton. Yet he was trusted by the Londoners and understood their business viewpoints. The board of the railway readily agreed to name him "agent on behalf of the Company to treat with the Corresponding Committee in England concerning matters of importance which seem unexpectedly to have arisen in England. . . . "[7] From 1846 to 1855, Buchanan served as sole or joint London agent of the Great Western, for the railway soon found that it needed a permanent agent to act for it in London; personal negotiation was involved in many of the crucial business decisions which had to be made there in the company's early years. Peter Buchanan took on the position above all to foster the development of Hamilton and his business there, but as his involvement in the London syndicate showed, he was not uninterested in private profits should the opportunity to gain them arise. Although he showed no inclination to become one of the growing group in London of fulltime railway experts, he was attracted too by the chance to associate with leaders in finance and in the fast-growing London railway world.

In February, 1846, he began his career as agent by travelling to London to negotiate with the subscribers. Many of them proved moderately optimistic,

---

[6] M. Uzielli to Buchanan, Nov. 29, 1845; M. Cowan to Buchanan, Dec. 9 and 15, 1845; S. Laing to Buchanan, Dec. 16, 1845; Buchanan to Isaac Buchanan, March 2, 1846. 58-46041; 22/18536, pp. 38-41; 37/30413-6; 14/17000-1. L. H. Jenks, *The Migration of British Capital to 1875* (London, 1963), pp. 163-7.

[7] J. T. Gilkison to Buchanan, Jan. 24, 1846, 27/23328. See also M. Uzielli to Buchanan, Feb. 21, 1846; W. O'Brien to Sir A. N. MacNab, Nov. 29, 1845 (copy); M. Cowan to Buchanan, March 1, 1846. 58/46046-7; 46/37031-2; 22/18542-5. The Corresponding Committee was an organization of the scripholders.

anticipating that the share market would soon revive, and he sought to assist this group in its debate with those who favored a wind-up of the company. At the same time, he counselled the directors in Canada that any attempt to compel shareholders to pay on their shares would lead to legal action which would destroy the company, and he advised the directors to modify the company's charter to meet the demands of the Londoners for security. For a time, in the summer of 1846, the stock market again looked promising and his efforts seemed rewarded, but by the end of 1846 there was clearly little hope of the line's going ahead.[8] From 1847 to 1849, conditions in the financial world precluded any further effort to raise funds in England. The company conducted surveys with the deposits it had received, but it could not compel the shareholders to pay up or forfeit their shares. The shareholders in turn were unable to secure repayment of deposits. Periodically Peter Buchanan discussed these issues with the London Corresponding Committee, concentrating his efforts largely on keeping the company in existence in London.

In August, 1846, Buchanan had been committed more deeply to the syndicate of London backers by his brother Isaac, acting for him in his absence in Canada. As a result, through these years Peter Buchanan held 3680 shares in the company, on which five shillings deposit had been paid. This reflected the difficulty of disposing of shares rather than any desire for long term investment. Shares were an unremunerative investment to a merchant with an expanding business.[9] Through these years, Peter Buchanan was also helping to promote the Trust and Loan Company of Upper Canada in Britain; in this he worked with Robert S. Atcheson, an Englishman who also began to take an interest in the affairs of the railway company. In 1849, as part of a general effort to revive the company, Sir Allan MacNab was replaced as president by R. W. Harris, Buchanan's leading Canadian partner at the time. A taciturn, rather withdrawn individual, with whom Buchanan nevertheless worked easily, Harris was a strong figure in the Hamilton business community and more able than MacNab to preside over a large business enterprise. His post as president and Buchanan's as agent reinforced one another, and this was one key to Buchanan's strength as agent in the early 1850's.[10]

[8] Buchanan to Isaac Buchanan, March 12, 1846 and n.d.; and to R. W. Harris, Aug. 31, 1849 (copy); Sir A. N. MacNab to Isaac Buchanan, Aug. 9, 1846; and to Buchanan, Sept. 3 and 18, 1846; R. S. Atcheson to Isaac Buchanan, Dec. 15, 1846. 14/11720-1, 11758; 67/52986-8; 46/37141-3, pp. 166, 170-1; 1/623.

[9] Buchanan to Harris, Aug. 31, 1849 and Sept. 27, 1850 (copies); and to T. Tilson, Sept. 20, 1850 (copy); Sir A. N. MacNab to Isaac Buchanan, Oct. 24, 1846. 67/52986-8, 53119-20; 66/52397-8; 46/37180.

[10] Buchanan to Isaac Buchanan, March 10, 1848; and to Harris, August 10 and 31, 1849 (copies), and Aug. 9, 1855; Atcheson to Isaac Buchanan, Dec. 15, 1846; Sir A. N. MacNab to Buchanan, Aug. 6 and 18, 1849, 14/11827; 67/52982-4, pp. 86-8; 15/12422-5; 1/623; 46/37202-4, pp. 6-9.

The Great Western now considered government aid, both in Canada and in Britain, as a necessary prerequisite to the all-important support desired from private individuals in Britain. The Canadian provincial and municipal governments agreed in 1849 to furnish aid, but an approach by Atcheson and Buchanan to the British government early in 1850 met a not unexpected rebuff.[11] Only in 1851 did the Great Western's prospects really turn upwards, and even then there were problems in bringing the many sources of funds together simultaneously. The municipalities along the route had agreed to take shares, selling their own bonds to pay for them, but it was not entirely clear that these bonds would sell. The contractors who would build the line would take shares in part payment of their contracts, but the share market could be upset if they tried to sell these shares too quickly. The American lines which would be linked by the Great Western confirmed their longstanding interest by beginning to pay for shares, but avenues of retreat were kept open. The Canadian Government's Guarantee Act, which permitted the sale of bonds whose interest was guaranteed by the government, once half the line was completed, meant that the company now need only raise funds initially to construct half its line. But it was still necessary to raise money in England to give the company the capital to build half the line.

In 1849, Peter Buchanan had advised that "a party resident in London of good standing would require to be appointed to try to get the public of this Country to come forward to take shares . . . ,"[12] and that such a party would have to be well paid. In reply, the board had asked him, with R. S. Atcheson, to do this, though only Atcheson resided in London, and little if any remuneration was offered. Throughout 1850 and 1851, the two men sought £200,000 in England, the sum estimated to be needed to complete half the line. Peter Buchanan continued to look for funds from the "old party," a number of shareholders and subscribers of 1845-6; this group now wanted paid up shares with a par value equal to the total deposits paid. Buchanan soon concluded that few members of the old party were really interested in the company, and he advised the board to threaten to declare the shares forfeit altogether, as it was empowered to do, unless the old subscribers took shares to an amount closer to that for which they had originally subscribed.[13] He and Atcheson now concentrated on a new promotion which would largely ignore the old party.

---

[11] Buchanan to Harris, March 22 and April 5, 1850 (copies). 66/52465-8, pp. 74-5.

[12] Buchanan to Harris, Aug. 10, 1849; also Sept. 21, 1849 and Jan. 11, 1850 (copies). Power of Attorney, Jan. 12, 1852. 67/52982-3, p. 992, 53032; 93/65346-8.

[13] A compromise may finally have been reached with a few of the earlier subscribers, for some remained active in the company after 1852, but it is not clear what were its terms. Buchanan to T. Tilson, Sept. 20 and Nov. 6, 1850; to Atcheson, Nov. 6, 1850; and to C. Devaux & Co., March 10, 1851 (copies). Memorandum of agreement between Buchanan and the English bond and shareholders, May, 1852 (copy). 66/52397-8, pp. 93-5, 52400-2; 68/53647; 93/65350-2.

They found that "there is a deal of money open for investment here" but "the moment . . . you talk . . . about Foreign undertakings they turn up their noses."[14] To persuade the British public to invest in a little known overseas venture it was clearly necessary to have the support of men of influence in Britain. Atcheson, who had some connection with Barings, concentrated on the two great banking houses of Baring and Glyn, the Canadian government's financial agents in London and active financiers of American and British railroads.[15] Although Glyns showed some interest, both houses replied consistently in negative or neutral terms, saying foreign securities would not sell. Buchanan took some part in these approaches, but concentrated his efforts on Manchester and Glasgow. In each, he recruited brokers to sell shares while he sought to influence public opinion. When these efforts failed, he approached influential figures among his own mercantile connections, hoping that they in turn would spur wider interest. At length, he secured subscriptions from several of those approached, but in September, 1851, the two agents had to admit privately that their efforts were unsuccessful; they had gathered reliable subscriptions for no more than 3500 of the 10,000 shares allocated to Great Britain.[16] They had perhaps created a modest reputation for the Great Western in concerned circles, but that was all.

Buchanan and others in the Great Western had at times discussed the problems of promotion with Samuel Laing and John Masterman Jr., from the line's 1845 syndicate; in 1851 he found them looking for new companies which they could promote in London. If the Great Western turned to these men, it was effectively abandoning hope for aid from Barings and Glyns, whose names were greater, but there seemed no alternative. To encourage their interest, Buchanan offered Laing two hundred shares for the price of one hundred and advised the board to make a similar offer to Masterman. Buchanan and Atcheson's decision to work with these men led almost at once to success. Laing, Masterman, and Masterman's brother-in-law, Isaac Braithwaite, a partner in the respectable stockbroking firm of Foster and Braithwaite, devised an alternative financial strategy, working swiftly and in great secrecy to avoid complication from rival schemes. There was no time for the matter to go to the board of directors in Canada; Buchanan, Atcheson, and R. W. Harris, in England at the time on business, negotiated for the company and authorized the Londoners to proceed.[17]

[14] Buchanan to Atcheson, May 24, 1851 (copy). 68/53745.
[15] Ralph W. Hidy, *The House of Baring in American Trade and Finance* (Cambridge, Mass., 1949), pp. 414-5, 423. H. G. Lewin, *op. cit.*, p. 262. Atcheson to Buchanan, June 4, 1851; Buchanan to Harris, June 10, 1851 (copies). 66/52429; 68/53758.
[16] Buchanan to Robert Barbour, Sept. 17, 1851; and to Harris, Sept. 19, 1851 (copies). 66/52493; 68/53858-60.
[17] *The Times of London*, Feb. 21, 1861, p. 5. "Samuel Laing," *Dictionary of National Biography* (reissue), vol. xxii, pp. 948-9. L. H. Jenks, *op. cit.*, pp. 130-4. Buchanan to Harris, Sept. 19 and Nov. 24, 1851 (copies) and Dec. 10, 1851; and to Atcheson, Dec. 25, 1851 (copy). 68/53859, 53909; 14/11961-2; 68/53964.

The Londoners proposed to abandon the effort to sell shares and instead to offer bonds to a similar amount, £200,000. They argued that the British investor, fearful of common stock in an unknown, unbuilt colonial enterprise, would, if the terms were right, buy bonds, whose returns appeared more certain and which were recommended by well-known brokers. Bonds committed the railway to a heavier fixed indebtedness, but the bonds which were offered could, until a specified date, be converted into common stock at par; if the anticipated dividends were realized, the stock would be more attractive, holders would convert, and the bonded debt would be shifted to equity ownership.[18] This feature of the Great Western's offer was a major factor in its success, and it later contributed to the Great Western's financial stability in the 1857 Canadian depression. Offered by Braithwaite late in December, 1851, the entire issue was oversubscribed at par in a few days by a margin wide enough to allow for the usual defaults. By early February, the full amount had been paid. The Londoners, of course, received commissions for their work, but the Great Western at last had its funds and some real stature with the investing public in Britain.

Within a few months of this success, Atcheson, who was plagued by ill health, retired from the railway and left Peter Buchanan as sole agent. He and the London group now planned a second issue. The Great Western had not yet been able to issue shares in Britain and wished to do so to establish a position on the stock exchange. In April, 1852, Braithwaite proposed to issue 8000 shares of common stock, par value £20/10s sterling; to make these more attractive, he proposed to offer £80,000 in ten year bonds bearing six per cent interest and convertible until 1856 into common stock, buyers of bonds being required to take double the value of their bonds in common stock. For managing this issue, Foster and Braithwaite would charge 2/6 per share and one per cent on the bonds, or £1800 in all. Many new railway schemes were developing as a result of favourable stock market conditions, and Braithwaite therefore chose an early chance, late in May, to launch the issue. Again it was oversubscribed, but by a narrower margin; one observer contended that the issue would not all have been taken up had Peter Buchanan not sold it so successfully among his friends in Glasgow.[19] The Great Western had now raised over £400,000 in Britain in less than five months. This success resulted from favourable market conditions[20] and the connection with influential Londoners, but the Great Western had had to

---

[18] Dorothy R. Adler," British Investment in American Railways, 1834-1898" (Ph.D. thesis, Cambridge University, 1958), pp. 30, 91-3, 99. L. H. Jenks, *op. cit.*, pp. 167-70, 205. Buchanan to Isaac Buchanan, Dec. 13, 1851; to Harris, Dec. 11, 1851 (copy); and to John Young, Jan. 2, 1852 (copy). 14/11966-7; 68/53926, pp. 74-5.

[19] Foster and Braithwaite to Buchanan, May 12, 1852; Buchanan to Harris, May 14, 1852; George Douglas to Isaac Buchanan, June 4, 1852. 26/22217; 14/11982-8; 24/20257-8.

[20] J. R. T. Hughes, *Fluctuations in Trade, Industry and Finance: A Study of British Economic Development, 1850-1860* (Oxford, 1960), p. 192.

be prepared to act quickly and it had required knowledgeable agents in London to act for it. In June, 1852, the name of the Great Western Railway of Canada began to be listed on the London Stock Exchange.

At this early stage in the company's development, it had many other uses for its London agent. Within a few years, the company would have experienced professional employees to do more of its work, and routines would in any case be more developed. Until that time, the founders of the company had somehow to make their own decisions. In 1851, the company had at last been able to begin construction. Atcheson and Buchanan were asked to buy the rails which would be required. Knowing little about railway iron, they turned to Samuel Laing. On his advice, and after several consultations with Buchanan, Atcheson in August, 1851, ordered 25,000 tons of iron rails from the Ebbw Vale Company. Deliveries were to begin at once, to be completed in 1852 and 1853; prices were £5/5s per ton in 1851, £5/10s in 1852, and £6 in 1853. Payment was to be half in cash and half in bonds or shares of the company at par; this reflected the company's relatively high standing, for despite a depression in trade, ironmasters were still very reluctant to take securities of overseas railway companies. Peter Buchanan proclaimed the contract "a first rate one" and was astounded to learn that the board of directors had refused to confirm it.[21] He suspected jobbery on the part of some directors who were interested in another supplier and rail type, though one valid objection did come forward; the board feared that the Ebbw Vale Company might be able to claim payment in government guaranteed bonds rather than the company's own. At length, after a number of trips to Wales by Buchanan and Atcheson and a visit to England by the company engineer, called over for advice on rail types, a new contract was signed in the spring of 1852.[22] Buchanan now had quickly to find shipping to carry the iron to Canada. For the next three years he continued to play a role in the company's large purchases of iron and locomotives, especially by negotiating part payment in company securities.

Late in 1851, with funds in hand and much work developing in Britain, Peter Buchanan decided to open a permanent office for the company in London. As office manager, he engaged a man recently retired from a post in a London banking house, George Harkness; his knowledge of office work and business propriety relieved Buchanan of the routine duties associated with correspondence, interest payments, handling of invoices on shipments, and maintenance of the share and bond registers of the company. To assist Harkness with some of these tasks, Buchanan appointed his own brother-in-

---

[21] Dorothy R. Adler, *op. cit.*, pp. 31, 66-7. Buchanan to Isaac Buchanan, Aug. 27, 1851 (copy) and Oct. 15, 1851; to Atcheson, Oct. 2; to Harris, Oct. 3; and to Samuel Laing, Oct. 23, 1851 (copies). Copy of contract for iron, Aug. 26, 1851. 68/53850-1; 14/11956-60; 66/52447-8; 68/53873-4, pp. 82-3, 855-6.

[22] Buchanan to Harris, May 14, 1852; and to J. T. Gilkison, June 11, 1852 (copies). 14/11982-8, pp. 91-2.

law, George Douglas, a retired army officer who welcomed additional income; Buchanan contended to critics that because Douglas was known in Hamilton he was ideal for the post.[23]

The American investors in the Great Western had insisted on the right to name two company officers and three directors. The English bond and stock holders were naturally anxious also to protect their investments. After discussion with his London connections, Buchanan, wishing to preserve the confidence of these investors while ensuring that the Americans and certain Canadian directors did not dominate the company, proposed that the board offer the English party in the company the right to appoint the chief full-time officer of the company, who would be styled Managing Director. Buchanan in any case felt that the company needed more professional and experienced staff, and he wished to avoid any appointment of a shareholders' committee in London which would restrict his own freedom of action. The board agreed, and in August, 1852, Buchanan was able to announce this offer in a circular to the bond and stockholders.[24] Later, he played some part in appointing C. J. Brydges, the young secretary of the London and Southwestern Railway, to this post. Brydges, on arrival in Canada in 1853, quickly extended his control over most of the Great Western's operations. Nominally an appointee of the British party in the company, he soon demonstrated his independence by quarreling publicly with Samuel Laing. He did, however, maintain a steady correspondence with Peter Buchanan, and, though no subordinate, he proved a strong ally of Buchanan and Harris for at least two years.[25] This did not prevent his developing other connections in Britain, and he ultimately helped to drive the Buchanan group from the company.

By the end of 1852, therefore, the Great Western was going rapidly ahead, much aided by its set of influential connections in Britain, which included Laing, Masterman, Braithwaite, and the Ebbw Vale Company. Masterman at this time was also selling Canadian municipal debentures issued to support the Great Western, and Braithwaite was managing the sale of contractors' shares, which were now finding their way to London.[26] Through 1852 and

[23] Buchanan to Isaac Buchanan, Dec. 13, 1851; to J. T. Gilkison, Dec. 19, 1851 (copy); to George Harkness, March 10, 1852 (copy); and to Harris, May 14, 1852 (copy). 14/11966-7; 68/53946, 54058-9; 14/11982-8.

[24] For this issue in general, see A. W. Currie, "British Attitudes Toward Investment in North American Railroads," *Business History Review*, xxxiv (1960), pp. 213-4. Harris to Isaac Buchanan, Nov. 5, 1852; Circular to English holders of shares and bonds, Aug. 4, 1852. 30/25171; 94/65438-9. (These records cited hereafter as C.N.R. Records.)

[25] Summary of Buchanan-Brydges correspondence for 1853; Buchanan to Isaac Buchanan, Dec. 16, 1852; Brydges to Buchanan, Dec. 24, 1853. 68/54118-21; 14/12096; 5/2844-50. P.A.C., Canadian National Railways Records, Vol. 2, Minutes of the Board of Directors, Great Western Railway, June 25, 1853. (These records cited hereafter as C.N.R. Records.)

[26] Buchanan to Harris, June 28, 1851 (copy); Isaac Buchanan to Harris, June 1, 1852 (copy); J. Masterman, Jr. to Isaac Buchanan, June 15, 1852. 68/53775; 30/25165; 27/23382.

1853, Peter Buchanan's influence in the company was at its peak. No longer facing the problem of launching the company, he now focussed equally on further questions of strategy and general policy and on the innumerable details of finance and purchasing. He relied greatly for advice on this London group and for routine work on Harkness. But of all this group, he was the only one known and trusted by the board in Canada, and this was the basis of his influence. Remarks of various parties in the company illustrated his role and its value. C. J. Brydges wrote at one point, "I mention these matters to you confidentially because I think you, as a Director of the Co., and the only one in England that I could address upon the subject, ought to know...."[27] J. B. Smith, M.P., a leading shareholder who was advocating appointment of a man to keep some check on Brydges, argued "what we want particularly is a man of character *we can depend on* [in Canada]. Canadian morals are sickening."[28] To men such as Smith, Peter Buchanan was some guarantee that Canadian morals alone were not governing the company's affairs. The importance to a company of its agent was emphasized in connection with a bank loan to a company affiliated with the Great Western. Samuel Laing, arranging the loan, wrote "as the Board [of the railway] are in Canada and unknown to them [the London bank] they would require you as representing them in this country to give your own security."[29] A known individual British businessman could readily have a higher credit standing in London than an incorporated Canadian company.

As the company developed, money became easier to find, but the need for it increased very rapidly. Construction costs far exceeded estimates, partly as a result of the general Canadian price rise and decisions to build branches and make other improvements. During 1852, the Great Western at last qualified for aid under the Main Trunk Act, the revised version of Hincks' earlier Guarantee Act, and the first of three lots of guaranteed bonds that would be issued between 1852 and 1855 was forwarded by the Canadian government to its agents, Barings and Glyns, for sale on behalf of the Great Western and on the advice of its agent, Peter Buchanan. In the state of the financial market in 1852, Buchanan had merely to agree to the timing and terms of sale and to remit the funds to Canada once Barings and Glyns had sold the bonds.[30]

Sale of the Great Western's own securities was less straightforward. In December, 1852, Buchanan, Braithwaite, and Laing decided a new issue for about £200,000 might sell, Braithwaite proposing to offer up to 6000 shares, par value £20/10s sterling, and between £100,000 and £120,000 in bonds. Buchanan urged the board to agree, and on receipt of its agree-

[27] Brydges to Buchanan, May 5, 1855. 5/2905.
[28] Smith to Buchanan, June [July] 10, 1855. 55/43785.
[29] Laing to Buchanan, Dec. 12, 1854. 37/30466-7.
[30] John Young to Isaac Buchanan, Oct. 22, 1852; Harris to Isaac Buchanan, Nov. 5, 1852 (copy). 63/50216-7; 30/25172-3.

ment in mid-January, the issue was offered to existing shareholders. It was proclaimed a success, but in fact Buchanan and George Douglas subscribed for seven hundred shares while Foster and Braithwaite took much of the issue themselves. As late as March, 1853, the brokers were supporting the price of Great Western stock by buying shares offered at or near par. At one time they held over £70,000 in Great Western securities. At this time too the Ebbw Vale Company was selling its Great Western holdings, Foster and Braithwaite managing this sale as well to avoid disrupting the market. Only in the summer of 1853 was the entire issue worked off without depressing the market too greatly. Clearly Foster and Braithwaite had considerable confidence in the Great Western, and this was principally a confidence in Peter Buchanan, who to the Londoners virtually was the company.[31]

Late in 1853, the Great Western prepared to open its line. Money to complete and equip it was very scarce, and Buchanan sought to issue further shares. Foster and Braithwaite declined, saying shares were unsaleable until dividends had begun to be paid and suggesting a new issue of £250,000 in twenty-two year convertible bonds, to be offered to shareholders. Foster and Braithwaite agreed to take up to one quarter of the issue themselves, and they would be paid a commission of one per cent on the amount issued. Buchanan judged the market favourable and without waiting for the approval of the board authorized the brokers to go ahead with the issue. Offered early in January, 1854, the issue was a considerable success, over £230,000 being taken up.[32] In taking such responsibilities on himself, Peter Buchanan again demonstrated an agent's value to the company. He concluded that the company now had enough money to complete its line; further sums, if needed, could be raised under the Main Trunk Act. The Great Western, with his assistance, had in two years raised about £900,000 on the London stock market, an amount exceeding that which it raised through the Canadian government's aid and far exceeding that provided by the other sources of funds for the line.

Buchanan considered his duty to the company largely fulfilled, but he dared not resign until a related project in which he was involved had been completed. Late in 1852, the Hamilton and Toronto Railway Company had been chartered and the Great Western was convinced that it needed to control this company to ensure access to Toronto and lines eastward from

[31] It was standard practice for established companies to issue shares through current share-holders. Harold Pollins, "The Marketing of Railway Shares in the First Half of the Nineteenth Century," *Economic History Review*, 2nd ser., vii (1954-5), pp. 234-9. Re this issue see Buchanan to Isaac Buchanan, Dec. 10, 1852; George Douglas to Isaac Buchanan. Feb. 11, March 4 & 11, 1853; Foster & Braithwaite to Buchanan, Jan. 16, 1856. 14/12024; 24/20279-82, pp. 86, 89; 4/2222-5.

[32] Buchanan to Harris, Dec. 16, 1853; George Douglas to Harris, Dec. 16, 1853 and to Isaac Buchanan, Jan. 13, 1854; George Harkness to Buchanan, Jan. 12, 1854. 14/12102-3; 24/20402, p. 8; 46/37327-8.

there. In November, 1852, Peter Buchanan went to London to discuss means of financing this line. Samuel Laing suggested that financing be done immediately, since a better time to raise funds was unlikely to occur. He suggested that George Wythes, a reliable English contractor with whom he was connected, be given a contract to build the line, so that investors could be guaranteed that the line would be built immediately before costs rose further.

Buchanan, for the Great Western, Laing and Masterman as intermediaries, and Wythes as the contractor signed a contract on November 30, 1852 by which Wythes agreed to buy the land, the iron, and the rolling stock and to build the line, sheds, stations, and telegraphs to a standard equal to that of the Great Western. For this he would be paid £328,000 sterling, the authorized share capital of the line. Meanwhile, Wythes would subscribe all the shares in the company when offered in Canada to secure control to the English promoters, who would then sell the shares to raise funds to pay Wythes. Construction would commence at once, to be complete by July 31, 1854. On December 1, the promoters issued a prospectus, and the company's scrip was at once taken up. A separate agreement signed at the same time provided for the division of various "commissions," "expenses," and profits among the four signers of the contract and Sir Allan MacNab, who had incorporated the company and was on his way to England to promote it; free shares would be given to those who would serve as directors of the company to keep them compliant. Ultimately it was intended to sell or lease the company to the Great Western. The line was evidently expected to cost less than £328,000, and the four signers envisaged further joint ventures in North America should this one succeed.

Peter Buchanan was essential to this arrangement, because he had vital connections in Canada and in the Great Western. He would be "agent" of the Hamilton and Toronto, as he was of the Great Western, although his duties in the new line were expected to be routine, since funds had been raised already. For his services, he expected to gain at least £8000. He admitted that he had been swept along by Laing in this arrangement, but he argued that the deal was good for Canada and the Great Western. Although the cost might seem high, it was not so, in view of the rapid escalation of construction costs in Canada and the advantages derived from the support of powerful figures in London. He did worry that Canadians might complain of jobbery, for this could affect his business standing in Britain, but having signed the contract and issued the prospectus, he saw no choice but to press on.[33] He worried that MacNab, unaware of these developments, might protest on his arrival, but an offer to MacNab by Laing of £5000 for labour and expenses in connection with the company mollified him. MacNab's view

---

[33] Buchanan to Isaac Buchanan, Nov. 30 and Dec. 16, 1852; and to Harris, Dec. 3, 1852. Copies of contracts, Nov. 30, 1852. Prospectus, Hamilton and Toronto Railway. 14/12003-4, 12095-6, 12012-5; 94/65774-8, 65854-5, 65782.

was that "much has been done, but unfortunately every step has been illegal – however there is nothing left for us to do, but *adopt their proceedings and perfect them.*"[34]

Contrary to the Londoners' expectations, MacNab had not formally organized the company before leaving: legally, the Hamilton and Toronto did not yet exist. Although scrip for a large part of its bonds and shares had been sold, Buchanan and the Londoners could not hope to deliver securities until late spring of 1853. News of the promotion had quickly reached Canada, accusations of corruption followed at once, and organization of the company was further delayed. Working through MacNab, R. W. Harris, Isaac Buchanan, T. G. Ridout, cashier of the Bank of Upper Canada, and Thomas Galt, the Great Western's lawyer, and with the tacit agreement of Francis Hincks, the Canadian premier, Peter Buchanan was able even so to secure control of the company, but only at further cost to its reputation in Britain.[35] Only the influence of the Londoners kept the scrip and then shares of the Hamilton and Toronto afloat on the London Stock Exchange through most of 1853. Fearing lawsuits by subscribers, the Londoners postponed construction. Provided they held the funds, they could always return subscriptions. Laing and Peter Buchanan concluded that an agreement by the Great Western to lease the Hamilton and Toronto, which would secure the position of the investors in the latter, was a necessary prerequisite to construction. Without much difficulty, given their positions in the Great Western, they soon persuaded the board and a meeting of the Great Western's British shareholders to approve an agreement to lease on completion of the line. Even so, delays, principally those imposed by unfavourable rumours in Britain, prevented the start of construction before early 1854. Costs rose sharply, the anticipated profits dwindled and then vanished, and the line was only completed eighteen months later than initially planned. Peter Buchanan, fearing a challenge to his actions in the Hamilton and Toronto, considered it essential to remain active in both companies until he was secured by the completion and leasing of the Hamilton and Toronto. During his remaining years as railway agent, the Hamilton and Toronto was his chief, though not his only, concern.[36]

During 1853, Buchanan, like others in the Great Western, had also to

---

[34] MacNab to Isaac Buchanan, Dec. 14, 1852. See also Buchanan to Isaac Buchanan, Dec. 10, 1852. 46/37245; 14/12024.

[35] Isaac Buchanan to J. C. Morrison, M.P.P., Dec. 23, 1852 and to T. G. Ridout, Feb. 19, 1853 (copies); Buchanan to Isaac Buchanan, Jan. 21, 1852 [1853]; T. G. Ridout to Isaac Buchanan, Feb. 1, 21, and March 18, 1853; Harris to Isaac Buchanan, April 15, 1853. List of shareholders, Hamilton and Toronto Railway, April 23, 1853. 48/39171-2, 52/41739-40, pp. 44-5; 14/11973; 52/41735-8, pp. 51, 65-7; 30/25192; 94/65865.

[36] Buchanan to Isaac Buchanan, May 20, 1853 and Jan. 20, 1854, and to Harris, Jan. 6, 10, and 24, 1854; George Douglas to Isaac Buchanan, Feb. 11 and March 11, 1853; Samuel Laing to Buchanan, Oct. 26, 1853. 14/12049, pp. 133-4, 124, 127, 137-8; 24/20279-80, p. 88; 37/30441-2.

respond to the challenge posed by the Grand Trunk Railway, which was launched in April with powerful backing in Canada and Britain. The Grand Trunk threatened to challenge the Great Western in its own territory west of Toronto and Hamilton. British interests in both companies, knowing of the problems of unchecked competition, were anxious to avert this. At once, therefore, a party from the Great Western led by Samuel Laing but also including Peter Buchanan, John Masterman, and R. W. Harris, negotiated a territorial agreement with George Carr Glyn and others representing the Grand Trunk.[37] Both sides soon encountered difficulties in keeping their Canadian allies to the agreement; the Canadians in the Great Western, led by C. J. Brydges and Isaac Buchanan, contended that the Grand Trunk was merely buying time and that Laing would betray the Great Western. Peter Buchanan tried repeatedly but ultimately unsuccessfully to keep the Canadians from breaking the letter or spirit of the agreement by buying steamships to operate on Lake Ontario and promoting a branch from London to Sarnia. In 1854 he continued to support Laing, who was trying to hold the Grand Trunk to the May, 1853 agreement, while he sought to keep the Canadians informed on and in agreement with the actions taken in London.[38] The London negotiations eventually collapsed, but throughout the period 1853 to 1856 Peter Buchanan spent much time in dealings with the London party in the Grand Trunk.

As the Great Western was completed and began operation, the position of agent began to change. As a result of the agent's work, regular sources of supply and finance were developed. The company acquired its own staff, organization, and routine, and channels of communication between Canada and Britain other than the agent naturally developed. Laing and Masterman began to withdraw, the former staying until 1855 when the Hamilton and Toronto was secure, and the latter being forced by his over-involvement in Belgian railways to withdraw early in 1854.[39] Peter Buchanan now dealt more with longterm investors in the company, his chief aim being to maintain harmony between them and the Canadians in the company. The shareholders, from British experience, considered all branch lines to be mistakes. The directors, however, lacked such experience, and in Canada there were innumerable rumours of branches, rivals, and strategic manoeuvres. Anxious to forestall competition from the Grand Trunk, perhaps at times corrupted by the pressures of contractors, and inadequately aware of the difficulties of finding funds in Britain, the Canadians in the line proposed a series of

---

[37] George Douglas to Isaac Buchanan, April 15, 22 and May 5, 1853. 24/20304-5, pp. 9, 12-14.

[38] George Douglas to Isaac Buchanan, Nov. 4, 1853; Harris to Buchanan, Nov. 19, 1853; Buchanan to Harris, Dec. 30, 1853 and Feb. 3, 1854 and to Brydges, Jan. 13, 1854 and May 12, 1854. 24/20372-8; 30/25202-3; 14/12121, pp. 151-3; 46/37322-3; 5/2865-7.

[39] Buchanan to Brydges, Feb. 17, 1854 (copy). 5/2852. C.N.R. Records, Vol. 10, *Minutes of the English Board*, Aug. 6, 1855.

extensions and branches. Two such proposals, both involving the contractor Samuel Zimmerman, to buy the Erie and Ontario Railway and to build a branch from London to Sarnia in competition with the Grand Trunk, provoked resistance by shareholders in late 1853.

Hitherto, Peter Buchanan had used circulars, occasional general meetings with shareholders, and the English railway press to reach investors, but pressure from them for a formal institutional voice mounted. While preferring English control to American, Buchanan hoped that proxies alone would provide this; he feared that an organization in London would limit unduly his independence and that of the company's officers while giving little positive control to the investors. Nevertheless, important shareholders were so disturbed by the Erie and Ontario that he deemed it essential to form a committee of shareholders specifically to investigate this purchase. Accepted by the board on his advice, this committee consisted of himself; Laing; James Baird, of the great Scottish ironmaking family, which had sold Zimmerman the iron for the Erie and Ontario in the first place; J. B. Smith and Robert Gill, emerging as leaders of the shareholders group; and John Harris and, C. Makins.[40]

Peter Buchanan had few problems now with the routine duties of the London agency. He still took a considerable part in financial matters and was individually responsible for the Great Western's funds in London. To allow work to go on smoothly in Canada, he several times negotiated short term advances of up to £ 50,000, secured by currently unsaleable company bonds, from the London Joint Stock Bank, with which his relations were very cordial. In the autumn of 1854, he advised Barings and Glyns on their sale of £ 300,000 in Canadian government guaranteed bonds for the Great Western. During the year, still working closely with Foster and Braithwaite, he gradually issued the last available shares and bonds in the company, taking individual responsibility for issuing the bonds at a slight discount despite the apparent illegality of this under the company's charter.[41] As well, he helped in the sale of further Canadian municipal bonds on the company's behalf.

By the end of 1854, the shareholders' committee had become a board of directors, consisting of Buchanan, Laing, Gill, and J. B. Smith; it was legally subordinate to the board in Hamilton, but still had much power. The board immediately took over supervision of the London office and in the spring of

[40] George Douglas to Isaac Buchanan, July 8, 1853; Buchanan to B. Baker, n.d. (copy), to Harris, Jan. 10, 1854 and to Brydges, Jan. 13, 1854 (copy); G. Harkness to Buchanan, Jan. 12, 1854. 24/20343; 2/844; 14/121278; 46/37322-3, p. 37327. C.N.R. Records, Vol 1, Minutes of general meeting of shareholders, June, 1854, p. 48.

[41] Buchanan to Brydges, May 12, 1854 (copy); Brydges to Harris, August 11, 1854; Thomas Bigly to Harris, July 5, 1854 (copy); W. Longsdon to Buchanan, Jan. 17, 1855. 5/2864, 2886; 3/1714; 39/32294. C. N. R. Records, Vol. 5, *Minutes of Finance Committee*, June 15, 1854.

1855 Peter Buchanan handed over responsibility for the company's funds, giving up his last duty as agent. Now simply a director, he retained considerable influence, but it could easily vanish; gratitude was never a characteristic of the company. As the board met weekly, often for merely routine duties, Buchanan attended fewer of its meetings.[42] Increasingly, J. B. Smith became its dominant figure. Though he consulted Buchanan and the other English board members, he played the larger role in another sale of bonds guaranteed by the Canadian government in the spring of 1855. As a result of the Great Western's very successful first year of operation, these went off at a handsome premium. At the same time, the Great Western after much delay received legislative permission to expand its share issue. Smith now managed the sale to shareholders on a one-for-one basis of over 40,000 shares, which almost doubled the company's share issue in Britain within a week.[43] In 1856, the shares were at a large premium and, without consulting Buchanan, the board offered to current shareholders all the remaining shares which the company was authorized to issue. Peter Buchanan protested that this discriminated against shareholders in the Hamilton and Toronto, which was about to be amalgamated with the Great Western, but failed to reverse the decision.[44] His influence had greatly diminished in a single year.

He had never possessed as much influence in the line's Canadian affairs. Although R. W. Harris, who generally accepted his advice, continued to work hard for the company, he was content to allow Brydges to dominate the day-to-day affairs of the company. And Buchanan had been unable to keep his own brother and Brydges from denouncing Laing even in 1853. In 1854 and 1855, he vainly urged the board to refrain from too many extensions. At the same time, he tried to persuade the English to accept some of the branches. On this issue he sought primarily to interpret the views of each side in the company to the other side.

During 1854, construction at last went forward on the Hamilton and Toronto. The last obstacle was a supervising engineer assigned by the Great Western to the project, who was blamed by J. C. Street, Wythes' Canadian agent, for delays in getting work under way. The engineer was finally dismissed after Street appealed to Wythes, Wythes to Laing, and Laing to Peter Buchanan, who asked Harris and Brydges to investigate.[45] The delays in

---

[42] Buchanan to Harris, Aug. 9, 1855. 15/12422-5. C.N.R. Records, Vol. 2, *Minutes of the Board of Directors*, Dec. 19, 1854 and March 16, 1855; vol. 10, *Minutes of the English Board*, May 9 and July 24, 1855 and Feb. 13, 1856.

[43] J. B. Smith to Robert Gill, June 13, 1855 (copy) and to Buchanan, July 30, 1855. 55/43788, p. 98. C.N.R. Records, Vol. 10, *Minutes of the English Board*, June 25 and Aug. 6, 1855.

[44] Extracts from *Minutes of the English Board*, March 4 and 11, 1856; J. B. Smith to Buchanan, March 8, 1856 and Buchanan to Smith, March 10, 1856 (copies); Buchanan to Harris, April 11, 1856. 93/65268, pp. 272-8; 55/43818, pp. 20-1; 15/12598-601.

[45] S. Laing to Buchanan, Feb. 3 and 24, 1854 (copies); Buchanan to Isaac Buchanan, Jan. 20, 1854 and to Brydges, Feb. 24, 1854 (copy). 37/30457-9, p. 61; 14/12133-4; 5/2855-7.

starting proved fatal to profits, and under the 1852 contract, Buchanan had to pay for shares he had been given and to return £8000 which he had received in commissions. This naturally distressed him especially because he regarded this sum as consolation for the responsibilities, the risks, and the worries which had been involved in the Hamilton and Toronto.[46] Even so, he continued to be on friendly terms with Wythes. Through 1854 and 1855 he gradually issued the company's remaining bonds and stocks, but he still worried about the legality of many of the promoters' acts. Allan MacNab, seeking payments he said he had been promised in 1852, tried to play on this when he threatened in 1856 to demand a public investigation into the whole history of the company.[47] By this time, however, Buchanan felt secure. Laing and he had decided that total amalgamation with the Great Western would make them more secure, since the Hamilton and Toronto would disappear as a separate legal entity.[48] In view of the Great Western's profitability in 1855 and 1856, the Hamilton and Toronto investors readily agreed, as did the Great Western's London directors. The shareholders in the Hamilton and Toronto, under the leasing agreement, had been guaranteed a six per cent return, while sharing in any higher dividends declared by the Great Western; amalgamation removed the guarantee.

Even early in 1855, the Great Western's London board was discussing detailed matters relating to the Hamilton and Toronto, reflecting its interest in amalgamation. By fall, 1855, the question was whether Wythes, trying to avoid a heavy loss, would hand over the line, nominally to the board of the Hamilton and Toronto, but in practice to the Great Western. The London board of the Great Western handled negotiations with Wythes, and in December, with the line about to be opened, it agreed to compromise the array of issues in dispute by offering £20,000 in cash to Wythes. Peter Buchanan was only one member of the London board, which in any case knew something of his involvement in the Hamilton and Toronto and was unanimous in favor of the compromise. Buchanan did attend most meetings at which the Hamilton and Toronto was discussed, however, to be sure that all went well.[49] This agreement was accepted by the Canadian board and the company's shareholders in February, 1856, and was implemented in May. With relief Peter Buchanan handed over his Hamilton and Toronto accounts to the Great Western and ceased altogether to be a railway agent. He was rapidly selling off his shares at this time, at a large premium, and this

[46] Buchanan to Harris, Jan. 6 and Oct. 27, 1854 and Sept. 7, 1855. 14/12124, p. 278; 15/12439-42.

[47] MacNab to Buchanan, Jan. 12, 1856. 46/37387-90. See also J. B. Smith to Harris, Aug. 16, 1855. 55/43800.

[48] *The Times of London*, Feb. 21, 1861, p. 5; April 2, 1861, p. 5. Buchanan to Harris, March 17 and April 6, 1854. 14/12185-8, 89. C.N.R. Records, Vol. 2, *Minutes of the Board of Directors*, April 5, 1854.

[49] Extracts from *Minutes of the English Board*, Nov. 6, 1855 and March 4, 1856. B. Baker to Brydges, Nov. 7 and 9, 1855 (copies). 93/65258, pp. 266-7; 5/2924-6.

confirms his stated intention not to run for re-election as a director of the Great Western in the fall of 1856.[50] His departure from the company was, however, embittered by an affair arising during the summer in which he was involved by his brother Isaac.

There was a shorter route than the Great Western's, known as the southern route, from Buffalo to Detroit, and a railway built along it could deprive the Great Western of its valuable through traffic. In 1856, it was rumoured that the Grand Trunk, with its apparently limitless government support, and Samuel Zimmerman would combine to acquire two companies, the Amherstburg and St. Thomas and the Woodstock and Lake Erie, which between them had powers to build the southern railway. In July, J. S. Radcliff, the vice-president of the Great Western, and Isaac Buchanan determined to forestall this combination by themselves buying control of the two charters. Working hastily and secretly, Isaac Buchanan made the purchases with funds from his business, and Radcliff then drew bills on the Great Western in London to reimburse him.[51] Acting on the written advice of C. J. Brydges, who considered the threat illusory, the London board refused by a vote of two to one to accept the drafts, despite the advocacy in writing of Radcliff and in person of J. B. Smith. Peter Buchanan and R. W. Harris, both in ill health, unaware of their partner's financial involvement in the question, and believing that the Great Western could not afford to build the southern line, had not attended the meeting. They were astonished to learn a few days later that their business would lose over £50,000 in the matter unless the decision was reversed. Peter Buchanan then rushed to London, with Harris in tow, only to find that Smith had resigned and there was no chance of reversing the opinions of Gill and Alexander Beattie, the other two directors. With little hope, they launched a proxy battle.[52] Zimmerman, himself in England, denied any plot, while such friends of Peter Buchanan as Wythes argued that there was no real threat in any case since no money was available. Wythes declined to give his proxies to Buchanan's opponents, but he said he could not in conscience vote for the matter either.[53] Thus the proxy battle was lost. At a meeting in October, the English shareholders voted non-confidence in Harris and Radcliff, whose terms as president and vice-president were just finishing.[54]

[50] Kerr, Anderson and Brodie to Buchanan, April 25, 1856 to Feb. 12, 1857. 36/29717-41.

[51] Isaac Buchanan to Buchanan, July 17 and 21, 1856; Agreement between Isaac Buchanan and J. S. Radcliff, July 14, 1856; Agreement between Isaac Buchanan and William Wallace, July 15, 1856. Draft circular, J. S. Radcliff to the Shareholders, July 17, 1856. 10/9135, p. 40; 71/55112, pp. 116-9; 94/65503-9.

[52] J. B. Smith to Buchanan, Aug. 5, 1856. 55/43884-7. C.N.R. Records, Vol. 11, *Minutes of the English Board*, August 5 and 6, 1856.

[53] Wythes to Buchanan, Aug. 31 and Sept. 1, 1856. 63/43834-40. C.N.R. Records, Vol. 11, *Minutes of the English Board*, Sept. 23, 1856.

[54] Buchanan to Robert Gill, Oct. 24, 1856 (draft). 28/23564-6. C.N.R. Records, Vol. 11, *Minutes of the English Board*, Aug. 14 and 22, Sept. 12, 1856; Vol. 1, *General Meeting of the English Shareholders*, Oct. 14, 1856.

As a result of Isaac's actions, Peter Buchanan and Harris's final exit from the company, which had been planned for October in any case, became inglorious and ignominious.

During his railway career, Peter Buchanan made money from the railway in a variety of ways. In the early period he probably showed at least some net profit from his involvement in the original share speculation. Until mid-1852, however, he does not seem to have been paid by the company for his expenses and services. By this time he had begun to secure some profit from the company by having the Montreal and Liverpool branches of his business made local agents for the Great Western.[55] Much of the shipping, insurance, and forwarding of the company's supplies to Canada were done through them. After his retirement from the company, his firm's charges were strongly challenged by the Great Western, the agency was taken from it, and its last account was not paid. The charges were, he admitted, higher than those charged by shipping agents, but he said his firm provided more services than such agents, and shipping agents earned most of their revenues from discounts on insurances and freights which they kept, whereas his firm had passed all such discounts on the company. Slightly disingenuously, in view of his influence in the company, he argued finally that his charges had been approved by the boards in Hamilton and London. His aim in setting charges at this level was to earn what he considered a reasonable return for the time and effort of his employees. Though in a position to seek iron supply contracts for the Great Western he made no effort to do so because the profit could not justify the work and the risks.[56] Once, when the company had surplus cash in hand, he arranged to lend £5000 to his Glasgow firm, arguing that if he did not use the funds, they would be deposited in the company's account at Masterman's banking house, and Masterman would use them.[57]

In 1852, the company agreed that he was entitled to a "negotiating commission" of 2½ per cent on sums which he raised for the company. Out of this he had to pay Foster and Braithwaites's commission plus any sums which were given to Laing and others with a claim to have aided in the issue.[58] Thus his clear profit was only 1 or 1½ per cent, probably paid in shares,

[55] Buchanan to John Young, Jan. 23, 1852 (copy). 68/54009.

[56] Buchanan to Isaac Buchanan and Harris, May 16, 1854; to Harris, May 26, 1854 and June 1, 1855; and to G. Borthwick, June 14, 1857 (copy). B. Baker to Buchanan, Harris and Co., Feb. 9, 1857 and Buchanan, Harris and Co. to B. Baker, Feb. 16, 1857 14/12211, pp. 19-20; 15/12405-6; 4/2115-6; 2/964, pp. 966-8.

[57] Buchanan to Harris, Jan. 29 and March 23, 1852 (copies). 68/54021, p. 77.

[58] Atcheson to Buchanan, March, 1850 (copy); Buchanan to Isaac Buchanan, Dec. 10, 1852; to Harris, Dec. 16, 1853 and May 16, 1854; and to Harris and Isaac Buchanan, May 16, 1854. George Douglas to Isaac Buchanan, March 11, 1853. 66/52469-70; 14/12024, 12104, 12203, 12211; 24/20289. It is not clear whether the commission, when it began to be paid, was made retroactive to December, 1851. By 1854, the company was moving away from a commission system, since it was well enough established that middlemen played a much smaller role in its financing.

amounting to perhaps £5000 or £6000 in 1852. He argued that "the *comn* [commission] is no object to me,"[59] and overall it is clear that these various sources of profit from the company were not his primary concern in becoming involved. His income from his own business was considerably greater than all his railway earnings, and growing rapidly through this period. Yet he considered his charges legitimate ones which the company would have had to pay someone else if not him. He valued his agent's commissions too as recognition of his services and as partial recompense for much time invested. Many of those who involved themselves in railroads took this view, though others involved themselves primarily to gain such profits. The concept of conflict of interest in corporations was clearly embryonic as yet, even in England. R. W Harris's views conflicted with Buchanan's on this point, for he viewed his work for the railway as a form of public service. Harris steadfastly refused all remuneration for his services, even declining to cash cheques given him for his duties as president.[60]

In his decade of involvement with the company, Peter Buchanan was instrumental in launching one of Canada's major railways. It is clear that he, and a number of others, were more vital to the company than those such as Isaac Buchanan and Sir Allan MacNab whom the public then and the historians since have credited with the leading roles.[61] MacNab rendered many political services, but these could not sell shares or lay rails, and he was well paid for his services at that. What the Canadian historian has underestimated is the complexity, and perhaps even the importance, of London finance. The role played by linking figures such as Peter Buchanan was essential to bridging the large gap interposed by the Atlantic. Peter Buchanan's holding role prior to 1851 and, more important, his major contributions in the next few years emphasize this. His subsequent swift decline from power in the company, while partly of his own choosing, reflects also the rapid shift of the company's perspectives and needs as it moved from projection to operation.

---

[59] Buchanan to Harris, May 20, 1853 (copy). 14/12056. See also Buchanan to Isaac Buchanan, March 2, 1846 and to Harris, Jan. 24, 1854 (copy). 14/11701, 12137.

[60] Harris to Isaac Buchanan, Aug. 23, 1855; Isaac Buchanan to Sir Thomas Dakin, June 20, 1872 (copy). 30/25227; 22/18976-7.

[61] See, for example, Stevens, *op. cit.*, p. 98 or Marjorie Freeman Campbell, *A Mountain and a City, The Story of Hamilton* (Toronto, 1966), p. 95. J. T. Gilkison, a longtime supporter of the Great Western who was squeezed out of his post as company secretary in 1853, published a circular contending that the whole railway operation was in the hands of Peter Buchanan, but it is clear that he rather exaggerated Buchanan's power. J. T. Gilkison, "To the Shareholders of the Great Western Railway Company," July 28, 1853. 94/65471-3.

The Burlington's Struggle for a Chicago-Twin Cities Line, 1870-1890

R. C. Overton, Professor of History, University of Western Ontario

Years ago there used to be a cartoon that appeared regularly in the papers entitled: "It happens in the best of regulated families." This is not a very scholarly sentiment, but it is the best sub-title readily available for this chapter. If one looks at the overall 121-year history of the Burlington, it is clear that more often than not it was characterized by propriety, prudence, and prosperity. Like most railroads, it started as a purely local venture way back in 1849 when the farmers and merchants of the little town of Aurora, thirty-eight miles west of Chicago, decided to build a twelve-mile branch so as to tap the only railway then running west from Chicago. Characteristically enough, these local people were the most solid men of the village, and, rather than adopt some fancy title such as "The Aurora, North-west and Pacific," were perfectly content to name their railroad The Aurora Branch, which is just what it was; eventually this became the Chicago, Burlington & Quincy. Meanwhile, the Aurora Branch paid its way, something which, in those days, was as much the exception as the rule. As a result, they attracted the attention of a group of Boston entrepreneurs who were heavily interested in the Michigan Central (between Buffalo and Chicago by way of Detroit) and who were looking about for a western feeder.[1]

So it was that in the winter of 1852-53, John Murray Forbes and his associates acquired the little Aurora Branch. Forbes, a pillar of Boston society, and, among other things, agent for Baring Brothers in London, had associated with him then and later such men as Erastus Corning of Albany, John C. Green of New York, John W. Brooks, Sidney Bartlett, Nathaniel Thayer, and John Denison of Boston, J. N. A. Griswold of Newport, and James F. Joy of Detroit. For nearly half a century this group controlled the destiny of the Burlington, and when they sold out in 1901, they did so not to any individual speculator or to the market place at large, but to that shrewd Canadian-born empire builder, James J. Hill, and his associates. These were, of course, the men who controlled the Great Northern and the Northern Pacific, and these two railways have, consequently, controlled the Burlington ever since. In fact, in February 1970 the three lines obtained authority to merge into one company, to be known as Burlington Northern Lines.[2]

Ever since 1852, then, the Burlington has been managed by only two entrepreneurial groups. It has grown from twelve miles to nearly eleven

---

[1] Richard C. Overton, *Burlington Route* (New York, 1965), pp. 3-5, 10-14. Hereafter this volume is referred to as *BR*.

[2] *BR*, pp. 26-31, 255-263, 580.

thousand in fourteen different states, it has never defaulted on an obligation, and it has paid dividends without a break for over a century. It has been progressive too: it has a long list of "railway firsts," including operation of the first Diesel streamline train in America and the introduction of the Vista-Dome car.[3] Hence one thing that fascinates is why an enterprise so eminently proper, prudent, and prosperous on the whole could possibly have got into as many difficulties as it did when, between 1879 and 1890, it tried to accomplish the straightforward task of acquiring a line of its own between Chicago and the Twin Cities. But that is precisely what happened, and the mere improbability of the story is one reason it is worth telling.

A second reason is that a story like this illustrates the ramifications of transportation. Admittedly, any account of how goods and people move from here to there is fascinating in its own right, but that is only the beginning. The Spring issue of the *Business History Review* in 1965, devoted entirely to transportation, exhibits the ramifications of the subject. One of the seven articles explored the loyalty of St. Louis to the Mississippi River and described the ambivalence that characterized its civic leaders when railways offered an alternate means of transportation. A second paper discussed how railways, suddenly faced with large-scale problems of management, simply had to devise from scratch means for mobilizing, controlling, and apportioning capital, for operating a widely dispersed plant, and for supervising thousands of specialized workmen strung all over the countryside. A third talked about the ethics of a prominent railway president, while a fourth untangled the confused story of an amateurish attempt on the part of Congress to regulate a highly technical transportation problem. The fifth paper described the early twentieth century agricultural development programs of the railways, the sixth studied the specialized financial problems of the aircraft industry, and the seventh described how the enormous Canadian National has gone about solving the problem of managing its huge store of records.[4] Transportation, in other words, inevitably involves much more than simply moving goods or people from here to there.

This applies forcibly to the present subject. The Burlington finally did get its line built and that, to be sure, was quite an achievement. But the significant part of the story is what happened to the character of the company in the process. After all, if anyone of us manages to survive at all, we grow bigger and older – and sometimes uglier. But it is what we are like that counts. Just as in the case of humans, those characters are often formed, and certainly vitally affected, by one or more traumatic experiences. In acquiring its line from Chicago to St. Paul between 1870 and 1890, the Burlington had its full share of such experiences, experiences that made a lasting difference to its structure and its nature as a business concern.

[3] *BR*, pp. 393, 495-496.

[4] *Business History Review*, "Special Transportation Issue," Vol. XXXIX, no. 1, Spring, 1965.

THE RIVER ROADS, 1870-80

With the help of the map on page 220, let us set the stage. By the end of January, 1856, the main lines of the Chicago, Burlington and Quincy connecting the cities named in the title had all been completed, and were securely under the control of the Forbes group. Corporate consolidation under the company existing until 1970 took place on June 24, 1864, and it is worth noting that, with characteristic prudence, the title of the company exactly described its location.[5] Meanwhile, on February 15, 1859, another enterprise controlled by the Forbes group, the Hannibal and St. Joseph Railroad, began operations between the cities named in its title, and early the next year the Quincy and Palmyra linked it with the C.B. and Q., except for a bridge across the Mississippi.[6] During the Civil War, of course, building on the system was at a minimum, but once the conflict ended it was apparent that not only the Burlington but other railways in the promising Midwest would resume expansion under heartily competitive conditions.

That the C.B. and Q. would be in the forefront of this scramble was guaranteed by the election of James F. Joy to the presidency on July 12, 1865. Able lawyer, brilliant strategist, consummate diplomat when it came to dealing with public authorities, he had, for nearly twenty years, enjoyed the implicit confidence of Forbes and his eastern associates. Partly because of this unique combination of talents, and partly because the other members of the Forbes group were preoccupied, in varying degrees, with the many other ventures in which the group was interested, Joy was given a virtually free hand to determine Burlington policy as he saw fit. This he proceeded to do with energy and imagination. By the end of 1869 the Burlington had built the first bridge over the Missouri at Kansas City and linked that metropolis with the Hannibal and St. Joseph. Meanwhile it had bridged the Mississippi at Quincy, thus providing the first all-rail service between Chicago and Kansas City, bridged it again at Burlington, and financed extension of the Burlington and Missouri River Railroad into Council Bluffs where, by ferry, it made connection in 1869 with the recently-completed Union Pacific to the coast.[7] But for Joy this was no time to rest on his laurels. As he told his stockholders in 1869, "In a country like the West, it is impossible to remain stationary. If the companies owning and managing roads there do not meet the wants of the adjoining country and aid in its development, other alliances are sure to be found which end in rival roads, and damage to existing interests."[8] For one thing, the rich farmland of northern Illinois was a tempting market indeed; between the close of the Civil War and the end of 1872, the C. B. and Q. laced it with a series of branches which increased the

[5] *BR*, p. 71.
[6] *BR*, p. 55.
[7] *BR*, pp. 90-96.
[8] C. B. and Q. R. R. Co., *Annual Report* for 1869, p. 20.

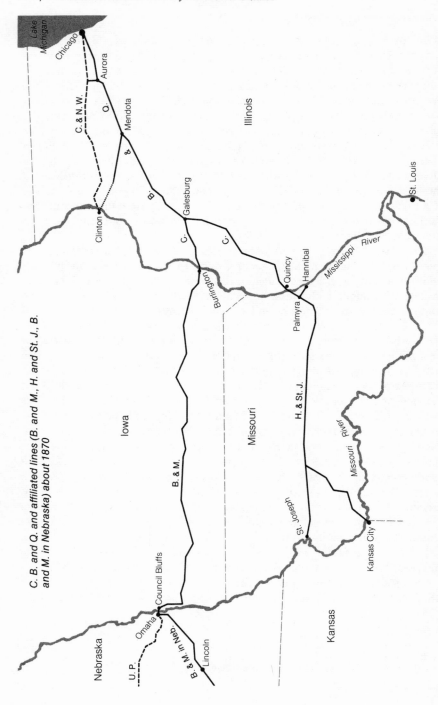

C. B. and Q. and affiliated lines (B. and M., H. and St. J., B. and M. in Nebraska) about 1870

system's mileage in that state from just under four hundred miles to over eight hundred.[9]

But what about the Twin Cities? By the beginning of 1870, the Burlington had established two principal through routes from Chicago, one to Kansas City, the other to Council Bluffs. And it had already started on its extensive branch line expansion in the home state of Illinois. That Joy should therefore seek to box the compass by looking toward the Northwest was not only logical but perhaps inevitable. Already, predecessors of both the Milwaukee and the Northwestern had penetrated the area, and Joy was determined that the Burlington should have a share of this region's promising business.

Because of the fact that the C.B. and Q.'s main stem in Illinois followed a southwesterly course across the state, however, the first step would be to control roads in a northwesterly direction. Fortunately, various local enterprises in the area made this comparatively simple. In particular, the Chicago and Iowa Railroad, together with a smaller company which it absorbed, completed a line between Aurora and Oregon in the spring of 1871. Over a year earlier, and at Joy's behest, the C. B. and Q. directors had voted to allow the Chicago and Iowa to use Burlington tracks between Aurora and Chicago in return for seventy per cent of the gross earnings on C. and I. business over that stretch and had, at the same time, authorized Joy to make whatever arrangements might be necessary to secure the business of the C. and I. in perpetuity.[10] Consequently, when the line was finished to Oregon, the C. B. and Q. agreed to set aside forty per cent of gross earnings realized over its own line from business to and from the Chicago and Iowa for investment in C. and I. bonds. In return, the C. and I. agreed to send all its business over the C. B. and Q. and to turn over to it half of its capital stock.[11] This was a sort of "pay-as-you-go" means of acquiring lines that Joy had devised and practised successfully for over a decade.[12]

So far, so good; control of a line from Aurora to Oregon was a promising first step, but it still fell far short of the Twin Cities. Again, however, local projects farther along the route suggested an answer. West of the Mississippi a company called the Chicago, Dubuque and Minnesota (soon to be known colloquially as the Upper River Road) was projected between Dubuque and La Crescent, just opposite Lacrosse, Wisconsin (see map, page 222). A second company, the Chicago, Clinton and Dubuque (soon to be called the Lower River Road) planned to cover the short stretch between Dubuque and Bellevue, to which point the Chicago and Iowa intended to build.[13] If the Burlington could get control of these River Roads, it would be well on its way toward the Twin Cities.

[9] *BR*, p. 121.
[10] C. B. and Q. R. R. Co., *Directors' Minutes*, Vol. 2, p. 312.
[11] *BR*, pp. 122-123; C. B. and Q. R. R. Co., *Annual Report* for 1872, p. 20.
[12] *BR*, pp. 70-71.
[13] *BR*, p. 124.

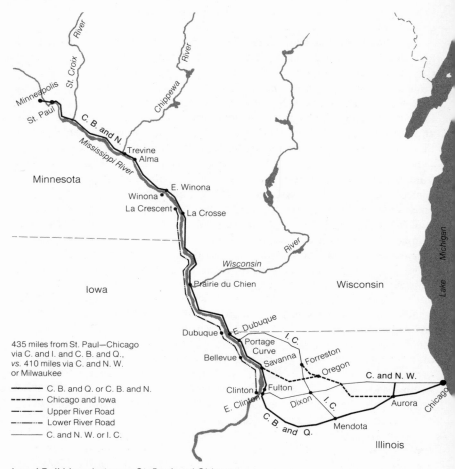

435 miles from St. Paul—Chicago
via C. and I. and C. B. and Q.,
vs. 410 miles via C. and N. W.
or Milwaukee

——— C. B. and Q. or C. B. and N.
-------- Chicago and Iowa
—·—·— Upper River Road
·········· Lower River Road
——— C. and N. W. or I. C.

Local Rail Lines between St. Paul and Chicago

As of the spring of 1871, however, several traffic agreements already in effect stood in the way. For one thing, freight business currently originating at Dubuque and destined to Chicago passed over the Illinois Central to Mendota and thence over the C. B. and Q. to Chicago; passengers took the Illinois Central to Dixon and thence the Northwestern. This meant that the Chicago and Iowa – which the C. B. and Q. hoped to use as the first segment of its route to the Northwest – was being by-passed so far as business to and from Dubuque was concerned. On the other hand, the Chicago and Iowa had already agreed with the two River Roads to build westwards to Bellevue to provide them with a southern outlet.[14] Yet this, if carried out, would benefit the C. B. and Q. only by increasing the amount of business exchanged with the C. and I. over the short haul between Aurora and Chicago.

This was just the sort of challenge that Joy relished. Fortunately, he had a golden opportunity to do something, because the Chicago and Iowa, in order to build westward to the river, was extremely anxious to market a million dollars worth of bonds and was hoping to persuade Joy, the super-salesman, to help out. The terms on which he offered to do so are fascinating:

1. Instead of continuing westward to Bellevue, the Chicago and Iowa should terminate its line at Forreston (on the Illinois Central) with the understanding that all business, both freight and passenger, originating on the Upper River Road would be routed over the Illinois Central to Forreston, there handed over to the Chicago and Iowa, and by them delivered to the C. B. and Q. in Aurora.
2. Since termination of the C. and I. at Forreston would preclude its building to Bellevue, the Lower River Road should extend to Clinton, Iowa, to which point the C. B. and Q. would build a branch that would bring all business from the Lower River Road *as well as* any business originating west or north of the Upper River Road to the main line of the C. B. and Q. at Mendota.
3. Joy would personally market a million dollars of C. and I. bonds if the C. and I. would give half its stock to the C. B. and Q.
4. The C. B. and Q. would make a contract with the Lower River Road by which that company could pay its adverse traffic balances with its own bonds, provided it gave half its stock to the C. B. and Q.
5. The C. B. and Q. would make a similar contract with the Upper River Road but without any provision to obtain stock.[15]

---

[14] *BR*, ibid.

[15] *BR*, p. 125; J. Foy to Sidney Bartlett; February 22, 1875 (Burlington Archives). The chief collection of primary sources concerning the River Roads is in the Burlington Archives on deposit at the Newberry Library, Chicago; see Elisabeth Coleman Jackson and Carolyn Curtis, *Guide to the Burlington Archives in the Newberry Library 1851-1901* (Chicago, 1949), pp. 243-245. These archives are referred to hereafter as BA.

This fifth point deserves scrutiny. For years it had been the established policy of the Burlington not to make any contract with a new road unless there were a provision for obtaining eventual stock control. But because all traffic originating on the Upper River Road itself would first travel eighty-three miles over the Illinois Central to Forreston, then about the same distance over the Chicago and Iowa to Aurora, and for only thirty-eight miles over the C. B. and Q. into Chicago, Joy could hardly demand a half stock interest in that company.[16]

The question, then, was how the C. B. and Q. could take control of the Upper River Road and thus warrant acceptance of that company's bonds in lieu of traffic balances. In Joy's estimation, there was but one solution. Early in 1871 the Upper River Road had made a contract with a construction company under which the latter agreed to build the 118 mile line between Dubuque and La Crescent in exchange for bonds *and* stock of the railway. There was nothing unusual about this arrangement; it was common procedure at the time. What *was* unusual was the fact that once the construction company had spent its assets (including its own capital stock of $300,000) it was to be released from any further liability. In other words, if the construction company should run out of money without completing the road, the line as it then stood could be turned over to the railway company with no further obligation whatever on the part of the construction company. Perhaps this is the place to add that the Lower River Road, in the fall of 1870, had also arranged with another construction company to build its line in exchange for bonds and stock, and it is notable that the contract included no such escape clause as existed in the case of the Upper River Road. What should also be noted is that the president of both construction companies was one and the same man, and before long he became president of both railways as well. His name was J. K. Graves.[17]

This, then, was the situation when Joy completed his complicated traffic contracts and reached the conclusion that the only way the C. B. and Q. could ever control the Upper River Road was to acquire the construction company that was to receive its stock. Accordingly, on April 27, 1871, Joy persuaded Sidney Bartlett, John Brooks, John Burnham, J. N. Denison, and Nathaniel Thayer – all directors of the C. B. and Q. – to join him in buying control of the construction company building the Upper River Road. Since the construction company would be paid for its efforts partly in the stock of the Upper River Road, this meant that these six directors of the Burlington (constituting just half the board) would eventually gain control of that company. But, whether they knew it or not, they had acquired control of a construction company which was not obligated to finish the job at hand. At

---

[16] *BR*, pp. 125-127; Joy to Nathaniel Thayer, Sept. 10, 1875, quoted in T. C. Cochran, *Railroad Leaders 1845-1890*, (Cambridge, 1953), p. 369.

[17] *BR*, pp. 126-127.

any rate, early in June the Burlington directors approved the traffic agreements Joy had worked out, and furthermore issued a circular recommending $1,500,000 of Upper River Road bonds to C. B. and Q. stockholders. A month later, the Lower River Road agreed with its construction company to build all the way from Dubuque to Clinton as Joy suggested but, following the Upper River Road model, it was further provided that once the construction company's stockholders had spent their assets, including their own capital stock, the construction company was to be released from any further obligation. Finally, on July 29, 1871, the same six Burlington directors who had bought stock control of the construction company building the Upper River Road purchased the majority of shares in the construction company building the Lower River Road.[18]

This, then, was the situation: through the operation of the traffic contracts the C. B. and Q. would certainly acquire bonds of both the River Roads and the stock of the lower one. Furthermore since half the C. B. and Q. directors also controlled the two construction companies, it was apparent and obvious that stock control of both River Roads would be in the hands of men interested in the Burlington, if not in the hands of the company itself.

Now, from the vantage point of 1970, and, indeed, in view of the prudent and prosperous record of the C. B. and Q. up to 1871, this sort of flimsy arrangement appears not only of dubious propriety, but out of character. Yet one must visualize matters as they stood nearly a century ago; competition was intense, times were booming, and there was nothing to indicate that any director of the Burlington was inclined to put his personal interests ahead of those of the company. The C. B. and Q. wanted to get to the Twin Cities and the River Roads were already projected as logical links. Indeed, if the Burlington did not acquire them, they might provide stiff competition for whatever other line the company might build. The way to support new railways was to make traffic agreements which would give them a market for their bonds. If the C. B. and Q. were going to do that, it quite naturally wanted to gain control through stock ownership. And since, under these particular circumstances, the only way to get hold of the Upper River Road was to acquire the construction company that was building it, it apparently seemed ridiculously obvious to Joy that he simply had to do what he did, and to bring in enough of his associates so that he could share the financial burden and be certain of co-operation on the C. B. and Q. board if and whenever that should be needed.

The dangers, of course, are plainly apparent to us with our twenty-twenty vision of hindsight. Whereas James Walker, elected president of the C. B. and Q. on July 11, 1871, a confidant of Joy, and a seventh member of the directorate, of course knew that six of his fellow-directors had invested in the construction companies, it is highly probable that the other five did not.

---

[18] *BR*, pp. 127-129; *Chicago Inter-Ocean*, February 25, 1875, BA.

Certainly neither Forbes nor his colleague John C. Green did.[19] Second, if boom times should turn into depression, or if Graves spent his money not wisely but too well, there was the risk that neither of the River Roads would be completed. In that case, the Burlington as well as its stockholders might well be left with bonds of bankrupt companies.

Unfortunately, that is precisely what happened. As proceeds of the sales of the Upper River Road bonds became available, they were turned over to the president of that road, Graves. Then, as president of its construction company, he proceeded to spend the money. During 1871-72 he built most of the Upper Road's main line, began work on some unnecessarily elaborate shops at Dubuque, and, unbeknown to anybody in the East, spent some $173,000 on a totally unrelated project in which he alone was interested. To the easterners who had entrusted their money to him, only two facts were visible: the burst of activity in and north of Dubuque, and the lack of it to the south. Naturally enough, in view of their anomalous position, they became understandably nervous.[20] Early in 1872, for example, Brooks wrote Joy urging him to have work prosecuted vigorously on the Lower River Road. He reported that he and Thayer and Bartlett were wondering how the money was being spent and whether the Northwestern, when the time came, would permit use of its vital bridge at Clinton to connect the Lower River Road with the Burlington across the river. About the same time Denison, who was remitting proceeds of the Upper Road's bond sales to Graves, wrote rather frantically to Joy: "Mr. Graves," he said, "acted upon his understanding with you and with us here and went wild .... We ought never to put our money into another man's hands without constant supervision and control. Excuse our anxiety; we are very sore."[21]

Thus Joy was fully aware how anxious were his colleagues who had invested with him in the two construction companies. But somehow he must have quieted their fears, because early in February all of them, along with Walker (thus constituting a majority of the Burlington board) offered another million and a half in bonds of the Upper River Road and a similar amount of bonds of the Lower River Road to stockholders of both the C. B. and Q. and of the subsidiary B. and M. in Nebraska. Obviously, no mention was made of the fact that neither construction company had to finish what they had started; because of the C. B. and Q. endorsement, the bonds found ready purchasers. How much money Graves eventually received is difficult to determine, but by the summer of 1872 he had taken in, from various sources, close to $6,000,000. Even this was not enough, and during the fall the C. B. and Q. advanced some $180,000 more, taking preferred stock of the River Roads in exchange. The only concession to prudence occurred in January

[19] *BR*, pp. 129-131.
[20] *BR*, p. 129.
[21] John N. Denison to Joy, January 25, 1872, quoted in Cochran, *op. cit.*, p. 307.

1873, when, at the insistence of Brooks, five of the six men who were doubly involved, along with Walker and another C. B. and Q. stockholder named Hunnewell, were elected directors of the River Railroads. By this time Graves had indeed finished the entire Upper River Road, but only about four-fifths of the Lower Road. Furthermore, the Northwestern flatly refused to permit the use of its bridge at Clinton. And, finally, both construction companies had used up all their funds, considered their obligations discharged and stopped all work.[22]

By the spring of 1873 it was apparent that neither River Road could pay the interest due on its bonds on June 1. So as to prevent default, all six men who were doubly involved, as well as Walker, voted – as C. B. and Q. directors – to have the Burlington pay these coupons when presented to the extent of some $237,000. Hopefully, the River Roads promised to repay this amount by the first of January 1874, but no notice whatever was given to the public of this arrangement. The head offices of the C. B and Q. and of the River Roads were both in the Sears Building at Boston, so that it was a simple matter for the River Roads treasurer to pay the coupons and reimburse himself at once from the C. B. and Q. Later on it was explained that this was done to preserve the credit of the River Roads and simply as a temporary expedient.[23]

Needless to say it is highly unlikely that the C. B. and Q. board would have acted as it did had either Forbes or Green – both of them directors – been present. But Forbes had been on an extensive trip, while Green of New York City had also, for various reasons, been absent. Ironically enough, Forbes wrote to an inquiring stockholder in mid-1873 that although the C. B. and Q. had undertaken a tremendous amount of construction in the years immediately preceding – so much so that despite an increase in revenues of more than fifty per cent during 1871-73, net income per share had declined from $14.55 to $10.62 – he felt that these investments were on the whole wise and that he hoped "*the loose era* of railroad building" had come to an end.[24] Actually, Forbes, once more back in Boston, was far more worried than his letter to the stockholder would indicate. He wrote Green that he thought it might be necessary to issue more than $20,000,000 of C. B. and Q. bonds shortly, and that long years of prosperity and rich dividends had apparently tended to make those in charge far too casual in the spending of money. "I *do* think the time has come for us to know something more about the property of which we are the managers than any others here in the East do know. . . . I hope and believe that if *we don't* investigate the road, our stockholders at our next meeting will insist on doing it."[25]

[22] *BR*, pp. 130-131; *Chicago Tribune*, February 24, 1875, BA.
[23] *BR*, pp. 131-132; *Memorandum* of February 20, 1875, BA; *Chicago Tribune*, February 24, 1875, BA; C. B. and Q. R. R. Co., *Directors' Minutes*, Vol. 2, pp. 361, 363.
[24] John Murray Forbes to a Stockholder, mid-1873, BA.
[25] Forbes to John C. Green, June 16, 1873, BA.

Suiting action to words, in the fall of 1873 Forbes, taking Brooks and Walker and Griswold with him, went west on an inspection trip. With them also was Charles E. Perkins, then vice-president of the B. and M. in Nebraska. On November 7, Graves took them all by special train over the Upper River Road to La Crescent and back again to Dubuque. On this journey Graves and Perkins fell into conversation, and quite casually Graves disclosed the fact that Joy, Brooks, and various other C. B. and Q. directors were stockholders of the two construction companies as well as of the River Roads themselves. Perkins was flabbergasted, for although, as he put it later, there was nothing necessarily wrong in construction companies building railways or even the fact that C. B. and Q. directors were their owners, it was of the first importance, in view of the various money advances and bond endorsements that the C. B. and Q. had made, there should be the utmost frankness about the entire matter. Consequently, when he had the chance, he told Forbes the entire story.[26]

Forbes was not only flabbergasted, but furious. That evening he and Griswold, in the presence of Brooks and Walker, tried their best to get Graves to explain precisely what he had done with the millions of dollars entrusted to his care and why. But Graves, apart from admitting that he had spent some $173,000 for his own purposes, refused to name the stockholders of the construction companies or to tell anything about those companies except that both were completely out of funds.[27]

Naively enough, the first thing Forbes did was to report to Bartlett what little he had been able to find out, never dreaming that Bartlett himself was as deeply involved as anybody else.[28] Bartlett, naturally, forwarded Forbes's letter along to Joy. From that point on, a serious split within the C. B. and Q. board became increasingly likely. Whereas Bartlett, Brooks, Burnham, Denison, and Thayer all later alleged that they were completely innocent of the outrageous contracts between the River Roads and the construction companies, and were horrified by Graves's misapplication of funds, Joy himself took an entirely different position. He told Walker that neither Perkins nor Forbes were friends of his, and that Forbes himself was not strong enough to "revolutionize the C. B. and Q." even if he wanted to. Obviously Joy had no intention whatever of retreating.[29] And since, for reasons that have never been explained, Forbes did not approach Joy directly, a showdown was inevitable.

Throughout 1874, however, Forbes tried to avoid open conflict. In vain he tried to get those directors of the Burlington who were also holders of

---

[26] *BR*, pp. 133-134; C. E. Perkins, *Memorandum*, November 2, 1901, in *Personal Letter Book*, Vol. 18, pp. 600-609 in Cunningham-Overton Collection, see *Guide, op. cit.*, p. 331. This collection is hereafter referred to as C-O.

[27] *BR*, p. 134; see also *Perkins Memorandum* noted in footnote 26.

[28] Forbes to Bartlett, November 9, 1873, BA.

[29] Joy to James M. Walker, November 17, 1873, BA.

River Road bonds to repay to the C. B. and Q. the interest that the latter company had paid out to them. Equally in vain he tried to get the C. B. and Q. directors to turn over their River Road stock to the bondholders of those companies so the latter could protect their interests. But all he was able to accomplish was to get the River Road directors (six out of nine of whom were also C. B. and Q. directors) to lease the River Roads to the C. B. and Q. until the net earnings of those roads were sufficient to pay off all debts to the Burlington. As the result, the C. B. and Q. took possession of the River Roads and began to manage them on October 1, 1874.[30]

But even this was of doubtful help, because the Burlington had to pour in more funds to complete the properties and to try to bring order out of chaos. In mid-January 1875 the obviously bankrupt River Roads were placed in the hands of a receiver, and a committee of bondholders was immediately formed to investigate the entire situation. Clearly such an investigating committee would, as indeed they did, uncover not only the infamous contracts between the River Roads and the construction companies that built (or rather failed to build) them, but also the fact that six C. B. and Q. directors controlled those construction companies so that they might, quite understandably, be charged with using C. B. and Q. funds to protect their investments. During the early days of February, 1875, Forbes worked literally day and night in an attempt to persuade at least Bartlett, Brooks, and Thayer to turn over their River Road stock to the investigating committee, but without success. So it was that on February 14, 1875, Forbes reached the reluctant conclusion that for the sake of the Burlington, the only solution was to reform the board of the C. B. and Q.[31]

Once he had made this crucial decision, events moved rapidly. Working closely with Griswold and Green, he carried out a whirlwind campaign for proxies to be voted at the annual stockholders' meeting of the C. B. and Q. scheduled for Chicago on February 24. For the sake of harmony and continuity, he was eager to make as few changes as possible, but was adamant that Joy would have to go. Three days later, on February 27, the bondholders of the River Roads met to hear the report of their investigating committee. Item by item the sorry story was revealed. Joy, with his customary courage, was present. But despite sharp questioning, he refused to admit that he had concealed any relevant facts at any point. Thereupon the other C. B. and Q. directors that had acted with Joy deserted him and sprang to their own defence. Brooks, Bartlett, Burnham, Thayer, and Denison published a lengthy statement in a Boston paper in which they placed the entire blame for the imbroglio squarely on Joy, claiming that they had relied throughout upon his judgment and integrity. Joy did not reply publicly, but in a private letter to Bartlett simply said that he had acted in the only way possible to

[30] *BR*, pp. 135-136.
[31] *BR*, pp. 136-137; Forbes to John N. A. Griswold, February 14, 1875, BA.

guarantee control of the River Roads for the Burlington, and hence access to the Northwest. Joy, in effect, nailed his flag to the mast.[32]

When the Burlington stockholders' meeting convened on February 24, the room was packed and filled with agents of the press. It was agreed that the size of the board should be increased from twelve to thirteen . But two slates were offered for the thirteen positions available. Nine names appeared on both: Bartlett, Brooks, Colton, Corning, Forbes, Green, Griswold, Thayer, and Walker. On the old ticket, the names of Burnham, Denison, Joy, and Moses Taylor of New York also appeared, whereas the new ticket, proposed by Forbes, included T. Jefferson Coolidge, William J. Rotch, J. H. Clifford, and Charles J. Paine, all of Boston.[33]

It should be noted carefully that in the new slate proposed by Forbes, three C. B. and Q. directors who had been involved in the River Roads (Bartlett, Brooks, and Thayer) were included as candidates for re-election. In the circular soliciting proxies, Forbes and Griswold explained why they were keeping these men on the board. For one thing, they said, they were anxious to make as few changes in the directorate as possible and were inclined to feel that these men had made their mistake because of over optimism about the future of the River Roads rather than because of any intent to abuse their position as directors. Furthermore, all three men had had long experience as Burlington directors as well as substantial interests in the company's stock. Hence it was felt they could be useful and, indeed, serve as watchdogs over the "reformed majority" that Forbes and Griswold hoped to have elected. Under the circumstances, Forbes and Griswold were asking the stockholders to retire only Joy and the two associates of his who could best be spared, namely Burnham and Denison.

The outcome was a foregone conclusion. Except for the election of Denison rather than Coolidge, the entire new ticket was swept into office, and Denison's election was only because Griswold had misunderstood Green's instructions. But that was a detail. Joy and Burnham were out; Forbes and his like-minded associates were in firm and complete control of the Chicago, Burlington and Quincy.[34]

Courageous and eloquent as ever, Joy made a touching speech of retirement. He recalled the long years during which he and others present had worked together to solve the countless problems of the early railway and said he hoped the new administration would do as well as the old. Thereupon the stockholders unanimously passed a motion indicating their undiminished regard for him, and voted their thanks for his past services.[35] His departure that evening for his home in Detroit marked the end of an era. However one

[32] *BR*, pp. 137-138.
[33] *BR*, p. 138.
[34] *BR*, pp. 138-146; *Chicago Tribune*, February 25, 1875, BA.
[35] *Chicago Tribune*, February 25, 1875, BA; *Chicago Inter-Ocean*, February 25, 1875, BA.

may characterize his involvement with the River Roads, he more than any-one else had figured out in the early 1850's how to weld together the original C. B. and Q. in Illinois. Thereafter, for twenty years, he mobilized the efforts of local business men, secured favorable action in state legislatures, staked out the territory the Burlington should control, and devised means for oc-cupying and holding it. Throughout he had thought in large terms and acted accordingly.

But now his overly intricate schemes and casual methods of control had cost him his leadership. Yet the "Revolution of 1875" was far more than a struggle between two strong men, Joy and Forbes. Even though what had happened in respect to the River Roads was more characteristic of the age than exceptional, for the Burlington, at least, such dubious practices now stood condemned; the "Revolution" shook the administration, and broke old friendships. But in the process it established a higher standard of integri-ty. At the very first meeting of the reconstituted board of directors on March 4, 1875, it was resolved, in effect, that any person in the service of the company who acted in a dual capacity was to be immediately discharged. Furthermore, the new post of General Auditor was created, and the occu-pant ordered to make a detailed examination of books and accounts in all departments. All cash not needed for current business was transferred to Boston where it was under the direct care of the board. In brief, the old casual ways of doing business were brought to an abrupt end.[36]

Perhaps, in view of that statement, a word of explanation should be made as to why J. M. Walker, who had become president of the C. B. and Q. on July 11, 1871, and was thus in office throughout the River Roads affair, was allowed to remain at his post. It is perfectly true that Walker was a "Joy man," and was probably aware of much that was going on in respect to the River Roads from the beginning. For one thing, he had been present during that fateful meeting in Dubuque on November 7, 1873, and had been pre-sent and voting at the C. B. and Q. board meetings at which assistance had been given to the River Roads. On the other hand, he had not owned any of the construction company stocks. Furthermore, Forbes felt (quite rightly as it turned out) that Walker, being by nature a follower rather than a leader, would carry out the majority wishes of the reformed directorate just as assiduously as he had previously followed Joy's directions. Thus, rather than create any further upheaval, it seemed wise to retain him in his post, at least for the time being.[37]

One question that could not be postponed, however, was what to do with the River Roads. At the time of the "Revolution" everyone apparently assumed that the C. B. and Q. would extend them to the Twin Cities and take over their management. Indeed, in April 1875 Perkins told Forbes that

[36] *BR*, pp. 139, 147-148.
[37] *BR*, pp. 143-144.

if the properties were carefully handled, they should gross about half a million dollars a year. But when Perkins himself was offered the opportunity to take charge of them, he declined. Just why he did so deserves further research, but quite probably there were several excellent reasons. For one thing, Perkins was "on the way up" in the parent C. B. and Q., as well as the dominating figure in the B. and M. lines west of the Missouri River. He thus not only had all he could handle – especially in view of the running fight with Gould that was then at its peak – but also because it would have been a needless risk to exchange his secure status on the well-established key lines for a post on the trouble-laden River Roads. Secondly, the hectic affairs of those roads between 1870 and 1875 had given rise to a series of law-suits; to untangle the mess was hardly an inviting prospect. Thus he left the job to others.

As it turned out – quite probably in view of the hopeless complications – all parties agreed, by mid-1877, to dismiss all pending suits and, in hopes of making a fresh start, to cancel the complex traffic agreements Joy had so ingeniously worked out in 1871. Sentiment on the Burlington then shifted toward disposing of the properties. True enough, the C. B. and Q. branch from the main line at Mendota had been extended through Prophetstown to East Clinton, but the Northwestern still adamantly refused to share the use of its bridge at that point so that, if the Burlington were to have its own link to the River Roads, it would have to build another expensive bridge over the Mississippi. Accordingly, the River Roads were reorganized, consolidated early in 1878, and in 1880 sold to the Milwaukee.

What the C. B. and Q. itself as a corporation lost on the entire River Roads transaction will probably never be known; a combined accountant and detective would require months, if not years, to find out. Yet probably the monetary loss was not more than $150,000, and perhaps nothing at all, since the sale to the Milwaukee more than offset direct monetary advances. What the affair had cost in time and anguish, however, was another matter. And furthermore, as of 1880, the C. B. and Q. was no nearer the Twin Cities than it had been some eight years before. Of course, the C. B. and Q. was still exchanging business and slowly acquiring control of the Chicago and Iowa which extended between Aurora and Forreston by way of Oregon. But it was over three hundred miles from either East Clinton or Forreston to the Twin Cities and – now that the River Roads had been sold to the Milwaukee – there were no local companies in between that might be used as stepping stones.[38]

Thus ended the sorry story of the River Roads. As time went by there were some revealing second thoughts. On February 1, 1897, for example, Perkins, in a letter to the president of the Michigan Central, observed: "I believe and always have believed that if he [Joy] instead of Mr. Brooks and

[38] *BR*, p. 148.

Mr. Walker had been at that meeting in Dubuque when the trouble began, there never would have been any trouble, because Mr. Joy would have told the whole story with the frankness and courage which characterized him. It was the refusal of the others to tell anything which changed the course of history. . . . "[39] Four years later Perkins said flatly that the sale of the River Roads to the Milwaukee had been "a blunder – the C. B. and Q. should have taken them and extended the line to St. Paul."[40] But hindsight, as always, was easier than foresight. As of 1880, the Burlington was still a long way from the Twin Cities.

Meanwhile, however, administrative changes on the Burlington suggested that this situation would soon be remedied. After the storm created by the "Revolution" had blown over, Forbes himself, on May 25, 1878, had assumed the presidency of the C. B. and Q. But he did so with the distinct intention of holding the post for only a few years until the up-and-coming Charles E. Perkins (then only thirty-seven years old) could, with the blessing of the directors, take over the job. This is precisely what happened; on September 29, 1881, Perkins, then forty, became president of the C. B. and Q.[41] With this energetic character in command, it was not long before the Twin Cities project was revived with a vengeance.

THE C. B. AND N., 1882-90

In October, 1882, Perkins wrote Forbes that there was a growing feeling around Burlington headquarters that the company "ought to get the line to St. Paul, the Kansas City of the North."[42] He pointed out that St. Paul business was growing rapidly and would increase even faster when the Northern Pacific was completed. Consequently, he suggested building up the east side of the Mississippi River and urged that preliminary steps be taken before the company's plans were suspected by the railways already serving the area, notably the Northwester and the Milwaukee.[43]

For the moment, nothing was done, but in the summer of 1883 Perkins authorized the first of several quiet surveys along the east bank of the Mississippi, and in August of that year saw to it that the Wisconsin Legislature incorporated a railway with the innocent-sounding name of Winona, Alma and Northern which would neatly serve the Burlington's purposes in that state. By November he jubilantly told Forbes that both Oakes Ames of the Northern Pacific and James J. Hill of the St. Paul, Minneapolis and Mani-

[39] Perkins to Henry Ledyard, February 1, 1897, C-O.
[40] Perkins Memorandum, "The Revolution in C. B. and Q.," November 1901, C-O.
[41] *BR*, pp. 162, 176.
[42] Perkins to Forbes, October 16, 1882, C-O. The chief collection of primary data concerning the C. B. and N. is in BA; see *Guide, op. cit.*, pp. 228-243.
[43] *Ibid., BR*, p. 190.

toba, in which he had confided, were willing to share their terminal facilities at the Twin Cities.[44]

By now it was fairly obvious to everyone what the Burlington had in mind. In mid-November 1883 a new railroad with appropriate authority was incorporated in Illinois, and the next month the C. B. and Q. directors authorized a full-fledged survey to St. Paul. Early in 1884, the State of Minnesota granted a charter for a line from the Wisconsin border to St. Paul itself. All that remained was to determine the final route. After considering several possibilities, the company decided to extend the Chicago and Iowa twenty-seven miles from Oregon to Savanna, and then build 288 miles along the east bank of the river so as to provide a through route 435 miles in length. This, to be sure, would be twenty-five miles longer than either the Milwaukee or the Northwestern, but this was only six per cent more for the entire distance. Of far greater importance, the C. B. and Q., at water level, would have by far the easiest grades and thus be the best fitted for through business. It was estimated that the new railway, including terminal grounds at St. Paul and Minneapolis, a seventeen mile branch to link Savanna with Fulton, motive power, and contingencies would cost approximately $10,-000,000.[45]

The incentives to build were obvious: the Twin Cities were already the largest commercial centre west of Chicago and St. Louis except for San Francisco, while the country surrounding them was rapidly being settled by an enterprising population. Secondly, once at St. Paul, the C. B. and Q. could tap the business brought in from the north and west by the Northern Pacific, the Manitoba, and the Canadian Pacific. Thirdly, there was the pine being cut along the banks of the St. Croix, the Chippewa and the Wisconsin; the proposed C. B. and Q. line could and would intercept this timber as it floated down to reach the Mississippi. Finally, local business from the intermediate stations along the route was promising indeed.

On the other hand, there was one notable risk involved: the Burlington would be invading a territory which had hitherto been regarded as the special preserve of the Northwestern and of the Milwaukee. But the fact that the Rock Island had just, in 1882, completed a round-about route between Chicago and the Twin Cities, and that the Wisconsin Central was heading in the same direction, were regarded as removing the onus from the Burlington of being the first to challenge the hegemony of the Northwestern and the Milwaukee. The Burlington, as a matter of major strategy, decided to go ahead.

For nearly a year, construction was delayed while Perkins hammered out the financial and administrative tactics. The company by then had already

---

[44] BR, p. 191; C. B. and Q., Documentary History, Vol. 1, pp. 1486-1488; Perkins to Forbes, November 1, 1863, in PLB Vol. 6, pp. 468-469, C-O.

[45] BR, pp. 191-192; George S. Morrison to Perkins, June 3, 1884, BA.

spent some $800,000 in making surveys and acquiring rights of way. What Perkins wanted to do first was to complete the line without committing further Burlington funds. Furthermore, he realized that outright ownership would add substantially to the managerial responsibilities of the C. B. and Q. staff; hence his second tactical objective was to create a controlled line that would not put a burden on the Burlington administration. Not until the summer of 1885 were these twin problems solved to his satisfaction.

The key to the arrangements lay in Perkins's success in persuading A. E. Touzalin to leave his post as vice-president of the Sante Fe to become president of the new Twin Cities road. Touzalin had worked for the B. and M. in Nebraska from 1869 to 1882 (except for a year spent with the Santa Fe) and had then served as vice-president of the C. B. and Q. from 1882 to 1883. Thus he needed no introduction to Burlington directors and, as Perkins told his stockholders at the time, was a man of character and energy. Touzalin, in turn, was able to bring with him George B. Harris as vice-president and general manager. Harris had started out with the Hannibal and St. Joseph in 1866 and had spent seventeen years on various Burlington family roads before going to the Santa Fe with Touzalin in 1883. Therefore he too was well known within the family.[46]

The matter of finances was somewhat more complicated, perhaps in part because the Burlington directors were determined to avoid any such situation as had arisen with the River Roads. It was agreed that the three local companies should be merged into one concern to be known as the Chicago, Burlington and Northern with a capitalization of $18,000,000 divided equally between stocks and bonds; the bonds were convertible into stock. According to long-standing practice, the C. B. and Q. promised to invest half its net profits from all business interchanged with the new company in bonds of the latter which could, of course, be converted into stock. This would help provide the new company with cash during its formative years, and at the same time pave the way for eventual C. B. and Q. ownership. So far as actual construction was concerned, a professional outside concern was hired to build the line for $25,000 per mile in stock and $25,000 per mile in bonds of the railway. In order to provide the contractor with ready cash at the outset, and also to make sure that the Burlington would indeed eventually control the new company, it was agreed that the contractor would immediately sell 30,000 shares of its C. B. and N. stock (that is, one third of the total) to the Burlington for cash at twenty cents on the dollar. Finally, the contractor was to allow individual C. B. and Q. stockholders to buy, within forty days, 45,000 additional shares of C. B. and N. stock and 75,000 bonds. The net result of all this was that the C. B. and Q. would hold a one-third stock control at the beginning, with the assurance that as time went on

[46] *BR*, p. 192, C. B. and Q. R. R. Co., *Annual Report* for 1888, p. 23; *Biographical Directory of Railway Officials* (Chicago, 1906), p. 256.

it would acquire more stock through conversion of bonds taken on account of traffic balances, and with the possibility that individual C. B. and Q. stockholders would hold most of the remaining stock. Thus although the C. B. and Q. corporation itself did not technically control the C. B. and N., it was actually in a position to call the tune with only a minor outlay of cash and, hopefully, without imposing a burden on its managerial staff.[47]

During the summer of 1885 these various arrangements were carried out as planned, and Touzalin went to work with vigour. As a matter of fact, the speed and extent of his activities caused Perkins some concern. As he bluntly pointed out, neither the Northwestern nor the Milwaukee could be expected to welcome any newcomer; Perkins consequently advised Touzalin to consult and negotiate with them and other established roads in an effort to keep relations on a friendly basis and, more specifically, to assure them that the C. B. and N. would not upset the established rate pattern. Perkins also told Touzalin that he would be well advised to organize his board of directors as soon as possible and to get its members to share responsibility with him.[48]

But Touzalin, energetic and independent, plunged ahead pretty much on his own. Indeed, the Illinois Central tried to prevent the C. B. and N. from sharing the narrow shelf of land they both had to occupy between Portage Curve and East Dubuque; the matter was settled only when the C. B. and N. gained a favourable court order. Fortunately, other arrangements proceeded more smoothly. Before the end of 1885, Hill agreed to let the new company use his line between St. Paul and Minneapolis as well as his terminals at both points. And in 1886 the C. B. and N. arranged to use the existing bridges at Winona and Dubuque, thus avoiding the necessity of building new ones. On August 23, 1886, the entire line was opened for freight, and on the last day of October inaugurated regular passenger service. There could be little doubt about Touzalin's energy.[49]

As Perkins had foreseen, however, the problem of rates was a thorny one. In a nutshell, Touzalin and Harris thought that the C. B. and N. should be a freelance for a year, and then, after its traffic-carrying capacity had been established, perhaps enter one of the established pools. But Perkins felt that the C. B. and N. should at least try pooling first. What he was afraid of, of course, was that the C. B. and Q. would be held responsible for whatever rate-cutting the C. B. and N. might do despite the fact that technically the C. B. and N. was not under the C. B. and Q. corporate control. If the C. B. and Q. were held responsible, then the Milwaukee and Northwestern might retaliate by cutting rates in, say, Iowa and Nebraska.[50]

[47] *BR*, pp. 192-193; *Perkins Memorandum*, July 30, 1885, C-O; C. B. and Q. R. R. Co., *Directors' Minutes*, Vol. 3, pp. 208-210.

[48] *BR*, p. 193; Perkins to A. E. Touzalin, October 6, 1885, C-O.

[49] *BR*, pp. 193-194; John H. Hobart, "The History of the Chicago, Burlington and Northern Railroad," unpublished thesis, Yale University, 1945, pp. 27, 39-43; C. B. and Q., *Corporate History*, pp. 117-123.

[50] T. J. Potter to Perkins, July 30, 1886, BA.

What actually happened during the first few years the railway was in operation was enough to try the patience of Job. Although the C. B. and Q. and the C. B. and N. had agreed not to make any through rates except by mutual consent, they were continually at loggerheads as to what such rates should be. In the fall of 1886 the C. B. and N. was persuaded to join the newly-formed Northwestern Freight Association which included all the companies serving the Twin Cities. As Touzalin feared, the Milwaukee and Northwestern were given the lion's share of prospective earnings. Even more to the point, the Association fixed a first-class rate of seventy-two cents per hundredweight between the Twin Cities and Chicago, while the C. B. and N. was perfectly willing to carry the business for forty cents. To complicate matters further, the Interstate Commerce Act became effective on April 5, 1887; it so happened that the provisions of that Act prohibiting pooling and making it illegal to charge more for a short than a long haul dovetailed neatly with the desires of the C. B. and N. But these two clauses were highly objectionable to the other lines serving the Twin Cities and, just as Perkins had foreseen, whenever the brash new C. B. and N. differed with the established lines, the blame was thrown squarely on the Burlington. Consequently as early as March, 1887, Perkins urged upon his board the outright purchase of the C. B. and N. But Griswold, among others, frankly opposed any such action until the new company had proven itself on its own merits. The C. B. and N. stockholders were willing enough to sell, but, fully aware of their strategic position, demanded $110 per share, a price that the C. B. and Q. board thought wholly unrealistic in view of the fact that the new line had not yet begun to make any money at all.[51]

As time went on Perkins became increasingly exasperated at Touzalin's independence. He told Forbes that Touzalin acted as if the C. B. and Q. were made for the C. B. and N., instead of the reverse. "The C. B. and N. is making C. B. and Q. lots of trouble, and I wish we could absorb it," he wrote in November 1887.[52] Shortly thereafter the tough-minded Touzalin, whose health had been failing, resigned, but the conflict of interests remained: charges by the C. B. and N. per hundredweight between Chicago and the Twin Cities had varied between forty and eighty cents during the first fifteen months of operation, and despite disclaimers by Perkins, the Burlington was being held squarely responsible. By the late summer of 1888 the situation was as ridiculous as it was serious. The C. B. and Q. directors still refused to purchase the C. B. and N., yet because of its essential strategic value they did agree to lend it $700,000 to keep it from bankruptcy.

In the fall of 1889, Perkins tried to get the Pennsylvania Railroad to join the Burlington in acquiring control of both the C. B. and N. and Hill's

---

[51] *BR*, pp. 194-195; Peter Geddes to Forbes and Perkins to Forbes, July 28, 1887, C-O; C. B. and Q. R. R. Co., *Directors' Minutes*, Vol. 3, p. 388; "Statement on behalf of the C. B. and N. in Arbitration before George R. Blanchard," Boston, 1887, pp. 11-12.

[52] Perkins to Forbes, November 17, 1887, in PLB, Vol. 8, p. 307, C-O.

Manitoba line. But Hill, now determined to build his own line to the Pacific, had no disposition whatever to sell his property. And unless the C. B. and N. could serve as a link to the Manitoba, the Pennsylvania refused to share with the C. B. and Q. the cost of acquiring it. Faced with these realities, the C. B. and Q. board finally, on March 12, 1890, authorized purchase of enough additional C. B. and N. stock to gain outright corporate control, provided that it could be obtained at not over $40 a share. With Touzalin gone and deficits mounting, the C. B. and N. shareholders likewise realized the realities of the situation. By the end of 1890, the Burlington succeeded in buying over ninety-eight per cent of the Northern's stock so that from then on the property could be run wholly in the interests of the C. B. and Q. even though actual corporate consolidation did not take place until several years later (1899).[53]

Thus, at long last the Burlington by 1890 controlled its own line between Chicago and the Twin Cities. Unlike the first chapter involving the River Roads, the second chapter concerning the C. B. and N. was completely above-board and without any breath of scandal. Actually, in allowing the C. B. and N. and Touzalin virtual autonomy, Perkins had simply been trying to relieve the managerial and financial burdens of the C. B. and Q. Yet despite his earnest intentions, and largely because Touzalin was just as tough-minded as Perkins, his plan simply did not work. After twenty long years, the C. B. and Q. finally learned that if it wished to exercise full authority, it would inevitably have to assume full responsibility as well.

CONCLUSION

Fortunately the story eventually had a happy ending. The C. B. and N. was consolidated with the C. B. and Q. in 1899, and during the twentieth century the Twin Cities line has proven to be a major and successful portion of the Burlington system. Indeed, today it carries its full share of all freight and the largest share of all passenger traffic between Chicago and the Twin Cities. And it was on this line that the nation's first Vista Dome went into regular operation. But perhaps the 1965 floods on the Mississippi and the three or four million dollar repair bill could be regarded as a sobering reminder that between 1870 and 1890 the perfectly straightforward desire to control a railroad between Chicago and St. Paul could cause plenty of trouble "even in the best of regulated families." Certainly this story shows that the history of transportation involves far more than simply explaining how goods and people move from here to there.

[53] *BR*, p. 196; C. B. and Q. *Corporate History*, p. 125.

The Fine Arts of Lobbying and Persuading: The Case of the B.C. Electric Railway, 1897-1917

Patricia Roy, Assistant Professor of History, University of Victoria

Documenting the relationship between Canadian governments and businesses is difficult. Governments generate public records; politicians die, sometimes bequeathing papers to archives, but corporations can live indefinitely, keeping their files under close control. Thus, knowledge of the relationship between government and business has had to rely on public records or on "official" company histories which may not reveal the whole story. Only in unusual circumstances are company records open to the public. As a result of the expropriation of the British Columbia Electric Railway Company by the British Columbia government in 1961, the early records of this public utility have become available. Because the B.C.E.R.'s policies were made in its London office, its records are particularly detailed. They are especially interesting in their revelations about the lobbying techniques used in seeking favours from governments.

British capitalists led by R. M. Horne-Payne had organized the B.C.E.R. in 1897 by re-financing the small electric street railway and electric lighting companies in Vancouver and Victoria. Through the B.C.E.R.'s London office, Horne-Payne carefully directed all of the company's policies. By 1914 the B.C.E.R. had grown with the province to become one of the largest privately-owned electrical enterprises in the British Empire. It produced and distributed hydro-electric power and gas on southern Vancouver Island and throughout the Lower Mainland of British Columbia; it ran street railways in Victoria, Vancouver and New Westminster; and it operated the "largest single intercity electric railway system in Canada."[1]

A striking feature of the company's history was its constant concern for maintaining good relations with all three levels of government – federal, provincial and municipal. The B.C.E.R. quickly developed effective techniques to cope with "the lobbying and wirepulling" which the first general manager complained were "necessary in order to get a favourable hearing from the ruling bodies."[2] The methods and success of lobbying varied somewhat according to the level of government. With the federal government, the company

---

[1] John F. Due, The Intercity Electric Railway Industry in Canada, *Canadian Studies in Economics*, (Toronto, 1966), Vol. 18, p. 104.

[2] Johannes Buntzen to Francis Hope, December 12, 1903, General Manager's Letter Book. [Unless otherwise specified, this and all other references are from the British Columbia Electric Railway Company Papers in the Library of the University of British Columbia.]

concentrated on key politicians. Federal politicians could afford to grant favours; the B.C.E.R. was only one of many supplicants. At the provincial level, the company, the largest single enterprise in British Columbia, also worked on key leaders. Because of the province's dependence on London for developmental capital, provincial officials were vulnerable to company hints of financial retaliation. Municipal office-holders could not be easily lobbied. For them, the B.C.E.R. was a convenient and popular subject for attack on grounds of inadequate service, exorbitant rates and exploitive profits. Since each municipal ratepayer was also a customer of at least one of its services, the B.C.E.R. had to cultivate good will. This was difficult and not always successful. The company had only one major advantage over local politicians. Since its future did not depend completely on the wishes and whims of the electorate, it could usually afford to bide its time.

There was considerable "talk" in Vancouver of developing a municipal hydro-electric power plant but the only serious challenge to the B.C.E.R.'s monopoly in this field came from a private firm, the Stave Lake Power Company. In order to forestall the expansion of this rival, the B.C.E.R. called on the good offices of the federal government. In the process of persuading the federal politicians to grant it access to Lake Coquitlam's water, the B.C.E.R. demonstrated the effectiveness of its lobbying techniques.

In 1900 a number of Vancouver businessmen including J. J. Hendry, a prominent lumberman, organized the Stave Lake Power Company to develop the hydro-electric power potential of the Stave River and to sell cheap power in Vancouver and surrounding districts. For eight years the company intermittently worked on the project but as long as it lacked strong financial backing, the Stave Lake Company was not a serious threat to the B.C.E.R. Then, in 1909, the Bank of Montreal, having acquired a large interest in the Stave Lake Company, re-organized it into the Western Canada Power Company in which the Bank and Max Aitken's Royal Securities Corporation each held a one-third interest. Among the individual shareholders of the new company were Sir Thomas Shaughnessy of the C.P.R. and C. R. Hosmer of the Bank of Montreal.[3] With such formidable financial support, the Western Canada Power Company was likely to be able to develop the Stave River quickly. The B.C.E.R. was justifiably worried but rejected an overture for a merger of the two companies. Then the W.C.P. Company endeavoured to prevent the B.C.E.R. from gaining access to the water of Lake Coquitlam which was necessary to expand the hydro-electric facilities at the B.C.E.R.'s near by Lake Buntzen plant.

The question of Lake Coquitlam water rights was unusually complicated.

---

[3] Hosmer also held a few shares in the B.C.E.R.

Although there was uncertainty about the jurisdiction of the federal and provincial governments over water rights in the railway belt,[4] the federal government had permitted the city of New Westminster to use Lake Coquitlam as the source of its domestic water supply. In its efforts to obtain access to Lake Coquitlam, the B.C.E.R. exercised its lobbying talents to their full extent. Through the work of Colonel A. T. Thompson, a professional lobbyist; F. R. Glover, the B.C.E.R.'s executive trouble shooter;[5] and Ralph Smith, M.P. (Liberal, Nanaimo), the B.C.E.R. secured Orders in Council cancelling the land grant around Lake Coquitlam to New Westminster. The same order authorized the Minister of the Interior, Frank Oliver, to lease these lands to the Vancouver Power Company, a wholly-owned subsidiary of the B.C.E.R. After visiting the lake in October 1909, the minister confidentially informed Glover that he would approve the leasing of the lands to the Vancouver Power Company as soon as the Public Works Department approved the dam plans. All seemed well. Then, the city of New Westminster, its Board of Trade and the neighbouring municipalities of Coquitlam and Richmond – probably encouraged by Hendry of Western Canada Power, who was present – met Oliver at a meeting lasting for more than three hours and outlined their objections to the dam. Oliver did not find their arguments convincing, but agreed to let them have until December 1, 1909, to present a case to a cabinet committee.[6] Hendry told several federal Liberals that his company would spend up to $100,000 to prevent further development of the lake by the B.C.E.R. Through its Montreal financial backers, the W.C.P.

---

[4] The railway belt was a strip of land, twenty miles wide on either side of the C.P.R.'s main line through British Columbia. The federal government's reassertion of its claim to certain water rights in the railway belt caused a lengthy judicial fight which ended in 1910 when the Judicial Committee of the Privy Council ruled that ungranted land in the railway belt was Dominion Crown land. For details on the land question see Robert E. Cail, "Disposal of Crown Lands in British Columbia, 1871-1913," University of British Columbia, M.A. Thesis, 1954, pp. 225-235.

[5] Thompson, a lawyer, had served as Liberal M.P. for Haldimand-Monck, Ontario, from 1900 to 1904. He became the B.C.E.R.'s agent in Ottawa in 1907 and retained this position until his death in 1939. During the Borden regime, the B.C.E.R. used Thompson's law partner, Robert A. Pringle, Q.C., a Conservative and "intimate personal friend" of Borden, McBride and Bowser, as its Ottawa agent. (R. H. Sperling to Hiram Williams, November 9, 1911, Letters from the General Manager, 1911.)
Glover, a B.C.E.R. employee, became so closely identified with Liberal politics that Senator Hewitt Bostock and William Templeman (M.P., Victoria, B.C. and Minister of Inland Revenue and Minister of Mines) invited him to stand for the Liberal nomination in Yale-Cariboo. Glover declined on the grounds that his work with the B.C.E.R. would prevent such an arrangement. (Senator Hewitt Bostock to F. R. Glover, August 3, 1911; William Templeman to F. R. Glover, August 5, 1911, Letters from the General Manager, 1911.)

[6] F. R. Glover to R. H. Sperling, September 8, 1909; B.C.E.R. (Vancouver) to B.C.E.R. (London), October 18, 1909, Box 719.

also seemed to have influence with Hon. William Pugsley, Minister of Public Works.[7]

In the meantime, Hugh Guthrie, M.P. (Conservative-Wellington South), acting for the city of New Westminster, submitted evidence suggesting that the cancellation of the land grant to the city was illegal. Most members of the federal government, including Sir Wilfrid Laurier, seemed sympathetic to Oliver and the B.C.E.R. Pugsley, however, tended to agree with Guthrie's interpretation of the law. And, as time passed, the Prime Minister appeared less sympathetic. The B.C.E.R.'s lobbyists – Glover, Smith and Robert Kelly, a leading Vancouver Liberal – interviewed influential members of the House to press their case. They told several members that if the Liberals were to make any progress in British Columbia – the party held only two of the province's seven seats – "it would have to stand by its friends."[8] Unfortunately, the B.C.E.R. papers contain no precise information to indicate the extent of its favours to the Liberals.

Certainly the British Columbia Liberals expected favours from the B.C.E.R. The lobbying tactics outlined below illustrate the need of the company to gain the favour of the government and the government's attempt to use the company for partisan political purposes. It is well to remember too that the B.C.E.R., like Canadian voters, could simultaneously support opposing political parties at the federal and provincial levels. At the same time as the B.C.E.R. was courting the Liberals in Ottawa, it was working with the Conservatives in Victoria on matters of provincial concern.

One of the continuing problems of the provincial Liberals was the lack of a party newspaper in Vancouver. Laurier refused to use national party funds to provide financial backing for such an organ. William Templeman, the senior Liberal in the province and the major shareholder of the Victoria *Times*, decided to start a new Liberal daily in Vancouver with himself as managing editor. Kelly reported that if some of the B.C.E.R.'s friends would take $25,000 worth of stock in the newspaper, Templeman would go with Glover and get the matter settled "at once." "In other words," Glover explained to R. H. Sperling, the general manger of the B.C.E.R., "the prime minister who was anxious to see the party strengthened in B.C., would set aside his scruples regarding the cancellation of the Coquitlam Lake land grant, and for the good of the Liberal cause accept the way out of the difficulty which the Justice Department has furnished." Sperling favoured the proposition; the B.C.E.R. Board, after several days' deliberation, reluc-

[7] F. R. Glover to R. H. Sperling, January 5, 1910; F. R. Glover to R. H. Sperling, January 7, 1910, Box 717. Hendry had spoken to Senator Bostock, Hon. William Templeman and Ralph Smith.

[8] F. R. Glover to Sperling, December 3, 1909; F. R. Glover to R. H. Sperling, January 3, 1910; F. R. Glover to R. H. Sperling, January 5, 1910, Box 719.

tantly cabled that if participation in the newspaper were "absolutely essential," they would consent in return for some additional concessions.[9]

Laurier, contrary to Glover's expectations, showed greater concern for justice than for the political situation. He would not uphold an illegal cancellation of the land grant to New Westminster. Desiring to find a solution, he promised to refer the matter to the cabinet where only he and Pugsley opposed the B.C.E.R.'s case. After reviewing the evidence, Laurier and Pugsley agreed to reconsider. Glover and his friends put direct pressure on Pugsley. The next day, Templeman and Kelly interviewed the Minister but got little satisfaction. Then Ralph Smith, advising Pugsley that the B.C.E.R.'s case was just, presented an ultimatum: he would fight to the finish and, if necessary, "change his attitude on certain matters which Pugsley was having some difficulty in getting through the Public Accounts Committee. . . . " Smith also warned that "he resented New Brunswick interference in a purely B.C. matter, which all the western members and the responsible minister were supporting and candidly added that he considered Pugsley's attitude indicated a support of other interests which are opposed to ours." Smith also arranged for Pugsley's chief supporter in New Brunswick to convey the ultimatum. Glover had two interviews with Pugsley's son, a Montreal lawyer and "an exceedingly nice young chap," and offered him "either a good fee or a position on our legal staff at $1500 per annum, if he could induce his father to see our case through."[10] Pressure on Pugsley and the promise of aid to a Liberal newspaper led the cabinet to approve the B.C.E.R.'s application for access to land around Coquitlam Lake and to confirm the cancellation of the grant to New Westminster.[11] The B.C.E.R.'s lobbyists had succeeded. And, in the long run, the cost was low. The Liberals were unable to establish a newspaper in Vancouver immediately. Hence, neither the company nor its "friends" seem to have been called upon to take up stock in the journal.

Because the B.C.E.R. decided that having a federal charter for its interurban railways would provide few advantages and might raise the contentious ques-

---

[9] F. R. Glover to R. H. Sperling, January 7, 1910; B.C.E.R. (London) to R. H. Sperling, January 11, 1910, Box 717. For details on the Liberals in B.C., see Melva J. Dwyer, "Laurier and the British Columbia Liberal Party, 1896-1911: A Study in Federal-Provincial Party Relations," University of British Columbia, M.A. Thesis, 1961.

[10] F. R. Glover to R. H. Sperling, January 11, 1910; F. R. Glover to R. H. Sperling, January 13, 1920; F. R. Glover to R. H. Sperling, January 17, 1910, Box 717.

[11] In order to pacify New Westminster and to prevent the city from appealing the Order in Council, the B.C.E.R. voluntarily proposed to improve the city's street railway service and to reduce interurban fares slightly. Nevertheless, the negotiations with the city dragged on over several years as civic politicians attempted to make political capital out of the situation.

tion of provincial rights,[12] the federal government had little direct effect on the company. The provincial government, on the other hand, could exercise considerable direction over the company. The province owned most of the undeveloped land in British Columbia, including land immediately adjacent to the growing city of Vancouver. The Legislature could regulate the operations of the company and could control municipal legislation. The municipalities, in turn, issued most of the franchises without which a public utility could not operate.

As part of its concern for cultivating public support and in order to exert direct influence on the provincial and municipal governments, the B.C.E.R. established a Local Advisory Committee in 1905. This Committee consisted of three leading British Columbians: F. S. Barnard, a B.C.E.R. shareholder who had extensive business interests in the province and was a former Conservative M.P. for Victoria; R. G. Tatlow, a popular Vancouver M.L.A. and Minister of Finance in the McBride government; and Mayor W. H. Keary of New Westminster. In return for an annual payment of $2,000, each advisor was expected to give his "personal influence" and "advice on all matters" referred to the Committee by the local management.[13] The Committee which met about once a month also acted as a sounding board to keep the management informed of likely local reaction to company policies. After Tatlow's death in 1910, the Committee was disbanded. There had been some public criticism of possible conflict of interest. Replacing Keary and Tatlow with other politicians who would be useful to the company would only arouse public hostility.

As a cabinet minister, Tatlow had been a particularly useful member of the Committee. In addition, the B.C.E.R. employed a Victoria lawyer to watch for any provincial legislation which might affect it. Whenever a serious matter arose, however, the B.C.E.R. usually negotiated directly with Premier Richard McBride. The general manager could easily visit Victoria from his office in Vancouver. As well, the anglophilic McBride frequently visited London where the directors of the B.C.E.R., especially Horne-Payne, made a point of seeing him.

The B.C.E.R. developed its friendship with McBride during his first election campaign as premier. During the election of 1903 the company donated $1,000 to Conservative funds. In line with its policy of courting all possible supporters, the B.C.E.R. also gave the Liberals $200.[14] Although these are

[12] Zebulon A. Lash to R. H. Sperling, May 6, 1907, Box 8A, File 130.

[13] Johannes Buntzen to F. S. Barnard, June 5, 1905, *General Letter Book*, #13; Johannes Buntzen to F. S. Barnard, May 31, 1905, *General Manager's Letter Book*, 1905; R. H. Sperling to George Kidd, January 26, 1909, *Letters from the General Manager*, 1909; George Kidd to R. H. Sperling, February 17, 1909, Box 11A, File 180. See also the *Minute Book of the Local Advisory Committee.*

[14] Johannes Buntzen to Francis Hope, October 29, 1903, *General Manager's Letter Book*, 1903.

the only fully documented examples of substantial contributions to party funds, they are most probably not unique.

McBride, who was usually sympathetic to B.C.E.R. requests, was also a very astute politician. During the 1907 provincial election, for example, he delayed negotiations with the B.C.E.R. over a proposed land grant in Point Grey for fear of stimulating opposition. He bowed to pressure from labour unions and introduced a Tramways Inspection Act after an accident on the interurban lane killed fifteen workmen. On the whole, however, McBride was anxious to co-operate with the company. He agreed with the B.C.E.R. that the province depended on the confidence of British investors to maintain the pace of her economic expansion and he recognized the close relationship between prosperity and political success.

During the years under consideration, a major concern of the B.C.E.R. was its franchises in greater Vancouver. One of the lengthiest and most complex franchise disputes involved Hastings Townsite and District Lot 301, two tiny unorganized districts under direct provincial administration. The controversy over these franchises, though relatively minor itself, reveals the company's interest in long term street railway franchises, its belief that it could influence British investment in the province and its dependence on the favour of McBride.

In 1908 the McBride government granted the B.C.E.R. a perpetual – but not exclusive – street railway franchise in these districts. When the city of Vancouver annexed these areas in 1911 it wanted to alter their franchises so they would expire simultaneously in the city franchise in 1919. The directors of the B.C.E.R. opposed any interference with their plan to surround the city with a series of street railway lines on private rights of way or very long term franchises. Since the provincial government retained responsibility for the two franchises, the management of the B.C.E.R. negotiated directly with the cabinet.

Acting on the advice of his directors, Sperling reminded the cabinet of the importance of maintaining good relations with the company in order to preserve the credit of the province and its industries in the London markets. He noted "the harmful effects" on the credit of Ontario of the cancellation of the rights of the Electrical Development Company. Through Tatlow, the B.C.E.R. got McBride's assurance that he would do nothing to "disturb the excellent relations which have always subsisted" between the company and the province. McBride, however, found no similarities between the Ontario case and the local situation and yielded to pressure from the city. He accepted a cabinet recommendation for a compromise which replaced the perpetual franchises with ones expiring in 1929, that is, ten years after the expiration of the main Vancouver franchise.[15]

---

[15] For the Ontario situation, see Merrill Denison, *The People's Power,* (Toronto, 1960), ch. 9.

The B.C.E.R., unable to do anything about this "breach of contractual rights" refused to return its copy of the original agreement for revision. The directors argued that such a concession would endanger the company's legal rights on which every appeal for capital had been made. They advised Sperling to warn the government and the leading men of Vancouver that "confiscatory legislation in these matters means absolutely not a penny of British capital for all Vancouver enterprises for four or five years and this is not in the power of the directors either to avert or affect." Through William Mackenzie of the Canadian Northern Railway, and by appealing to McBride during his visit to London in the spring of 1912, the B.C.E.R. convinced the premier of the need to retain the perpetual franchise pending "a friendly adjustment."[16]

Neither the B.C.E.R. nor McBride took any action until Sperling interviewed the premier in January 1913. At this time, the B.C.E.R. was willing to consider a twenty-one year franchise in return for certain concessions including the relaxation of the Tramways Inspection Act. In spite of this modification of the company's position, Sperling repeated his earlier warning of the effects any mistreatment of the B.C.E.R. would have on British investment in the province and threatened to reduce company expenditures if the government passed hostile legislation. These arguments were particularly effective since the pre-war depression was already being noticed. McBride advised the B.C.E.R. to cultivate the good will of the city and agreed to delay altering the franchise. As the depression deepened and the war came, the question faded into insignificance. The B.C.E.R. with its ready access to the premier and its awareness of his financial vulnerability had preserved its franchises.

The company's problems were only just beginning. Its methods of seeking provincial government assistance remained the same; the company continued to stress the relationship between the prosperity of the company and the maintenance of British investment in the province. Its lobbying efforts were directed mainly towards the provincial government but it worked simultaneously on the city of Vancouver.

The new problem was the jitney. These privately-owned ordinary passenger automobiles began seeking passengers along major thoroughfares in Victoria and Vancouver in November 1914. The jitneys were not subjected to any public regulations, they had no fixed routes or schedules and, unlike the B.C.E.R.'s street railway, they operated only in densely populated areas and during rush hours. Their speed provided faster service than the street railway

---

[16] R. H. Sperling to W. R. Ross, Chief Commissioner of Lands and Works, February 3, 1911, Letters from the General Manager, 1911; B.C.E.R. (Vancouver) to B.C.E.R: (London), February 6, 1912; Box 23B, File 331; B.C.E.R. (London) to B.C.E.R. (Vancouver), February 8, 1912, Box 23B, File 331; William Mackenzie to Richard McBride, February 13, 1912, Richard McBride Papers (in the Provincial Archives of British Columbia), B.C.E.R. *Vancouver Daily Province*, June 19, 1912, p. 23.

and a cheap thrill. By the end of January 1915, there were over two hundred and fifty jitneys operating in Vancouver causing an average daily loss of $2,000 to the B.C.E.R.

Although the B.C.E.R. had previously opposed government regulation of business, Kidd now asked Attorney-General W. J. Bowser to regulate the jitneys by imposing strict safety rules and by forcing jitney operators to contribute to the cost of maintaining the streets. To strengthen this request, Kidd twice visited Premier McBride and had Horne-Payne remind the premier of the unfairness of "unregulated competition," and its effect on the company's ability to expand and to maintain employment. A week later, Horne-Payne cabled the premier that "the price of the Company's stocks is the Stock Exchange's barometer of British Columbia conditions and general credit. . . . " He hinted that the company might have to default on debenture interest which "would be a lasting catastrophe for the province."[17]

To reinforce the financial argument, the key to the campaign for jitney regulations, the B.C.E.R.'s London office prepared a press release which was published early in 1916 in many British newspapers. This statement, which drove down the prices of B.C.E.R. shares and bonds, was designed to make British investors aware of the situation in British Columbia in the hope they might exert pressure on McBride's government. Kidd also attempted to get the Canadian Bank of Commerce, the government's banker, to intercede on the B.C.E.R.'s behalf. The Bank, however, was unwilling to commit itself to such action. William Mackenzie of the Canadian Northern Railway was not so reticent when he reminded the premier of the B.C.E.R.'s problems. To indicate popular support, the B.C.E.R. also requested the unions of its employees, the Trades and Labor Council and the Boards of Trade to press the government for action. Editorials sympathizing with the B.C.E.R. on the jitney question appeared in the Vancouver *Province* and the Victoria *Colonist*.[18]

McBride, who sympathized with the B.C.E.R.'s arguments, could do little because of divisions within his cabinet. Attorney-General Bowser, who was reported to be having serious policy differences with McBride over the financing of the Pacific Great Eastern Railway,[19] refused to legislate against

---

[17] George Kidd to W. J. Bowser, December 11, 1914; George Kidd to R. M. Horne-Payne, December 30, 1914; R. M. Horne-Payne to Sir Richard McBride, January 7, 1915; Box 62A, File 1163. R. M. Horne-Payne to George Kidd (to be handed to McBride), February 1, 1915, *London Letters Inward*, #2. Horne-Payne sent a similar cable to William Mackenzie who passed it on to McBride.

[18] George Kidd to Michael Urwin, January 28, 1915, Box 62A, File 1163; William Mackenzie to C. N. Wilde (Canadian Northern Railway, Vancouver), February 10, 1915, *McBride Papers, Premier's Official Correspondence*, 143/15.

[19] A. T. Goward to George Kidd, March 8, 1915; A. T. Goward to George Kidd, March 11, 1915, Box 131. See also Brian R. D. Smith, "Sir Richard McBride: A Study in the Conservative Party of British Columbia, 1903-1916," Queen's University (Kingston), M.A. Thesis, 1959, pp. 296-298.

the jitneys under the Motor Traffic Act. Bowser would agree only to empower the municipalities to pass jitney regulations. McBride could do no more.

In the fall of 1915, after returning from a visit to England where he met B.C.E.R. officials, McBride invited the mayors of Victoria, Vancouver and New Westminster and the reeves of the adjacent municipalities to a confidential meeting to discuss the serious position of the B.C.E.R. "caused, it is claimed, by jitney competition." At this meeting, Kidd described the jitney problem and warned of the possible need to shut down certain unprofitable street railway routes. In a subsequent letter to the mayors and reeves, he presented statistical evidence showing the sharp decline in revenue and demonstrating that the company had never made an excessive profit.[20] The idea of securing municipal co-operation through the premier's office came to naught. When Sir Richard McBride retired as premier in December 1915, his successor, W. J. Bowser, never a friend of the B.C.E.R., expressed sympathy for the company but did nothing to assist it.

When attempts to get the provincial government to regulate jitney competition seemed likely to fail, the B.C.E.R. resumed agitation through newspaper advertisements and by encouraging civic groups to have the Vancouver City Council impose jitney regulations. At the municipal level, Kidd again stressed the relationship between the B.C.E.R.'s prosperity and the credit of the community. However, he rejected Horne-Payne's proposal that friends of the company should refuse to buy Vancouver or Victoria municipal securities until the cities regulated the jitneys. Kidd advised that financial arguments would not sway municipal councillors who were "irresponsible in the sense understood in England, without personal funds and almost entirely dependent on their aldermanic salaries." Of greater long term consequence was the fact that London was declining as a source of municipal funds; the city of Vancouver had already raised money in New York.[21] Eventually, Kidd's work seemed to succeed. In January 1917, the City Council, after much debate, passed a by-law requiring jitneys to offer a regular service and to

---

[20] George Kidd to Sir Richard McBride, September 10, 1915; Sir Richard McBride to Mayors and Reeves, September 20, 1915; Sir Richard McBride to Mayors and Reeves, October 18, 1915; L. D. Taylor to Sir Richard McBride, November 1, 1915; *McBride Papers, Premier's Official Correspondence*, 10/15. Notes for a meeting with Mayors and Reeves, November 5, 1915; George Kidd to Mayors and Reeves of Vancouver, New Westminster, North Vancouver, South Vancouver, Point Grey, Burnaby, North Vancouver District, Victoria, Oak Bay, Saanich and Esquimalt, November 15, 1915, Box 62A, File 1163.

[21] George Kidd to Michael Urwin, February 17, 1915, *Letters from the General Manager, 1915*; "Draft of speech which the Chairman proposed to deliver at the annual general meeting of the British Empire Trust Company, May 1915," Box 62A, File 1163; George Kidd to Michael Urwin, May 25, 1915, Box 62A, File 1163; George Kidd to R. M. Horne-Payne, April 29, 1915, Box 68.

undertake certain safety measures. The measure was ineffective; the jitneys continued to operate.

In the meantime, the provincial general election of 1916 had resulted in the election of a Liberal government under H. C. Brewster. Brewster was unwilling to have the province act against the jitneys but he did not oppose municipal regulations.[22] Kidd then publicly suggested that the province establish a Public Utilities Commission which might deal more favourably with the company than political bodies such as the Legislature and municipal councils. A Public Utilities Commission which would be an expense for the province was, however, low on Brewster's list of immediate priorities. Not until after a street railwaymen's strike and the subsequent report by Dr. Adam Shortt on the economic conditions of the B.C.E.R. did the provincial government undertake to establish a Public Utilities Commission.

The change in government did not alter the B.C.E.R.'s lobbying techniques. During the election campaign, it apparently donated $2,500 to Liberal funds.[23] In an endeavour to gain entrée to the Liberal caucus, the company hired F. J. Stacpoole, a Liberal lawyer, as its legal advisor in Victoria. The B.C.E.R., however, did not immediately develop with Brewster, a businessman himself, the kind of rapport it had had with McBride. And, because British Columbia was now looking to New York rather than to London for new capital, the B.C.E.R. shibboleth about endangering British investment had lost its effect.

In lobbying the federal and provincial governments, the B.C.E.R. concentrated on courting the support of individual politicians; in dealing with the municipalities, it focussed most of its attention on the general public. The history of the Local Advisory Committee is a clear reflection of its concern for public opinion. The company, however, did not rely on general means of cultivating good will; it sought to have "friends" on Council and it participated in by-law campaigns which affected it.

Of the three levels of government, the municipal was the most important. Without municipal franchises, utilities such as the B.C.E.R. could not operate. Except in outlying municipalities where the sparseness of the population did not make the introduction of electric lights and street railways

---

[22] H. C. Brewster to W. H. Tonks (a B.C.E.R. shareholder in England), February 5, 1916, *H. C. Brewster Papers, Personal*, Provincial Archives of British Columbia.

[23] George Kidd to Michael Urwin, May 17, 1917, *Letters from the General Manager, 1917*. The charge about the contribution was made during a by-election in June 1917 by Dr. Ernest Hall, an Independent Liberal who was running against the Hon. John Hart, the new Minister of Finance, in Victoria. Hart admitted that the B.C.E.R. provided $2500 of the Liberals' $8500 campaign fund but argued that it went entirely for the supervision of the soldier vote. (*Vancouver Daily Province*, June 21, 1917, p. 4; August 16, 1917, p. 12).

an immediately attractive investment, municipal politicians drove hard bargains.

Because of its fear that the city of Vancouver might take advantage of the option in its franchise to purchase the city street railway lines in 1919, the B.C.E.R. sought to make the city lines themselves unattractive by surrounding the city with a series of suburban lines on long term franchises. This explains the company's concern for the franchises in Hastings Townsite and District Lot 301 and is responsible for its great interest in the South Vancouver and Point Grey franchises.

Of the suburban municipalities, South Vancouver was the most important. A paradise for real estate speculators, it was being rapidly settled by workingmen and artisans. By 1911 it claimed to be the third largest "city" in the province.[24] When South Vancouver asked for an extension of the existing B.C.E.R. street railway line in the municipality and for the construction of other lines, the B.C.E.R. used the opportunity to insist on a forty year franchise. Behind the scenes, the B.C.E.R. won over a recalcitrant councillor, added the names of one hundred and twelve "friendly" ratepayers to the voters' list and got the Council to submit a new "very advantageous" tramway agreement to the electors. The ratepayers, anxious for improved transportation facilities, approved by a handsome majority of 881 to 151.[25]

In the adjacent municipality of Point Grey, the B.C.E.R. had a more difficult time which required it to use its powers of persuasion to their fullest extent. Many of the early settlers of the Eburne district of Point Grey were staunch advocates of municipal ownership. When the B.C.E.R. offered to build street railway lines in the municipality in exchange for a forty year franchise, the Point Grey Ratepayers' Association began discussing a plan to construct a municipally-owned tram line or to invite the Stave Lake Power Company to operate such a line. For over a year, the B.C.E.R. and the Point Grey Council discussed the franchise. Eventually, after the B.C.E.R. and the C.P.R. (which owned much of the land in Point Grey) assisted in the election of Frank Bowser as reeve and of several councillors who favoured a forty year franchise, the Council and company agreed on the terms of a forty year franchise. As part of the compromise the B.C.E.R. agreed to reduce the fare to Eburne and to accept regulations about the frequency of service and the speed of the cars.

After the ratepayers approved the agreement, several residents criticized the exclusiveness of the franchise and complained of irregularities in the voters' lists as the result of the inclusion of voters who had recently purchased land from the C.P.R. These dissident ratepayers appealed to the

---

[24] Its population was 16,126. (Canada, *Census*, 1921, Vol. I, p. 217). A. H. Lewis, *South Vancouver, Past and Present*, Vancouver, (Western Publishing, 1920), pp. 12-18.

[25] R. H. Sperling to George Kidd, March 25, 1909; R. H. Sperling to George Kidd, May 19, 1909; *London Letter Book*, # 6.

courts which upheld their argument. The B.C.E.R. immediately stopped construction work and suspended service on all existing lines within the municipality except those on private rights of way. On the latter lines, the company cancelled special settlers' fares. While the B.C.E.R. prepared an appeal to the Privy Council, the Point Grey Council presented a new by-law to the ratepayers.

The vote on the new by-law was preceded by a lively campaign. Both the dissident ratepayers and the B.C.E.R. organized their supporters. The Point Grey Citizens' Campaign Committee claimed that the franchise gave the B.C.E.R. "practically" an exclusive forty year franchise without compelling the company to build on any routes other than those specified in the agreement. The Committee also objected to the lack of a profit-sharing arrangement as in the city of Vancouver, and to the absence of any means of forcing the company to provide adequate service. If its candidates were elected, the Committee promised it would co-operate with the other municipalities to get a better agreement.[26] The Point Grey Committee was assisted in its campaign by moral support from members of the Vancouver City Council who were anxious to have a consolidated street railway agreement for all of greater Vancouver. According to Sperling, the company exerted every possible effort to secure the election of a favourable council and the passage of the by-law:

> Through our instrumentality and initiative a large hall was secured in the business centre [of Point Grey], a campaign manager, secretaries and canvassers appointed and with the assistance of an influential business men's committee, the organization of which we also arranged, and the provision of special writers, a very complete machine was put in action. Pamphlets were prepared and delivered or sent to each ratepayer, and each day special articles setting out the advantages of the by-law to the municipality, were published in the Vancouver papers. The Point Grey "Gazette" and "Clarion" were also secured in our support. While primarily responsible for the whole organization, matters were so arranged that no reference to our part in the campaign was made at any of the meetings.[27]

These efforts were in vain; by a narrow margin, the voters rejected the by-law. Lobbying had failed. Only after Point Grey residents tired of walking and petitioned their council for a new by-law did the B.C.E.R. resume service in the municipality. In the second by-law campaign, the B.C.E.R. played no part. The withdrawal of service had succeeded where traditional lobbying techniques had not.

[26] See the open letter of the Point Grey Citizens' Committee, January 12, 1912. Copy in Box 23, File 331.
[27] R. H. Sperling to Michael Urwin, January 17, 1912, Box 23, File 331.

The B.C.E.R. was also politically active in the city of Victoria where it desired to have a firm guarantee that the city would not attempt to compete in the light and power business without offering to buy out the B.C.E.R. Such a guarantee was particularly desirable since both Mayor A. G. Morley and his successor, Dr. Lewis Hall, advocated municipal ownership and had plans for amending the city charter to allow the city to produce and distribute electricity.

In order to gain support for this guarantee, or the "protective clause" in the City Charter as the B.C.E.R. described it, A. T. Goward, the local manager, quietly campaigned among members of the Council and placed extra advertising in local newspapers.[28] Goward, however, carefully avoided having the "protective clause" become an issue in the 1909 civic election campaign which was won by Dr. Hall. Privately and individually, the new councillors expressed sympathy for the B.C.E.R. but as a group were reluctant to commit themselves publicly. The Council consented to the "protective clause" only after Goward promised certain concessions: the construction of a hydro-electric plant at Jordan River; the reduction of rates; and the expenditure of $250,000 within three years on extending the B.C.E.R.'s operations in the Victoria area. Then, the Council dallied. Finally, the local management threatened to withdraw the promised concessions. The threat worked; the Council presented a by-law to the ratepayers.

In the subsequent campaign, the B.C.E.R. played a discreet but active role. The company financially supported a citizens' committee which sent out circulars – even a special one to lady voters – citing the advantages of the agreement, sponsored public meetings, canvassed voters and arranged transportation to the polls. Banners supporting the by-law were stretched across the principal streets and a favourable press was secured; even the Victoria *Times* which normally favoured public ownership supported the by-law. After the heaviest poll ever for a by-law, the voters accepted it by a three to one majority.[29]

This victory was an expensive one. In contrast to its usual caution, the B.C.E.R. had promised to spend $250,000 without having a clear idea of where this money would be used. It did not deny reports that it would build an interurban line on the Saanich peninsula. Over a year later, rumours circulated that the company would not build the Saanich line. Victorians were deeply concerned. The Council complained that the B.C.E.R. was sacrificing the interests of Victoria in order to concentrate on developments on the Mainland. Premier McBride confidentially advised Horne-Payne that if the rumours were true, there would be:

---

[28] F. R. Glover to George Kidd, May 29, 1908, *London Letter Book*, #5; A. T. Goward to R. H. Sperling, November 18, 1908, Box 29A, File 408.

[29] A. T. Goward to R. H. Sperling, August 26, 1909; A. T. Goward to R. H. Sperling, August 3, 1909, Box 29A, File 408.

A most disastrous effect on the standing of your corporation in British Columbia . . . should it now occur that there is a disposition on the part of the corporation to avoid the responsibility which should be looked upon as a moral as well as a legal one, it would be impossible at this time to forecast what pressure may be brought upon the government and what action as a result we may eventually have to determine on.[30]

In contrast to the usual situation, the premier, who was anxious to win votes by building railways,[31] was warning of dire consequences to the B.C.E.R. Within a month of receiving this letter, the directors of the B.C.E.R. approved the construction of the Saanich line. Two years later, on June 18, 1913, McBride drove the last spike on the Saanich line which cost considerably more than $250,000 to build and which never made a profit. The B.C.E.R. had got its "protective clause" and it preserved the support of the premier, but the price was a high one.

Drawing wide-ranging conclusions from a single case study is difficult and possibly dangerous. This essay has endeavoured to do no more than illustrate and document the techniques by which one company sought the support of the various levels of government and to explain its relative success with each level of government. Nevertheless, it is possible to make a few observations about the B.C.E.R.'s relationship with governments.

The success of the B.C.E.R.'s lobbying activities tended to vary inversely according to its distance from the level of government with which it was working. Dealing with the federal government was relatively straightforward. The company simply had to retain one of the professional lobbyists operating in Ottawa and follow his advice. In the few transactions the B.C.E.R. had with the federal government, it secured what it wanted. Granting a favour to one company on a distant coast cost federal leaders very little. The B.C.E.R. was an unlikely election issue but B.C.E.R. cash could be useful in political wars. In negotiating with the provincial administration, the B.C.E.R. copied many of the techniques it used in Ottawa. At Victoria, however, company personnel rather than professional lobbyists did this very delicate work. Provincially, the B.C.E.R. was potentially a prime political issue. It was advantageous for both Premier McBride and the company to avoid having the B.C.E.R. become a subject of election debate. Thus, in spite of his sympathy for the company and his fear of its threats to turn British investors away from the province, McBride sometimes rejected B.C.E.R. requests. The company reluctantly accepted these rejections as sacrifices necessary to maintain harmony with a basically friendly provincial

---

[30] Richard McBride to R. M. Horne-Payne, January 27, 1911, Box 40, File 629.

[31] For McBride's railway policies see my M.A. thesis, "Railways, Politicians and the Development of the City of Vancouver as a Metropolitan Centre, 1886-1929," University of Toronto, 1963.

government. The B.C.E.R. also appreciated the fact that McBride's longevity as premier gave a continuity to negotiations which was conspicuously lacking at the municipal level where the B.C.E.R. was often the major political issue. Lobbying federal and provincial governments cost little more than the time and effort of some company officials and occasional contributions to party funds. Gaining municipal support required not only the discreet expenditure of company time and effort on direct political activities but also expensive bribing of the electorate. Not all concessions to municipal voters were as expensive as the construction of the Saanich interurban line but the acceptance of municipal regulation of street railways and the reduction of certain fares inhibited the company. Moreover, because of the size of the constituency, the B.C.E.R. was never certain of its success in persuading local governments to grant its wishes.

The amount of attention the B.C.E.R. gave to lobbying the federal and provincial governments and to swaying municipal voters suggests that businesses in this period of Canadian history were subjected to considerable informal governmental control. The existence of formal regulatory agencies does not tell the entire tale. Because it operated wholly within the province, the B.C.E.R. did not have to come under the Board of Railway Commissioners. Prior to 1919 when an abortive Public Utilities Commission was established, the province in British Columbia had no corresponding regulatory body. Through their control of essential franchises, municipal electors effectively restricted the activities of the B.C.E.R. Although the B.C.E.R. had efficient lobbying techniques to use in working with the federal and provincial governments and was well-practised in the art of persuading municipal voters, it never succeeded in gaining a completely free hand in conducting its business. The informal influence of public opinion at the provincial and municipal levels of government and the company's concomitant fear of antagonizing the electorate were as effective in controlling the company as any official regulatory body was likely to be. Individuals could be lobbied; the general public could not.

International Nickel: The First Fifty Years

O. W. Main, Director of the School of Business, University of Toronto

In April 1902, International Nickel Company was incorporated in the United States to carry on the business of mining and refining nickel. The story of Inco in the next fifty years is a story of the company's struggle to maintain its dominant position in the industry, and the control which that position gave.

The company was the result of a merger of the Canadian Copper Company which had copper-nickel mines in the Sudbury district and the Orford Company which refined Canadian Copper's matte. Before the merger these two companies had a long history of co-operation based on the mutual dependence of each other. Canadian Copper owned the largest mines and Orford had an economical method of refining the metal and, more importantly, the market contracts.[1]

When nickel became an important ingredient in the development of superior armour-plate at the turn of the century, the armour-plate manufacturers, seeking to control a supply of nickel, bought into the nickel companies in Europe and in the United States. J. P. Morgan and Company, New York financial bankers, which had recently formed the United States Steel Corporation set up a nickel syndicate which took over control of the Orford-Canadian Copper combination. The new company, International Nickel, came under the financial control of Morgan and the administrative control of the United States Steel Corporation. The first president, Ambrose Monell was formerly with Carnegie Steel, and five of the directors were United States Steel officers.[2]

The merger was the logical outcome of developments in the industry which had been taking place since the discovery of nickel-copper ores in the Sudbury district in 1886. The complex nature of the ores had put a heavy premium on a feasible and economical method of separating the nickel from the copper. Canadian Copper, one of the first companies in the district, had been fortunate in discovering large ore reserves, and in having exclusive refining contracts with the Orford Company, which had an economical method of refining nickel. Orford, in turn, was fortunate that its owner, Colonel R. M. Thompson, had contacts with the United States Navy, which had a keen interest in the possibilities of nickel in the manufacture of armour-plate. This combination was able to withstand numerous attacks on its dominant posi-

[1] For a detailed account of the early history of the industry see O. W. Main *The Canadian Nickel Industry* (Toronto, 1955).
[2] *Engineering and Mining Journal*, LXXIII, April 2, 1902.

tion during the 1890's and had emerged relatively unscathed, except for the entrance of an English company, the Mond Nickel Company, which also had a refining process and contracts in the European market. By 1902, the market for refined nickel was shared by agreement among Inco, Mond and the European producers led by Le Nickel, using New Caledonian and Norwegian ores.

Nickel is a product which might be considered ideal for monopolistic control. Since it is used in a wide variety of alloys, it is important for both peace-time and war-time use. The amount used in each alloy is so small that wide changes in price do not affect the demand for the product. It has such unique properties that it is extremely difficult to find suitable substitutes for it. Under these conditions, the price could be set to maximize the profits of any producer having monopoly control over it. In addition the relatively few large-scale deposits available and the small number of refining processes in existence would make control over the production of the metal relatively easy. At best, the industry would be dominated by a few firms, and the tendency to monopoly or cartel control would be extremely strong.

Although the nickel industry might be considered to be an ideal example for monopoly theory, the history of the industry does not fit the traditional pattern of behaviour expected of a monopolist. The reasons can be found in the uncertainties of its control and the constant attacks upon any monopoly position, both from potential competitors and from governments.

The period from 1902 to World War I found International in the role of a captive monopolist. Although it had control of the United States market and an agreed share of the European market, it was under control of the armour-plate manufacturers and its price policy was dictated by their needs rather than by the desires of Inco to make monopoly profits. Indeed, it was at this time that Mond Nickel Company was able to obtain a foothold in the Sudbury district and to get a share of the market with the Steel Manufacturers' Syndicate in Europe as well as contracts with the British government.[3]

In the pure theory of monopoly, one might expect that the entrance of Mond would be greeted by a price war, or by attempts to block the company from securing contracts. While Mond did have some economic power, it was political considerations in Canada which led to the acceptance by Inco of Mond Nickel Company's entrance into the Sudbury district. In 1900, the Ontario Government had passed the Mining Act to place a royalty on the exportation of nickel ores and matte. The fear that this Act might be proclaimed led Inco to welcome Mond as British proof that Inco was no "foreign monopolist". Inco hoped that the presence of Mond would cause the nationalistic cries for Canadian control of refining to die down and that it would be free to follow its own policies.

Thus, from the beginning, the two companies operated in close co-opera-

---

[3] Mond Nickel Company, *The Story of Mond Nickel*, privately printed, 1951.

tion. In 1904, when Inco's smelters burned down, it was Mond which came to the rescue and leased a smelter to Inco. Also, in 1910, when the cry of "monopolist" was again raised against International it was Mond which entered the fight on the side of Inco to show that no monopoly existed![4]

Other companies which challenged Inco in the same period did not have the same degree of good fortune. The Lake Superior Corporation (later Algoma Steel Corporation), the brain child of a noted American entrepreneur, F. H. Clergue, tried to enter the industry but, despite help from the Ontario Government, it failed to find the necessary finances and its venture into the nickel business ended in failure. The Nickel-Copper Company tried to interest American Mining and Smelting Company in picking up its properties but the move was blocked by J. P. Morgan and Company when it was revealed that Inco and Le Nickel held the market under long-term contracts. In evidence before the Select Standing Committee on Mines and Minerals, in 1910, John Patterson of Nickel-Copper Company laid the cause of his failure in the industry to the protected market in the United States, the threat of the Ontario and Canadian governments to impose restrictions on the export of matte, and the powerful financial influence of J. P. Morgan in blocking financing.[5] Other companies also invaded the Sudbury district in the hope of getting a foothold. Some were nickel consumers urgently seeking a release from the nickel monopoly power. These included Thomas A. Edison, Sterling Boiler Company, Vickers, Maxim and Company, and American Mining and Smelting Company. They all withdrew from the district either because of their failure to find suitable deposits or from lack of financing.

The most serious threat to the dominance of Inco came from the British America Nickel Corporation, formed by Dr. H. F. Pearson, who was prominent for his promotion of Brazilian Traction, Mexican Light, and the Dominion Coal Company. He teamed up with the railroad entrepreneurs, McKenzie and Mann, to buy out the assets of the Dominion Nickel-Copper Company (a successor to Nickel-Copper Company), from the lumber magnates, J. R. Booth and M. J. O'Brien. Included in the sale were the rights to an electrolytic process for refining nickel, developed by a Norwegian, N. V. Hybinette.[6]

British America was potentially in a good position to threaten the dominance of Inco. It had ore bodies and it had a superior refining process. Although the grade of ore was not comparable to that mined by Inco, the superiority of the refining process made up for some of the difference. Unfortunately, it had no way of breaking into the market on a large enough scale

---

[4] *Report of the Royal Ontario Nickel Commission* (Toronto, 1917), p. 64.

[5] Canada, Select Standing Committee of the House of Commons on Mines and Minerals, *Proceedings* (Ottawa, 1910), pp. 43-56.

[6] *Nickel Commission* evidence of N. V. Hybinette. *Appendix*, pp. 84-85.

to make production possible. In turn, the lack of markets made it difficult to secure finances. Some assistance was obtained from J. H. Dunn, a Canadian financier, but capital had to be sought from the United States and England. Some backing came from Norway but by the outbreak of World War I, British America had not yet succeeded in getting into production.

The outbreak of World War I led to a serious disruption of the convenient market-sharing arrangements of Inco, Mond and Le Nickel. The war on shipping isolated the New Caledonia deposits and Canada became virtually the only source of supply of nickel. Governments took over the purchasing of nickel, breaking up the armour-plate syndicates and freeing the nickel industry from the steel manufacturers' control. Freedom for Inco, however, meant freedom from protection and the next few years in Inco's life proved to be stormy ones.

The latent nationalism which has beat in Canada's breast intermittently over the years burst forth with renewed vigour with the outbreak of war. In peace-time attempts of Canadian entrepreneurs to raise the "American monopolist" cry had only limited success because of political fears of the consequences of the withdrawal of capital. War-time, however, brought a new patriotic dimension to the "foreign monopolist" cry. Not only was Inco foreign but it was also controlled in a neutral country which could sell valuable nickel to the enemy.

The press began the attack with a clamour for a ban on the export of nickel matte, followed by more strident demands for government ownership and control of the nickel mines and the erection of a nickel refinery in Canada. Inco's action in shutting down its mines and smelters temporarily at the outbreak of war while Mond continued production added fuel to the fire. It was claimed that Inco had been supplying the enemy all along and that Inco was under the control of German interests.[7]

To counteract the bad publicity, the Canadian Government issued an unusual memorandum denying that the company was under German control and stating further that adequate precautions had been taken to ensure that the nickel did not fall into enemy hands. Inco, however, again disturbed public opinion by refusing even to consider the possibility of refining its matte in Canada, suggesting that, if Inco had to move its refining plant to Canada, there would be unfortunate consequences for the Sudbury district. These threats and assurances did not quell the storm. Boards of Trade passed various resolutions urging that nickel be refined in Canada and the opposition press continued its outcry for investigation.

In typical reactions, both the Ontario and the Federal governments set up commissions. The Dominion Munitions Resources Commission recommended that the federal government insist that Inco refine in Canada and

---

[7] *Toronto Telegram*, Dec. 27, 1914. *Toronto Star*, Dec. 9, 1914. *Mail & Empire*, Dec. 10 and 11, 1914.

also that financial aid be given to British America to help it establish a refinery in Canada. The Ontario government set up the Royal Ontario Nickel Commission, which also urged that nickel be refined in Canada.

To underline the urgency of the situation, the Canadian public was shocked in the summer of 1916 to read reports that the German submarine "Deutschland" had taken back from the United States a cargo of nickel. The exploit was repeated in November. To the public, there was only one source of nickel, Ontario, and only one company – International Nickel – could be responsible. Denials were brushed aside and governmental insistence replaced mild urgings. If Inco refused to give up its protected position behind the United States tariff wall, it might find its mines expropriated at the worst, or financial support given to its competitors at the best. Inco succumbed with a hasty announcement that it would refine its matte in Canada.

The closing of the Nickel Question brought a new dimension to government power in influencing entrepreneurial decisions. Inco lost heavily in the deep distrust it had engendered and it lost even more heavily in the pocketbook. The Mining Tax Act of 1917, directed against the nickel industry, and against Inco, in particular, was the direct result of the years of frustration of the Ontario government in trying to get some public benefit from the operations of the nickel industry. During war-time the monopoly power had swung from the company to the government. Inco finally recognized the precarious position it had placed itself in. The next few years were devoted assiduously to an active development of good relations with the Canadian public.

Armistice brought renewed troubles to the beleaguered company. British America Nickel Corporation, with support, had reached the production stage just as the post-war depression came and disarmament conferences reduced the demand for nickel for war purposes. British America started to seek markets aggressively. Inco retaliated by cutting prices. Prices fell from the maintained contract price thirty-five cents a pound to twenty-one cents a pound. By 1924, British America was in difficulties and went into bankruptcy. The assets were bought by Inco and another threat to its dominance was thwarted.[8]

Market control brought some blessings to Inco but it also brought some serious responsibilities. The switch to peace-time meant a drastic decline in the demand for nickel. If Inco was to prosper, it had to develop new uses for the metal. Monopoly control over a dwindling market brought no profits. Inco, along with Mond, embarked on a campaign of research to widen the use of the metal. The twenties was a period of consolidation and diversification in use. Price cutting would not help improve sales, since the demand for the metal was inelastic. Inco's salvation lay in moving its demand curve by promoting new uses. In this endeavour, Inco's leadership changed with

---

[8] *Canadian Mining Journal*, May 15 and Sept. 15, 1924.

the change in problems. The steel executives were replaced by the metallurgical experts.

Inco's new aggressive posture was, in part, a reaction to the aggressive behaviour of Mond. Mond had maintained good relations with Inco but the post-war period had brought to it the same set of problems. Mond responded by a vigorous invasion of the United States market. The old contract system was breached and Mond moved into the new areas of demand, by entering the nickel fabricating field. Since it had got a head start, Mond was much more successful throughout the period, in meeting the transition from war to peace. Mond developed into a major producer and became very active in seeking out new markets and new mining properties.[9]

Although the market for nickel expanded rapidly in the twenties, Inco's control over the best mining properties made it difficult for new competitors to enter. Its pricing policy was also designed to discourage the search for new properties. Throughout the period it maintained the same price, although it would have been possible to make better short-run profits by charging what the market would bear. It also improved its control by moving into the nickel fabricating field which freed it from its dependence upon a few large customers.

By 1928, Inco and Mond had reached the point in their mining operations that joint exploitation of the large Frood deposits, owned by both companies, was necessary. As a result of technical and other factors, Inco and Mond merged. The new Company, International Nickel Company of Canada arose from the merger. The move of Inco from American to Canadian incorporation was dictated by the fear that if the merger went through in the United States, Inco could have been charged with anti-trust violations. As a Canadian company, it was free from United States jurisdiction. Also, in Canada, it was not likely that any anti-combines action would be taken since Canadian consumers would not be affected to any degree. The merger of the two companies gave Inco complete control over the Sudbury district and virtually world-wide dominance of the nickel markets.[10]

Inco's dominance was short-lived. In 1930, Falconbridge Nickel Mines began production of nickel matte to ship to the Kristianssands refinery in Norway. The company, a subsidiary of Ventures, Limited, drew heavily on the technical staff brought together by British America Nickel and the financial support of a group of New York capitalists. It began in a small way by shading prices and moving into the cracks in the market. Despite its aggressiveness, it had serious difficulties in surviving the first years. Distrust of the quality of its product and the onset of the Great Depression proved almost too much for it. However, it did survive. Why was it not forced out as other competitors had been before it? Inco made no moves to engage it in a price

[9] Mond Nickel Company *Annual Reports.*
[10] *Financial Post*, Aug. 24, 1928.

war or to buy it out. It would seem that Inco's behaviour ran counter to what would be expected of a monopolist. However, the uncertainty of its position probably influenced Inco to allow Falconbridge to try its wings. First, Falconbridge was small and a price war would have meant large losses to Inco with little to gain. Second, Falconbridge probably could not survive, anyway. Third, if Inco had made any moves, it would have raised the cry of "foreign monopolist" all over again. In retrospect, the rise of Falconbridge to the position of a major producer, which was not foreseen, seems to suggest that Inco's tolerance may not have been in its own long-run interest.[11]

The gathering war clouds in the late thirties again threatened Inco's position. However, Inco had learned its lessons well and the cry for government control over the industry did not raise much response. The fear of disrupting a profitable industry during a depression which already had seen too much unemployment was not palatable either to governments or to the public. However, the war years of the forties and the aftermath did leave Inco in a weakened position in the industry. The chief was getting old and its position was being threatened more and more.[12]

Crises can often accomplish much more than years of pressure. The effects of World War II and the uneasy peace which followed made governments clearly aware of the strategic nature of nickel. The support for the discovery of new deposits and the encouragement of new producers weakened the controlling position of Inco. While Inco continued to dominate the industry, its market share had been slowly slipping, and its control of the markets, while still strong, was being quietly eroded.

A brief history of a period in a company's life cannot tell the whole story, any more than a snapshot of a person gives a complete understanding of the individual. Companies do not grow in a vacuum; their life-style and their goals are determined by their environment and by their leaders. Inco, the uneasy monopolist, displayed far different behaviour than the economists' models of monopoly might suggest. Like an individual, it learned that to survive, it had to adapt its behaviour to changing needs of the society it served. When it ignored them, it almost lost its existence. Its survival and continued dominance was adequate testimony to its ability to learn.

[11] W. Y. Elliott *et al., International Control in the Non-Ferrous Metals* (New York, 1937), p. 155.
[12] See *House of Commons Debates*, esp. 1934 to 1936.

4/The Study of Canadian Business History

Canadian Business History: Approaches and Publications to 1970.[1]

Frederick H. Armstrong, Associate Professor of History, University of Western Ontario

I would like to divide this discussion of the historian's approach to Canadian business into four sections: first an examination of some of the problems involved in the writing of business history in the Dominion and an estimate of the present state of Canadian business history; then some comment on the economic theories of Canadian development which lie behind so much of the writing in this field; next, an outline of the key works on the subject; and, finally, some suggestions for possible lines of future investigation.[2]

---

[1] This article grew out of a paper which was given at the Business History Conference held at London, Ontario, on 3-4 March, 1967, and later, in amplified form, was printed in the *Proceedings of the Fourteenth Annual Meeting of the Business History Conference*, edited by Richard C. Overton (London, Ont., 1967).

    The writer would like to thank Dr. R. C. Overton, of this University, Professor J. M. S. Careless, of the Department of History, University of Toronto, and several of his other colleagues at the University of Western Ontario, especially Professors R. A. Hohner and A. M. J. Hyatt. Miss Hilary Bates of the Western Library provided valuable bibliographic assistance. Mr. José Iguartua has been most helpful in making suggestions on Quebec bibliography.

    We would also like to thank the University of Toronto Press for permission to use the quotations from D. G. Creighton's *Harold Adams Innis, Portrait of a Scholar* and H. A. Innis' *The Fur Trade*; and McClelland and Stewart for permission to use the quotation from the introduction to Gilbert N. Tucker's *The Canadian Commercial Revolution*.

[2] For reasons of space it has been necessary to shorten some of the longer titles in both the text and footnotes below. Reference has been made to only a few important articles; many more will be found in *The Canadian Historical Review; The Canadian Historical Association Report*; and *The Canadian Journal of Economics and Political Science*, as well as other journals cited under specific headings. For further bibliographical information the best source is: Carl F. Klinck (ed.) *Literary History of Canada* (Toronto, 1965), Part III, p. 13; Kenneth N. Windsor "Historical Writing in Canada (to 1920)"

The history of Canada presents many problems for the business historian: it spreads over a 350 year time span; its peoples are divided into several regional groupings; the territory is vast, and sharply separated by natural barriers. There are, in addition, some political problems which must be considered if the development of Canada is to be understood. The country did not achieve Confederation until nearly a century after the United States declared its independence; it received equal status with Great Britain only under the Statue of Westminster in 1931, and did not add its last province, Newfoundland, until 1949. Thus, throughout most of its history, Canada has been governed, at least to some degree, from outside centres: first Paris, then London. Indeed, it still remains part of a complex international commonwealth.

Biculturalism has added further complications. To an extent business has been a preserve of the English-Scottish-Canadians, especially as far as the major commercial enterprises have been concerned; but there has still been a considerable development of French-Canadian business endeavour, which has until recent years been rather neglected by the French historians who have tended to turn their eyes to the pre-Conquest era and the political problems of the Province of Quebec since Confederation. Then too there is the question of state ownership, or state participation, in business. In a vast country with a small, widely scattered population, and little capital for developmental projects, it has been necessary from the very first for the government to play a major role in business. The idea of the Crown corporation, or the nationalized enterprise, is far more readily accepted here than it has been in the United States.

Thus Canadian historians are faced with a multitude of problems but, and herein lies the difficulty, there are few Canadian historians. Not only is the population of the country not large, but also there have been comparatively few centres of learning, and only small grants available for research. Canadian universities have certainly not specialized in setting up chairs of business history, there is no centre of studies such as that at Harvard, and business schools are interested in turning out future executives, not in probing the past. In history, as in many other fields, the University of Toronto was virtually dominant until recent years, with only slight competition from other

pp. 208-50; and "Canadian History and Social Sciences since 1920", Part IV, p. 27. William M. Kilbourn, "The Writing of Canadian History" pp. 495-519; and Henry B. Mayo "Writing in the Social Sciences" pp. 519-28. Another bibliographical source is Robin W. Winks, *Recent Trends, and New Literature in Canadian History*, Publication No. 19, Service Centre for Teachers of History, of the American Historical Association (New York, 1959). For short biographies of Canadian business figures see W. Stewart Wallace, *The Macmillan Dictionary of Canadian Biography* (Toronto, 1963). W. T. Easterbrook and M. H. Watkins have edited a collection of essays entitled *Approaches to Canadian Economic History* (Toronto, 1967) which includes an extensive bibliography by Easterbrook and an interesting essay by Watkins entitled "A Staple Theory of Economic Growth," which originally appeared in the *Canadian Journal of Political Science and Economics*, Vol. XXIX, May, 1963, pp. 141-58.

universities such as Queen's. Here, then, is the first difficulty facing the development of business history in Canada; it is only one of the many facets of history demanding investigation, and there are few qualified historians.

This, however, is only part of the story. In a nation that has slowly divested itself of the mantle of the motherland, naturally there has been a concentration of interest on constitutional and political issues. Further, in a nation that was a colony for so long, and continues to live under the shadow of a much larger neighbour, there has naturally been a search for a separate identity. These questions have turned many historians' eyes to such problems as biculturalism, northern approaches, and, fortunately for business history, the search for an economic framework into which an individual Canadian identity can be fitted. Thus, although political considerations continue to dominate Canadian historiography, economic theories have gradually assumed a more respected place. It is the consideration of these theories that will occupy the second part of this chapter.

Before going further into these theses, however, it must be noted that such work as has been done in Canadian economic history, and Canadian business history, always has been divided between two themes: continentalism and nationalism. This merely reflects the economic history of the nation in which demands for reciprocity have always been met with suggestions for an imperial zollverein, or, more recently, protection of the ownership of Canadian business. The discussion goes back well over a century and can still be heard in the conflicting statements of the two wings of the party at present in power in Ottawa.

As a result of these problems, what is the present state of Canadian business history? The best general evaluation is that made by Hugh G. J. Aitken in the introduction to the 1964 edition of Tucker's *Canadian Commercial Revolution*:

> ... very few collections of Canadian business records are available to historians and very few biographies of Canadian businessmen have been written.... One could wish that one-tenth of the energies that have been lavished on the arcane details of the Canadian fur trade had been diverted to other sectors of the economy. Where, for example, is our history of trade and shipping on the Great Lakes? Where are our studies of the nineteenth-century Canadian government finance? The history of the Canadian canal system is still to be written; the beginnings of secondary manufacturing in Canada are shrouded in obscurity; our ideas of the nineteenth-century Canadian business cycle remain vague and impressionistic; and our statistics of price and output movements are spotty and unreliable. Canadian economic historians have won a high reputation in Europe and North America; not least among their achievements has been the erection of an imposing edifice of generalizations on decidedly inadequate foundations.[3]

---

[3] Tucker, Gilbert N., *The Canadian Commercial Revolution* (Toronto, 1964), p. xv.

Such charges will hardly please certain Canadian historical circles, but they do point up the fact that some theories have been accepted with very little re-examination. One of them, however, the Laurentian thesis, does provide a good starting point for an investigation of Canadian business history.

Any survey of Canadian business history must begin with Adam Shortt (1859-1931), the first major historian to devote considerable time to business problems. His career, like that of so many later Canadian business histori-ans, exemplifies the extent to which business history has normally been a part-time interest in this country. Shortt began his career as a philosopher, transferred to political science, moved to the civil service, and finally became Chairman of the Board of Historical Publications at the Public Archives of Canada. As well as his work on economics he wrote an excellent biography of Governor Sydenham, who arranged a union between Ontario and Quebec in 1841.[4] His most important work was his joint editorship of the monumen-tal *Canada and its Provinces*,[5] which contained the first extended survey of Canadian business development.

In the years following the appearance of that survey (most of the volumes were published just before World War I), the questions posed by the envi-ronmental theories of Frederick Jackson Turner began to make a serious impression north of the 49th parallel. Canadian historians had to answer the question of how far Canada, geographically a North American nation, was affected by the same environmental factors that had conditioned the develop-ment of the United States. Surprisingly the Turner thesis never found many outright supporters in this country. Walter N. Sage of the University of British Columbia was the most outstanding proponent.[6] The majority of Canadian historians, such as A. R. M. Lower of Queen's, pointed out that there were complicating factors in Canadian development, particularly the British connection, which meant that the Turner thesis required considerable modification before it could be applied to a Canadian setting.[7] A few histori-

---

[4] Shortt, Adam, *Lord Sydenham*, "Makers of Canada Series," (Toronto, 1908).

[5] Shortt, Adam and Sir Arthur G. Doughty, *Canada and its Provinces*, (23 vols., Toron-to, 1913-17). Volume 23 contains the general index, bibliography and chronology.

[6] See particularly his two articles in the *Canadian Historical Association Report*: "Geo-graphical and Cultural aspects of the Five Canadas," 1928, pp. 28-34, and "Some Aspects of the 'Frontier in Canadian History'," 1937, pp. 67-72. These were repub-lished as a pamphlet *Canada from Sea to Sea* by the University of Toronto Press in 1940.

[7] There are several interesting articles on this theme in the *Reports of the Canadian Historical Association*. See particularly, A.R.M. Lower, "Some Neglected Aspects of Canadian History," 1929, pp. 65-71; and "The Origins of Democracy in Canada," 1930, pp. 65-70. Also, John L. McDougall, "The Frontier School and Canadian Histo-ry," 1929, pp. 121-25, which provides a strong attack against the use of the thesis in Canada. Two more recent discussions are in the *Canadian Historical Review*: Morris Zaslow, "The Frontier in Recent Historiography," 1948, pp. 153-67; and J. M. S.

ans, however, did apply it to particular phases of Canadian history.[8]

Then, in the mid-1920's, came a reaction to Turnerism that led to the prime Canadian thesis on the economic development of the country. The man responsible was not a historian, but an economist, Harold Adams Innis (1894-1952), for many years Chairman of the Department of Political Economy at Toronto. Innis added a special touch to Canadian environmentalism: a touch that has become known as the Laurentian thesis because it is based on the development of the St. Lawrence River-Great Lakes economy. His theory, evolved while he was preparing his doctoral thesis on the Canadian Pacific Railway for publication,[9] was, to quote his disciple and biographer, Donald G. Creighton, that Canadian economic development to that date, including his own work, had:

> ... presented what now seemed to him to be an unhistorical and artificial interpretation of Canadian national development. They [the Canadian historians] had viewed the achievement of Canadian unity, through the creation of Confederation and the building of the Canadian Pacific Railway, as an unnatural achievement, an act of men, done in defiance of geography. Innis was now firmly convinced that this idea was false. He had come to realize, as he worked on his thesis, that the Canadian Pacific Railway had simply recaptured, through the medium of rail transport, a much older Canadian economic unity which had been based on water communication. Canadians had not, as they kept insisting with senseless parrot-like iteration, been "fighting geography"; geography had been fighting for them. "The present dominion," Innis wrote later, "emerged not in spite of geography but because of it."[10]

Spurred on by this theme Innis began his great studies of the fur trade and the cod fisheries which developed the Laurentian theme. His idea, basically, was that Canada had developed in response to the British need for staples rather than in reaction to American expansionism. The economic axis of the country, as he saw it, did not stretch north-south, but rather along the St. Lawrence and the Great Lakes, spreading on to the western hinterlands on one side and across the Atlantic to Europe on the other. Along this back-

---

Careless, in "Frontierism, Metropolitanism and Canadian History," 1954, pp. 1-21. The latter article is discussed below. Michael S. Cross has just edited a book on this subject for Copp Clark's "Issues in Canadian History Series," entitled *The Frontier Thesis and The Canadas: The Debate on the Impact of the Canadian Environment* (Toronto, 1970).

[8] For example, A. L. Burt, "The Frontier in the History of New France," *Canadian Historical Association Report*, 1940, pp. 93-99; and Fred Landon, *Western Ontario and the American Frontier*, (Toronto, 1941).

[9] Innis, Harold A., *A History of the Canadian Pacific Railway*, (London, 1923).

[10] Creighton, D. G., *Harold Adams Innis, Portrait of a Scholar*, (Toronto, 1957), pp. 57-8.

bone he visualized the evolution of a Canadian economic system that was both transcontinental and transoceanic at the same time.[11]

His first staple industry was, of course, the fur trade, which led the explorer and trader up the St. Lawrence and Great Lakes, across the wilderness of northern Ontario, and on to the Great Plains and the far northern waters. Innis expounded this thesis in his *The Fur Trade in Canada: An Introduction to Canadian Economic History* (New Haven, 1930). He then continued his work with an investigation of the eastern fisheries, paying particular attention to the factors which bound the economy of the St. Lawrence to England. A decade later this research resulted in *The Cod Fisheries: The History of an International Economy* (New Haven, 1940). Innis's energy and diligence were phenomenal; he consulted vast numbers of documents in archives on both sides of the ocean, though unfortunately the Hudson's Bay Company records were closed to him. Also, like Francis Parkman in an earlier period, he travelled many of the fur traders' routes, partly in his own canoe. His style, unfortunately, did not resemble Parkman's. His books are undoubtedly among the most difficult to read in Canadian historical writings, the despair of the conscientious student. Footnotes and statistics clog the text, and as Creighton admits, Innis often did not indicate clearly the steps which had led him from his detailed evidence to the sweeping generalizations of his theses.[12] Possibly for this reason some of his conclusions have never been sufficiently contested. Professor Aitken's statement on the foundations of Canadian economic theses may well be specifically applied to much of Innis's grand conclusion in the long run. Take for example the following statement from the *Fur Trade*:

> By 1821 the Northwest Company had built up an organization which extended from the Atlantic to the Pacific. The foundations of the present Dominion of Canada had been securely laid. The boundaries of the trade were changed slightly in later periods but primarily the territory over which the Northwest Company had organized its trade was the territory which later became the Dominion. The work of the French traders and explorers and of the English who built upon the foundations laid down by them was complete. . . . The Northwest Company was the forerunner of confederation and it was built on the work of the French *voyageur*, the contributions of the Indian, . . . and the organizing ability of the Anglo-American merchants.[13]

These assertions raise certain questions. Had international treaties laying down boundaries really been so unimportant? Were the foundations really so secure? Certainly neither the Colonial Office nor Sir John A. Macdonald was convinced. These problems cannot, however, be considered here.

---

[11] Creighton, *Innis*, p. 105.
[12] *Ibid.*, p. 101.
[13] Innis, Harold A., *The Fur Trade* (Toronto, 1962), p. 262.

Innis's work was amplified and carried on by Creighton, the most magnificent stylist of all Canadian historical writers, in his first book, *The Commercial Empire of the St. Lawrence, 1760-1850* (Toronto, 1937), which was reissued in 1956 with exactly the same text, but without the word *Commercial* in the title. Creighton's theme, as he restated it in his new preface, was the central point of his interpretation of Canadian history as the idea of an east-west transcontinental system based both politically and commercially on the St. Lawrence.[14] The work is an examination of the trade in the various Canadian staples: fur, timber, potash, wheat, up to the time of the decline of the old British commercial system in the late 1840's.

More recently the Laurentian thesis has been redirected by J. M. S. Careless, Creighton's successor as Chairman of the History Department at Toronto. His suggested revision appeared not in a book, but in an article in the *Canadian Historical Review* in 1954.[15] Entitled "Frontierism, Metropolitanism, and Canadian History" this short discussion must be considered as one of the most significant contributions to Canadian historical writing. In it Careless first examines the various schools of Canadian historiography, including the works of the supporters of Turner and of the Laurentian thesis. He then points out that the second group had actually turned the frontier thesis backward and substituted in its place a metropolitan focus for Canadian history centred upon London, England, and the cities of the St. Lawrence system. After noting that we should be careful not to substitute a metropolitan determinism for a frontier one, Careless concludes that for Canada the study of the role of the metropolis might well lead to a more satisfactory explanation of our development than could be obtained by merely borrowing the frontier concept from the United States. He is presently writing a history of the rise of Canadian cities to 1914 which will amplify his theories on this subject. With his work we come to the end of the theories of Canadian economic development that have received major consideration by the historians.

Let us now turn to an examination of the individual monographs that have been specifically written on various aspects of Canadian business history. Following the above discussion of the theories of Canadian economic development these may be classified under several headings: first, general works and those which discuss some particular theme; secondly, monographs dealing with phases of Canadian business development which might be said to amplify the Laurentian thesis; thirdly, works which are more aligned to

[14] Creighton, D. G., *The Empire of the St. Lawrence* (Toronto, 1956), p. iii.

[15] Careless, J. M. S., "Frontierism, Metropolitanism and Canadian History," *Canadian Historical Review*, XXXV (1954), pp. 1-21. Two of his other essays should be mentioned "Metropolitanism and Nationalism," in P. Russell, ed., *Nationalism in Canada*, (Toronto, 1966) pp. 271-83; and his Presidential Address to the Canadian Historical Association "Somewhat Narrow Horizons," *Canadian Historical Association Annual Report*, 1967, pp. 1-10.

Canadian-American relations (these are far fewer in number), and, finally, discussions of other staples, other types of business, histories of individual companies, and biographies of individual entrepreneurs, none of which really falls into the other categories. Such a classification, of course, is arbitrary; many of the works discussed might well be placed elsewhere, but the arrangement does have the advantage of pointing up some of the major contributions to Canadian business history, and also of demonstrating the extent to which Canadian research has followed certain lines.

The father of Canadian business history, as noted before, was Adam Shortt.[16] The twenty-three volume collection *Canada and its Provinces*, which he edited jointly with Sir Arthur Doughty in 1913-17,[17] still stands as the one great survey of Canadian life. Not content with merely preparing a history of the political evolution of the nation – which is basically what is attempted in the new eighteen volume Centenary Series now making its appearance[18] – Shortt and Doughty designed a work that embraced all aspects of Canadian growth. Specific sections were devoted to business, and volumes nine and ten deal with nothing but post-Confederation industrial development. Shortt himself contributed the sections on banking. Some of the essays in *Canada and its Provinces* are now outdated, but the collection will always form an invaluable reference for business historians, as well as for students of all other phases of Canadian history. In 1926 Shortt also edited a two-volume set of documents on currency, exchange and finance during the French Régime.[19]

Innis made many other contributions to Canadian business history, among them his *Problems of Staple Production in Canada* (Toronto, 1933), and the two-volume *Select Documents in Canadian History* (Toronto, 1929-33) which he edited with Arthur Lower. A few other particularly important studies of specific aspects of Canadian economic development should be noted at this point. They have a dual interest, for the careers of the historians involved again demonstrate the fact that Canada has never developed a special discipline of business historians. One of the most valuable of these is the *History of Transportation in Canada* (Toronto, 1938), by G. P. de T. Glazebrook, who has divided his career between the History Department of the University of Toronto and the Canadian Department of External Affairs. He has also

---

[16] For a biography see W. A. Mackintosh, "Adam Shortt, 1859-1931," *Canadian Journal of Economics and Political Science*, 1938, pp. 164-76; and for a bibliography R. F. Neill, "Adam Shortt: A Bibliographical Comment," *Journal of Canadian Studies*, 2 (1967), pp. 54-61.

[17] See note 5.

[18] This series, edited by W. L. Morton and D. G. Creighton and published in Toronto by McClelland and Stewart, began to make its appearance in 1963; six volumes have appeared to date.

[19] Shortt, Adam, ed., *Documents Relating to Canadian Currency, Exchange and Finance during the French Period* (2 vols., Ottawa, 1925-26). Yet another contribution was his *Documents Relating to Currency and Finance in Nova Scotia, 1675-1758* (Ottawa, 1933).

written the standard survey of Canadian external relations.[20] Another is the already mentioned *The Canadian Commercial Revolution 1845-51* (New Haven, 1936), by the late Gilbert N. Tucker who wrote in addition the history of the naval service in Canada.[21] Mention should also be made of D. C. Masters' *The Reciprocity Treaty of 1854* (London, 1937); this author, like Glazebrook, has written on an amazing variety of historical subjects. In spite of such basic works, there are few satisfactory one-volume surveys of Canadian economic history; W. T. Easterbrook's and H. G. J. Aitken's *Canadian Economic History* (Toronto, 1956),[22] is an extremely clear presentation.

In the second category, works dealing with topics related to the Laurentian thesis, there is an unusually rich amount of material. This can be discussed under the three headings of the fur trade, transportation and communications, and finance. Beginning with the fur trade a good general history is Paul C. Phillips, *The Fur Trade* (2 vols., Norman, Okla., 1961), and for Canada more specifically E. E. Rich has recently written *The Fur Trade and The Northwest to 1857* (Toronto, 1967), for the Centenary Series. There are also some area studies such as Henry C. Biggar *The Early Trading Companies of New France* (Toronto, 1901 – republished 1965), and Wayne E. Stevens *The Northwest Fur Trade 1763-1800* (Urbana, Ill., 1928).

In the field of biography there has been a recent surge of research on the early French merchants – whose interests were often broader than just the fur trade – and their place in the Colonial community, which may be seen in Cameron Nish's *Les Bourgeois – Gentilshommes de la Nouvelle-France 1729-1748* (Montreal, 1968), and Jean Hamelin *Economie et société en Nouvelle France* (Quebec, 1960). The publication of the first two volumes of the *Dictionary of Canadian Biography* covering the period 1100-1740 has resulted in the appearance of biographies of such early business figures as Charles Aubert de la Chesnaye (1632-1702) by Yves F. Zoltvany. For more recent figures and individuals involved more completely in the fur trade, Innis has contributed a life of Peter Pond, one of the more murderous early traders.[23] Other major biographies connected with the fur trade are Arthur S. Morton's *Sir George Simpson* (Toronto, 1944), the life of the greatest of the Hudson's Bay Company governors, a recent biography of Lord Selkirk by

---

[20] Glazebrook, G. P. de T., *A History of Canadian External Relations*, (Toronto, 1950). More recently Glazebrook has authored several new works, including *Life In Ontario: A Social History* (Toronto, 1968).

[21] Tucker, Gilbert N., *The Naval Service of Canada, its Official History* (2 vols., Ottawa, 1952).

[22] Older surveys are A. W. Currie, *Canadian Economic Development* (Toronto, 1942); and Mary Q. Innis, *Economic History of Canada* (Toronto, 1943). Space does not permit a discussion of books related to specific economic periods or problems, rather than more directly to business history; the Easterbrook bibliography mentioned in footnote 2 and the references in Easterbrook and Aitken's text can be consulted in this regard.

[23] Innis, Harold A., *Peter Pond, Fur Trader and Adventurer* (Toronto, 1930).

John Gray, the President of Macmillan's of Canada,[24] and Marjorie E. Campbell's study of William McGillivray in *McGillivray, Lord of the Northwest* (Toronto, 1962). Unfortunately there is no full biography of the latter's uncle, Simon McTavish, the Montreal merchant who for many years before his death in 1804 was the key figure of the Northwest Company. There is, however, a short study, along with other interesting papers, in *The Pedlars from Quebec* (Toronto, 1954), by W. Stewart Wallace (1884-1970), for many years Librarian of the University of Toronto.

In the field of corporation history the Hudson's Bay Company has been the subject of more studies than any other Canadian – and I suspect English or American – organization.[25] Among the best is *The Honourable Company: A History of the Hudson's Bay Company* (Indianapolis, 1936), by Douglas MacKay, who for several years was the editor of the official magazine of the company, *The Beaver*,[26] which is itself a valuable source of information on the history of both the company and the Canadian North. More recent is a study of the political activities of the organization by John S. Galbraith, *The Hudson's Bay Company as an Imperial Factor 1821-1869* (Toronto, 1957). The official history is *The History of the Hudson's Bay Company 1670-1870* (2 vols., London, 1958-9), by Edwin E. Rich, the company archivist.[27] In addition to these secondary sources many documents are now available in the series published by the Hudson's Bay Record Society.[28] There are also histories of its rival in *The North West Company*, by Marjorie E. Campbell (Toronto, 1957), and C. Gordon Davidson's work with the same title (New York, 1967).

Thus, as Aitken says, the fur trade has been the subject of the most detailed examination in all its phases, and new material is constantly coming out. Certainly it provides a romantic topic which has attracted many amateur historians as well as taking up a disproportionate part of the available time of the few Canadian business historians. It has also, unfortunately, spilled over into the public school text-books. As a result, generations of Canadian

---

[24] Gray, John M., *Lord Selkirk of Red River* (Toronto, 1963).

[25] Among the most frequently encountered earlier works are: Beckles Willson, *The Great Company* (1661-1871) (2 vols., London, 1900); George Bryce, *The Remarkable History of the Hudson's Bay Company* (Toronto, 1900); and Agnes C. Laut, *The Conquest of the Great North-West* (2 vols., Toronto 1908); and *The 'Adventurers of England' on Hudson Bay; A Chronicle of the Fur Trade in the North* (Toronto, 1914). Arthur S. Morton, *A History of the Canadian West to 1870-71* (London, 1939), provides a general history of the region under the company.

[26] *The Beaver* is a quarterly which was first published in 1920.

[27] These originally appeared as volumes 21 and 22 of the Hudson's Bay Record Society series but have now been reissued separately. Rich has also edited other works in this series and has recently published a small volume of lectures: *Montreal and The Fur Trade* (Montreal, 1966).

[28] There are now 27 volumes in this series (published in Toronto and London, 1938-69). The first 12 were published jointly with the Champlain Society.

students have had their interest in Canadian history killed by the stories of innumerable traders, whose names could be neither spelled nor pronounced, paddling in all directions on a vast number of rivers with equally unintelligible names.

Next to the fur trade the history of the transportation industry has received more attention than any other division of Canadian business history. Its treatment, however, has been unbalanced, for most of the historians' energy has been concentrated on the railways, which have been the favorite topic of transportation historians. Innis's history of the Canadian Pacific has already been mentioned; a more recent examination of the same subject is John M. Gibbon's *Steel of Empire* (Indianapolis, 1935).[29] The Canadian National Railways have received fine treatment in Colonel G. R. Stevens' history,[30] two volumes of which appeared in 1960-62; a third is under way, as well as a single-volume summary to be published as part of the "Railways of America" series edited by Tom Brewer, which will also contain a history of the C.P.R. by W. Kay Lamb, who recently retired as archivist of Canada. In addition A. W. Currie has written a history, *The Grand Trunk Railway* (Toronto, 1957), discussing one of the most important predecessors of the C.N.R., and the construction of another predecessor is described by the engineer who was responsible: Sir Sandford Fleming, *The Intercolonial* (Montreal, 1876).[31] There are also important works on land policy and railways in James B. Hedges', *The Federal Railway Land Subsidy Policy of Canada* (Cambridge, Mass., 1934), and on railways and nationalism in Leonard B. Irwin, *Pacific Railways and Nationalism in the Canadian-American Northwest, 1845-1873* (New York, 1968). Railway nationalization aroused as much interest as railway construction and has left a considerable number of government committee reports and private opinions.[32]

The railway builders have also attracted attention; they form a particularly interesting group as their entrepreneurial activities involved so many aspects of both business and politics. There is one rather early collective survey of their activities in *The Railway Builders* (Toronto, 1915), by Oscar D.

[29] Other popular histories of this railway are: Keith Morris, *The Story of the Canadian Pacific Railway* (London, 1916); R. G. MacBeth, *The Romance of the Canadian Pacific Railway* (Toronto, 1924); and J. Lorne McDougall, *Canadian Pacific: a Brief History* (Montreal, 1968).

[30] Stevens, G.R., *Canadian National Railways* (Vol. 1, 1836-1896, Vol. II, 1896-1922, Toronto, 1960-62).

[31] For minor railway lines there are many articles and several monographs, such as Howard Fleming, *Canada's Arctic Outlet; A History of the Hudson Bay Railway* (Berkley, 1957). Details of minor railways may be obtained in Robert Dorman, *A Statutory History of Steam and Electric Railways in Canada* (Ottawa, 1938); and T. P. G. Shaw, *Handbook and Catalogue of Canadian Transportation Postmarks* (Shawinigan, Que., 1963).

[32] For example William H. Moore, *Railway Nationalization and the Average Citizen* (Toronto, 1917).

Skelton, the biographer of Prime Minister Sir Wilfrid Laurier. Skelton himself was later Undersecretary of State for External Affairs. Other older biographies are L. J. Burpee's *Sandford Fleming, Empire Builder* (London, 1915), and Walter Vaughan's *The Life and Work of Sir William Van Horne* (New York, 1920).[33] There are at least five accounts of Lord Strathcona's career,[34] and one of his cousin and associate Lord Mount Stephen: Heather Gilbert, *Awakening Continent, The Life of Lord Mount Stephen: Vol. I, 1824-1891.* (Aberdeen, 1965). With regard to recent figures there are also biographies of Sir Henry Thornton and Sir Edward Beatty, the presidents of the C.N.R. and the C.P.R. respectively in the 1920's and 1930's.[35] There is even a certain amount of autobiographical material such as the reminiscences of D. B. Hanna, the first president of the C.N.R.[36]

Compared to railway history the subject of shipping has been almost completely neglected. The general surveys are still William Wood, *All Afloat*, (Toronto, 1915), and an extended article by M. J. Patton "Shipping and Canals" in *Canada and Its Provinces*.[37] Steamships were specifically covered by James Croil, *Steam Navigation in Canada* (Toronto, 1898). With such a dearth of general material it is not surprising that there are no histories of even such large corporations as the Canada Steamship Lines and virtually no examinations of the major ports.[38] The Great Lakes have received a great deal more attention than any other Canadian waters, though much of the material is of a rather romantic nature. Basic histories are James O. Curwood, *The Great Lakes* (New York, 1909, reprinted 1967), George A. Cuthbertson, *Fresh water* (Toronto, 1931), and Harlan Hatcher, *The Great Lakes* (New York, 1944). Except for Fred Landon's *Lake Huron* (Indianapolis, 1944), "The American Lakes Series" edited by Milo M. Quaite in the mid-1940's is rather disappointing. *Inland Seas*, the quarterly journal of the Great Lakes Historical Society, which has been published since 1945, is a mine of useful information to the business historian.

The story of the Canadian canals is much the same as that of the other aspects of Canadian shipping. Patton's above mentioned article (1914) is still

[33] Other works on leading engineering figures who did much of their work on the railways are Ludwik Kos-Rabcewioz-Zubkowski and William E. Greening, *Sir Casimir Stanislaus Gzowski: A Biography* (Toronto, 1959); and Frank N. Walker, ed., *Daylight Through the Mountains: The Letters and Labours of Walter and Francis Shanly* (Toronto, 1957).

[34] The most frequently encountered of these are W. T. R. Preston, *The Life and Times of Lord Strathcona* (Toronto, n.d.) Beckles Willson, *Lord Strathcona* (London, 1902); and John Macnaughton, *Lord Strathcona* (London, 1926).

[35] D'Arcy Marsh, *The Tragedy of Henry Thornton* (Toronto, 1935); and D.H. Miller-Barstow, *Beatty of the C.P.R.* (Toronto, 1951).

[36] David B. Hanna, *Trains of Recollection* (Toronto, 1924).

[37] Vol. X, pp. 475-624.

[38] For Montreal there is Laurence C. Tombs, *The Port of Montreal* (Toronto, 1926); and Esdras Minville, *Montréal Économique* (Montréal, 1943).

the most recent overall examination. Two earlier, but still interesting, histories are William Kingsford, *The Canadian Canals*, (Toronto, 1865), and Thomas C. Keefer, *The Canals of Canada* (Montreal, 1894).[39] In addition there are two studies of specific canals, Aitken's, *The Welland Canal Company* (Cambridge, Mass., 1954) and Robert Legget's more popular *Rideau Waterway* (Toronto, 1955).

With regard to more recent methods of transportation, the history of *The Intercity Electric Railway Industry in Canada*, (Toronto, 1966), by John F. Due of Illinois has just been published. General works on the theme of transportation include: A. W. Currie, *Economics of Canadian Transportation* (Toronto, 1959); J. C. Lessard, *Transportation in Canada* (Ottawa, 1956), a valuable survey of recent developments published by the Royal Commission of Canada's Economic Prospects; and H. A. Innis, ed., *Essays in Transportation in Honour of W. T. Jackman* (Toronto, 1941).

In the field of communications a certain amount of attention has been paid to the evolution of Canadian journalism. There are two histories, *A History of Canadian Journalism 1859-1959* (2 vols., Toronto, 1909-59), and the recent Wilfred A. Kesterton's, *A History of Journalism in Canada* (Toronto, 1967), and there is also M. E. Nichols, *(CP): The Story of the Canadian Press* (Toronto 1948). Not surprisingly, several editors have written their autobiographies or reminiscences and there are a fair number of biographies of prominent editors. Most of these, however, are of more value for political and social studies than for business history.[40]

In a more technical area there is no history of the telegraph and very little on the telephone. There are biographies of Alexander Graham Bell, such as Thomas B. Costain, *The Chord of Steel* (New York, 1960), but no history of the Bell Telephone Company. Nationalization, however, again called forth a protest in James Maera, *Government Telephones: The Experience of Manitoba, Canada* (New York, 1916). The post office has, however, received more complete treatment with William Smith, *History of The Post Office in British North America, 1639-1870* (Cambridge, 1920), and a more recent article by A. W. Currie on the post-Confederation period.[41] A mod-

---

[39] A short biography of Keefer, who was an important figure in canal and railway building as well as reciprocity, may be found in D. C. Masters, "T. C. Keefer and the Development of Canadian Transportation," *Canadian Historical Association Report* (1940), pp. 36-44.

[40] Examples of works in the first category are: Wilfred Eggleston, *While I Still Remember* (Toronto, 1968); Arthur R. Ford, *As The World Wags On* (Toronto, 1953); J.H. Cranston, *Ink on My Fingers* (Toronto, 1953); and Hector Charlesworth, *Candid Chronicles* (Toronto, 1925), *More Candid Chronicles* (Toronto, 1928), and *I'm Telling You* (Toronto, 1937). Biographies include G. Ramsay Cook, *The Politics of John W. Defoe and The Free Press* (Toronto, 1963); Ross Harkness, *J.E. Atkinson of the Star* (Toronto, 1963); and C. Frank Steele, *Prairie Editor: The Life and Times of Buchanan of Lethbridge* (Toronto, 1961).

[41] "The Post Office since 1867," *Canadian Journal of Economics and Political Science*, XXIV, (1952), pp. 241-50.

ern overview of communications in Canada is John A. Irving, editor, *Mass Media in Canada* (Toronto, 1962).

Canadian financial institutions form a third link which unites the nation, but comparatively little research has been devoted to their development, even though their story would do much to clarify the advance of Toronto and Montreal. A. B. Jamieson, *Chartered Banking in Canada* (Toronto, 1953), is a standard work, and the more recent *Canadian Monetary, Banking and Financial Development* (Toronto, 1961), by R. Craig McIvor provides a balanced history of Canadian finance and does not relegate the pre-1900 period to a few pages. An earlier, and still valuable examination of this field is Roeliff M. Breckenridge, *History of Banking in Canada* (Washington, 1910). Another recent addition to this branch of Canadian economic history is Edward P. Neufeld ed., *Money and Banking in Canada: Historical Documents and Commentary* (Toronto, 1964). With regard to individual banks Neufeld has also written the *Bank of Canada Operations 1935-54* (Toronto, 1955).

The most extended works in this field are Victor Ross and A. St. L. Trigge, *A History of the Canadian Bank of Commerce* (3 vols., Toronto 1920-34), which includes the histories of the many banks the Commerce had absorbed since its establishment in 1869, and Merrill Denison's disappointing *Canada's First Bank: A History of the Bank of Montreal*, (2 vols., Toronto, 1966-67), which becomes more sketchy as it progresses.[42] Another source of banking history is *The Canadian Banker* (formerly *The Journal of the Canadian Bankers' Association*) which has appeared regularly since 1893. For trust companies and insurance companies there is almost nothing, although a few life insurance companies have prepared authorized histories.[43] There is also a fine short history of Canada's leading firm of auditors, A. J. Little, *The Story of the Firm, 1864-1964; Clarkson, Gordon and Co.* (Toronto, 1964).

The captains of finance are much more poorly represented in the biographical field than the tycoons of the railways, many of whom were, of course, also interested in finance. The connections of Lords Strathcona and Mount Stephen with both the CPR and the Bank of Montreal is a good example. There are, however, a few books that were written as memorials,

---

[42] There are some official histories of other banks which provide much useful information, for example: *The Centenary of the Bank of Montreal 1817-1917* (Montreal, 1917); *The Dominion Bank 1871-1921* (Toronto, 1922); Joseph Schull, *100 years of Banking in Canada, A History of the Toronto-Dominion Bank* (Toronto, 1948); and T. Taggart Smyth, *The First Hundred Years: History of the Montreal City and District Savings Bank, 1846-1946* (n.p., n.d.).

[43] For example, Harris, George H. *The President's Book: The Story of the Sun Life Assurance Company of Canada* (Montreal, 1928); and, more recently, Campbell, James A., *The Story of the London Life Insurance Company* (2 vols., London, Ont., 1965-66); and the Canada Life Assurance Company's, *Since 1847, The Canada Life Story* (Toronto, 1967).

but are still mines of information, such as the Rev. R. G. MacBeth, *Sir Augustus Nanton* (Toronto, 1931), the story of Winnipeg's leading financier. His Toronto associates, the Oslers, who were prominent in so many fields of endeavour, have two family histories: W. A. Craik, *A Short History of the Osler Family* (Toronto, 1938), and Anne Wilkinson, *Lions in the Way, A Discursive History of The Oslers* (Toronto, 1957).

Business history in what might be called the field of Canadian-American relations has been far less productive of major works. Foreign ownership of Canadian industry is discussed in Hugh C. J. Aitken, *American Capital and Canadian Resources* (Cambridge, Mass., 1961), in a collection of essays published by the Duke University – Commonwealth Studies program, *The American Economic Impact on Canada* (Durham, N.C., 1959), and, most recently, in A. E. Safarian *Foreign Ownership of Canadian Industry* (Toronto, 1966). There is also I. Brecher and S. S. Riesman, *Canada-United States Economic Relations* (Ottawa, 1957). Some histories of American corporations have included a chapter on "Canadian operations"; moreover, there are biographies of American captains of industry which contain information on Canadian industrial development. John W. Jenkins' *James B. Duke* (New York, 1927), is an example, as the author discusses Duke's role in the development of Quebec power. There are also a few works which study a specific Canadian-American operation such as Carl Wiegman's *Trees to News* (Toronto, 1953), an examination of the operations of the *Chicago Tribune* through the Ontario Paper Company. J. A. Gutherie, *Newsprint Industry* (Cambridge, Mass., 1941), should also be noted in this field.

There are good surveys available on the tariff, particularly Orville Mc-Diarmid, *Commercial Policy in the Canadian Economy* (Cambridge, Mass., 1946), and John H. Dales, *The Protective Tariff in Canada's Development* (Toronto, 1966),[44] and various opinions on specialized topics; for example, the relatively large number of books on Imperial Unity which appeared in the 1880's and 1890's, written by a variety of people from an ex-governor-general to Canadian emigrants to the United States.[45] Any of these topics could provide a basis for an interesting study, and they extend from prob-

[44] There is also the older Edward Porrett, *Sixty Years of Protection in Canada, 1846-1907* (London, 1908); and three more recent works, J. H. Perry, *Taxes, Tariffs and Subsidies: A History of Canadian Fiscal Development* (2 vols., Toronto, 1955); G. A. Elliott, *Tariff Procedures and Trade Barriers: A Study of Indirect Protection in Canada and The United States* (Toronto, 1955); and Gordon Blake, *Customs Administration in Canada: An Essay in Tariff Technology* (Toronto, 1957).

[45] This included the question of an imperial *zollverein* as a counter to reciprocity of some form with the United States. Among the books written were: The Marquis of Lorne, *Imperial Federation* (London, 1855); James Douglas, *Canadian Independence* (New York, 1894); and Colonel George T. Denison, *The Struggle for Imperial Unity* (London, 1909). The actual relationship with Britain is best covered in Douglas R. Annett, *British Preference in Canadian Commercial Policy* (Toronto, 1948).

lems over a century old to former Finance Minister Walter Gordon's recent statements.[46] An early example is the group of speeches entitled *Isaac Buchanan on the Relations of the Industry of Canada with the Mother Country and the United States* (Montreal, 1864). Buchanan had these gathered by Henry J. Morgan, the first Canadian specialist on dictionaries of biography. They provide a valuable insight into the outlook of an early Hamilton merchant who was also a leading member of Parliament.

One of the greatest contributions to an understanding of Canadian-American business relations is to be found in some of the volumes of the series which appeared between 1936 and 1945 under the editorship of J. B. Brebner and J. T. Shotwell. Entitled "The Relations of Canada and the United States" and sponsored by the Carnegie Endowment for International Peace, the series naturally included many manuscripts concerned with matters other than Canadian business history, or with purely Canadian affairs. The quality of the works included was far from even, but the importance of these volumes cannot be overestimated. Three of them have already been noted as among the most significant works in Canadian business history: Innis's *Cod Fisheries*; Creighton's *Commercial Empire of the St. Lawrence*; and Glazebrook's *History of Transportation in Canada*. Another outstanding contribution to the understanding of a Canadian staple industry was A.R.M. Lower's *The North American Assault on the Canadian Forest: A History of the Lumber Trade Between Canada and the United States* (Toronto, 1936). Mention should also be made of Herbert Marshall, F. A. Southard and K. W. Taylor's *Canadian-American Industry: A Study in International Investment* (Toronto, 1936), William J. Wilgu's *The Railway Interrelations of the United States and Canada* (Toronto, 1937), and N. Ware, H. A. Logan and H. A. Innis, eds. *Labour in Canadian American Relations* (Toronto, 1937).

Two other staple industries of Canada, wheat and mining, should be discussed. For the grain trade there are two works by D. A. MacGibbon, *The Canadian Grain Trade* (Toronto, 1932), and *The Canadian Grain Trade, 1931-1951* (Toronto, 1952), as well as G. E. Britnell, *The Wheat Economy* (Toronto, 1939), and two works by Vernon C. Fowke, *Canadian Agricultural Policy: The Historical Pattern* (Toronto, 1946), and *The National Policy and the Wheat Economy* (Toronto, 1957). These last two authors have collaborated on a more specialized study, *Canadian Agriculture in War and Peace, 1935-1950* (Stanford, 1962). There are also biographies of the family which developed Marquis Wheat in Elsie M. Pomeroy's *William Saunders and his Five Sons* (Toronto, 1956), and of the leading figures in the establishment of the wheat pools in W. K. Rolph's *Henry Wise Wood of Alberta* (Toronto, 1950). For corporation biography there is George Ste-

---

[46] Gordon, The Hon. Walter L., *A Choice for Canada, Independence or Colonial Status* (Toronto, 1966).

vens, *Ogilvie in Canada – pioneer millers, 1801-1951* (Montreal, 1952). For general agricultural history there are several regional studies including Robert L. Jones, *History of Agriculture in Ontario 1613-1880* (Toronto, 1946), and Firmin Létourneau, *Histoire de l'agriculture (Canada français)* (Montreal, 1950).[47] William G. Phillips, *The Agricultural Implement Industry in Canada: A Study of Competition* (Toronto, 1956), should also be noted.

In the field of mining G. B. Longworth has written *Out of the Earth: The Mineral Industry in Canada* (Toronto, 1954), and Donat M. LeBourdais *Metals and Man; the story of Canadian Mining* (Toronto, 1957).[48] LeBourdais – who has produced several works in this field – has also written the story of nickel in *Sudbury Basin: The Story of Nickel* (Toronto, 1953), a topic again examined by O. W. Main in *The Canadian Nickel Industry* (Toronto, 1955). Also to be noted are W. J. A. Donald, *The Canadian Iron and Steel Industry* (Boston, 1915), and a short history of petroleum, Victor Ross, *Petroleum in Canada* (Toronto, 1917).[49] Virtually nothing is to be found on individual mining corporations. Leslie Roberts' *Noranda* (Toronto, 1956), is an exception, covering the history of a large concern engaged in mining copper and other minerals.

Moving from staples to what might be called categories of business, Canadian manufacturing needs much more analysis, both in the overall picture and in the individual branches. A few histories in this class have been noteworthy, such as Phillips' work on the agricultural industry; and there are some others, for example T. Ritchie's history of construction in Canada, *Canada Builds, 1867-1967* (Toronto, 1967), but very little is available, and all too much of the information must be obtained from what might be called "official histories," commissioned by various companies and often far from representative. These, of course, have largely been written by professional writers and vary greatly in value. The most prolific exponent of this field is Merrill Denison, already mentioned in connection with the history of the Bank of Montreal. In recent years he has also written; *Harvest Triumphant: The Story of Massey Harris* (Toronto, 1948); and *The Barley and the Stream, the Story of Molson's Brewery* (Toronto, 1955). Few professional historians flourishing today have written in the field of corporation history, but William Kilbourn is an exception; his *The Elements Combined* (Toronto, 1960), a history of the Steel Company of Canada, is a model of both

[47] Agriculture in Quebec is also discussed in several excellent regional economic histories noted below. Mention should also be made of another area study, Stanley N. Murray, *The Valley Comes of Age: A History of Agriculture in The Valley of The Red River of The North 1812-1920* (Fargo, N.D., 1967).

[48] Older and popularly written, but still useful, is Arnold Hoffman, *Free Gold: The Story of Canadian Mining* (New York, 1946).

[49] Two useful works deal specifically with oil in Alberta: A. A. McGillivray and L. R. Lipsett, *Alberta's Oil Industry* (Edmonton, 1940); and Eric J. Hanson, *Dynamic Decade* (Toronto, 1958).

scholarly research and lucid style, as is his more recent *Pipeline* (Toronto, 1970), an examination of the development of the controversial Trans-Canada Pipe Lines. Some biographies of manufacturing families also exist such as Mollie Gillen, *The Masseys: Founding Family* (Toronto, 1966), naturally a popular account. Unfortunately Canada's former Governor-General, Vincent Massey, only makes brief reference to business affairs in his autobiography *What's Past is Prologue* (New York, 1964). Soon to appear will be Alfred Dubuc's "Thomas Molson, entrepreneur Canadien," which should cast much light on the badly neglected Montreal business community.

The story is the same in the mercantile field, which has witnessed the flowering of a great many official histories, many on the eulogy level. One difference from the manufacturing field, however, is that these tend to be histories of individuals as often as of companies. An early example is the Rev. Hugh Johnston's, *A Merchant Prince: Life of Hon. Senator John Macdonald* (Toronto, 1893), the story of the great Toronto dry goods wholesaler. That this type of writing can reach a very high level can be seen by such works as G. Alan Wilson's *John Northway, a Blue Serge Canadian* (Toronto, 1965), the tale of a somewhat later Toronto merchandizing tycoon. At the other end of the scale are the almost countless glorifications of the Eaton family beginning with *Golden Jubilee 1869-1919* (Toronto, 1919).[50] Recently, however, they have produced a fine aid to the social historian in George T. de P. Glazebrook, Katharine B. Brett and Judith McErval, eds., *A Shopper's View of Canada's Past; pages from Eaton's Catalogues, 1886-1930* (Toronto, 1969). Their rival, the Robert Simpson Company, is represented only by C. L. Burton, *A Sense of Urgency: Memoirs of a Canadian Merchant* (Toronto, 1952). Newfoundland makes one of its few appearances in Canadian business history in this area with David Keir's *The Bowring Story* (London, 1962), the story of that province's leading mercantile family. One of the earliest merchants to be discussed is Aaron Hart in Raymound Douville, *Aaron Hart récit historique* (Trois-Rivières, 1938). At a very different level of merchandizing there have been *exposés* of not so fine Canadian merchandizing practices in Pierre Berton, *The Big Sell* (Toronto, 1965), and Coriolis, *Death Here is Thy Sting* (Toronto, 1957).

Mention must also be made of the various publicly-owned corporations that have played such an important role in Canadian development. On the federal level there is a new book on the corporations generally, Charles A. Ashley and R. G. H. Smails, *Canadian Crown Corporations* (Toronto, 1965); but there is very little on the individual companies, though Ashley has also written *The First Twenty-Five Years* (Toronto, 1963), the story of the Trans-Canada Airways, now Air Canada. There is also a biography of the

50 Other examples are George G. Nasmith, *Timothy Eaton* (Toronto, 1923); *Memory's Wall: The Autobiography of Flora McRea Eaton* (Toronto, 1956); and Mary-Etta Macpherson, *Shopkeepers to a Nation: The Eatons* (Toronto, 1963).

man who was responsible for the creation of so many of these corporations by Leslie Roberts: *C.D., The Life and Times of Clarence Decatur Howe* (Toronto, 1957), and William Kilbourn is now preparing a second study which will be based on Howe's papers.

In the provincial field, the Ontario Hydro has been the subject of a vast amount of discussion, particularly at the time when it was first created through the efforts of Sir Adam Beck. The most recent history is Merrill Denison, *The People's Power; The History of the Ontario Hydro* (Toronto, 1960). Among the more frequently seen of the earlier works are: R. P. Bolton, *An Expensive Experiment* (New York, 1913); E. B. Biggar, *Hydro-Electric Development in Ontario* (Toronto, 1920); James Mavor, *Niagara in Politics* (New York, 1925); and *The Hydro-Electric Power Commission of Ontario, Its Origins, Administration and Achievements,* (Toronto, 1928). In addition, W. R. Plewman has written a biography of Sir Adam in *Adam Beck and The Ontario Hydro* (Toronto, 1947), and a retired official, Edward M. Ashworth, has left his reminiscences in *Toronto Hydro Recollections* (Toronto, 1955). The development of hydroelectric power in Quebec, which has followed quite a different course, has been written up by John H. Dales in *Hydroelectricity and Industrial Development: Quebec 1898-1940* (Cambridge, Mass., 1957). There are even a few works devoted to municipally owned corporations, such as The Toronto Transportation Commission's *Wheels of Progress* (Toronto, n.d.).

In such a regionalized nation as Canada it is surprising that so little has been written on business development in the individual areas of the country. Possibly this is because so much business enterprise spreads right across the country, but still the evolution of individual regions is a point of great interest. Some specialized works – such as those mentioned on agriculture – do fall into this field, however, much of what there is comes under the heading of economic surveys, often sponsored by a government body.[51] Not surprisingly, much of the most interesting work on regional economic and social development is being done in Quebec. Jean Hamelin's *Economie et société en Nouvelle France* (Quebec, 1960) has already been mentioned and an earlier analysis is Joseph-Nöel Fauteux, *Essai sur l'industrie au Canada sous le régime Français* (2 vols., Québec, 1927). Fernand Ouellet has written the equally interesting *Histoire, économique et sociale du Québec 1760-1850* (Montreal, 1966) and now Jean Hamelin and Yves Roby are preparing an economic history for the period 1850-96. There is also A. Faucher and M. Lamontagne's "History of Industrial Development" in Jean C. Falardeau, ed., *Essays on Contemporary Quebec* (Quebec, 1953), and Robert Comeau, ed., *Economie Québécoise: Les Cahiers de l'Université du Québec* (Montréal, 1969).

---

[51] The Ontario Department of Economics, *Ontario Economic and Social Aspects Survey* (Toronto 1961), is an example.

Finally, a word should be said on labour history. N. Ware, H. A. Logan and H. A. Innis, *Labour in Canadian-American Relations* (New Haven, 1937), has already been noted, but the most prolific writer in this field was the late H. A. Logan who wrote *The History of Trade Union Organization in Canada* (Chicago 1928), *Trade Unions in Canada: Their Development and Function* (Toronto, 1943), and *State Intervention and Assistance in Collective Bargaining: The Canadian Experience 1843-1954* (Toronto, 1956). There is also a short account by Stuart Jamieson, *Industrial Relations in Canada* (Ithaca, 1957), and Doris French's *Faith, Sweat and Politics: The Early Trade Union Years in Canada* (Toronto, 1962). Eugene A. Forsey of Ottawa has now nearly completed his history of Canadian labour, which should provide us with a definitive reference in this area. Specialized and regional studies which should be noted are D. C. Masters, *The Winnipeg General Strike* (Toronto, 1950), Gad Horowitz, *Canadian Labour in Politics* (Toronto, 1968), and Paul A. Phillips, *No Power Greater; a Century of Labour in British Columbia* (Vancouver, 1967).

As one can see, Canadian business history is still in its infancy, even if its origins reach back quite far into the past. It is not yet possible to effect a separation of business history from economic history because so much remains to be done in both fields. The day when sufficient information is available so that business history can be studied as part of the entrepreneurial process is far in the future.

If this is the present state of business history, what is the future of the field in Canada? Professor Aitken's list of unexplored aspects of Canadian economic history provides an outline of how much is waiting to be done; certainly any graduate student looking for a topic will have a wide area of selection. In addition, although there is a scarcity of documentary sources, those collections that exist have hardly been fully examined. The William Hamilton Merritt Papers in the Ontario Archives and the Public Archives of Canada are a typical example. Merritt was one of our most important early entrepreneurs, promoter of both canal building and reciprocity as well as an influential member of Parliament for three decades before his death in 1862. Yet, in spite of the availability of both his papers and those of many of his contemporaries, the only biography of him is that prepared by his son in 1875.[52] Research on entrepreneurial documents, however, will be greatly facilitated by two recent publications: The Public Archives of Canada, *Union List of Manuscripts in Canadian Repositories* (Ottawa, 1968), and the Achives du Québec, *État Général des Archives Publiques et Privées* (Québec, 1968).

Thus both topics and documents await examination, but it remains problematical how many Canadian historians will turn their attention to business

---

[52] Merritt, J. P., *Biography of The Hon. W. H. Merritt, M.P.* (St. Catharines, 1875).

history in the near future. Social history is becoming more popular, political and constitutional problems remain as important as ever, and there is no shortage of figures in these fields for whom it would be relatively easy to prepare a biography. Biculturalism and separatist problems from Quebec are also continuing sources for argument. Further, even with the growth of graduate schools, there is no evidence that there will be a surfeit of competent Canadian historians in the next few years. In view of these circumstances can we expect any breakthrough in business history in Canada in the near future? There are two possibilities that appear to hold particular promise.

The first of these lies in the field of biography. Thanks to the generous bequest of the late James Nicholson of Toronto, ample funds are available for the publication of a multi-volume *Dictionary of Canadian Biography*. By arrangement of the first editor, the late George W. Brown (d. 1963) of the University of Toronto, the *Dictionary* is appearing in both English and French under the auspices of the universities of Toronto and Laval.[53] The very compilation of this dictionary itself is resulting in a vast increase in our knowledge of the careers of all the major Canadian entrepreneurs, and provision has been made to include biographies of figures who are not of the first rank of importance.[54] An allied project promises equally salutory results. This is a plan for a series of biographies of leading Canadian figures of secondary rank, which will be prepared by the authors who will write the articles on the same individuals in the *Dictionary*. The selection will include business figures, and G. Alan Wilson of Trent University, one of the editors of the series whose work on Northway has already been mentioned, is particularly interested in this field.[55] It can be further hoped that these biographies will stimulate interest in the corporations controlled by the individuals selected and the field of business history expanded accordingly.

Certainly the development of biographical studies in the field of business could lead to a much needed analysis of the place of the business men in Canadian history and answer many questions such as class influence on politics, inheritance of wealth, the effect of interlocking directorates. Although the irregularity of the appearance of early biographical dictionaries would create problems for the nineteenth century historian, in this century such works have become far more frequent. Examples of the type of work that would provide an excellent source are W. R. Houston's *Directory of*

---

[53] The first volume, containing biographies of those figures who died from 1000 to 1700 appeared in 1966, the second (1701-40) in 1969, and volumes are currently under way covering 1741-70 and 1871-80.

[54] An example of the type of entrepreneurial analysis that can rise from research for the *Dictionary* is Y. F. Zoltvany's "Some Aspects of the Business Career of Charles Aubert de la Chesnaye (1632-1702)," in *The Canadian Historical Association Historical Papers, 1968*, pp. 11-23, which developed out of his above mentioned *Dictionary* article.

[55] Wilson's idea on the need for biographies of secondary Canadian figures may be found in "Forgotten Men of Canadian History," *Canadian Historical Association Report*, 1965, pp. 71-86.

Directors in Canada (Toronto, 1906), and The Financial Post *Directory of Directors*, which was published biennially from 1931-1957 and has appeared annually since 1959.

As yet the literature in this field is very thin. Gustavius Myers, one of the American muckraking school of historians, put out *A History of Canadian Wealth* (Chicago, 1914), which is not too reliable, and in recent years sociologists have been taking an interest. John Porter's *The Vertical Mosaic* (Toronto, 1965), is the outstanding work in this area; it is subtitled "an analysis of social class and power in Canada." The only attempt at a collection of business biographies is Peter C. Newman, *Flower of Power: Intimate Portraits of Canada's Great Businessmen* (Toronto, 1959).

The second possibility for the expansion of business history in the near future lies in the suggestion of Professor Careless that we examine the role of the metropolis in order to arrive at a better understanding of our separate development. With the continuing search for a Canadian identity it is probable that more emphasis will be placed on this theme in the years to come, and an understanding of the role of the metropolis will certainly add greatly to our knowledge of Canadian business history. The field is a fascinating one that has virtually been unexplored. It may seem that Toronto and Montreal would dominate such an investigation, but no real attempt has yet been made to understand the significance of such centres as Halifax, Winnipeg, or Vancouver, let alone more recent rivals such as Edmonton. Their interaction with each other is not understood, nor is their relations with contiguous metropolitan areas south of the border.[56]

In conclusion I would like to suggest the type of materials that are available for one such study, using Toronto as an example. In spite of the importance of the city there is no authoritative history of Toronto, let alone a history of the business establishment; the same may be said for Montreal.[57] Beginning with the secondary sources, we have a considerable amount of work on Toronto. The late Percy J. Robinson wrote a *History of Toronto under the French Régime* (Toronto, 1933), which provides much information about the French and Indian trade from 1615 to 1793. For the period from the founding of the modern metropolis by Governor Simcoe in 1793 until its incorporation as a city in 1834, Edith G. Firth of The Toronto Public Libraries has prepared two volumes of documents with excellent in-

---

[56] For an analysis of the state of Canadian urban history and a bibliography of some of the more important works, see F. H. Armstrong, "Urban History in Canada," *Urban History Group Newsletter*, No. 28, (1969), pp. 1-10.

[57] The most extensive history of Toronto is Jesse E. Middleton, *The Municipality of Toronto, A History* (3 vols. Toronto, 1923); and of Montreal, William H. Atherton, *Montreal, 1535-1914* (3 vols. Montreal, 1914). Two enjoyable histories of Montreal are: Stephen Leacock, *Montreal Seaport and City* (Toronto, 1948); and John I. Cooper, *Montreal: A Brief History* (Montreal, 1969). Professor Gerald Tulchinsky of Queen's is now examining the entrepreneurial development of Montreal in the 1850's.

troductions and sections on commerce.[58] For the last years of the nineteenth century D. C. Masters' *The Rise of Toronto 1850-1890* (Toronto, 1947), provides a survey of the city's growth. This work is particularly important because Masters suggests the application of the metropolitan thesis of Norman S. B. Gras (1884-1956) as a yardstick in studying Canadian metropolitan development. Gras, an early graduate of the University of Western Ontario, did most of his work at the Harvard Business School. He believed that towns pass through certain definite stages in their growth to metropolitan status, an argument which he based on the study of London, England, and brought it forward in his *Introduction to Economic History* (New York, 1922).

With regard to what might be called semi-secondary material, the most scholarly picture of the early city was provided by Canon Henry Scadding in his *Toronto of Old*; a sort of historical guide book, based on both extensive research and personal reminiscences, which appeared in 1873 and has been a mine for all later writers on early Toronto. There is also an authorless *History of Toronto and the County of York*, dating from 1885, which includes short histories of every major business then existing in the city. The information it contains, some of it going back a half a century, is quite accurate to the extent that it can be checked against other sources. Finally the six volume *Landmarks of Toronto*, published by John Ross Robertson of the *Toronto Telegram* in 1894-1914, is another, though less accurate, source of information. Beyond these printed works, however, there are the extensive manuscript collections of the Ontario Archives, the City Archives, the Library of the University of Toronto, and, above all, the Toronto Central Library.

Using these data a historian could prepare a commercial history of Toronto which might well answer many important questions; how the city became independent of Montreal, why it rose to dominate Ontario, what its trade connections were with both the St. Lawrence cities and with New York State, how British policies, or later those of Ottawa, channeled its growth, and to what extent it dominates Canadian commerce and finance today.

For such future analysis it is to be hoped that some improvements will be effected in the level of writing business history. As noted, there has been some excellent work done by a few professional historians, such as William Kilbourn and Alan Wilson, but a great deal of the writing has been done by amateur historians, some good, some merely grinding out one history after another on a commission basis. In addition many companies are overly suspicious of the business historian, thinking of him only in the framework of the muckraker searching for scandals, rather than the scholar attempting to analyse his country's economic growth. There are all too many cases of the historian who was refused access to century old records because some official

---

[58] Firth, Edith G., *The Town of York*, Vol. 1, 1793-1815, (Toronto, 1962), and Vol. II, 1815-1834 (Toronto, 1966).

feared damage to the corporate image. There has also been too great a tendency for some companies to see a history as merely a glossy type of advertising brochure turned out by a journalist, or a eulogy for the founding family. Conversely, other companies have spent a great deal of money, allowed unlimited access to records and received a far worse history than they deserved in return.[59] Other weaknesses can result if the history is written by an employee, who usually lacks the literary excellence of the journalist, but at the same time often does not present a more coherent history.

A classic example of how Canadian business history should not be written can be found in *A Family of Thirty Million* (New York, 1934), the seventy-fifth anniversary history of the Metropolitan Life Insurance Company by Louis I. Dublin, Ph.D., Third vice President and Statistician. Dedicated to the Chairman of the Board and the President (with full page autographed pictures of both) and bearing acknowledgements to the First and Second Vice-Presidents, Actuary, Associate Actuary and Economist, it includes a chapter "The Company in Canada" which is only slightly longer than "The Company on the Pacific Coast." In this we learn that the history of both countries "reflects the vigour of the people, their intelligent initiative, their love of family life, and their devotion to democratic ideals."[60] Though such a history may be a fine example of the bad side effects of foreign ownership, it is certainly no worse than many local productions.

For an idea of what business history should do one can look not only at the works of the authors cited immediately above, but also at some much happier American precedents. For a survey of the evolution of business history in the United States there is an excellent article by Harold F. Williamson, Secretary of the American Economic Association, entitled "The Professors Discover American Business"[61] which is a must for the would-be writer of business history in Canada. Older works by N.S.B. Gras are the *Development of Business History up to 1950* (Ann Arbour, 1962), and a short guide to the would-be author: "Are you writing a business history?"[62]

In summary, then, Canadian business history is still an undeveloped field. In the past, business historians have tended to concentrate their researches on a few staple industries, and on an examination of the development of communications. Many of their theories will have to be re-examined, and almost all aspects of Canadian business history require further investigation. In our search for a national identity, however, economic development holds out

---

[59] See Michael Bliss' review of Merrill Denison's *Canada's First Bank: A History of The Bank of Montreal*, in Vol. II of the *Canadian Historical Review*, XLIX, (1968), pp. 288-89.

[60] Page 279.

[61] This appears in Ross M. Robertson and James L. Pate, eds. *Readings in United States Economic and Business History* (Boston, 1966), pp. 25-34.

[62] N. S. B. Gras, "Are you writing a business history?" *Business Historical Society, Bulletin*, XVIII (1944), pp. 73-110.

interesting possibilities. By exploring new paths, particularly along the lines of the metropolitan thesis suggested by Careless, we may arrive at a different economic interpretation for the evolution of the nation; one that will possibly be less nationalistic, but more realistic, than that of the Laurentian school.

Business Records: The Canadian Scene

John H. Archer, Principal, Regina Campus, University of Saskatchewan

Canadian historians have not generally used the term historical manuscripts to include the records of business concerns and the private papers of businessmen. Historians in Canada, especially those who wrote in the nineteenth century, were preoccupied with political history. This has been Canada's loss, for business records are part of the history of the country, and the failure to appreciate this truth led inevitably to the neglect of the resource. As a consequence of neglect much of the documentation for the early economic history of our country has disappeared and can never be replaced.

Canada's large basic business in the nineteenth century had to do with shipping, shipbuilding, lumbering, milling, distilling, fishing, railroad building and banking. Canada was a young nation rich in raw resources – a fertile field for the magnate with imagination and money. In the stern competition of the day the more powerful firms battened on the weaker, swallowing the small and merging with the larger. There was no call for, and little thought of, making public, details of business dealings. At the parish level were to be found the blacksmith, the brickmaker, the shoemaker, the storekeeper, the innkeeper and the miller. Historians and local historical societies generally ignored the records of such small businesses for these were family businesses and not national businesses. Not until the turn of the century was there rapid industrialization and then it was concentrated in Ontario and Quebec.

It was at the turn of the century, also, that there developed a stirring of interest in the history of commercial enterprise in Canada. There is some expression of this interest in the first report issued by the Bureau of Archives of Ontario for 1903. The archivist writes: "The importance of the early collecting of data concerning the business development of the Province has been urged by several correspondents, and in consequence of the representations made to me I have begun a collection of papers, maps, pamphlets, reports, surveys, etc. in connection with the promotion and construction of railways and canals in Ontario, and the hearty-co-operation promised by those with whom I am in communication shows a keen interest in this line of research."[1]

The Public Archives of Canada, an institution founded in 1872 for the express purpose of gathering the historical records pertaining to Canada, also took in business records, though these were thought to be secondary in importance to the records of an industrialist's public life. To some degree at least the national archival institution gathered business records by inadvertence. The Provincial Archives of British Columbia gathered the personal,

---

[1] Bureau of Archives of Ontario, *First Report of the Bureau of Archives for the Province of Ontario, 1903,* (King's Printer, 1904), p. 11.

and hence the business papers of commercial leaders in the fur trading, lumbering, mining, and transportation industries, for these latter were so much a part of the early history of the province. At one time or another every public archival institution in Canada has accessioned the records of businessmen and the records of business firms. But at no time has there been a consistent pattern of collecting. Business records have not fitted easily into the acquisition policies of public archival institutions in Canada.

The explanation does not lie in the fact that business records are not official government records. Archival statutes governing each public archival institution have at least one element in common – authorization to collect, process and preserve historical manuscript material other than public records. The explanation is much simpler. Business records were not considered to be historical records by either the archivist or historian of the nineteenth century. Since the existing public archival institutions of the period invariably turned to the historian for aid and advice it is reasonable to assume that the oversight was intentional.

Unquestionably the archivist of that day was aware, as his contemporary of today is aware, of the problems attendant in the collecting of business records. One great problem in the handling of business records is their bulk, which is usually out of all proportion to their historical value. In the absence of a company archivist or records manager the burden of weeding, stripping, and selecting for permanent preservation falls on the archivist in the depository invited to house the collection. Few archival institutions have the space and other resources needed to tackle large collections of unsifted material if these come in any number. A second problem with business records is the matter of access. There are legal and financial requirements demanded of businesses, and corporate bodies must keep records to satisfy these even though the records are private or business records and not public records. Because these records have been earmarked by the company they have generally been treated as restricted items not open to outside researchers. There is about company offices still a suspicion of enquirers and a suspicion of governments. Unless this is offset by a realization of the potential research value of the collection, the records generally remain closed. Short of space and of staff and with other, seemingly more fruitful lines of endeavour open to him, the archivist understandably came to look on business records as a future, rather than a present area for investigation.

There came a change in the thinking of historians at the turn of the century. The fixation on political and constitutional history began to give way to an interest in economic history. Significant of this changing climate was the establishment in 1917 of a Bureau of Historical Publications under the Chairmanship of Adam Shortt, a noted historian at Queen's University. Shortt was very much aware of the importance of the economic factor in history. He determined that others should be made aware of it also. Under his direction the Bureau published a volume of documents on Banking. The staff of the Bureau, among them Arthur M. Lower, were trained and constrained to seek out the economic influences on Canadian history. It is not surprising that in the decades following, a considerable number of volumes should be published marking the development and influence of the great staple industries of Canada and marking also, the influence of the St. Lawrence River on Canada's economic development.

If scholars are to understand and appraise the historical role of private enterprise in Canadian society, they simply must have access to business records. Business leaders may justly complain that Canadian history texts accent politics, wars, and dates and pay little attention to economic history save perhaps for beaver skins and wheat. No one, however, can adequately describe the role of business in Canada's history without access to business records. The only certain way to ensure that business records are preserved and administered for research purposes is to establish business archives.

There is a large reservoir of support for the argument that a corporation is not only responsible for living within the law of the host country but should, in addition, contribute to the country's general welfare. John Andreassen calls this the factor of "historical accountability" in his paper entitled "Canadian National Railway Records" written in 1963.[2] This is a good term; translated into active citizenship, it means either the opening of a company's records to accredited researchers or the deposit of records in an archival depository, where they become available to responsible scholars under whatever terms of access the company sets.

If archivists emphasize "historical accountability," which is another term for a sense of history and tradition, then surely company officers will emphasize security and confidentiality. This is understandable. There are trade secrets, there are competitors, there are muckrakers. Fortunately the days of excess seem to be of the past, and archivists can offer safekeeping. Company officers today recognize a changing climate of opinion.

Many companies have come to terms with the present in the matter of giving access to records. Private enterprise cannot keep enterprise "private" by closing its records. A developing sense of maturity permits company presidents today to admit that excesses took place and that mistakes were made. Dark areas have occurred in business history, but the historian is not seeking evidences of a shocker for the sake of shocking. He is interested in the whole story, in the whole context.

Some businesses have financed the writing of their histories. Merrill Denison's *History of the Bank of Montreal* is a prime example of a carefully researched and well documented history of an institution. It proves to the historian at least that the institution's records still exist. The historian re-

---

[2] John C. L. Andreassen, "Canadian National Railway Records," *Business History Review*, Spring, 1965, pp. 115-119.

spects the history as a reference tool but he is not likely to be completely satisfied with it as the definitive work on the subject. He will want to go over the same records that Denison worked through – and for an equally legitimate purpose. A business concern should not expect a history to be a satisfactory substitute for access to the original records. Nor should the company administrators feel free to throw out records once the history of the firm is published. A history, no matter how complete, is yet but one man's view. No historian will be satisfied to rely on memory or on a second-hand source.

The Hudson's Bay Company is a prime example of a business enterprise with a tradition, a sense of history, and a sense of historical accountability. Canadian history and Canadian scholarship generally would be much the poorer, but for the enlightened policy of the officers of the Company who saw to the preservation of the records and who made those records available for the researcher. The Hudson's Bay Record Society's publications, various volumes of the Champlain Society series, and the spate of works, fiction and nonfiction that have dealt with the Hudson's Bay Company are indisputable proof of the interest of scholars in the records produced in the course of day-to-day operations of the enterprise.

If a private chartered enterprise of long standing recognizes the factor of historical accountability so readily one would expect at least as marked an appreciation of history from a crown corporation, which is a public business. It comes as something of a shock to learn the the Public Archives of Canada does not have control over the records of crown corporations set up by the Canadian Parliament. The corporations in this respect are treated as private business concerns. It is to the credit of the officials of some of these corporations that they have voluntarily requested advice and assistance from the Public Archives and have made arrangements for the deposit of records in that institution. It is very much to the credit of the Dominion Archivist that he should command such implicit trust. One corporation does deserve special mention. This is the Canadian National Railways, which signed a formal agreement with the Public Archives of Canada. One man who deserves much credit for this arrangement is John C. L. Andreasssen, who was engaged as Systems Archivist of the CNR in 1962. He is now University Archivist at McGill.

Voluntary agreements voluntarily arrived at bespeak a mature attitude. But one wonders whether voluntary arrangements with federal crown or public corporations are good enough. Crown corporations' records are every whit as "public" as are the records of a department of government. Should the safekeeping of these records, then, depend on the interest evinced by executive officers and the tactful diplomacy of the Dominion Archivist? If there is any validity to the proposition that a private business making its "living" in Canada owes to its host the safekeeping of its records for scholarly research, then surely there is the strongest case for ensuring that the public records of public or crown corporations come under adequate controls to prevent wanton destruction.

Provincial governments in Canada have been much more forthright in this respect than has the Federal Government. Perhaps this is because the common type of crown corporation at the provincial level, the public utility, affects the lives of most citizens. In most instances there is but an indistinct line of demarcation between department and corporation. The majority of Canadian provinces have passed legislation bringing crown corporations within the compass of established public records programs. The development of public records programs at the provincial level, however, has been uneven. Many public utilities were set up before there was any thought of public records programs or records storage centres. Since these bodies were accountable to legislative committees for moneys spent, essential records were kept and records programs installed.

The Atlantic provinces show a mixture of public and private ownership in the utilities field. The Nova Scotia Power Commission was set up in 1919 as a publicly owned utility. The Nova Scotia Light and Power Co. functioned as a private concern. The New Brunswick Electric Power Commission is a public corporation and, both Nova Scotia and New Brunswick are served by privately owned telephone companies. The records of crown corporations in Nova Scotia, New Brunswick, Newfoundland, and Prince Edward Island come under legislation dealing with public records.

Quebec has passed no legislation dealing with public records. The Quebec Hydro-Electric Commission, a crown corporation, has contracted with the Records Management Co. of Canada for the management of its records. In Ontario the records of crown corporations, except for the Hydro-Electric Power Commission of Ontario, come under the legislation covering departmental public records. Ontario Hydro was excepted because it had developed a comprehensive and efficient internal records program, with the records open to scholarship.

In Manitoba, Saskatchewan, and Alberta crown corporations are specifically included in legislation covering public records. The Saskatchewan Power Corporation has developed a satisfactory records program internally and this is fully integrated with the general public records program of the province. When British Columbia Electric Co. was taken over by the provincial government, the company's records became the property of the Provincial Archives. British Columbia Telephones, a private concern, has a records program administered by a records management institute in New York.

The development of records programs for provincial crown corporations if uneven is, nevertheless, impressive. It will be more impressive yet for there has been a quickening of interest in archival matters at the provincial level with the result that every province now has a functioning archival program. Ten years, twenty years from today, such will be the imbalance as between the quantity of records of crown businesses and those of private businesses that there will be the danger of a wrong interpretation of the facts of Canadian business as it operated for the first century of confederation. Historians, perforce, must turn to the resources available and historical writings usually reflect the scope and depth of resources researched.

A close perusal of the *Union List of Manuscripts in Canadian Repositories*[3] gives considerable point to the warning voiced in the preceding paragraph. The Union List was produced in 1968 by the Public Archives of Canada. It is the result of years of field work and office work directed by the Public Archives of Canada, but made successful through the co-operation of archivists, librarians, museum curators, officials of historical associations and private collectors who reported holdings. While it is not always possible to distinguish between collections of business papers, the records of an enterprise, and business records, an integral part of the private papers of an individual, the format of the Union List makes it possible to give a considered estimate. It appears that Canadian depositories report some fifty-five significant collections of business papers. These are other than crown corporation records. The Public Archives of Canada has thirty of these though it reports in addition, other business records, part of collections of private papers. The provincial archival institutions report fourteen collections in all. There are eleven collections in university archival collections – in particular at Queen's and at the University of Western Ontario – in Glenbow Archives, in McCord Museum, and the New Brunswick Museum, and in the historical collection gathered by the Lennox and Addington Historical Society.

There are a few significant collections that have been accessioned since the *Union List of Manuscripts in Canadian Repositories* was published. The University of Waterloo received the records of the Home Bank which went into receivership in the nineteen-twenties. This banking firm had much to do with financing early farmer organizations in Western Canada and is an essential companion piece to the *Crerar Papers* held at Queen's University since Crerar was a director of the bank at one time, and was president of the United Grain Growers', a farmers' association that had considerable financial dealings with the Home Bank. Queen's University has recently accessioned records of the Kingston Shipping Company and the Fairbanks Morse Plant that recently closed down in Kingston.

The collections reported in the *Union List* cover such basic businesses as fishing, lumbering, general merchandising, banking, fur-trading, railway building, shipping, mining, distilling, iron-foundries, and brewing. Eighteen of the businesses were of the pre-Confederation era. The great majority were of the 1890-1925 period. There was only one firm that had been active after 1929. It is significant that there are very few records of later manufacturing companies or food processing companies or clothing firms. But before the

---

[3] A joint project of the Public Archives of Canada and the Humanities Research Council of Canada. Published in Ottawa in 1968.

too earnest researcher begins to compute the percentage of firms whose records have been saved, he should remember that many, many early firms were absorbed by larger firms. The Bank of Montreal, for example, absorbed numerous smaller banking concerns. Canada Steamship Lines, founded in 1913, took over twenty-six constituent companies, some going back to the 1850's. These records have survived, but they are not in archival institutions.

Though the picture set out above is somewhat austere, the present holds some promise of better things. There is a noticeable increase in the interest shown by business concerns in business archives. I do not refer to records programs here, but rather to archives such as the T. Eaton Company Archives, the Molson Brewing Company Archives, the Walker Museum and Archives in Windsor. In these last few years other concerns, including banks and other financial institutions, have followed this lead. Usually the business archives begins as an archives-cum-museum agency. Few, if any, would qualify as thoroughgoing archival institutions. They may become such, but it will be years before most companies switch from records to programs to company archives. Economic factors justify records programs. There must be present in the company, in addition, a strong sense of history and tradition before the officers will set up a company archives and, through it, make the firm's records available for research. I do not think that there will be any rush in this direction. A much more probable development will see universities clamouring for the records either as lone wolves or in more orderly fashion, under the umbrella of some national organization. For the sake of convenience to scholars I hope it is the latter.

It is very probable that universities in Canada will be, in the future, the dominant partner in gathering business records. Such is the competition for research materials in the humanities that no graduate faculty will feel itself well equipped unless it has a collection of historical manuscripts or literary papers or business records, all in addition to the library resources required. Universities are in a strong position when seeking the records of business concerns – particularly strong if the university has established university archives. Universities have a reputation for pursuing disinterested research. A university archivist can offer security, disinterested professionalism and a select user clientele. Certainly public archival institutions have no less a professional approach, and, in the main, offer a greater experience in archival methodology. But there has been evidenced in the past a certain reluctance on the part of some business concerns to turn over all their records to a governmental agency. While such a reluctance is understandable it is not one that can be defended from example, for the reputation for security and discretion in public archival institutions is of a high order. Nevertheless it seems certain that universities will press the search more vigorously and argue the need more forcefully than will competitors. Archivists in public archival institutions, acutely aware of space problems, have been very selective in the intake of business records.

Archival methodology as developed in public archival institutions in Canada is now generally applicable to university archives. The leadership shown by the Public Archives of Canada in extending the group principle of arrangement to include non-governmental material has made it comparatively easy for an archivist to deal with manuscript collections. Business records fit readily into such an arrangement. The nature of business records, however, precludes any compulsory transfer to governmental centres. They are a resource to be sought in an open arena. The university archivist has an advantage over his competitors in the matter of processing costs for a great deal of such work can be done in university archives by graduate students, working under his direction.

Records programming has become a much talked about topic this past decade. The relationship of records management to archival work frequently comes under discussion. Richard H. Lytle's article raises the important matter of a widening isolation between the two professions as apparent in the United States.[4] As a Canadian archivist who has been the chairman of a public documents committee and also a university archivist, I read the article with deep interest, but not with the same concern evidenced by some university archivists in the United States. Because of the tradition of public archives in Canada most archivists in the public service, whether at the provincial or federal level, are involved in records programs and in archival programs. Every public archival institution in Canada, save one, acts as a public records office and as an archival repository for historical manuscripts. At the higher levels at least, every archivist in the public service in Canada, provincial or federal, is betimes both records manager and archivist.

This tradition has not carried over completely into the university field in Canada, but it is still strong. Again, the reasons are to be found in our history. The older universities in Canada – McGill, Queen's, Laval, Dalhousie, the University of Toronto, and the University of Western Ontario – were established, and had their own libraries and graduate schools before most provinces had established public archival institutions. These university libraries acquired manuscripts and the librarians worried these treasures, and worried themselves, in their efforts to manage them. Only at Queen's and at Laval was a conscious decision made to establish a University Archives which would be both a records office for the institution and a repository for research materials in manuscript form. McGill and the University of Toronto each established an archival institution but circumscribed the role to that of a records office for the university served. Only at McGill was the Univer-

⁴ Richard H. Lytle, "The Relationship between Archives and Records Management: an Archivist's View," *Records Management Quarterly*, April, 1968, pp. 5-8.

sity Archivist made a ranking officer of the university, reporting directly to ths Principal.

Lytle, in his article, writes of the preoccupation of university archivists with the needs of scholarship. Quite frankly, though I was at once a professor of History and University Archivist, I did not hold such a preoccupation. Certainly Queen's University Archives was a rich resource for graduate research in the humanities, and I was concerned that the holdings in the Archives be processed for users. But I considered my primary task as Archivist to be the establishment of the Archives as the records office for the university. Such a project would mean a thorough-going records management program covering all offices in the university. I did not expect any serious arguments from my colleagues in history, nor did I expect any insurmountable resistance from the administration.

No single Canadian archival depository has strong collections of business records, sufficient to support a broad graduate program of research. The *Union List of Manuscripts in Canadian Repositories* is a most valuable research tool in this connection, for it lists business papers from all depositories in Canada; and, where family papers have a business connection, this aspect is mentioned. Still, the total is disappointingly small, and the rate of intake very slow. There are not sufficient business archives established to give any assurance that business records will be preserved for research purposes without further effort on someone's part. We must do better than sit in contemplation of this scene.

Records programs there are in the business world, and even the most skeptical archivist will welcome these. But, if a records program means that the essential records of a company are to be preserved and locked away from scholars, then one's joy can be restrained. Even here, if there is a choice between a records program operated by a records management concern, or no program, archivists will of course opt for the program. As a matter of fact, a records program operative in a company makes the ordering of the records of the company, should these come to an archival institution, a simple matter. Indeed, the mass quantity of business records will not be so great a problem in the future as records programs become the rule rather than the exception.

There are scores of businesses, however, which hold old records, unused, stowed away in second-grade storage. Some of these businesses have changed hands and the old records have been forgotten. Some old records have been deliberately forgotten. In some instances family businesses have been discontinued, and the mute evidence of the history of such enterprises moulders in attic and warehouse. Fire, mildew, vermin, and souvenir hunters will eventually erase the last evidence of such remnants of Canada's economic history.

Even when old records in bulk have been rescued by some enterprising sleuth and deposited in an archival institution, the struggle is not over. The staff of that institution is faced with the long, dirty, expensive task of sorting, cleaning, and arranging the collection. Few archival institutions have the staff or budget or space to cope with many large deposits of old records. The problem will be less pressing in the future if records managers have their way. It seems to me reasonable that the archival institution taking in old records in bulk, and making them available for research, should receive outside financial assistance. Whether such assistance comes from a foundation or in the form of a special grant from a corporation makes little difference. True, the institution receiving the records, if it is a university institution, thereby acquires unique resources that may be a factor in attracting faculty and researchers. That increment, it seems to me, might balance off the costs of servicing and housing a collection that had been acquired through a records program. But a large collection of old unsorted records is another matter.

This still does not make good a noticeable lack in Canada's archival resources. No haphazard program is likely to result in a concentration of similar resources in one or more places where researchers may do comparative studies or research in depth. Perhaps this lack may be made good through the work of a council representing the national interests of business and scholarship. Perhaps this will be the role of the Business Archives Council of Canada. It would seem that such a council would be acceptable to the business community and to the community of archivists. In any event the formation of the Council is a sign of vigour and good intentions in an area that has lain fallow for many years.

The Business Archives Council of Canada, as it is presently constituted, seeks to apply the American concept of specialized repositories for business records. To this American concept the Council would apply the British device of a voluntary self-supporting organization with a head office, to act as a co-ordinating agency. The head office would carry on correspondence and negotiations at the national level; the regional depositories would carry on the practical work of deposit, processing and use.

As a pilot project only and certainly not with any intention of pre-empting region or precedence, the Council, in 1968, designated Queen's University Archives as a depository. Queen's has a strong archival tradition and a nucleus of trained archival staff. From such a base it was hoped that Queen's University Archives might become a depository for business firms operating in the St. Lawrence region. The Council envisages that other depositories will spring up in the Atlantic Provinces, in Quebec, in Northern Ontario, in the Niagara Peninsula, in the Prairie Provinces, in British Columbia – anywhere that space, staff, resources and opportunity unite to make for a feasible operation. It is not considered to be the purpose of the Council to control the policies of the depositories. The Council, it is expected, would be concerned with general policy; the depositories would be autonomous, acting in unison through the Council to the greater advantage of all.

The role of the Council as outlined above should have an appeal to researchers. When fully operative it would concentrate resources of business records in regions, bringing together records from business concerns operating in each region. I cannot see such a concern as the Saskatchewan Wheat Pool agreeing to send its records to a depository in the Atlantic Provinces, but there would be a good argument for depositing these records in the prairie region. If this were done, and if other business concerns cooperated, the records of the Wheat Pool would be held along with the records of farm implement companies, milling concerns, meatpacking businesses, and a number of service industry records. Of course the Council would encourage companies to establish internal archives.

It is a great Canadian pastime to lay the blame for sins of omission on our ancestors, while outlining grandiose plans for our progeny. Well may we ask with a former distinguished Canadian historian, George W. Brown: "What would we not give for the early records of the Cunard Company or of the Canada Company, burned as junk?" And we can agree with him when, on learning that the early records of an important Canadian industry were cut up for toilet paper for the company's employees, he remonstrated that "such a measure is hard to justify even as a war-time economy." But are we any less guilty than our predecessors? We have resources of money, staff and techniques never dreamed of by the men of old. Our capacity to pay lip service to the importance of history seems unlimited. But, if it had not been for the work of public archival institutions in housing some business records, our cupboards would be bare indeed. We must now do more.

Any panoramic view of business records in Canada must seem to be edged in black, though rays of optimism may occasionally gleam through the dusk. A closer examination, however, seems to indicate that the period of neglect may be nearly over. Canadian businesses are concerned with systems of records management. Of a list of thirty firms chosen to give wide coverage of both size and interest, thirteen had, on examination, instituted some system of records management. Seven concerns had taken the further step and had organized archives staffed in each case with at least one full-time person. Ten concerns had made no special effort to preserve vital records or to maintain older, dormant records. Not altogether black! If the trend toward records managers and archivists continues and if we can provide the vehicle to get business records into the mainstream of research we may yet salvage much of our economic past. Whether the researcher uses the records in a business archives or some other archival institution will not be a major concern. It will be important, however, that resources are made known through some central facility. If we can plant deep the appreciation of, and the need for business archives, as we cater to the needs of scholars who would research business records, we will have accomplished much. Perhaps then we may be permitted to leave to the next generation the problems of record storage centres for industry and business, the concentration of research resources, and the dissemination of information on resources made available.

Appendix

A selection of significant collections of Business Archives listed in the *Union List of Manuscripts*, with details of the contents and locations of these collections. The papers are listed in order to give some idea of the range of material which is available for research.

1. Anderson, Alexander Caulfield, 1814-84. Chief trader, Hudson's Bay Company, and Commissioner of Fisheries. Correspondence, journals, certificates and notes of the period 1836-84, including letters to and from prominent business personalities (e.g. Sir George Simpson) and mostly concerning the affairs of the Hudson's Bay Company, *Provincial Archives of British Columbia, Victoria, B.C.*

2. Bank of British North America (established 1836). Audit books, ledgers, and minute books of director's meetings, 1836-1918; Minutes of the daily committee of directors, 1837-1918; correspondence of the New York Agency, 1873-1918; superintendent's records. *Public Archives of Canada, Ottawa.*

3. Baring Brothers and Co. Records, 1781-1878, relating to the economic development of Canada, the United States, and Latin America, including correspondence from agents and private individuals and letterbooks, maps and printed material. *Public Archives of Canada, Ottawa.*

4. Bernard, Leslie Gordon, 1890-1961. Author. Manuscript short stories, plays, speeches and addresses, c. 1932-61; correspondence and unfinished manuscripts; travel notes and diaries, 1917 to and 1960. *McGill University Library, Montreal.*

5. Buchanan Family Papers, 1697-1883. Merchants and politicians; Correspondence and papers relating to land and legal matters, 1697-1887; account books; business papers relating to general trade, wholesale-retail and agency business and railway promotion, c. 1884-1890. *Public Archives of Canada, Ottawa, and Hamilton Public Library, Hamilton, Ontario.*

6. Calvin Co., Garden Island, Kingston. Timber merchants, ship-builders and forwarders. Letterbooks, account books, 1837-1913. *Queen's University Archives, Kingston,* and the *Public Archives of Canada, Ottawa.*

7. Canada Company 1824-1953, held in the *Ontario Department of Public Records and Archives, Toronto,* and in the *Public Archives of Canada, Ottawa.* These records include correspondence, 1824-1953, minute books, letters of credit, reports, maps and plans, correspondence of John Galt, Robert Wilmot and other officials of the Company, share records, etc.

8. Canadian National Railways. Original minute books, correspondence, letterbooks and miscellaneous records of over three hundred railway, land and steamship companies, dating from the period 1848-1950, absorbed by the C. N. R. *Public Archives of Canada, Ottawa.*

9. Cartwright Family, Kingston, 1779-1913. Merchants and politicians. These records include letterbooks of Richard Cartwright, 1793-5, and correspondence on business matters, 1825-44, 1858-1907, as well as miscellaneous business papers. *Public Archives of Canada, Ottawa; Ontario Department of Public Records and Archives, Toronto; Canadian History and Manuscript Section, Toronto Public Library; Archives of Queen's University, Kingston, Ontario.*

10. Chamberlin, Brown Papers, 1818-1894. Author and Queen's Printer. Correspondence and other papers relating to private, business, and political affairs, and to the Canadian Commission for the International Exhibition in London in 1862. *Public Archives of Canada, Ottawa.*

11. Co-operative Union of Canada, 1906-1952. By-laws, minutes and correspondence of the Union, with account books and financial records. *Public Archives of Canada, Ottawa.*

12. S. A. Crowell and Co, 1870-1911. Merchants in Yarmouth, Nova Scotia. The records include correspondence, 1870-1900, letterbooks, 1876-1902, circulars, price-lists, orders received and account books, 1870-1911. *Public Archives of Canada, Ottawa.*

13. Davidson Family, New Brunswick, 1765-1955. Businessmen and lawyers in the province, with interests centred on Newcastle and the Miramichi. Correspondence, 1784-1902, land grants, 1786-1854, diaries and personal papers, *New Brunswick Museum, Saint John, New Brunswick.*

14. Dixon Brothers, Maple Creek, Saskatchewan, 1863-1922. Storekeepers and general merchants. Papers relating to business, political and family affairs. *Saskatchewan Archives Board, Legislative Library, Regina, Saskatchewan.*

15. Ellice Papers, 1770-1880. Merchants, landowners, and politicians in Lower Canada and London. Correspondence 1764-1875; documents relating to property holdings and diaries; papers concerning the North West Company. *National Library of Scotland, Edinburgh; Public Archives of Canada, Ottawa; Ontario Department of Public Records and Archives, Toronto; Canadian History and Manuscript Section, Toronto Public Library.*

16. Ermatinger Family, 1759-1876. Fur traders, merchants and magistrates in Montreal. Correspondence of Lawrence Ermatinger, 1765-80; account book, journal of the Clallum Expedition (Puget Sound), 1828; letters relating to police and militia work, 1854-63. *Public Archives of Canada, Ottawa; Provincial Archives of British Columbia, Victoria, B.C.; Special Collections Division, University of British Columbia Library, Vancouver.*

17. Flavelle, Sir Joseph Wesley, 1858-1939. Financier and industrialist. Records relating to the Munitions Board, 1915-38, and to the Grand Trunk Railway, 1917-38. *Public Archives of Canada, Ottawa.*

18. Gilmour and Hughson Ltd, 1845-1926. Timber and general merchants. Correspondence, 1847-1924, letterbooks, 1877-1921, account books, 1873-1925. *Public Archives of Canada, Ottawa.*

19. Great West Sadlery, Winnipeg, Edmonton, and Calgary, 1899-1956. Files, business correspondence and legal papers, Edmonton 1907-31, current account ledgers, Calgary, 1899-1946. *Glenbow Foundation, Calgary, Alberta.*

20. Hudson's Bay Company. Transcripts and original papers, 1671-1906, including minute books, 1671-1707, factory journals and correspondence, accounts, invoices and trading and financial records, legal papers and business correspondence. *Public Archives of Canada, Ottawa; Provincial Archives of British Columbia, Victoria, B.C.; Special Collections Division, University of British Columbia Library, Vancouver; Ontario Department of Public Records and Archives, Toronto.*

21. Kerry and Chace Ltd, 1887-1938. Toronto manufacturers, Specifications and reports, 1887-1926, appropriations, 1910-38, specifications and contracts, 1909-29. *Public Archives of Canada, Ottawa.*

22. Kirkpatrick Nickle Papers, 1840-. Legal firm in Kingston, Ontario; various records of the firm of Thomas Kirkpatrick, (later Nickle and Nickle), from 1840 to date. *Queen's University Archives, Kingston, Ontario.*

23. Lester – Garland Family, 1761-1834. Timber and fish merchants of Poole, Dorset, England, and Trinity, Newfoundland. Extracts from diaries and letterbooks, (microfilm). *Public Archives of Canada, Ottawa.*

24. Lowe, John, 1848-1913. Politician, journalist and editor. Correspondence relating to farming interests in Manitoba, to the Department of Agriculture, to the British American Bank Note Company, 1867-1901, and letterbook of the Evening Telegraph, 1860-68. *Public Archives of Canada, Ottawa.*

25. Matador Land and Cattle Co., 1905-1924. Letterbook, 1906-1909, correspondence regarding sale, 1920-24, and on ranching operations, cattle sales and shipments. *Saskatchewan Archives Board and Office, Regina.*

26. McLachlan, Duncan W., 1909-1961. Engineer and civil servant. Correspondence, 1909-61, including material and diaries on the St. Lawrence Seaway. *Public Archives of Canada, Ottawa.*

27. Merritt Papers, 1775-1897. Merchants in the Niagara district. Correspondence, 1804-60,

notebooks and diaries, 1808-1855; ledgers and stock books of the Welland Canal Company, 1829-46. *Public Archives of Canada, Ottawa.*

28. Newman, Hunt and Co., 1774-1899. Importers, (formerly Robert Newman and Co.) at Harbour Breton, Newfoundland. Ledgers, account books, and letterbooks relating to the port wine and codfish trade, (microfilm). *Public Archives of Canada, Ottawa.*

29. North West Company. Correspondence, accounts, inventories, agreements, Beaver Club Minute Book, journals, letterbooks, and other records, c.1780-1860. *Public Archives of Canada, Ottawa; Provincial Archives of British Columbia, Victoria, B.C.; Ontario Department of Public Records and Archives, Toronto; Canadian History and Manuscript Division, Toronto Public Library; Department of Rare Books and Special Collections, University of Toronto Library.*

30. W. and J. Sharples Reg'd, 1854-1923. Merchants in Quebec. Correspondence and memoranda, 1854-1917, accounts, 1866-1921. *Public Archives of Canada, Ottawa.*

31. Western Stock Growers'Association, Calgary, Alberta, 1896-1960. Constitution and minutes, 1896-1960, Directors' correspondence, 1920-46, general correspondence, 1920-54, financial records, 1912-53, and records of the Stock Growers' Protective Association of Western Canada. *Glenbow Foundation, Calgary, Alberta.*

Significant collections of Business Archives not listed in the *Union List of Manuscripts.* These are held by the companies concerned.
1. Bank of Montreal (Montreal)
2. Bell Telephone (Toronto, Montreal, Fredericton, Halifax)
3. British Columbia Electric (B.C. Archives, Victoria)
4. Canada Steamship Co. (Montreal)
5. Canadian Pacific Railway (Montreal)
6. Crerar Papers (Queen's University, Kingston)
7. T. Eaton Co. (Toronto)
8. Home Bank of Canada (Waterloo University, Waterloo)
9. Merrill Denison Papers (Queen's University, Kingston)
10. Molson's Brewery (Montreal)
11. Montreal Board of Trade (Montreal)
12. Quebec Hydro (Quebec and Montreal)
13. Saskatchewan Power Corporation (Regina)
14. Saskatchewan Telephones (Regina)
15. Saskatchewan Wheat Pool (Regina)
16. Robert Simpson Co. (Montreal)
17. Sun Life Assurance Co. (Montreal)

EDITOR'S NOTE
To the lists of papers above, provided by Dr. J. H. Archer, the following important collections might be added.
1. Records of William Forsyth and Co, general merchant in Halifax c.1785-1798, *Public Archives of Nova Scotia.*
2. Papers of James Keith, of the North West and Hudson's Bay Company, c.1800-1851, *Archives of Davidson and Garden, Aberdeen, Scotland.*
3. Records of R.R. Thompson, merchant, of Shelburne, Nova Scotia, 1801-1871, *Public Archives of Nova Scotia.*
4. Correspondence of James Dunlop, Montreal merchant, 1792-1815, *Scottish Record Office, Edinburgh.*
5. Melville Papers, with many references to the timber and general trades, in the *Scottish Record Office and the National Library of Scotland, Edinburgh.*

6. Boyd Papers, 1832-1940 relating to lumbering, transportation, and agriculture in Ontario and Saskatchewan.

In addition to the collections listed above, the *Union List of Manuscripts in Canadian Repositories*, published by the Public Archives of Canada, Ottawa, contains many references to smaller groups of business records and of family papers which often contain material relating to business. Two examples of such entries are:

1. The Papers of William Edgar, Montreal fur trader and exporter in the period 1750-84, and China trader in New York from the latter date. These are held in the National Archives.
2. The Papers of John Abell of Woodbridge, Ontario, (1822-1903) manufacturer of agricultural implements. These include the accounts of the firm for the period 1857-1913, and the collection is held in the Ontario Department of Public Records and Archives, Toronto.

Numerous other entries of this type are to be found in the *Union List*, which is a mine of information about existent sources for the study of business history.

Problems and Traditions of Business History: Past Examples and Canadian Prospects

Alan Wilson, Professor of History, Trent University

Few historians will accept Professor William Kilbourn's attempt to define business history by example: he suggested that the best business history written in Canada, or anywhere else, is E. J. Pratt's long narrative poem on building of the C.P.R., *Towards the Last Spike*. Certainly, in research, understanding and grandeur in execution, Pratt puts most of us to shame. But historians, from want of talent or material, adopt more prosaic forms and humbler imagery than Pratt, and many see little poetry and less sense in special attention to business history. Many historians dispute the value of tracing single-unit company history, and economists share their scepticism; such history seems only a sub-branch of micro-economics, with few landmarks beyond static economic theory and pointless chronology. Many historians dismiss business history in the same breath as economic history: as one earlier historian put it, "After all, we are all economic historians," and that half-truth seemed to put an end to the subject. H. A. L. Fisher declared that history cannot be made of laundry bills, and few challenged the implication that laundry bills have nothing to do with history.

Study of the history of business and businessmen appealed to a few muckraking American historians, but even serious Marxist students have not pursued its possibilities for their purposes. Many intellectuals capped their contempt for the businessman himself with a rejection of his activities as a fit field for historical study. They agreed with the wag who remarked that the difference between the professions and business was the difference between great learning and no learning.

Indeed, business history as it was written until quite recently frequently and deservedly had a bad press. It was too mechanistic, too isolated, too prone to ignore theoretical questions of importance to the economist, and too ready to pass over questions of business's relationship to social, intellectual, environmental and other so-called "external" conditions.

But it is only forty years since the field was first systematically begun in Europe and the United States, and it was perhaps unreasonable to expect a philosophic dimension to arise immediately. Broad vistas do not come to pioneers whose heads are bowed over the stumps and the plough. More sophisticated business history writing would depend upon the extent and nature of the sources available to study past business activity, and the process

Note: This chapter was presented as a Killam Lecture at Dalhousie University, Halifax, on March 22, 1971, during the author's residence as Senior Killam Fellow 1970-71.

of collecting business records was formidable. Perhaps this collection process itself helped to limit the historian's horizon; in any case in Canada we have not yet seriously undertaken this first stage of establishing business archives. There may be a lesson for us, then, in looking at beginnings and developments elsewhere.

In fact, failure to accept the value of business studies arose from two circumstances: first, the lack of sufficient materials and the businessman's reluctance to yield up his records; second, the paradox of too little early definition of the field, and too much.

Large-scale preservation of business history records preceded large-scale research and publication, even in Europe where both first began. Interest in the Fuggers and Welsers is old; the Fugger banking archives in Augsburg and the Cotta publishing archives in Stuttgart are long-established sources for studies of merchants in the Renaissance setting. But at the end of the nineteenth century the Germans established more widely other types of archives useful to economic and business historians. Incidentally, the Austrians, Dutch and Swiss followed the German lead in most respects.

The first, and least systematically assembled in Germany, are family archives, the private papers of business and labour figures. These, perhaps the papers of greatest interest to the entrepreneurial historian, are still the thinnest remains. The second are public archives, state and municipal, which in Germany have a particular value. Late eighteenth and early nineteenth century Germany frequently witnessed greater government than private enterprise in ventures such as mining, iron, salt and china production; in Prussia the state assumed control of the railroads and of the Saar mines; in many places there was a heavy emphasis upon public utilities. A mixed economy naturally enhanced the importance of public archives. Moreover, another influence derived from the German historical school of economists, many of them bureaucrats, whether teachers or administrators: few of them were socialists, but in advocating state coordination of economic and social resources, they prompted the centralization of economic activity and records. For quite different reasons, the Nazis called for similar steps; later, after the Nuremberg investigations of the Krupp empire, there emerged a huge collection of German business materials.

More recently, in East Germany the Marxist doctrine of economic determinism, and the law, both require that all businesses deposit their records in state archives, to be used as fodder in the production of general history and of edifying "factory histories" which are used as the means of "socializing" the workers. A greater prostitution of Clio would be hard to find – unless it is one of those cloying, adulatory company histories produced in the west for public relations.

A third form of German business archive, the *Betriebsarchiv*, or "house archive," is the large corporation's own depository of its extensive earlier records. The first was the Krupp archives, begun in 1906 and soon copied by other companies in the Ruhr area; others included the I. G. Farbenindustrie collection, the Siemens electrical museum-archive in Munich, and the Daimler-Benz in Stuttgart. This movement flourished in the thirties, often with a very practical purpose. Germany had produced no schools of business administration, but some firms wanted an internal house history to serve their operational review and improvement – a case method, on-the-job training for their executives, backed by a corps of commissioned historians and archivists of high calibre. But many other firms offered conditional access to independent historians. For the company concerned a certain prestige attaches to having its own archives, but there is also practical benefit from more efficient records-management programs. The example has been followed elsewhere, and large corporations such as Ford, Hudson's Bay, Lloyd's and Swift's have established archives and commissioned house histories, often retaining their archival and historical advisers permanently. The commissioned historians and independent students alike have benefited materially.

Finally, in Germany there developed another class of archives, the *Wirtschaftsarchive*, or "regional archives." There were really joint commercial and industrial depositories set up on a regional basis. Often they were a kind of condominium set up by branch operational units of a single corporation, as if, say, the old Dosco had set up one records center for both its Sydney steel and its Halifax ship repair operations. In other cases, as in the Ruhr valley, where competition was blunted by overlapping ownership, the *Wirtschaftsarchive* were founded by seeming industrial competitors who combined their records and their photographic and technological exhibits; or again, Swiss and German banks, current competitors, pooled their non-current records for joint reference and for access by *bona fide* scholars.

But these *Wirtschaftsarchive* were commonly established also by regional chambers of commerce, assisted by the municipality, and starting with Cologne in 1906. After the usual period of growth in the 'thirties, the movement was resumed after the war, through close regional cooperation by business, municipal and university representatives. Bringing together non-governmental manuscript and printed material dealing with economics, business, and regional planning, these collections often reflect the metropolitan character and ambition of important cities and industrial valleys. The professional historian may have to tread carefully through forests of local pride and hyperbole, but embarrassing as such promotional literature may be, it is also evidence to the serious historian of the area's attitudes and identity.

Much of this German activity, which I have only sketched, established models and precedents in collecting. In Germany itself, it prompted an early production of business and allied economic histories, principally by the firms themselves. In 1956 at Munich there appeared the important business and economic journal, *Tradition*. American collecting and development parallelled and in some ways surpassed this German achievement.

In the U.S., business history was long synonymous with Harvard. Collections were begun at Harvard's Widener and Baker Libraries between 1910 and 1930. The appearance of the Harvard Commission on Western History encouraged librarians and economic historians to begin the systematic collection of business and allied family records. After its founding in 1908, Harvard's School of Business Administration mirrored the enterprise of the university's law school by adopting the historical "case method" of instruction. This move led to the development of the Slater Collection of economic, business and governmental materials relating to cotton and woollen manufacture. With the founding of a Business Historical Society at Harvard in 1925, the introduction of a quarterly (now *Business History Review*) in 1926, and the completion of the Baker Library in 1927, large-scale discovery and collation of business records was established. By 1970 the Baker's Manuscript Division held nearly 1500 separate collections, many of them extending to hundreds of volumes of manuscript business records. Significantly, however, business history at Harvard was still essentially functional and related to the new graduate purposes of the Harvard Business School, although there was cooperation from the university's academic departments of history and economics.

Harvard's pioneering work pushed it to the leading position in the world as a business records center, and justified its early presumption to be a national depository. But when conditions warranted, the university promptly recognized the need for decentralization. Harvard transferred to Yale, Michigan and elsewhere papers relating to other regions. The Baker now emphasizes its New England collection, but Harvard has not confined its collections to American records. It holds hundreds of volumes dealing, for example, with the Florentine fifteenth and sixteenth century wool industry, local records of nineteenth century Welsh industry, and fifteen volumes of manuscript material relating to German railway construction in China. Similarly, Columbia and Chicago's John Crerar libraries house important German business and industrial materials.

The most aggressive American institution, however, has been Northwestern, where, in addition to adopting the German depository practice, they have encouraged and gone beyond Harvard in adopting a *Betriebsarchiv* enterprise in cooperation with business firms. The university undertakes the writing of a company history, recommends an internal archival staff, charges a competent, specialized historian with the writing, which the company then finances under a strict, legally conditioned contract. The way is then open to establishing a permanent company archive and the production of supplementary histories by Northwestern's staff and graduates. No other American school operates so clearly on a business basis, and although the studies are often limited in scope, one result has been to strengthen the principle of university-centered activity in the field, and to make available to all students many more business records and studies.

The American collections have certainly been extensive, but they have not always been as systematic as one could wish. Many collections have arisen out of the research interests of particular scholars or schools, which has provided a valuable motivation and momentum, but it has not ensured a *national* program of recovery and of registration. In that regard we may have something to learn from British experience.

Although the British have shown only a fraction of the Germans' and Americans' enthusiasm for business training and for business history, they were not without their own prophets. They just ignored them. W. R. Scott and G. W. Daniels pioneered in business and industrial studies before 1920, and new momentum was afforded when Cunningham and Ashley laid the foundation of modern British economic history. But the unsystematic growth of British business histories is typified by the appearance in 1924 of George Unwin's *Samuel Oldknow and the Arkwrights*, which was made possible by the chance discovery of a cache of papers found by a troop of Boy Scouts in an abandoned stable! (Of course, British mediaeval economic studies were an exception to this pattern.)

The chief problem in the modern fields in Britain was the absence of systematic collections of business records, although records of chartered companies were often lodged in public archives. Consequently, as the Depression took its toll of more companies and their records, there arose early in 1934 a Council for the Preservation of Business Archives under the distinguished auspices of Stanley Baldwin, W. H. Beveridge, and Professors J. H. Clapham, G. N. Clark and A. F. Pollard. These principals had considerable business backing and the support of the London School of Economics and London's Institute of Historical Research.

While the British Council advanced many sound reasons for preserving business records, one of the most novel has become increasingly appreciated since their first statement in 1937:

> Our present knowledge of much modern economic and business history rests largely on the various governmental inquiries, like those of the early factory conditions or on the crises of the nineteenth century. The immediate origin of such official inquiries has often been some pathological condition of business which aroused public comment. As a result our knowledge of normal business conditions and history is much less full, and, with the records in private possession and their existence frequently unknown to students, such knowledge is harder of attainment.

As David Macmillan once remarked, "To write business history from government enquiries, when industries are depressed and in difficulties, is like writing the history of marriage from the records of the Divorce Courts."

Although the British Council was never as well funded as the Germans and the Americans, it accomplished a great deal on slight resources. Winning the respect of many private companies, it began a series of regional enquiries soliciting from firms information on their records, asking the right of scholarly access, and the chances of independent deposit for company records – from which an impressive "Register" was steadily compiled. The war and its reminders of mortality prompted an even greater cooperation, and by 1954 a national register and a central library of company histories and entrepreneurial biographies were accomplished facts. Perhaps more important, there has since developed a broadening of university cooperation in discovery and deposit, notably at Liverpool, Manchester, Swansea, Glasgow and Edinburgh. British interest and achievement in the field has also advanced the establishment of company house archives in Britain. The British Business Archives Council has published an annual report of its activities (*Business Archives*), as well as occasional papers dealing with archival techniques and special projects. But it was not until 1958 that the journal *Business History* appeared as a complement to the Americans' *Review* and the Germans' *Tradition*. Significantly, *Business History* is published by a university (Liverpool), and boasts a board of leading businessmen and economic historians from the old and new British universities; a Scottish Business ·Archives Council was more recently formed, and it flourishes at Glasgow. Thus, the range and quality of British activity in business history has been greatly strengthened, the universities showing the greatest interest and promise.

I stress this last point because it leads to a principle inherent in American, British and Australian activity – and one which Canadians, who have done so little in the field, must face. Is a joint universities' archival project preferable to a scheme embracing the various state archives in Canada? The other councils enjoy a preponderance of businessmen and of university historians in their membership and direction. These advocates – and the Germans have moved further in this direction recently – see certain advantages in a university connection in the development of business studies and collections.

One of the strongest arguments for university repositories is simply that, in addition to providing readily available research and teaching materials, they have operated elsewhere with small staffs and at reasonable cost. Much of the classification has been assisted by scholars and research assistants, as well as by the participating companies themselves.

The case for university business archives also relates to the problem of mutual confidence. Experience elsewhere suggests that business is not so ready to cooperate with state archivists as with academics. Harvard, Northwestern, London, Liverpool, Glasgow, Sydney and Canberra have all set a pattern of confidentiality which has encouraged business firms to make the universities the repositories of their non-current records. Much has been required in academic statesmanship and cooperation, both with business and among the universities. The companies concerned have gained several assurances: that access would be given only to *bona fide* scholars; that sound rules would be set regarding publication and deposit; that these arrangements would reduce the chance of infringement of governmental regulations and tax practices, which might discourage transfer in the case of some state archives. Public records offices often have fairly prescribed policies regarding deposit, and there can arise difficulties in establishing restricted or closed collections in essentially public archives. On the other hand, too often state archivists collect state and bureaucratic papers so complacently and exclusively that they show little conviction and less initiative in tracking down other forms of historical record. General economic and business records, particularly at the provincial level, have often been among the most neglected by archivists in Canada, and the initiative shown by universities elsewhere ought to prompt Canadian universities to consider these matters closely.

The field of collections, however, cannot be divorced from the question of achievement in writing business history. I said earlier that lack of sources and differences over definition of goals were at the root of the failure of business history to gain greater recognition and respect from the non-specialists. By speaking at length about how the sources were marshalled I have run a risk, for in presenting so much information on the facilities for business history I may seem to beg the question of why it is worth doing in the first place. Tolstoy described the "new history" as a deaf man answering questions which no one had asked. To turn to the problem of definition may throw some further light on the question of motivation and of the broader utility of business history.

American business history early in this century was marred by the ponderous moralizing of the muckraking era. Ida Tarbell, Lincoln Steffens, and later, Matthew Josephson and the fervidly New Dealing Claude Bowers brilliantly condemned the so-called Robber Barons, and so seemed to have characterized all earlier business activity that there arose a common antipathy to its history. Decent people didn't care to think of the Barons. A more objective business history had yet to appear.

This neglect was challenged in 1927 when a Canadian, Norman Gras, became Harvard's first professor of business history in the Graduate Business School. Gras dominated the field for the next twenty years, and he also contributed to a constant debate over the nature of business history. In fact, if the business of business was business, the preoccupation of business historians was definition of their purpose. Although Gras had begun with a broad idea of business history – of the comparative, the generic, even the cultural study of business in history, everywhere – the Depression so struck at his resources that he was restricted to a narrower field of the history of business in America. By necessity and habit, then, he came to assume what one scholar has called a "strict constructionist" view of business history. In Gras's words, business history was "the study of the development of business administration." Gras denied even that business history was a new phase of economic history; in any event, he said, business history "has no more connection with economic theory than it has with psychology or politics." Notably, he insisted that business history was concerned only with the *private* aspect of economic development, and that public finance, agricultural, industrial and labour history were none of its affair. Perhaps his most revealing assertion was that, "Economic history has come to be associated with economic determinism, while business history looks more to economic libertarianism."

On this most difficult and controversial point, however, basing his position on a business-directed explanation of capitalism, on the myths of American individualism, and on the necessity of preserving free enterprise as the only atmosphere in which businessmen could pursue a creative role, Gras was most assertive and least persuasive. Whereas, for example, contemporary German entrepreneurial historians would include earlier Prussian state railroad officials in the ranks of the entrepreneurs – either for their technological or their administrative innovations and decisiveness – Gras would rule them out because they were not profit-seeking business capitalists.

Let there be no mistake, however, that from Gras's own work and influence there emerged a body of company histories remarkable both in numbers and quality. But the limited historical and philosophic perspectives within which he had come to work were bound to be challenged. In time his criticisms touched the absurd when he lamented that economic history might sully itself by moving too far from the counting room and executive suite, and into the town – the very unit he himself had isolated as the early nursery of business capitalism. "Economic history," he warned, "is edging off into social history. Scholars are studying economic history increasingly to get background for social practices and social changes. Underneath the surface this new association means that the historian is turning philosopher and working the economic interpretation of human activity very hard. Doubtless he is pursuing a fruitful course, but let that pass." Gras died in the fifties, before the demands of students for "relevance," but some of his most admiring professional colleagues had already begun to strike out along new paths.

Among them, none was more significant than Gras's Harvard colleague, Arthur Cole. Cole was located, however, on the other side of the Charles River, among the more strictly academic scholars in history and economics in Harvard Yard. He was no less interested in business history than Gras – he constantly crossed the river – but his approach was broader and less utilitarian. Gras had been essentially an administrative historian. By contrast Cole's interests and those of his colleagues in the growing Harvard entrepreneurial school were more eclectic. Problems of definition would challenge their cohesion, too, but with less dogmatism than Gras they remained associated for a fruitful period after the founding of Harvard's Center for Entrepreneurial Studies in 1948. During that coalition they opened up prospects of a more comprehensive and sophisticated synthesis of business, economic and cultural history. Men such as Thomas Cochran, Joseph Schumpeter, Leland

Jenks and Fritz Redlich joined with Cole, and although they shared Gras's interest in the individual entrepreneur's field of choice-making and specific decisions, their interest also lay in his social, class and cultural background.

The Cole group also allied themselves with (or were impelled toward) social scientists working in sociology and psychology, and to a lesser degree in political science. In their heyday they dominated the field of American business history and saturated its output with entrepreneurial biographies and specialized studies. European and British scholars were also active in the entrepreneurial field, but never so singlemindedly as these Americans on the entrepreneurial bandwagon in the fifties and early sixties.

Norman Gras had identified capitalism with business and profit, and saw the successful entrepreneur as the vital creative agent whose freedom must be protected against legislative and bureaucratic strictures. Although Gras was severely critical, he was also influenced by one aspect of the earlier work of Werner Sombart and Max Weber in Germany. Sombart had accepted Weber's wonderfully German hypothesis of an ideal type, a "homo capitalisticus," someone who epitomized the "capitalist spirit, " its *geist*, as Weber said. Capital ownership, according to Sombart, was less important than whether a man had this "capitalistic spirit." But while Sombart agreed with Marx that profit was the ultimate gauge of capitalism, Sombart saw that there was another value by which to judge; this was the entrepreneur's contribution to the supremacy of order, reason and efficiency in production and in administration. So, Sombart had shifted the centre of enquiry away from the institution of capitalist fulfilment to the individual, and his approach to business history would require a Richard Wagner, not an E. J. Pratt, to celebrate its success. But whereas the socialist Sombart saw this kind of capitalistic spirit, he maintained faith in the American breed of capitalism and in the continuance of its "homo capitalisticus." But Arthur Cole and the American entrepreneurial historians who succeeded Gras viewed the role and nature of the entrepreneur less simplistically, although they were just as obsessed with him as the central figure in the capitalist process. Their anthropomorphic view of the successful entrepreneur was bound to be almost as unsatisfying to the philosophic historian as Gras's, because they had not sufficiently faced a fundamental question historians must ask themselves; how much does causality owe to individuals? Put at its simplest, in their enthusiasm for entrepreneurialism they forgot the business cycle. And this neglect helped to widen the gap between themselves and the economic or general historian with sounder canons of historical explanation.

That is a harsh indictment, and it is only true of the most rigid of the group; moreover, it was a failing soon recognized by the best of them and which thereby hastened their dissolution. But they had left important lessons. They had successfully tested the application of certain research and analytic techniques drawn from the social sciences. More wary than Gras of their own implicit value judgements, they sought a scientific method by which, primarily, they could measure efficiency in business operations; but they were also conscious of the effect of political, social and cultural factors in forming the minds of their entrepreneurs, and in influencing business activity. In short, they borrowed something from the behaviouralists' approach. The present sensitivity to ecology had not arisen when they were already perceiving that business studies should be set in a more environmentalist framework. Led by Leland Jenks and supported by Cole they sought what Cole called "a historical sociology of entrepreneurship comparable possibly with existing studies of the church, or the immigrant, or the public school, . . . "

A close parallel arises in the studies by Merle Curti and Richard Hofstadter of the social ideas of American educators, in which they analyze the values brought by leading educators from their own backgrounds and the impact upon the educational system of their melding. Oscar Handlin's studies of immigration are clearly another model. Under these influences, business administration would not remain an exclusive and sufficient end for business historians; entrepreneurship could become a broad integrating focus for research in the conditioning, functioning and effect of business operations in society. Inter-disciplinary approaches might be further developed, although most of the Cole group were less interested in the social scientist's quantifying than in his conceptual approaches. Cole warned of the "infection of measurement," and Jenks remained a historian, but one skilfully using particular techniques and ideas from the social sciences.

The American entrepreneurialists had produced a vigorous movement, a huge literature, and an elaborate apparatus in a short time. But the lack of a more philosophic judgement of the relationship between individualism and historical causality weakened the authority and general usefulness of their achievement. By contrast, British and European business historians remained broader in interest, producing a history more *en philosophe*, and one more closely related to the methods and interests of other historians. This conclusion becomes apparent in comparing, for example, the range and type of articles appearing in the British *Business History* or in *Tradition* with those appearing in the American *Review*. But the best of the American business historians provided a sound foundation and a worthy tradition for good company history, and the leading entrepreneurialists capitalized upon their earlier experience to produce several outstanding books in a new dimension of social, cultural and intellectual history.

Where, for example, company histories are being written today, it has become apparent that single-unit histories are of greater value when they include a comparative dimension. The reader benefits when the historian measures the relative performance of two companies, and if he judges and comments upon decisions taken by comparable firms, whether these bear on technological innovations or on some financial or administrative decision. Further, it is far more valuable to judge a particular firm against the general pattern in the industry or branch of commerce of which it forms one unit.

The key is a matter of perspective, of introducing a broader backdrop into company histories: however microscopic, company history ought at least to provide a view of "economic process."

On the other hand business history should not become purely an economic discipline. There should be plenty of scope for psychological and social studies of entrepreneurial activity at the decision-making level, such as Alfred Chandler continues to encourage in the United States. Historians are interested in human behaviour, and even the political historian should be interested in the metaphor he finds in business studies.

A broader view of business history offers scope for Professors Hyde and Harris in England to build upon their sound studies of the Blue Funnel Line and Liverpool's other shipping companies until we have that sweeping portrait of the Merseyside world that they are so patiently building. Or, one can cite Elizabeth Armstrong's remarkable study, *Robert Estienne: Royal Printer*. Estienne was the outstanding figure of the Paris book trade during the French Renaissance when that trade was a crucial agency in disseminating scholarly and religious ideas. Her book examines the printing trade, the publishing business, the social and intellectual circles of a court printer; it is "history in the round" in the best sense, and yet it is still a business biography. How far have we in Canada even produced a check-list of our newspapers?

As further models of business history, let me cite three other writers, all American: Thomas Cochran, Robert Wiebe and Edward Kirkland. Cochran's list of books on railroad and industrial history is too large to bear mention. His importance rests in the attention he has directed toward the study of the mind of the businessman, and the value of social science techniques to the conventional historian. Wiebe's principal book, *Businessmen and Reform, A Study of the Progressive Movement*, is a thoughtful and rigorous examination of business values, of businessmen's statements about their private and public values, and about their attitude to reform. Edward Kirkland is a man one despairs of measuring himself by, for he applies professional excellence and wisdom to all he touches. These qualities emerge in his biography of Charles Francis Adams, Jr., in his brilliant *Dream and Thought in the Business Community*, and in his perceptive essays in *Business in the Gilded Age*. With Kirkland, as with the latest German biography of Jakob Fugger, we see how business history, when it focuses upon the men and the ideas involved, merges in intellectual and social history. It becomes purposefully a part of general history.

Is there a lesson here for Canadian and Maritime studies? Canadian business studies are not new, but a systematic development is barely in its infancy. We have established no university chairs of business history; we have no centres of historical business studies; there appears to be little coordination of interest and effort between disciplines touching on the subject. A Business Archives Council of Canada has been founded, but has yet to attract large-scale support. Many of our large corporations and some of the principal banks either refuse serious scholars access to their records, or look for authorized versions of their public virtues. Many firms in Canada do not understand the historian's old adage, "Every age writes its own history." If a "satisfactory" history has been written, they will destroy the records used to prepare it, or they will close them to use by other scholars.

On the scholarly side, one can only mutter *"mea culpa."* Hugh Aitken was one of the first and most prominent students at Cole's Harvard entrepreneurial centre, and he has co-authored the standard economic history of Canada, but no Canadian university has offered him such facilities that he would return to Canada. Yet, as he himself describes the state of Canadian economic and business history: " . . . very few collections of Canadian business records are available to historians and very few biographies of Canadian businessmen have been written. . . . One could wish that one-tenth of the energies that have been lavished on the arcane details of the Canadian fur trade had been diverted to other sectors of the economy. . . . " Staple theory history centering upon fish, furs and wheat should not be lightly dismissed, nor should we ignore the Laurentian thesis of Canada's growth. But our practice of going after wholesale syntheses before retail histories may confuse working hypotheses with hard conclusions.

Our entry into Canadian business history can profit by American example and caveats, as it should from British, European and Australian experience. A fruitful line may rest in comparative imperial and commonwealth studies: in working on the Canada Company based in London, for example, I was struck by the number of investors and directors who had also taken part in the East India Company and in similar Australian schemes. Perhaps a closer look at our early problems of under-capitalization, imperial dependence and geographic challenge as they affected business would be of value to students of recently emergent nations. Certainly the systematic examination of cultural and linguistic problems in Canadian business growth has a broader application in the age of the multi-national corporation. Recent French-Canadian studies of Quebec's economic, demographic and entrepreneurial history show great promise. There is a field for multi-national corporate history in Canada in its broad outlines, one which denies the charge of xenophobic business studies and which might give public opinion-makers such as the Waffle or the Committee for an Independent Canada either pause or satisfaction, depending upon the conclusions.

The field of business history gathers support in Ontario, but it will be important to ensure that there is interest and support from scholars and business people in other parts of Canada. This is particularly important in the Maritimes, because this region would appear to be especially promising for the development of business studies. We must act quickly, however, for the records are rapidly disappearing. In recent years new conditions have driven many older Maritime firms to the wall, and mergers and the failure of family continuity have also prompted the end of operations. In such circumstances the reticence of owner-managers to yield up their records should have been reduced, and the opportunity should be seized to consolidate collections. There is also cause for alarm over the effect of down-town renewal and suburban dispersal of long-established Halifax business firms. Progress has its price among the ancient shipping and chandlery houses of the Maritimes, and the moment of shifting operations is usually the one when dead records are dispatched to the city dump.

But Maritime business operations have so often been local and family-oriented that this circumstance enhances the possibility that secondary, personal and other corroborative material may be found to encourage the reconstruction of business history. The inter-connections of business, society and politics should project business history in the Maritimes into a wider dimension *sui generis*.

There is also a more indirect factor currently favouring Maritime studies – business or otherwise – arising from the resurgent interest in various forms of Maritime union. Even without full political union, measures of governmental coordination may be undertaken across the board in the Maritimes. In examining even this limited objective, questions arise regarding some significant elements: territorial and administrative operations of Maritime business and government agencies; operating conflicts inherent in maintaining separate provincial industrial development commissions and crown corporations; common agricultural production and marketing in marginal conditions; technical education and innovation in a fairly distinct labour area; coordination of fisheries subsidization and anti-pollution control; Maritime assumptions and claims in areas of jurisdiction such as the Territories of off-shore oil rights; and the nature of administrative and/or political re-arrangement with a view to union. All of these questions affect and reflect business interests to some degree. Our understanding of them must be enhanced by exploring their historical dimension, especially in the Maritimes where the pattern of eighteenth century beginnings, even in business location and operation, often remains remarkably apparent in the twentieth century.

I have presumed to suggest these Maritime applications of business history partly because so little has been undertaken in Maritime studies at universities outside the Maritimes themselves, and because so much needs to be done. Perhaps one or several of the Maritime universities may before long introduce a substantial programme of Maritime Studies, and I believe that more is involved than nostalgia, micro-history or a narrow provincialism in advocating Maritime business studies when the issues of Maritime Union and federal constitutional revision have both been raised. A systematic pursuit of the record, identity and prospects of the Atlantic region seems imperative, and social, economic and business history approaches may well deserve precedence over political and constitutional.

Appendix

FURTHER READING

Hugh G. J. Aitken, ed., *Explorations in Enterprise* (Cambridge, Harvard University Press, 1965), 420 pages.

Thomas C. Cochran, *The Inner Revolution, Essays on the Social Sciences in History* (New York, 1964), 187 pages.

Norman Scott Brien Gras, *Business and Capitalism, An Introduction to Business History* (New York, 1939), 408 pages.

——————————, *Development of Business History up to 1950*, ed. by Ethel C. Gras (Ann Arbor, 1962), 208 pages.

Fritz Redlich, "The Beginnings and Development of German Business History," in the Supplement to *Bulletin of the Business Historical Society*, September, 1952, 82 pages.

5 / Extra-National Control: An Early Case Study

The Wrights of Saint John: A Study of Shipbuilding and Shipowning in the Maritimes, 1839-1855

Richard Rice, University of Liverpool, England

Until now many of the economic and business aspects of Canadian shipping in the nineteenth century have remained virtually unexplored. This study is concerned with two brothers, William and Richard Wright, and their involvement with shipbuilding and shipowning in the Maritimes during this period.

From 1839 to 1855 it appears that Saint John was the most productive shipbuilding centre in North America, having overtaken Halifax as the first shipowning port in British North America.[1] During this time, the Wrights established themselves as the leading shipbuilders in Saint John, and from 1847 on proceeded to build an impressive fleet of ships.[2] The career of the Wrights falls into three areas of activity: shipbuilding, shipbuilding and shipowning, and finally, just shipowning; this study will attempt to examine each of these phases.

The sources relating to Canadian shipbuilding and owning in the nineteenth century tend to be somewhat scattered. Regrettably, for Canadian scholars, many are housed in England. However it is interesting to note that perhaps the most comprehensive collection of records relating to one firm, is that of John Ward and Sons of Saint John which are presently in the New Brunswick Museum. But no firm can claim to be as representative, or as significant, as that of W. and R. Wright in these outstanding years of Canadian shipbuilding.

Saint John shipbuilding suffered a severe depression in the years 1830 and 1831. In 1831, for example, only one vessel of any size was built. Things

---

[1] See Tables 1 and 2, pp. 328, 329.
[2] See Tables 2 and 3, pp. 329-331.

improved in the course of the decade, with a marked climax occurring in 1839 and 1840, the time of the Wrights' entry into the industry. It will be readily perceived that new ships, which because of their size took about nine months to build, were very much the result of the economic situation existing at the time of their initiation. This fact may help to explain the somewhat enforced cycle which came into play in building ships, and also how, during the extraordinary years of 1839-40 and 1853-54, the patterns of production were shaped. In these years there was a sharp peak, the production of each year rising well above the former, to be followed at the end of the second year by a sharp decline. It can therefore be assumed that there must have been an economically favourable climate in Courtney Bay, Saint John in 1839, when the Wrights began to build their ships.

It is extremely likely that the first vessels built by the Wrights were built under contract. Agreements were generally made whereby payments were handed over during the course of construction at specified stages by shipowner to shipbuilder.[3] The fact that the Wrights did not register their first vessels in their own name is not conclusive, as ownership frequently changed before registration, or re-registration (termed registration *de novo*) was effected.[4] However, the specialized nature of the first two vessels launched strongly suggests that they were designed and constructed for specific owners. That opinion is confirmed in a contemporary newspaper report which states that the whale ship was built for the Saint John Mechanic's Whale Fishing Company, and that the steamboat was intended for the Saint John to Boston run.[5] The evidence that the *Rival* was built under contract is more tenuous. There are indications that this and two other vessels of similar dimensions were ordered from W. and R. Wright by a Saint John merchant, John Walker. In 1839, Walker registered the *Ben Nevis*, built by George Thompson who seems to have constructed many ships for him. The link between Thompson, Walker, and the Wrights was provided by the apprenticeship of both William and Richard Wright to Thompson.[6] It may well be that one or both of the brothers had risen to become master shipbuilders for Thompson and thus well-known to Walker. During the period of strong demand for Saint John ships, there seems every likelihood that he contracted his shipbuilder's master shipbuilders for additional vessels.

In addition to these points, the general pattern in 1839 indicates that

---

[3] The memorandum of such an agreement is cited by Stanley T. Spencer, *Masters of Sail*, pp. 147-148.

[4] The first vessel was the 418 ton *Java*, the next a 207 ton paddle-wheeled steamer rigged as a schooner, the *North America*, followed by the 647 ton *Rival*. All details of the Wrights' vessels in this study have been taken from the Public Records Office, Board of Trade series 107 and 108. With exceptions, such as Liverpool registration, original registers and transcripts have been consulted..

[5] *Commercial News*, Saint John, N. B., September 16, 1839.

[6] Frederick W. Wallace, *Wooden Ships and Iron Men* (Boston, 1937), p. 78.

shipbuilders did not engage in speculative building. It is not without significance that of the twenty-five new vessels for which this writer has record of first registrations, none was registered by the builder. It is probably safe to assume therefore, that the Wrights were contracted for their first year's building program, if not for the second as well.

It is possible, for purposes of comparison, to assess the minimum capital requirements for the establishment of a shipbuilding business by consulting the papers of the long-established Saint John firm of John Ward and Sons. Several of their ships were built by Francis Bourneuf at Clare, Nova Scotia, including the 745 ton *Ward* in 1836, the *Maitland* in 1839, and the *Avon*, of over one thousand tons, in 1840. The *Avon*, which was the second largest ship built in 1840 in British North America, was constructed under contract.[7] From the letters directed to Bourneuf, it is clear that the Wards largely financed the building of the ship. They purchased and imported on their own account the very considerable quantity of materials needed for the ship's outfit. These included items such as, the ironwork, canvas, chain, special woods, and cordage, as well as other smaller items. The principal charges falling to Bourneuf included local timber, investment in the site, and cost of labour. However, to offset this Bourneuf apparently received heavy advances which presumably would have met his capital needs.

There must undoubtedly have been advantages in building in a location such as Clare, where the shipbuilder could operate the truck system, or at least include in wages the cost of board and lodging. Whichever system operated, the shipbuilder would have made substantial savings in labour costs. In the city of Saint John, the Wrights, in common with other shipbuilders, were exposed to a less set labour market, where wage fluctuations experienced in all seafaring activities also affected the shipyards.

There is also another obvious distinction to be made between the shipyard of an outport and one of a city, and that concerns the cost of the site. Located near timber resources, probably bought or leased, the country builder enjoyed a clear advantage over his city counterpart who was no doubt confined by land values to a small site, and would have had to buy all his timber.

Compared to the investment represented by a ship, the sites themselves were in all likelihood cheap. In 1854, for example, Thomas Hilyard bought a narrow but prime shipyard in Saint John for £3000, and that sum was paid off over a period of thirty years. It is not unreasonable to suppose that the cost of the site to Hilyard in the first year was about £400, and that thereafter about half that sum annually.[8] In any case, the purchase of a

---

[7] According to Wallace, *op. cit.*

[8] Calculated on the basis of a 5 per cent down payment, 30 equal, annual capital repayments, and annual interest on the outstanding balance of 6 per cent – a common interest rate given on ship mortgages in the late 1850's.

shipyard did not usually pose a problem, as it appears that merchants were willing enough to advance cash and credit.

It is possible to get a good idea of the Wrights' labour costs from the Ward collection, which includes information giving the number of employees, time employed, and rates obtained there. When, in the latter part of 1840, the shipping industry took a downward turn, Ward remarked in a letter to Bourneuf that wages in Saint John shipyards had been reduced by as much as 1/6 to 2/- a day.[9] During the seven months it took to construct the *Ward*, Bourneuf wrote that on July 1, 57 men were employed, on September 3, 40 men were engaged, on September 14, that 43 were working, and that three days later more men had been hired. With an average crew size of 45, and the Saint John daily rate of 3/6, the labour cost of the hull of the *Ward* works out at £2 per ton. Excluding the timber, iron, and sails, the cost of the Bay of Fundy ship at the time the Wrights began building would appear to have been £3.1.0. per ton. As long as the Wrights and their contemporaries remained solely shipbuilders, their income is relatively simple to estimate. The price at which newly built Canadian tonnage changed hands ranged between £7 and £12 per ton. Thus, depending upon the general economic conditions prevailing at the time, a figure can be accordingly selected from the range and multiplied by the quantity of tonnage built. The shipbuilding income of the Wrights can be estimated to have ranged between approximately £10,000 for 1272 tons of shipping in 1839, to about £1400 for 200 tons and a mortgage for 594 tons in 1843, to a probable high in 1853 for the 3654 tons of clipper shipping of about £55,000.[10]

From the Ward manuscripts it appears that it took about seven-and-a-half years to build and completely finish a 650 ton ship. With this information, and in conjunction with the shipping registers, it can be established with some certainty the continuity of operation at the Wright shipyard. In the sixteen-and-a-half years that the Wrights built ships, there appears to have been only about twenty months during which time the yard was closed, and this tended to be concentrated in the 1840's. From the spring of 1848 until the last ship was launched seven-and-a-half years later, the shipyard was probably in continuous operation.

Again from the Ward manuscripts, it seems that the ratio of workmen to a thousand tons of shipping under construction was about fifty. Employing that ratio the size of the workforce can be estimated. Beginning with about sixty, the number must have sunk to perhaps fifteen in 1842. This followed a period when the workforce had been non-existent for probably four months, a period equalled in 1840, and 1843, and exceeded in 1847. However, when

---

[9] Col. Ward, John Ward and Sons, to Francis Bourneuf, June 27, 1840.

[10] There is an excellent record of the price of Canadian shipping from 1850 onward in the C. W. Kellock Collection, recently deposited in the National Maritime Musuem, Greenwich. The Liverpool-based firm, C. W. Kellock and Co. were for a long time brokers to the Admiralty, and were probably the leading English shipbrokers for much of the nineteenth century.

the firm began building clippers, the number of employees in all likelihood expanded faster than the tonnage. Clipper ships were much larger in relation to their tonnage, and this can be seen when the Wrights' *Guiding Star*, registered at 1472 tons is compared with the larger *Beejapore* of 1672 tons. The latter, launched just before the revolution in hull design was only 182 feet long compared with 233 feet for the *Guiding Star*. With longer masts, yards, spars, and rigging requiring the best quality, and therefore more attention, the ratio of workmen to a thousand tons may have changed to as much as seventy per thousand tons. With the *White Star* and *Morning Light*, the best-known, and largest clippers, totalling between them 4716 tons, the number of men employed was possibly as many as 330.

Gathering all the available evidence from the ships owned by the Wrights, it can be seen that the progress of the firm was closely linked to the nature of their main Liverpool agent. Initially, the Wrights' business remained small as they built for Saint John owners who in turn operated as agents and brokers in the shipping and selling of vessels at Liverpool.

Involved in this same theme is the question of speculative building, that is, the shipbuilder building on his own account and hoping to meet the market at the highest price. By doing this, the middleman, in Saint John or Quebec, was eliminated, and further, speculation could be made in the purchase of a cargo of timber to be sold in England for a higher price, or at least earn the freight on the cargo, which on occasion amounted almost to the value of the timber itself.[11] There appeared therefore, to be a strong initiative for the builder to become owner, if only for a short time, in order to deliver the ship, plus cargo and freight to the market, Liverpool.

This situation, whereby ships could be constructed in major timber-exporting ports providing cheap building costs and a ready cargo, was much resented by some sections of the British shipping industry. The General Shipowners' Society waged a long campaign against British North American ships and shipbuilders. In a letter to the Select Committee on British shipping of 1844, the chairman of the Society, George Frederick Young, himself a partner in a Thames shipbuilding company, complained that this operated as:

> ... a direct bounty on Colonial shipbuilding amounting to from £3 to £4 per ton, and constitutes a serious disqualification to the competing British shipowner, who has to purchase either the dearer timber of this country, or the timber of the colonies enhanced by the cost of freight and charges of importation for the construction of his ship, which, when completed, he has to send to North America in ballast, to bring home the very timber which the colonial ship loads at the port of construction.[12]

---

[11] Col. Ward, John Ward and Sons, to Wm. Dawson and Co., Baltimore, October 3, 1840.

[12] "Report from the Select Committee on British Shipping, 1844," *Parliamentary Papers*, (545), VIII, 1, Appendix 1. p. 215.

The General Shipowners' Society was very similar to the Committee of Lloyd's Register, which for most of the nineteenth century accorded Thames-built shipping a much higher rating than shipping constructed in other British regions, particularly that built in British North America.[13]

Of the twenty-nine Wright vessels, only eleven were not clearly owned and registered by the Wrights. By tonnage, the Wrights registered in their own name 21,393 tons of their total production of 26,977. 1842 and 1843 were tough years for Saint John, and a common sign of the times can be seen in the number of mortgages appearing on ships registered by Saint John owners. The Wrights mortgaged their ship *Solway* within days of its registration in 1843 rather than hand her over to their English agents at a loss.[14] The ownership was transferred by deed of mortgage to David Cannon and Sons of Liverpool, with whom W. and R. Wright were commercially linked for ten years (this is the first evidence of the link).

The manner in which the Wrights expanded their business to eliminate the middleman can be seen from the number of times Richard Wright acted as master on their ships. Of the eighteen vessels registered by them, Richard was master on the maiden voyages of at least fourteen. The money saved from the wages bill was probably incidental to two other things. Firstly, the vessel with an appropriately skilled crew could, during the transit period to market, deliver the finishing touches to the ship before her sale on arrival. Second, and more important, Richard Wright was able to act as his own agent in Liverpool. If the ship were sold through a shipbroker, the standard fee was one per cent of the sale price, and it is difficult to deny the advantage in having the sale agent of the vessel as one and the same person as owner, master, and builder.[15]

Although the idea of "streams" as a term used by economists to describe the direction of business expansion is not a new one, it has some considerable bearing in the relationship between the Wrights and their agents, and the nature of their commercial expansion. By taking a "downstream" course, a shipbuilder expanded in the direction of ownership and operation of ships; the converse direction, "upstream" meant expansion towards the supply of the principal product. An example of the latter case is when Thomas Hilyard, a shipbuilder of considerable reputation, expanded into sawmilling.

Without the records of those who made the decisions, one can but speculate, or at least note some of the striking features of the Wrights' course of expansion. Their agent at Liverpool through most of the 1840's and early 1850's was the firm of David Cannon and Sons, who in 1850 were the

---

[13] R. S. Craig, "British Shipping and British North American Shipbuilding in the Early Nineteenth Century, with Special Reference to Prince Edward Island," in H. E. S. Fisher, ed., *The South-West and the Sea*, Exeter Papers in Economic History, 1, pp. 21-37.

[14] PRO, BT, Series 107.

[15] The fee was the usual one charged by C. W. Kellock and Co., in common with two other leading brokers, Stitt, Coubrough and Co., and Cunard and Munn.

largest importers of timber into Liverpool. There are two significant observations to be made about the major timber importing firms which aid in accounting for the Wrights' commercial activities. First, the timber merchants, unlike other specialized merchants, particularly cotton importers, were heavily involved in shipowning. Second, the main timber importers were large importers of cotton as well, an aspect developed only in the 1840's. Cannon and Sons imported cotton not only from the United States, but in substantial quantities from India as well.

It is therefore not surprising to find the Wrights' ships involved in the trades engaged in by their principal agent. Cotton freights were on occasion decidedly profitable. A surviving crew list from the Wrights' *Queen*, on the Liverpool to Mobile run, describes the ship as carrying ballast, or a small general cargo on the outward trip, and loading up with cotton on the inbound leg. The normally proper, puritanical, and close-lipped Wards were moved to uncharacteristic exuberance when their small barque *Clarence* was sent from Savannah to Liverpool with a cotton cargo instead of returning to Saint John with a cargo of hard pine as had been the original instructions. The Wards informed their Liverpool agents that the freight of £987, considering the smallness of the vessel, was "doing good business."[16]

The *Queen*, 1098 tons, which had been the largest ship built by the Wrights, was surpassed in size by the 1331 ton *David Cannon*, launched in the autumn of 1847. The growth in the size of the Saint John and Quebec ships in the 1840's might well have been due to the influence of the cotton trade, into which the Liverpool merchants had entered during the decade. The *David Cannon* was doubtless a better size of vessel for the cotton trade than the *Queen* because she remained under Wright ownership for four and a half years as compared to just under two years for the *Queen*. The *David Cannon* made ten voyages under Wright ownership. Outbound she sailed either directly to Mobile and back to Liverpool, or to New York and then to Mobile, Saint John, or Quebec, depending on which port held the promise of a better freight. Wage bills for the trips varied. Those for the westbound stages were usually lower than ones eastbound, in spite of the larger complement of the former. According to crew lists, seamen's wages in North American ports, like those of Australia, exceeded the wages of able seamen sailing from Liverpool.[17]

The specific roles performed by the brothers are not clear. Generally, William appears to have remained at Saint John during the shipbuilding period, and later, during the period 1855-1867 until the move to Liverpool, as a shipbroker and possibly ship's agent. Although he never had a master's certificate (which, after the Merchant Shipping Act of 1854, was necessary to gain clearance from a British port), Richard acted as master on many of the

---

[16] Col. Ward, John Ward and Sons, to Gibbs, Bright and Co., April 14, 1840.

[17] Crew lists, held by the PRO, begin in 1835 and continue to the present.

Saint John to Liverpool runs, and captained the *David Cannon* on her first voyage from England to Mobile. Perhaps a telling comment on the management of the shipyard is that while Richard was at Mobile it was only a matter of days before the shipyard at Saint John was to start up again after a six-month shutdown.

That the Wrights expanded their business "downstream" into the sphere operated by their Liverpool agent is supported in the evidence of the voyages of the *Dundonald*, which, over a period of four-and-a-half years made four voyages on the Liverpool-Bombay route. In light of this, it hardly seems surprising that after launching themselves into the East Indian trade with the *Dundonald*, the Wrights named three of their ships in succession, *Belochee, Beejapore*, and *Bhurtpoor*. In fact the Wrights filled out the builder's certificate for the *Belochee* just one week after the *Dundonald* returned from her maiden voyage to Bombay.

The collapse of the Liverpool shipowner, Edward Oliver, in the autumn of 1854 caused a strong reaction in shipping circles. Oliver had been particularly involved in speculating on Canadian ships in anticipation of even higher freight rates and tonnage values in consequence of the Crimean War. The Wrights were fortunate with the *Dundonald*. With the Lloyd's five-year classification expiring, the *Dundonald* arrived in Liverpool in early July, and four weeks later, while in dock, presumably discharging timber, was sold for £11,000.[18] This was a very high figure for a vessel which had apparently not undergone a refit, and was doubtless due not so much to the quality of her build, but to the current extraordinarily high prices.[19]

Up to 1851, the Wrights were clearly associated with David Cannon and Sons, and after 1855 just as clearly with the Fernie Brothers. It would appear, from ship registers, that during the intervening years, the Wrights were involved with a variety of other Liverpool houses. Three of their finest ships were sold to the one firm of James Beazley, the clipper, *Guiding Star*, was sold to another firm heavily committed to the Australian trade, and just over two-thirds of the *White Star* was sold to, if not built for, the owners of the White Star line. In addition, the Wrights sold another ship which they had just bought to the White Star line in 1855. The shared ownership of the *White Star*, and the sale of the second ship implies some form of continuing commercial relationship, but evidence indicates otherwise – that in fact the Wrights were actually operating under the umbrella of the agency of Fernie Brothers.

From ship registers, transactions, and crew lists, it appears that the Fernies were owners of a very large number of ships, managed by themselves, involved in the timber trade, American and Indian cotton routes, Australian

---

[18] C. W. Kellock Papers, National Maritime Museum, Greenwich, Sale Contract, August 2, 1854.

[19] *Ibid.*, Sale Contract for the Wrights' *Queen*, £7,000.

emigration, gold clipper trades, (the Red Cross line), and, beginning in the later 1850's, the coal and guano circumnavigatory routes. The firm must have come quickly into commercial prominence in the early 1850's because at the turn of the decade they are not recorded as having played any major part in the timber or cotton trades in Liverpool. However, by 1854, one of the Fernies was part of an important group of Liverpool merchants who acted as trustees in winding up Edward Oliver's shipping interests, and the Fernies may well have succeeded him in the role of merchant prince of Liverpool shipping. Many vessels purchased by Fernie Brothers or David Fernie (always listed on the registers as owner, whereas the former are given the title merchants) remained under Canadian registry for years.

During the only period of the 1850's when Canadian-built tonnage was leading the way in the premier merchant shipping route, William and Richard Wright, who set the standard for New Brunswick shipbuilding, were in close commercial connection with Fernie Brothers. Of the three clippers sold to James Beazley in 1852 and 1853 the role of Fernie Brothers can be seen only with one of the ships, the *Miles Barton*, but it is entirely likely that Fernies also arranged the sale of the other two as well. The *Guiding Star*, much the longest vessel built in Saint John until the *White Star*, was sold to the firm of Millers and Thompson. Despite the fact that from first registry on July 20, until registration by Millers and Thompson on October 26, the form releasing the crew at Liverpool on August 20, gives Fernie Brothers as owners. This form is not as reliable as the register itself, which was proof of property, but it does suggest that the Wrights had given up ownership of the *Guiding Star*, perhaps even before she sailed from Saint John, and there is similar evidence concerning the *White Star*. A very good indication of how a Liverpool agent could and did protect his clients' interests (not to mention his own), was provided by the ownership registrations of the *Guiding Star*. One year after Millers and Thompson registered her at Liverpool, they took out a mortgage for an undisclosed amount with William James Fernie and Henry Fernie. Two months later, a further mortgage was registered, this time with a Manchester merchant. It is not evident whether or not Millers and Thompson failed shortly after, but five weeks later Fernie Brothers registered two transactions in which they sold the vessel and acted as mortgager to the buyer. It is quite possible that the Fernies may have arranged the sale of the *White Star* to the White Star line because of their listing as owners of that vessel.

The new ship *Shepherdess* which arrived in Liverpool in September 1855, was bought by the Wrights from the builder and registered at Saint John. On board was a cargo of timber consigned to Fernie Brothers,[20] and the ship was then sold by them to John Pilkington and others in October 1855, in a

---

[20] *Gore's Advertiser*, Liverpool, October 4, 1855. Whether the Wrights owned the cargo is undetermined.

form of transaction which was commonplace at that time between a Canadian shipbuilder, his agent, and the purchaser. The sale to Pilkington was made by William James Fernie and Henry Fernie, attorneys for the Wrights under a Certificate of Sale. This was a sale contract which appears to have been a power of attorney, and which, if the vessel were sold by the attorneys, then became operative.[21]

With the launching of the *Morning Light*, somewhat unfairly termed a "monster New Brunswick ship,"[22] the Wrights unexpectedly found themselves owners of one of the largest clippers afloat. The number of a transaction, probably for a certificate of sale empowering the Fernies to sell the ship, was endorsed on the register in 1855. It stood for more than four years, but was finally cancelled in 1860, the power not having been exercised. The *Morning Light* had apparently been launched a year too late to take advantage of the very high prices of 1854.

In the transitional period from being shipbuilder to becoming just shipowner, there are three particular years which stand out during which the Wrights made major investments in ships – 1847, 1854, and 1856. The investment in the first two of the years was into their own ships, and the connection between shipbuilding and shipowning is evident. Unfortunately, the absence of the Wrights' business papers prohibits the distinction that might be made in later years as to which side of their business activities was mainly responsible for generating the capital which made expansion possible.

By retaining their two largest ships, the *White Star* and *Morning Light*, the Wrights added some 3000 tons during 1854 and 1855. Their rise to shipowners of some magnitude can be said to have occurred in 1856, when some 5000 tons were added without being offset by corresponding sales of tonnage.

It seems evident that the large jump in ownership in 1856 was simply the result of a transfer of capital resources from the shipbuilding program, which had been running at about 3000 tons per year for the previous four years, into the owning of ships. In that four years the Wrights had been building the most expensive kind of tonnage, whereas the shipping in which they invested was considerably cheaper because it was not of the clipper variety. This alone would have allowed the translation of the Wright tonnage of about 3000 tons into a rather larger amount of ordinary New Brunswick tonnage. Moreover, the very high prices of the early fifties dropped after the autumn of 1854 thus providing greater purchasing power. An example of this can be seen in the sale of the *Queen* which fetched £7.17.7 and £11.17.6 per ton (old measurement) on the two occasions she was sold in 1854 when she was seven years old. On the other hand, the *Chrysolite* fetched only £8.2.2 per ton (old measurement) when she was sold in 1858 at Liverpool, only two months after her launching at Saint John.

21 PRO, register transaction, BT, Series 109.
22 Basil Lubbock, *The Colonial Clippers*, (Lauriat Co., 1921), p. 105.

When the Wrights stopped building ships, they became not only shipowners to a new degree of specialization, but shipbrokers as well. In this way they came much closer in function to the Liverpool firm with which they were intertwined. With the institution in 1855 of the registration certificates of sale there exists a record of heavy dependence by the Wrights upon the Fernies. All the ships which they sold were either to or through the Fernies. As long as their ships were running in the timber, cotton, or guano trades, the Wrights probably managed them. But it appears that on the Australian route the ships were chartered to, or by, some other arrangement managed through Fernie Brothers. It was, however, in the area of capital that the reliance upon the Fernies can best be seen.

In the depression which started late in 1857 one of the bigger commercial casualties was the Borough Bank of Liverpool. This bank appears to have had considerable involvement in shipping, and one of its customers was Fernie Brothers. Although the bank failed, it continued to operate for at least four years before its assets were liquidated. The involvement of the Wrights with the Fernies, and the Fernies with the Borough Bank are not at all clear, but there is one evident pattern which emerges from the transactions of registry and the ship registers.

The Wrights were surviving their investment program of 1856 and 1857, and the depression, but the Fernie Brothers were not. Richard Wright may have made an emergency trip to Liverpool. At any rate he was there in December of 1857, and he re-purchased three ships that he and his brother had recently sold to the Fernies, and mortgaged two of them to the Fernies. A further three ships were also mortgaged, the sum mortgaged amounting to £39,038. A quick calculation reveals that the mortgaged value per ton was £7.14.11, and a direct application of this figure to the 12,205 tons owned by the Wrights gives their shipping a value of £94,466.14.0. However, there are several peculiarities about the situation. First, Richard Wright bought back three ships which they had already sold, one as recently as four weeks before the re-purchase. Second, the ships mortgaged by the Wrights were the vessels of least value and size. Third, and probably most significant, the mortgages given by the Fernies were immediately transferred to the Borough Bank of Liverpool, and there followed three more, somewhat smaller, mortgages in the next two years. It would thus appear that the Wrights had bailed out the Fernies.

To understand why the Wrights had come to the rescue of Fernie Brothers it would be necessary to know a good deal more about this situation in which the securities given up, and the obligations undertaken by the Wrights were doubtless only a small part. And to the Wrights, the events of late 1857 meant the end of a long period of sustained and unencumbered growth. The next year saw a complete stoppage of the buying and selling of ships by the Wrights, and the resumption of activity in 1859 was of a moderate level.

To go beyond 1859 exceeds the confines of this study. But it is relevant for narrative purposes to state that the firm recovered slowly from the depression of 1857 and experienced a steady growth through the 1860's in tonnage of shipping owned. The peak size of their shipping interests came in the year of Richard's death, in 1872, and thereafter declined, at first slowly, under William, and then rapidly following his death in 1878, when his nephew George Wright inherited the business.

Appendix

Table 1. Comparative Statement of Tonnage and Number of Vessels Registered at Saint John, New Brunswick, and Quebec, 1839-1855

Year	*Registered Tonnage*		*No. of New Vessels*		*Tonnage of New Vessels*	
	Saint John	Quebec	Saint John	Quebec	Saint John	Quebec
1839	73,837	32,451	—	—	—	—
1840	81,139	38,124	—	—	—	—
1841	80,853	46,755	—	—	—	—
1842	67,309	41,339	—	—	—	—
1843	64,709	44,104	40	43	8,745	12,776
1844	63,676	45,361	—	—	—	—
1845	69,293	51,018	—	—	—	—
1846	81,345	55,893	85	34	28,660	15,724
1847	91,267	57,910	83	65	38,112	28,098
1848	89,968	46,961	60	44	16,107	15,090
1849	93,192	43,759	73	70	25,784	25,845
1850	99,490	40,762	55	69	19,133	28,044
1851	94,810	50,087	60	62	28,628	35,536
1852	82,589	55,114	—	—	—	—
1853	89,574	70,588	83	74	47,178	36,833
1854	115,276	74,793	97	40	70,801	18,250
1855	110,451	71,553	75	86	39,486	26,650
		TOTAL	711	587	322,634	242,846

Source: P R O, B T 107-108, "Plantation Annual Lists," 1839-1855. This data was collected by the Collectors of Customs at Saint John and Quebec, usually too soon after the end of the year to account for all the vessels struck off the register. The totals cited here were tallied by the writer. For the Quebec figures, the number of new vessels and tonnage of new vessels include the totals for the certificated vessels in addition to those registered.

Table 2. Comparison of Largest Wright Ships with those of British North America

Year	Largest Quebec Ship	Tonnage	Largest Nova Scotia Ship	Tonnage	Largest Saint John Ship	Tonnage	Builder	Tonnage	Largest Wright Ship	Tonnage
1839	United Kingdom	1267			Glengarry		F. and S. Smith	1054	Rival	647
1840	Goliath	988	Avon	1013	Queen of the Ocean		F. and S. Smith	1196	Helen Mar	640
1841					Princess Royal		Geo. Thompson	1109	Eglinton	949
1842					Enchantress		John W. Smith	833	Corsair	717
1843	Ottawa	1152			Lord Ashburton		Jas. Briggs	1009	Solway	594
1844					Saint John		Owens and Duncan	985	Colonist	751
1845	Malabar	1175			William Penn		Owens and Duncan	1041	Milicete	899
1846	Sobraon	1280			Alfred		Jas. Smith	1073	Oregon	928
1847	Brandon	1196			Forest Monarch		Owens and Duncan	1542	David Cannon	1331
1848	none over 1200		Zetland	1283	The Duke	1283	Jas. P. Payne	1357	—	—
1849	Dalriada	1504			Dundonald		W. and R. Wright	1372	Dundonald	1372
1850	Martin Luther	1241	Montgomery	848	Welsford	848		1655	Belochee	967
1851	Ailsa	1457	Bourneuf	1495	Beejapore	1495	W. and R. Wright	1676	Beejapore	1676
1852	Ebba Brahe	1756	Catherine Glen	1327	Wanata	1327		1442	Constance	1106
1853	Boomerang	1823	Hotspur	1670	Clas-Meriden	1670	Thos. Hilyard	1598	Guiding Star	1472
1854	Lord Raglan	1888	Magna Carta	1466	White Star	1466	W. and R. Wright	2339	White Star	2339
1855	Acadia	2030			Morning Light		W. and R. Wright	2377	Morning Light	2377

Source: F. W. Wallace, *Wooden Ships and Iron Men*; E. C. Clarke, a typescript given to the writer; and "Register Transcripts," P.R.O., B.T.107 and 108.

Table 3. Wright Shipowning and Shipbroking Activities

Ship	Builder, or First Owner	First or Second Owner	Agent in Selling or Mortgaging	Date of Sale	Buyer or Mortgagor
Mary	built for	Richard Wright	William Wright	27.2.1856	David Fernie
Wigtownshire	built for or bought from builder, Wm. P. Flewelling, by	Richard Wright	William Wright (not sold) Richard Wright	17.12.1857	mortgage to Fernie Brothers
Florine	built for or bought from builder, unknown by	W. and R. Wright	Fernie Brothers	2.2.1857	David Fernie
Scottish Chief	built for or bought from builder, Nevins¹ and Irving by	W. and R. Wright	R. Wright C. of mtg	not exercised, as late as 1867	
Uncas	—	C. Boultonhouse	Wm Wright		Fernie Brothers
Morning News	built for	W. and R. Wright	?	?	Frederick Grant
Venus	built for or bought from builder D. Robertson, by	William Wright	Richard Wright	6.11.1857	David Fernie
Empress	built for or bought from builder, unknown, by David Fernie	William Wright	Fernie Brothers	1.12.1857	David Fernie

Ship	Builder, or First Owner	First or Second Owner	Agent in Selling or Mortgaging	Date of Sale	Buyer or Mortgagor
Sovereign of the Seas	built for or bought from Gass[2] and Stewart by	Wm. Wright, (52 shares)	—	28.11.1857	W. and R. Wright
Clifton Belle	built for or bought from builder, unknown, by	William Wright	mortgaged to		Fernie Brothers
Royal Saxon	built for, or bought from builders Nevins and Irving, by	Richard Wright	(R. Wright) mtg.	22.12.1857	Fernie Brothers
Rising Sun	(Gass and Stewart, builders)	Gass and Stewart	Fernie Brothers	?	Richard Wright
Statelie	built for, or bought from, builder unknown, by	William Wright	Richard Wright (not sold)		
Empire of Peace	built for, or bought from Gass and Stewart, builders, by	William Wright	Fernie Brothers	17.11.1859	David Fernie
Dawn of Hope	built for, or bought from the builders, Nevins and Irving, by	William Wright	Fernie Brothers	10.10.1859	Fernie Brothers

[1] James Nevins was probably the brother-in-law of Richard Wright. In 1837 the latter married Jane Nevins, and after his death in London in 1872, Jane and James Nevins had financial transactions with the surviving brother, William Wright.

[2] George Wright Gass was the nephew of William Wright who inherited the Wright business after William's death in 1879.

Table 4. Ships Built by W. and R. Wright

Name	Rig	Ton- nage	Date of Build or Launch	Date Lost	Detail	Life span
Java	s	418	10.9.1839	1855	sold for	15
North America	stm	207	11.9.1839	Dec. 1846	ashore	7
Rival	s	647	8.11.1839	1840	wrecked	1?
Helen Mar	s	640	23.5.1840	Jan. 1844	missing	4
Eliza Keith	s	537	4.7.1840	12.8.1885	hulk	45
Mary Stewart	brig	216	22.10.1840	30.3.1862	lost	21
Spitfire	sch	83	11.1.1841	9.2.1852	sold for	11
Eglinton	s	949	19.6.1841	25.11.1851	sold for	10
Corsair	s	717	24.5.1842	1850	missing	8
Canmore	barg	200	26.1.1843	16.6.1851	sold for	8
Solway	barg	594	7.8.1843	2.8.1855	condemn	12
Elizabeth	s	724	29.6,1844	Aug. 1848	aband'd	4
Colonist	s	751	10.12.1844	11.8.1833	bespoken	39
Milicete	s	899	13.8.1845	1856	lost	13
Oregon	s	928	15.4.1846	Aug. 1863	wrecked	17
Queen	s	1098	4.3.1847	31.7.1867	sold for	20
David Cannon	s	1331	30.10.1847	11.9.1854	wrecked	7
Dundonald	s	1372	14.4.1849	2.11.1858	burnt	10
Kitty Cordes	s	849	12.11.1849	Feb. 1862	aband'd	12
Belochee	s	967	24.6.1850	14.10.1869	lost	19
Beejapore	s	1676	19.2.1851	29.11.1869	burnt	18
Bhurtpoor	s	978	5.1.1852	Sept. 1852	ashore	1
Constance	s	1106	2.6.1852	24.12.1884	wrecked	33
Miles Barton	s	963	1.1.1853	8.2.1861	wrecked	8
Star Of The East	s	1219	8.2.1853	9.4.1861	wrecked	8
Guiding Star	s	1472	20.7.1853	1854	missing	1
David G. Fleming	s	1466	1854	1.1.1877	ashore	24
White Star	s	2339	1854	24.12.1883	ashore	30
Morning Light	s	2377	29.8.1855	1889	lost	34

L x B x D	Length Breadth	First Registration	Second Registration
110x25x19	4.4	1839 Trustees SJMWFC*	1847 James Kirk
156x22x12	7.1	1839 James Whitney & Co.	1840 James Kirk
131x27x21	4.9	1839 John Walker	
135x28x21	4.8	1840 John Walker	1840 John Wishart
121x27x20	4.5	1840 John Walker	1840 John Pollok
95x24x13	4.0	1841 John Pollok	1841 Daniel Baird
62x19x99	3.3	1841 Ratchford Bros.	1841 Alexander Cameron
150x32x22	4.7	1841 Munro & Wallace	1841 Gray & Roxburghs
134x29x22	5.0	1842 Richard Wright	1842 Robert Rankin
94x22x16	4.3	1843 James Malcolm	1843 Thos. Nimmo
122x27x21	4.5	1843 W. and R. Wright	1844 Chas. Walker
130x28x22	4.6	1844 Samuel Gardner	1844 John Haddon
138x29x22	4.8	1844 W. and R. Wright	1845 L. Frost
149x30x23	5.0	1845 W. and R. Wright	1845 Sharples and Jones
151x30x22	5.0	1846 W. and R. Wright	1846 L. Frost
154x32x21	4.8	1847 W. and R. Wright	1849 Geo. Seymour
168x32x21	5.4	1847 W. and R. Wright	1853 Wilson & Chambers
176x35x21	5.0	1849 W. and R. Wright	1854 W. J. Fernie
154x33x22	4.7	1849 W. and R. Wright	1850 D. Cannon, W.&R. Wright
163x32x23	5.1	1850 W. and R. Wright	1850 J. & T. Sinclair
182x36x29	5.1	1851 W. and R. Wright	1851 Willis, W.R. Wright
163x32x22	5.1	1852 W. and R. Wright	1852 Wilson & Chambers
174x32x23	5.4	1852 Richard Wright	1852 Jas. Beazley
170x31x22	5.5	1853 Fernie Bros.	1853 Jas. Beazley
205x37x22	5.5	1853 W. and R. Wright	1853 Jas. Beazley
233x38x22	6.1	1853 W. and R. Wright	1853 Millers & Thompson
191x38x23	5.0	1854 W. and R. Wright	1867 W. and R. Wright
259x40x28	6.5	1854 ?	1855 Pilkington & Wilson, and R. Wright
265x44x21	6.0	1855 W. and R. Wright	1867 W. and R. Wright

* Saint John Mechanic's Whale Fishing Company

Sources: Register Transcripts, P.R.O.,B.T. 107 and 108; and *Lloyd's Shipping Registers.*

Table 5. Shipowning, W. and R. Wright, 1839-1859

Year	Tonnage Owned as of December 31	Tonnage Built	Tonnage Bought	Tonnage Sold
1839	—	1,272 / 3*	—	—
1840	—	1,177 / 2	—	—
1841	—	1,248 / 3	—	—
1842	594 / 1	717 / 1	—	717 / 1
1843	751 / 1	794 / 2	—	200 / 1
1844	—	1,475 / 2	—	1,318 / 2
1845	—	899 / 1	—	1,650 / 2
1846		928 / 1	—	928 / 1
1847	2,4291	2,429 / 2	724 / 1	724 / 1
1848	2,429 / 2		—	—
1849	3,552 / 3	—	996 / 1	2,094 / 2
1850	3,039 / 2 $^{20}/_{64}$ths	2,221 / 2	—	1,488 / 1 $^{44}/_{64}$ths
1851	3,877 / 2 $^{52}/_{64}$ths	967 / 1	—	838 / $^{32}/_{64}$ths
1852	3,906 / 3 $^{20}/_{64}$ths	1,676 / 1	875 / 1	2,922 / 2 $^{32}/_{64}$ths
1853	3,674 / 3 $^{32}/_{64}$ths	2,084 / 2	1,427 / 1 $^{32}/_{64}$ths	4,350 / 3 $^{20}/_{64}$ths
1854	6,107 / 4 $^{32}/_{64}$ths	3,654 / 3	—	1,372 / 1
1855	6,427 / 4 $^{21}/_{64}$ths	3,805 / 2	1,596 / 1 $^{32}/_{64}$ths	3,653 / 2 $^{43}/_{64}$ths
1856	11,499 / 9 $^{21}/_{64}$ths	2,377 / 1	5,072 / 5	—
1857*	12,205 / 10 $^{20}/_{64}$ths	—	8,374 / 8 $^{20}/_{64}$ths	7,669 / 7 $^{21}/_{64}$ths
1858	12,205 / 10 $^{20}/_{64}$ths	—	—	—
1859	13,277 / 11 $^{10}/_{64}$ths	—	3,828 / 3	2,756 / 2 $^{10}/_{64}$ths

* Number after the stroke gives the number of vessels
** In this year the Wrights bought the same ship twice.

W. and R. Wright – Hypothetical Balance Sheet, 1839

Receipts

Java, 418 tons, reg 133 SJNB 28.9.1839: contracted £8.10.0 per ton:	£3,553.0.0	
North America, steamer, 207 tons, reg 128 SJNB 24.9.1839: contracted £7 per ton:	1,449.0.0	
Rival, ship 647 tons, reg 161 SJNB 14.11.1839: contracted £7.10.0 per ton	4,852.10.0	
	£9,854.10.0	

Reserve Fund

Transferred in, and balance:	£2,416.6.8

Expenditure

Vessel Building Schedule:
No 1, *Java*, 1 March to 20 Sept.;
No 2, *Rival*, 1 April to 13 Nov.;
No 3, *North America*, 21 May to 21 Sept.;
No 4, *Helen Mar*, 14 Nov. to 31 Dec.

Labour

March, 30 men @ 3/6 per day		126
1 April to 21 May: 55 men @ 4/ per day		528
21 May to 21 Sept. 65 men @ 4/ per day		1,326
22 Sept to 13 Nov: 35 men @ 4/ per day		314.16.0
14 Nov to 31 Dec: 35 men @ 3/6 per day		257.5.0
		2,551.13.0

Timber for vessels nos. 1-3, £1,200	
Outfits for vessels nos. 1-3, £1,200	
Iron for vessels nos. 1-3, £1,200	3,600

Fire insurance

Java, 5%/4mths/£2,926:	48.15.0	
North America, 5%/3mths/1,242	15.10.5	
Rival, 5%/6½mths/4,526	122.4.9	
Helen Mar, no insurance as frames not up		
	186.10.4	186.10.4

Site mortgage or lease	500
Withdrawal by partners	600
Transfer to reserve	2,416.6.8
	9,854.10.0

W. and R. Wright – Hypothetical Balance Sheet, 1840

Receipts

Helen Mar, 640 tons, reg 54 SJNB 1840,
contracted £7.10.0 per ton: £4,800.0.0

Eliza Keith, 537 tons, reg 87 SJNB 10.7.40
contracted £7.10.0 per ton: £4,027.10.0

Receipts £8,827.10.0

Expenditures
Vessel schedule:

4 *Helen Mar*, 1 Jan to 8 June;	£1,687.0.0
5 *Eliza Keith*, 1 Jan to 9 July;	180.0.0
6 *Eglinton*, 1 Nov to 31 Dec.;	370.0.0
7 *Mary Stewart*, 9 Nov. to 9 Dec.;	189.0.0
8 *Spitfire*, 1 to 31 Dec.	98.0.0
	189.0.0
	£2,413.0.0

Labour:
1 Jan to 8 June, 60 men @ 3/9 per day
9 June to 9 July, 30 men @ 4/ per day
1 to 9 Nov., 50 men 3/6 per day
9 Nov. to 1 Dec., 60 men @ 3/6 per day
1 to 9 Dec., 70 men @ 3/6 per day
9 to 31 Dec., 60 men @ 3/6

Timber, vessels nos. 4 & 5:	£1,050
Ironwork, vessels nos. 4 & 5:	1,050
Outfitting, vessels nos. 4 & 5	1,050
Purchase of brig *Mary Stewart*, 216 tons @ £3/10/0 per ton:	£708

Insurance, *Mary Stewart*,	£21.12.0
Fire Insurance, *Helen Mar*	£120/5%/6mths/4,800
Eliza Keith	£100.13.8/5%/6mths/4,027
Eglinton	£13.16.8/5%/2 wks/6,643
Spitfire	£1.7.8/5%/1mth/332
Site: mortgage or lease:	500
	£4,831.9.4

Expenditure 7,244.9.4
Transfer to reserve 1,583.0.8
£8,827.10.0

Reserve Fund:
From 1839: £2,416.6.8
Int @5% 120.16.2
Transfer in, 1840: 983.0.8
£3,520.3.6

(residue after £600 withdrawn by partners)

W. and R. Wright – Hypothetical Balance Sheet, 1841

Receipts

No 7, brig *Mary Stewart*, 216 tons,
reg 1 SJNB 6.1.1841:
sold @ £6 per ton   £1,296

No 8, schooner *Spitfire*, 83 tons,
reg 12 SJNB 25.1.1841:
sold @ £4 per ton   332

No 6, ship *Eglinton*, 949 tons,
reg 63 SJNB 9.7.1841:
sold at £7 per ton   6,643
   £8,271

Reserve Fund
From 1840:   £3,520.3.6
Int @ 5%   176.0.2
Transfer 1841:
1840:   1,387.11.4
   £5,083.15.0

Expenditure

Vessel Building Schedule:
No 8 *Spitfire*, 1 to 12 Jan.;
No 6 *Eglinton*, 1 Jan to 6 July:
No 9 *Corsair*, 1 Sept to 31 Dec.;

Labour
1 to 12 Jan.: 60 men @ 3/6
12 Jan to 6 July, 55 men @ 3/9
1 Sept to 31 Dec., 45 men @ 3/9

Timber vessels nos 8 & 6   £1,050   105
Iron vessels nos 8 & 6   1,050   1,485
Outfits vessels nos 8 & 6   1,050   860.12.6
   £2,450.12.6

3,150

Fire Insurance
Spitfire, 5%/12 days/332   0.11.8
Eglinton, 5%/6mths, 1wk/5,694   145.1.8
Corsair 5%/2½mths/3,585   37.2.10
Site   500
Paid to partners   600
Transferred to reserve fund   1,387.11.4
   £8,271.0.0

Further Reading

Writings on Business History: A Short List of Books and Journals. (For further items see the reading list at the conclusion of Alan Wilson's Chapter "Problems and Traditions of Business History: Past Examples and Canadian Prospects.")

Books:

Miriam Beard, *A History of Business*, Vol I; *From Babylon to the Monopolists*, Vol. II; *From the Monopolists to the Organisation Man*, Ann Arbor: University of Michigan Press, Ann Arbor Paperbacks, (Ann Arbor: 1963), obtainable through Longmans Canada Limited.
  Publications of the Business Historical Society, (Chicago).
Scott D. Walton, *Business in American History*, (Columbus, Ohio: Grid, Inc., 1971).
E. Samhaber, *Merchants Make History*, (London: Harrap, 1963).
Peter L. Payne, ed., *Studies in Scottish Business History*, (London: Frank Cass and Co. Ltd.)
Alan Birch and David S. Macmillan, *Wealth and Progress, Studies in Australian Business History*, (Sydney, Australia: Angus and Robertson Ltd).
The Business History Conference, *Proceedings of the Fourteenth Conference held at the University of Western Ontario*, March, 1967.

Journals:

Business History, published twice yearly by The University of Liverpool Press, Liverpool, England.
Business History Review, published quarterly since 1926 by the Harvard School of Business Administration. Special issues on important topics are issued periodically.
Explorations in Entrepreneurial History, published by the Research Center in Entrepreneurial History, Harvard University.
Tradition, (Journal of Business History and Entrepreneurial Biography), published four times a year by August Lutzeyer, Baden-Baden, German Federal Republic.
Hamburger Wirtschafts Chronik, (Research and writings from the Hanseatic Regions), published regularly by the Hanseatic Mercury Press, Hamburg, for the Business History Institute.
The Australian Economic History Review (formerly *Business Archives and History*), published twice yearly by Sydney University Press. Contains occasional articles and reviews on Business History.

Index

Date Due